**DO NOT REMOVE
CARDS FROM POCKET**

THE MODERNIZATION OF TURKEY

THE MODERNIZATION OF TURKEY

From Ataturk to the Present Day

Walter F. Weiker

HOLMES & MEIER PUBLISHERS, INC.
NEW YORK • LONDON

First published in the United States of America 1981 by
Holmes & Meier Publishers, Inc.
30 Irving Place
New York, N.Y. 10003

Great Britain:
Holmes & Meier Publishers, Ltd.
131 Trafalgar Road
Greenwich, London SE10 9TX

Library of Congress Cataloging in Publication Data

Weiker, Walter F.
   The modernization of Turkey.

   Bibliography: p. 281
   Includes index.
   1.   Turkey—Politics and government—1909–
2.   Turkey—Economic conditions.   I.   Title.
JQ1803   1980.W44   303.4'09561   80-24514
ISBN   0-8419-0503-7

Manufactured in the United States of America

7065341

For Miriam, Daniel, and Gail

Contents

List of Tables   ix

Acknowledgments   xi

Guide to Pronunciation   xii

Introduction   xiii

1   Overview: The First Half-Century   1

2   The Development of Modernizing Leaders   19
     The Ottoman Legacy
     National Political Leaders
     Local Political Leadership
     The Bureaucracy
     The Economic Elite
     The Military
     Students
     Conclusions

3   The Modernization of Turkish Followers   49
     Villagers
     The Urban Lower Strata
     Turkish Workers in Europe

4   Groups and Forces   87
     Interest Groups
     The Military
     Religion
     The Role and Status of Women

5   Political Parties in Turkish Modernization   119
     The Republican People's Party
     The Democrat and Justice Parties
     Minor Parties
     Party Activity, Organization, and the Party System
     Turkish Voting Behavior
     Conclusions

6   Socialization and Integration: Education, Communication,
    and the Arts   151
    Education
    Communications and Modernization
    Literature and the Arts

7   Economic Development   181
    General Overview
    Industry
    Agriculture
    Infrastructure
    Capital Formation
    Foreign Sources of Financing
    Balance of Trade and Payments
    The Problem of the Common Market
    Conclusions

8   Government Institutions and Organization   221
    Government Structure
    Local Government
    Regional Balance

9   The Modernization of Turkey: Today and Tomorrow   241
    Turkey's Achievements
    Turkey's Shortcomings
    Why the Achievements?
    Why the Shortcomings?
    Growth vs. Modernization, or the Functionality of Traditions
    Turkish Capabilities
    The Second Half-Century

Notes   255
References   281
Index   301

Tables

2-1 Population by Last School Graduated   20
2-2 Social Backgrounds of Turkish Deputies   22
2-3 Social Backgrounds of Deputies by Political Party   22
2-4 Social Backgrounds of Deputies and Local Political Leaders   28
2-5 Social Backgrounds of Officers and Noncommissioned Officers   38
2-6 University Entrance Examinee Survey, 1973–1974   41
2-7 Political Opinions of Sample of Students from Ten Faculties of Ankara
        University   45
3-1 Rural Population by Size of Community   53
3-2a Values and Attitude Characteristics of Villagers   55
3-2b Attitudes by Size of Community   56
3-3 Villager Characteristics by Literacy   58
3-4 Urban Population   65
3-5 Family Characteristics   70
3-6 Growth of Voluntary Associations   74
3-7 Voter Turnout by Type of Urban Area   75
3-8 Voting Behavior by Type of Urban Area   76
3-9 Workers Sent Abroad by Turkish Employment Service   80
4-1 Trade Union Activity   86
4-2 Business and Professional Associations   93
4-3 Agricultural Cooperatives   98
4-4 Religious Education   109
4-5 Women's Education and Employment   113
5-1 Regional Variations in Voter Turnout   144
5-2 Left-Right and Moderate-Radical Voting   145
5-3 Minor Party and Independent Voting   147
5-4 Regional Voting for RPP, by Levels of Development   149
6-1 Education   153
6-2 Literacy   154
6-3 Scholarization   156
6-4 Higher Education   160
6-5 Newspapers, Periodicals, Radio, Television   166
6-6 Circulation of Leading Istanbul Dailies   167

6-7 Periodicals by Subject   170
6-8 Television Programming   173
6-9 Books Published   175
7-1 Macroeconomic Targets and Achievements of the Development Plans   185
7-2 Selected Industrial Production   186
7-3 Sectoral Origin of GNP   187
7-4 Public and Private Manufacturing Plants   192
7-5 Agricultural Production—Selected Major Crops   197
7-6 Agricultural Productivity—Selected Major Crops   198
7-7 Agricultural Technology   199
7-8 Road Quality   203
7-9 Transportation and Mail Volume   204
7-10 Percentage of Transportation by Road and Rail   205
7-11 Government Finances   209
7-12 Foreign Financing   210
7-13 Balance of Payments, 1950–1978   215
8-1 Regional Differences   237

Acknowledgments

Writers on modern Turkey are fortunate to have available to them a great deal of assistance from Turkish written sources, and from Turks in many walks of life. Just as it has been impossible in the body of this study to cite all of the many written sources from which I obtained ideas, insights, and interpretations, limitations of space preclude me from listing all of those who were personally helpful. I do, however, want to mention a number of persons who were either asked to read parts of the manuscript, or were kind enough to provide me with unusually hard-to-obtain data. They include Professors William Zartman, Howard Reed, Feroz Ahmad, Jacob Landau, Mükerrem Hiç, Ilter and Gül Turan, Ergun Özbudun (who not only provided information but also hospitality during my recent stay in Ankara), Ruşen Keleş, Metin Heper, Deniz Kandiyoti, Çiğdem Kagıtçıbaşı, Suna Kili, Nermin Abadan-Unat, Mübeccel Kıray, Oya Tokgöz, and Talat Halman. Others who gave unusually generously of their time include Dr. Nuri Tortop of the Turkish Municipalities Association, and Altemur Kılıç and Gündüz Aktan of the Turkish Mission to the United Nations. Grants in aid from the Rutgers University Research Council are also gratefully acknowledged. I am particularly pleased that not only was I received warmly by all of the Turks whom I consulted, but that they were so open and frank and did not hesitate to offer insightful evaluations of their own country, even if these were sometimes critical. None of these people, of course, bears any responsibility for my views as expressed in this work.

Finally, I cannot neglect mentioning the great tolerance shown by my wife, Miriam, and my children, Daniel and Gail, for the countless hours I spent poring over data or at the typewriter. Their encouragement has been invaluable.

Newark, New Jersey
August, 1980

Guide to Pronunciation

For those not familiar with Turkish, the following guide may be helpful:

c — j as in *join*.

ç — ch as in *church*.

b, d — as in English, but at the end of a syllable they are frequently pronounced and often written p, t (e.g. Recep/Receb, Ahmet/Ahmed).
Both are correct.

ğ — soft g lengthens the preceding vowel.

ı — somewhat like u in *stadium*.

ö — like French word *deux*.

ş — *sh* as in *shout*.

ü — like French *lumiere*.

Introduction

Turkey has long held the interest of the West. Once it was the focus of attention because of its romantic fascination: an exotic land with sultans, harems, eunuchs and dervishes; a fierce and fearsome people who had twice knocked on the very gates of Vienna; the great mosques and monuments of Constantinople; the amazing Ataturk, who devastated mighty Britain at Gallipoli and then set out to turn his entire country around with one dramatic revolution after another. Then after World War II came the spectacle, almost unparalleled in modern times, of a ruling single party which not only allowed a free election, but acquiesced in its own defeat and quietly left power to become the opposition.

Today Turkey is still attracting the attention of observers, but for different reasons: It has completed a full half-century of a modernizing revolution, half of that period with democratic politics, a record achieved by few other "developing" countries. Its multiparty political system has been strong enough to survive two interventions by its armed forces. It has also managed to do well generally in checking radical challenges from both the right and the left, even while undergoing the strains of rapid population growth, the problems of rapid and massive urbanization, a vast increase in popular demands on both the political and economic systems, critical economic problems, and challenges from many directions in international relations. How and how well these problems have been met, and how the work of the first half-century of the Republic may have prepared Turkey for meeting the problems of the second, may tell us a great deal about both the potential for and the difficulties of the survival of democratic institutions in nations undergoing modernization. And while it is true that each society is in some way unique, perhaps it is not too much to hope that the ideas developed in this study might also be food for thought for other, later-modernizing nations.

To the visitor from the West, Turkey is a country of great paradoxes. One hears many complaints about the economy—rapid inflation, numerous shortages, aggravating inadequacies of public services—but at the same time most people seem to have a remarkable ability to adjust to their circumstances. To take but one small example, there is an amazing willingness to wait patiently for public transportation for what seems to the foreigner an extremely long time, and the orderliness of such queues is rarely disturbed. Stores are filled with goods and customers. Everyone has solutions to Turkey's problems, even if few have concrete ideas as to how those solutions are to be implemented.

Although I found many people who were pessimistic for the short run, I found almost nobody who was not also optimistic for Turkey's long-run future. Virtually everyone with whom I spoke foresaw good prospects for his or her personal future well-being and improvement. When I asked a cabinet minister what he considered to be the government's most serious problem, he replied that it was the seeming inability to persuade the general population how serious the country's problems really were. A rejoinder to this comment might have been (and indeed it was a rejoinder made to me by several nongovernment observers) that such persuasion has not really been tried, that the political parties continue to jockey for short-run positions in the midst of a highly competitive electoral atmosphere. To a considerable extent this does seem to be true.

And problems there are. Although political radicalism is confined to a small percentage of the population, the urban guerrilla violence which took well over a thousand lives in 1979, and continued to rise frighteningly as the 1980s began (and which has been accompanied by a noticeable increase in nonpolitical crime as well) is making everyone a great deal more wary in their everyday lives, particularly at night. Yet it must also be noted that the political violence for the most part is not random, but almost always has been directed at very specific and usually individual targets rather than being a generalized anti-society phenomenon.

On the economic scene, already critical shortages of foreign exchange are likely to get worse unless there are large new foreign credits, for which negotiations can be expected to be very difficult despite the apparent realization of Turkey's increased importance now that neighboring Iran has all but collapsed as an anchor of Western defense. Many of the decisions waiting to be made in this area are subject to troubling contradictory considerations: the price of gasoline in Turkey, for example, was long among the lowest in Europe, and while many say that it is kept low in order not to offend the government's upper-middle-class supporters, it must also be pointed out that the sharp increase which some experts advocate would likewise significantly increase the operating costs of industry and mechanized agriculture and, in turn, harm Turkey's already very difficult prospects for increasing exports.

On still another front, there is now beginning to be public acknowledgment that there are indeed some ethnic minority problems, which are being aggravated in part because they also coincide with regional imbalances, as with the Kurds in the eastern provinces. Other such problems arise from more traditional communal feelings, as with the Alevis, who are spread throughout many parts of the country and who are now also particularly concentrated in certain *gecekondu* areas of Turkey's rapidly growing large cities.

There is extremely high popular interest in politics in Turkey today, and a sharply increased degree of polarization in the press and parliament than was the case a few years ago. It is not clear, however, at least to this writer, whether the same degree of divisive feelings can be found among the general population, which is described by some observers as a good deal more moderate but also generally disillusioned with the performance of all the major political parties. Yet there is also considerable attachment to democracy, even if this attachment is partly on the basis that the prospect of authoritarian government revives memories of the gendarmerie and repression. Democratic institutions are seen by many as a means of bargaining, through which one can advance at least a part of one's interests. What is perhaps even more important is that for many Turks, democracy has become a *norm,* which, among other things, places Turkey in a different category than many other "developing" countries. There is some concern that failure to solve major problems may result in another military intervention (as in 1960 and 1971), but there is also a firm conviction that any such intervention would again be only a temporary and rather superficial interruption of political processes.*

Prediction about the future of any country is a risky enterprise, particularly if it is a "developing" one, and perhaps even more so if it is in the volatile Middle East. But as social scientists we must try to look ahead in at least a general way, particularly if our work is to be useful to policymakers as well as to scholars. Since this is not a who-done-it, there is no reason not to state at the outset my overall conclusion, which is positive, though it is not made without apprehension. I believe that if Turkey can overcome her short-term problems, the fundamental societal strengths which have been established augur well for her long-run stability and prosperity, and that the Republic's first half-century will indeed have prepared Turkey well for its second one.

There are many reasons for this potential for success, as will be pointed out in the following chapters and elaborated upon in the concluding chapter of this study. Some are ones for which Turkey cannot take particular credit, such as some favorable geographic and demographic conditions, and fortunate timing (both in the sense that enough time was available for adjusting to new situations slowly, and that Turkish modernization began in a period when there were not yet popular pressures for spectacular achievements, achieved immediately and all at one time). But there are also some indications of success which are clearly the work of the Turks themselves.

*A new military intervention did indeed occur on September 12, 1980, as this book was going to press. Significantly, it came only when guerrilla violence between right and left extremists had become so great that many leaders, political and military alike, agreed that "business as usual" was impossible. Early signs indicate that the officers again envision their action as an essentially short-run structural "repair job" to preserve the fabric of Turkish democracy to which they are committed.

One, of central importance, is having brought the great majority of the population into the social, economic, and political mainstream of national life. While this has led to a great increase in demands, to dislocation and sometimes frustration, it is also the case that a great many Turks (nonelites as well as elites) are now *agents* of continuing modernization, not merely objects of it. In fact, nonelites now have a major role in defining many of the objectives and general policies of the society. Another asset, corollary to this, is that virtually all of the responsible political leaders of Turkey have decided that it is both wise and feasible to accept a relatively slow pace of cultural and social change, and have learned to be comfortable with the survival of certain "traditions" while at the same time vigorously spurring modernization in some other spheres. Of course, these things have obverse sides as well, and it can be argued that the nonelites (followers, as I will call them) are the least well-equipped to make those difficult long-run decisions (even the most general ones) which are required for development, that some of the "traditions" are dysfunctional to the modernization process itself, and that the high rate of earlier economic growth has made it possible to avoid other problems of structural reforms which are currently very grave.

Criteria of Success

This study is based on the premise that the requirements for success in modernization include:

1. Maintaining a rate of economic growth which will be satisfying to the general population.
2. The minimization of social cleavages.
3. As little as possible psychological dislocation for the many individuals undergoing rapid social change.
4. Providing outlets for ambitions of social mobility and rewarding individual achievement.
5. Inculcating in leaders and followers alike new habits of work and thought appropriate to a technological, interdependent society.

Meeting all of these requirements presents some obviously difficult problems. Indeed they may entail contradictions. For example, minimizing psychological dislocation might call for slow change, while facilitating social mobility may demand that change in values and social institutions be rapid and great. It is clear, as well, that meeting some of the criteria requires not only that individuals change, but that the entire society be transformed, institutionally and in the values which it supports. Still further, it is quite possible that short-run needs such as visible improvement in the standard of living will clash with a longer-run need such as allocating resources to investment in infrastructure, a policy which can be inflationary as well as requiring that increased consumption be postponed. Such potentially troubling contradictions are all too clear in the case of Turkey.

The Basic Hypothesis

I will take as my general overall framework the concept of "modernization," and as my basic hypothesis that the relatively stable course along which Turkish development has proceeded during the Republic's first half-century has been related in considerable part to the emergence of combinations of "tradition" and "modernity" (or degrees of modernity, as some would prefer to put it) within individuals, groups, and Turkish society as a whole. Exploring the ways in which these combinations address various of the criteria of success just set out will be one of this study's major focuses.

In view of this approach, it is appropriate that the definition of "modern" and "traditional" be spelled out here as precisely as possible. The literature of social science now contains numerous such definitions, as well as critiques and analyses of the general concept and of its specific components. I will not try here to analyze these. I believe that the following general outline will be sufficient for this study's purposes.

On the Concept of Modernization

1. "Traditional" and "modern" are "ideal" concepts, not found anywhere in pure form.

2. There is no assumption of linear progression or unidirectional movement from "traditional" to "modern." Indeed, one of the important conditions facilitating personal and group adjustment to contemporary life and problems may lie in the ability to move back toward some greater degree of "traditionality," as well as forward to "modernity."

3. "Traditional" and "modern" are terms which may be applied to entire political and social systems, to smaller groups, and to individuals. All of these levels will be used in this study.

4. There is no assumption that "modernity" is necessarily more desirable than "tradition." In fact, it will be contended that for some purposes and in some situations a degree of "traditionality" can be both functional to resolving certain problems of development, and more satisfying psychologically to individuals undergoing rapid change than full "modernity" might be.

5. The characteristics of "modernity" can be grouped into two general categories, which I label "structural" and "social." "Tradition" can often be usefully defined as the opposite of "modern" on these indicators. Though some attempts have been made in the literature on modernization to analyze relationships among them quantitatively, *e.g.*, to try to determine what percentage of a society must be urban, educated, or in industrial occupations to justify the label of "modern," many of the indicators are not really quantifiable (e.g., fellings of equality, sufficiency of individual social mobility in terms either of individuals or the society as a whole.) Rather, it is the predominant thrust of each characteristic of modernization (either its actual existence or movement toward it) which should lead us to placing a society in one category or the other.

6. The structural aspects of modern society which are most important are:

   (a) It is urban.

   (b) It is productive; *i.e.*, it produces a significantly higher amount of goods and services than does a traditional society.

   (c) It is industrial.

   (d) It is technological and scientific.

   (e) It is mobile, geographically and socially.

   (f) It is literate and educated.

   (g) It has a high level of upward and downward communication.

   (h) It contains many centralized institutions, including government and private ones such as national trade unions, business and professional organizations, and such institutions result in a high level of penetration of traditional elements of a society by more modern ones.

   (i) A modern society contains a sizable and fairly steadily increasing middle class.

7. The social, value, or behavioral aspects of "modern" societies include:

   (a) A predominance of "voluntary association," *i.e.*, individuals associating themselves with persons other than those who share the characteristics with which they were born (kin groups, ethnic groups, religious groups, geographical groups).[1]

   (b) A modern society is achievement-oriented. A traditional society, in contrast, will be either based on ascription (*i.e.*, one's individual status and choices of leaders for the society or nation and for smaller units and groups within it are more determined by who you are—an elder, hereditary tribal leader, etc.—than by what you are), or, if it is based on achievement, it will be "traditional" achievement, *e.g.*, religious learning.

   (c) A modern society is secular. This does not mean the absence of religion, but implies that individuals are both willing and able to use "discovered knowledge," (as contrasted to "revealed knowledge") in many aspects of their lives and work.

   (d) Modern individuals are ambitious; *i.e.*, they have significant desires to raise their standard of living beyond the basic necessities. A "traditional" person, on the other hand, is much more easily satisfied, particularly in regard to what is often called "materialism."

   (e) Modern individuals have strong drives for upward social mobility.

   (f) A related value to many of the above is the desire of modern individuals that their society be more "equalitarian," and, corollary to this, a "modern" society is characterized by predominantly impersonal relationships between the governors and the governed, between individuals, and between many societal institutions.

   (g) To some extent a modern society will be more "individual-oriented," *i.e.*, there will be an increased degree to which one of the functions the society is expected to perform is enhancement of the capabilities and welfare of its individual members, as contrasted with the obligation of the individual to contribute to the welfare of the group.[2]

   (h) Modern individuals have the ability to be empathetic and to be future-oriented both in psychological and material terms. That is, they are able to conceive of what they might be in the future, and they have both the mental equipment and some of the material assets to work toward the future. This kind of ability may, of course, be affected by outside factors. For example, the ability and willingness to postpone current consumption or gratification for anticipated greater future welfare may well be influenced by the stability of the society (*e.g.,* confidence that there will not be events such as confiscation of bank assets by a revolutionary government, or that industry's record of stability makes it reasonable to expect that a firm in which one's money is invested will still be there when it comes time to reap the fruits of one's thrift).

Terms

In this study I will use the term "development" more or less interchangeably with "modernization."

Some Caveats

1. This study will not contend that Turkey is unique, that the problems, achievements, and situations of many other countries cannot be described in at least similar terms.

2. Comparisons with other countries will be made where possible and applicable, but this is not of major concern to the study. In part this is because I am seeking to appraise how well the experience of the Turkish Republic's first half-century has succeeded in preparing that country for the challenges of *its* future. I am also less concerned with trying to appraise whether readiness could have been greater. Among the reasons why this question, interesting as it surely is, is not emphasized is because its appraisal would involve much speculation, as well as measuring how other countries have done, and the latter in particular has so many variables that no more than nebulous observations are possible at this stage of social science knowledge. I hope, however, that this study will contribute to our ability to make better comparisons in the future, an enterprise in which I look forward to having a part.

3. On numerous topics, the data are inadequate in both quantity and quality, and it is necessary to use rather gross aggregates, to interpolate, and to make assumptions about the degree to which various specific data can be generalized. I have tried to do this, particularly on topics where all or most of the data available seemed to point in the same general direction. I have also tried, wherever possible, to use Turkish studies as primary data sources. It is certainly a great advantage to students of Turkey that that country's own social scientists are a most capable and impressive scholarly group.

4. It is always somewhat difficult to know how to handle historical matters. What I have done is to begin this study with an overall sketch of some important aspects of Turkish history, focusing on the Republic period, and then go on to present more specific historical background in conjunction with relevant individual topics discussed in the subsequent chapters.

ONE

Overview:
The First Half-Century

The Ottoman Empire died with World War I, after an existence of some five centuries. Although it passed away in disgrace, it had had many glorious periods and it left its successor, the Turkish Republic, with considerable assets with which to undertake the process of modernization. These assets included a capable army and bureaucracy, the rudimentary beginnings of modern economic and social institutions, and a group of publicists and politicians who were veterans of several periods of struggle against Sultanic absolutism. Men like Namık Kemal and philosophers like Ziya Gökalp had already begun to propagate doctrines of Turkish nationalism and to éstablish contact with the Turkish masses through such methods as the simplification of the Ottoman language to conform more to the popular Turkish speech. In fact, many of the reforms which Kemal Ataturk implemented were facilitated by events and trends of the Ottoman period. Some were even begun at that time. Actually, reformers had come to power in the Young Turk revolution of 1908, but were able to achieve little in the way of development because (among other things) Turkey was soon beset by the Balkan Wars and World War I.

It remained for the Ottoman general, Mustafa Kemal (Ataturk)[1] to widen, deepen, and quicken many of these changes. The son of a minor bureaucrat, he was born in Salonica in 1881, and educated in Ottoman military schools. He served in various commands in the Arab countries, the Balkans and Thrace, was briefly active in politics during the Young Turk period, spent some time as military attaché in Bulgaria, and had traveled in Europe. He became an outstanding hero when he commanded the successful defense of Gallipoli against formidable Allied armes in 1915–1916. An unusually perceptive, energetic, and determined man (see Rustow, 1969: a very insightful article), he soon began to lay plans for the wholesale reform of his country. When he was sent by the Sultan to Anatolia in 1919 as inspector of what remained of the defeated Turkish armies, he campaigned not only against the allied armies which had occupied part of the country, but against the Istanbul

1

government as well. Mobilizing the armies, he waged the War of Independence to its successful conclusion in late 1922.

Simultaneously Ataturk began political organization. Defense of Rights Societies (which later became the nucleus of the Republican People's party) were organized and brought together in Congresses at Sivas and Erzurum in 1919. From these Congresses issued the National Pact, declaring Turkey's intentions to remain sovereign and intact and the formation of a Representative Committee to take charge of the affairs of the state pending the "liberation" of the Sultan's government, which was then in Allied-occupied Istanbul. Ataturk was the committee's leader. To the surprise of practically no one, it shortly took on all the attributes of a provisional government, including the convening of a Grand National Assembly at Ankara on April 23, 1920. At the peace conference at Lausanne in 1923, it was the Ankara government which represented Turkey.

From that point things moved rapidly. With the overwhelming support of his military and bureaucratic colleagues, Ataturk persuaded the Assembly to proclaim a Republic and abolish the Sultanate in 1923 and to end the Caliphate in 1924. He made it clear that even more momentous reforms were to follow, and his new People's party achieved strong domination of the Second Assembly in 1923.

In the years that followed, Ataturk, now President of the Republic, set out to turn Turkey's face toward the modern West. New civil, commercial, and penal codes based on European models were adopted. The Western calendar, style of dress, and other such symbols were introduced. One of the most important steps in this process was adoption, in 1928, of the Latin alphabet in place of the Arabic-Ottoman script, a reform ostensibly designed to facilitate the acquisition of literacy (and it is true that Ottoman is very difficult to learn), but which also had the effect of cutting the new generation off from most of its literary past. (For one detailed description of these dramatic reforms see Shaw, 1977. The best analytical discussion remains that of Bernard Lewis, 1961. Briefer and/or more popular accounts include Geoffrey Lewis, 1955; Davison, 1968; and Kinross, 1965.)

Another area of major attention during this period was secularization. Denying frequent charges that he was opposed to religion and asserting only that Turkey must be freed from some of the "backward-looking institutions" of Islam, Ataturk proceeded to disestablish the *ulema*. Religious schools and courts were abolished and replaced by secular ones. Religious orders, lodges, and brotherhoods were closed. Clerics were forbidden to wear ecclesiastical dress outside religious premises. *Vakifs* (pious foundations), a primary source of revenue for religious activities, were nationalized, and the call to prayer from the minaret of a mosque was mandated to be made in Turkish, not the traditional Arabic. Although resistance to these measures was sternly suppressed, traditional religious feelings remained strong among much of the populace. Indeed, the drastic nature of these religious reforms was to become an extremely divisive issue after World War II when the multiparty period began.

Another aspect of the reform era which would later lead to difficult repercussions was the existence of only one political party (though other parties had not been declared illegal). Under the Republican People's party's (RPP) stewardship, the new modernizers moved to take control of all aspects of public affairs. Drawn in large part from the bureaucracy, army, and intellectuals, they installed their supporters in all important official posts and ran roughshod over all dissent, although officially declaring freedom of speech and the sovereignty of the Grand National Assembly.[2] RPP penetration also included seeking to politicize private organizations such as the craft guilds, and making the new corps of village school teachers *ex officio* members of Village Councils.

Social and economic reform, on the other hand, was at the beginning largely institutional and primarily to the benefit of urban areas. Some land reform legislation was passed, but little was implemented, partly because of a dearth of funds and personnel, but partly also because in many rural areas the RPP was dominated by traditional local notables who were willing to give support to many reforms only in exchange for tacit neglect of implementation of measures which might result in drastic changes in rural social or power structures. Furthermore, resources for the expansion of education, health, and other social facilities were inadequate even for the needs of urban areas, to say nothing of the needs of the rural regions. Some infrastructure was begun, consisting in the early years of things such as railroad and harbor expansion, which simultaneously increased military mobility. Economic development had been discussed extensively at the Izmir Economic Congress of 1923, and resulted in primary focus being placed on the encouragement of Turkish private entrepreneurs. But because many non-Muslim minority entrepreneurs had left the country during and after World War I and the War of Independence, and the remaining foreign concessionaires were being phased out as rapidly as possible, it was necessary to rely on the still small and weak Turkish entrepreneurial groups with the result that there was only slow growth, and little of it spreading beyond a few urban places.

However, by the end of the 1920s much institutional reform had been accomplished, and in 1930 Ataturk felt ready for another momentous step, loosening the political structure. Impelled in part by confidence that his basic reforms had taken root and also by the feeling that "a new infusion of life was needed in the political and governmental apparatus in order to deal with urgent problems, chiefly economic in nature" (Weiker, 1973:55), he persuaded several loyal colleagues of long standing to organize an opposition party. The announcement of this party in August 1930 aroused great excitement, and the Free Republican party (*Serbest Cumhuriyet Fırkası*) under the leadership of Fethi Okyar (one of Ataturk's closest colleagues) quickly moved into high gear. Strongly supporting all the basic reforms but advocating more liberal economic policies and criticizing the lack of accountability and free debate within the single party, the Free party quickly gathered adherents in many parts of the country. Having only rudimentary organization, however, the party's leaders were able to exercise only superficial control over its growth. In short order the growing number of people who proclaimed themselves Free party members came to include religious and other groups who opposed the revolution as a whole, as well as many who were loyal to it but had valid complaints against the conduct of the authorities or who advocated the alternative economic policies articulated by the opposition party's official leaders. As a consequence, the Free party aroused determined resistance from the RPP leadership and organization. When violence and signs of deep hostility to the Ataturk reforms appeared along with the approach of local elections, even Ataturk began to have doubts about the wisdom of the venture, and the Free party "voluntarily" disbanded after a life of ninety-nine days (see Weiker, 1973, chapters III–X).

But effects of the Free party experience were to be felt for many years. Sources of opposition to the Kemalist revolution itself had been identified. At the same time, however, legitimate complaints and shortcomings had had a chance to be aired. In response, Ataturk initiated a set of new steps intending to "tutor" the nation toward eventual democratization and to full acceptance of the reforms.

Some of these steps were designed to make the members of the RPP more responsive to criticism and pressure. Success was spotty. Organization of a group of "independent deputies" in the Assembly was not productive. Many of the independents were forceful and well-informed speakers who occasionally made some public impression and raised valid criticisms, but it soon became clear that they had no prospect of attaining effective power to force either policy or leadership changes (Weiker, 1973, chap. XI). The RPP was reorganized as another step toward decentralizing authority and developing local leadership which would be more effective in popularizing the party and the revolution, and which, it was hoped, would display less offensive attitudes than those which had caused resentment during the period of the most militant reforms. But here, too, there was little real change until true decentralization and attention to popular feelings became unavoidable with the opening of the multiparty period in 1946 (Weiker, 1973, chap. XIII. See also chapter 5 of this study).

A far larger and more visible venture was establishment in 1931 of a network of People's Houses *(Halkevleri)* and People's Rooms *(Halkodarları)* across the nation. Eventually numbering 479 houses and 4,322 rooms, they became community centers. They conducted cultural activities, adult education courses, health and welfare programs, libraries and popular publications, and sought to promote interchange between townsmen and villagers. The success of these cultural and social endeavors was considerable, but as with the other reform policies, the more directly political activities which the *Halkevleri* sponsored were less so. The lectures on cultural, historical, and political topics (discussion of the principles of the revolution, of citizenship and its duties) were attended mostly by the better-educated groups which had least need to hear them, although there was also probably some "spillover" effect among the general population. Although membership was open to all, and all could share in the houses' administration, the houses quickly became what might be called wholly-owned subsidiaries of the RPP. They were centers of indoctrination more than they were training grounds for institutional self-government or for open debate on public affairs. Here, too, direct political tutelage for democracy proved elusive (Weiker, 1973, chap. XII; Karpat, 1963).

The final political venture resulting from the Free party experience was efforts toward development of Republican ideology. Most of the principles of what was to become known as Kemalism had been outlined during the 1920s, but after the Free party these ideas were elaborated upon and formalized. In 1937 the "Six Arrows," as they came to be called, up to then only a part of the RPP program, were inserted into the Turkish Constitution, a move which stirred some resentment because it was seen as a step toward making the views of the party those of the entire nation. However, inserting these principles in the Constitution subsequently also made it possible for anyone adhering to the principles, often rather loosely interpreted, to qualify as loyal to the revolution. The "arrows" varied both in their degree of precision and in the degree to which they were to settle important political issues.

Republicanism was the most rigid "arrow." It provided for the demise of the Sultanate and Caliphate and their replacement by the sovereignty of the nation as expressed through the Grand National Assembly. These precepts were never to be seriously challenged.

Nationalism also had some aspects not open to subsequent challenge. One was that by defining the borders of the state largely as constituted at the end of the War of Independence[3] it effectively ruled out of consideration irredentist ambitions as expressed in doctrines like pan-Ottomanism, pan-Turkism or pan-Islam. Somewhat more controversially, until 1960 nationalism was also invoked to prevent expression of "internationalist" ideologies, outlawing not only communism (which is still illegal) but even frowning on inclusion of the word "socialism" in any political programs. (See chapter 5 below on the Turkish labor party.) On a more populist level, nationalism became the basis for numerous efforts and exhortations to heighten Turkish self-esteem and pride.[4] There were, for example, the language and history reforms. Following the 1928 adoption of the Latin alphabet, the Turkish Language Society included in its work the replacement of as many Ottoman words as possible with "native Turkish" (*öz Türkçe*) ones, and the Turkish Historical Society embarked on major research and publication efforts to stress the greatness of the Turkish race through history and to deemphasize Ottoman history, which had chiefly been concerned with the activities of the sultans. At times these and related efforts went to extremes in placing national passions at the service of national pride. But it is to the credit of the Turks that chauvinism eventually was quietly deemphasized and that a relatively balanced and sensible orientation to history soon began to prevail and continues so.[5]

Populism stressed "popular sovereignty," mutual responsibilities of the state and individuals toward each other, and the absence of social classes in

Turkish society (Weiker, 1973:244). Popular sovereignty in principle was not to be disputed. The 1961 Constitution added some institutional checks and balances to the governmental structure, however, rather than continuing the Assembly's unchecked powers through which popular sovereignty was expressed until then (see chapter 8). The concept of mutual obligations became (among other things) the basis for insisting that officials take pains to listen to popular opinion, though during the single party period populism in practice was more often "government for the people" to the relative neglect of "by the people." The Kemalist assertion that Turkish society is composed not of social classes, but of individuals who belong to various occupational groups was ideologically democratic but also politically utilitarian in that it helped to legitimize the single party as the sole representative of all elements of society. Turkey has never been a classless society, of course, but the acceptance of the idea that there were to be no inherently privileged elements made it easier to encourage equality.

Secularism was certainly the most dramatic Kemalist doctrine, and for many years the most controversial. (Secularism is considered in detail in chapter 4.) On the one hand, no responsible Turkish leaders have dissented from its basic principles: there should be no state religion, Islamic functionaries should not *per se* take an official part in politics, and there should be secular control of both law and education. On the other hand, there continues to be controversy over the role which the state should play in such matters as financing the building and maintenance of mosques, training of religious personnel, and paying their salaries. Secularism became a subject of intense controversy in part because Ataturk insisted on interpreting its requirements rigidly and often gave the impression of being antireligious (even though he always asserted that he favored Islam if only it were "enlightened"). It also became the area which provided the aspiring Democrats in 1946 with some of their most potent political ammunition. Only as economic and social issues became the primary concerns of a majority of the Turkish people did the issue of secularism begin to wane in relative importance.

Etatism, the doctrine that the state should play an active role in economic development, was added to Kemalism in 1931 (in contrast to the previous four principles which had been part of the program since the 1920s) in conjunction with new efforts at economic development. It stressed the primacy of the public sector in industrialization, though it also stated that there was to be encouragement of private enterprise. *Etatism* soon became the primary government economic policy. The civil bureaucracy became dominant in Turkish industry, and the State Economic Enterprises received the bulk of public investment. *Etatism* was to become the "arrow" most quickly and directly challenged by the opposition Democrats, and it provided the country with a useful "modern" issue for political debate in addition to more value-rooted social and cultural issues (which also were prominent in 1946–50). In part this was possible because *etatism* had never been made into normative doctrine, but had been kept, rather, on the pragmatic level as the most effective way to rapid economic development, which indeed it was during the 1930s when the Turkish private sector was still quite weak. It is also to be noted that during the multiparty period neither side was to go to extremes on this point, and that although program emphases have differed greatly, both public and private economic sectors have been strongly supported side-by-side (see chapters 5 and 7).

Revolutionism was the final "arrow," and the second explicitly added in the 1930s. Of all the "arrows," this principle was the vaguest. The Republicans generally took it to mean the summation of the great Ataturk reforms, but they would later be challenged by others who said that the true revolutionaries were those people who implemented popular sovereignty during the multiparty period by reflecting the "will of the people."

All in all, Kemalism served a double purpose. It established general principles which provided the outer limits of permissible dissent, but many of the principles were also flexible enough in their operational interpretation so that they could be legitimately debated. It was therefore at least nominally possible to dissent without putting the legitimacy of the entire Revolution in danger, and without tarnishing the image of Ataturk, who had become the very symbol of modern Turkey.

It should also be made clear, however, that important as these ideological matters were, social change and political and economic development were also largely responsible for such things as diminution of extreme views of secularism and the pursuit by the elites of political support from nonelites. One can also say that the early, sometimes extreme and often very partisan interpretations of what Kemalism required, and the identification of the RPP with those interpretations, were among the factors leading to the deep gulfs opened in 1946 between the RPP and its potential opposition. One can only speculate whether planting the seeds of what became a dialectic process was avoidable, e.g., whether secularism would have been just as firmly implanted if it had not been first made so dramatically divisive, or whether Ataturk could have done a better job controlling the bureaucracy to which he had assigned such gigantic tasks.

In addition to the various steps just discussed, two other spurs in the 1930s to the foundation for multiparty politics must be mentioned. One is that many of the Ataturk policies noted above sent out constant, if often tacit signals that democracy remained the ultimate goal. These signals were taken as virtual promises, which the RPP was to be called upon to redeem in 1946. A second element was economic and social growth and change, a process which had accelerated during the post-Free party years and which at the end of World War II, after the Republic's first quarter-century, confronted Turkish leaders with a nation in which the general population was rapidly becoming politically mobilized to make demands both for the fruits of economic growth and for a voice in guiding the nation's policies. Although a great deal still remained to be done, and although villagers were still only little affected in these spheres, there is no doubt that in cities and towns the number of persons involved in the processes of change was becoming sizable, and would continue to grow.

Ataturk died in 1938, and his place as President was taken by Ismet Inonu, who had been prime minister for all but a few brief periods of the Republic. Inonu guided Turkey through neutrality in World War II[6] and his domestic policies were similar to those of his predecessor. At the end of the war, however, Turkey faced additional pressures for political liberalization. One such pressure was the fact that the United Nations was being sponsored largely by Western democracies, and Turkey's being nondemocratic was a potential political embarassment. A second was that much of the nation was chafing against martial-law restriction of free expression imposed as a security measure during the war, and against the economic austerity made necessary by the international situation. A third was that people who had accepted Ataturk's policies as containing signals that his ultimate goal was democracy now were ready to see it realized—and there was nobody of the stature of Ataturk to dampen their enthusiasm.

In the summer of 1945 the RPP expelled four prominent deputies who had demanded some political liberalization. In January 1946 the ousted deputies founded the Democrat party (DP). Considerable debate took place within the RPP as to whether the new party should be permitted. There was much vacillation, but the liberals finally gained the upper hand. The Law of Associations was amended to strike the prohibition on associations having a class basis. Some changes were made in the electoral law to move toward stronger guarantees of secrecy of the ballot. In the words of one writer, "In a matter of months the Republicans abolished or greatly liberalized many of the restrictions that took them twenty-five years to impose" (Karpat, 1959:159).

The RPP organization was not, however, entirely ready to give up the fight. The general election scheduled for 1947 was moved up to July 1946, thus severely limiting the Democrats' efforts to organize and to prepare for the election. When despite these handicaps and the fact that most of the election machinery was still in the hands of the RPP, the Democrats won 65 out of 465 Assembly seats, the handwriting on the wall was plain enough for everybody to read. In July 1947 President Inonu, long a leader of the proponents of liberalization, tried once more to reconcile the conservatives through negotiation. When he failed, he issued the formal public "Declaration of July 12," which recognized the full legitimacy of any opposition party using legal methods and declared that on that basis "I consider myself, as the head of state, equally responsible to both parties" (Karpat, 1959: 191). In the ensuing three years the DP continued to organize and criticize, often aided by liberals within the RPP. The RPP continued to make concessions, such as softening some secularist practices, and started decentralization of the party to match the increased power which the DP was offering its local supporters.

For the party of Ataturk, the results of Turkey's first free election in 1950 were a surprise nevertheless (as well as, of course, a bitter blow). The RPP won only 39 percent of the votes and 69 Assembly seats, compared to 53 percent and 408 seats for Democrats (due to an electoral system which gave the party winning a plurality in any province all of that province's seats). Some observers speculated that the government and the army would intervene to nullify the election results, but that did not happen. The RPP quietly moved to the opposition side of the chamber. Adnan Menderes, a wealthy landowner from the Aegean region who had first come to prominence in the Free party and who had been personally recruited into the Assembly by Ataturk on the basis of that performance, became Prime Minister. The Presidency was taken over by Celal Bayar, whose political activity dated back to the Young Turk period and who had been for some years Ataturk's Economics Minister, Prime Minister for a short period, and who had also been Inonu's most direct personal political rival during almost the entire period of Ataturk's presidency.[7]

In some ways there was general continuity from the old government to the new. As Dodd has remarked, ". . . the economic policies of the People's Party and the Democrat Party differed in emphasis, not in direction; and much the same might be said . . . of their social policies" (1969:25). Thus, while a great deal more favorable treatment and assistance was given to private entrepreneurs, little reduction was made in the State Economic Enterprises, though other important economic changes did take place, including a large increase in imports and more deliberate attention to agricultural development. In the social sphere, softening of secularist policies had already begun under the RPP, and although there was a decided change in the "tone" of official attitude toward religion, and major increases in such things as government funding for building mosques and training religious personnel, the basic Kemalist policies of a secular state were not reversed. (This interpretation of Turkish secularism in this period is discussed more fully in chapter 4.)

Eventually the Democrats resorted to policies (discussed in chapter 5) which led to severe political and social conflict and which brought their rule to a violent end in 1960. It must also be said that some of the DP's economic policies are open to question as to their long-term wisdom, as I will discuss in later chapters. There is no denying, however, that the DP presided over a period of growth and change which was to have extremely significant effects on Turkey's future. In economics, both agricultural and industrial production grew rapidly and factories began to spring up across the land. Imports were also massive, and included large numbers of tractors and other amenities for the rural sector. One important characteristic of these accomplishments was their high visibility. As Simpson has observed, "the rate of economic growth between 1950 and 1955 (Menderes' 'boom years') was no more rapid than between 1936 and 1939," but it occurred "without forced savings" and was "characterized by *high consumption* " (1965:145, 146, emphasis added). Another factor was the government's ability to provide many consumer goods with rather little readily apparent cost to the public. The DP had available to it sizable surpluses accumulated from the World War II period when few imports were obtainable. In addition, large-scale foreign aid was beginning to come in. Exceptionally good crop weather combined with high world wheat prices and the DP's willingness to engage in a great deal of deficit financing added to the surplus. The real cost of these policies began to appear only toward the end of the decade, in the form of severe inflation. (Much of the peasantry was not yet sufficiently integrated into the national economy, however, to be greatly affected, and thus the Democrats lost support mainly in the cities.) The cost was further evident in the growth of foreign debt, to the point where in 1958 the World Bank, acting in the name of most of Turkey's creditors, forced the government to undertake a "stabilization program" and currency devaluation, a blow to Menderes' prestige.

Unfortunately for the government, these problems came just at the time when the DP was also having domestic political troubles over other matters, because socially Turkey was changing rapidly as well. One spectacular phenomenon was rapid urbanization (see chapter 3). Part of this was due to a high rate of population increase, almost 3 percent a year. A major contributing cause was rapid expansion of transportation and communications (see chapter 6), with many new facilities serving villages which had never before had easy connections with urban areas.

All of these growth areas were to be developed even more during the 1960s, but for several reasons the changes of the 1950s were particularly significant. For one thing, they were highly visible and large-scale, and thus presented a great contrast to what had taken place during the single-party period. Second, they took place under a government which although socially conservative was doing its utmost to stress how much more "democratic" it was than its predecessor. The latter claim, of course, had much truth to it, and there is little doubt that the policies of rapid growth in standards of living and of relaxation in the pace of social reform were viewed favorably by most of the population. The DP's favorable image was further enhanced by the decentralization of a good deal of power into the hands of local leaders. These new powerholders did not hesitate to intervene whenever possible on behalf of their supporters in dealings with the bureaucracy. Those who acquired political power in the provinces and local communities were often the economic leaders, small merchants and artisans (*esnaf*), who had traditionally been powerful there. With this kind of double-barreled support from influential local groups and the open use of patronage and selective financing of local public works projects to reward supporters and publish opponents, the DP succeeded in forging a powerful political base.

In the election of 1954 the DP increased its majority, winning 57 percent of the votes (only about 3 percent more than in 1950) and gaining 490 out of 535 seats. The victory was followed, somewhat inexplicably, by a series of repressive measures, including strengthened press censorship (stressing among other things heavy penalties for criticism of any public official), laws giving the government the power to arbitrarily retire judges and university professors, and regulations making it more difficult for small parties to qualify to enter elections.

By the time of the 1957 election, tensions were becoming severe. Resentment against many DP measures had begun to mount among the urban intelligentsia. The economic boom of the early 1950s was showing signs of waning. Inflation and shortages were becoming evident. A group of some thirty DP deputies had rebelled in 1955 to form the Freedom party, and although its electoral showing was poor (3.8 percent of the votes), its appearance on the political scene had sharpened the sense of threat which the Democrats had begun to feel. The DP's fears grew when the RPP vote in 1957 increased from 35.3 percent to 40.9 percent, and the conservative Nation party's support rose from 4.9 percent to 7.2 percent. The governing party was reduced to less than a majority (47.7 percent), even though its control of the Assembly remained overwhelming with 424 seats compared to 186 for the combined opposition. The government was further embarrassed the following year by having to agree to the World Bank's stabilization program (the loan portion of which was promptly used by the government to continue many of the questionable practices which the International Monetary Fund had criticized). In late 1959 tensions increased even more sharply when the government began to arrest journalists and dissident students, and to move toward direct repression of the RPP. After a number of violent clashes in Ankara, Istanbul and Izmir, the armed forces moved to overthrow the Menderes regime on May 27, 1960 (Weiker, 1963: 8–20; Ahmad, 1977: 63–7; Dodd, 1969:26 ff.).

The military commanders ruled Turkey for the next eighteen months only, keeping their promise to return the country to democratic politics as quickly as possible. There were several reasons for this. One was that the armed forces since Ataturk's day had been schooled to keep military and political affairs separate (see Chapter 4). A second was that there were disagreements within the army on goals and policies. A third was tactical. From the outset the National Unity Committee (NUC), as the junta called itself, had proclaimed clearly limited goals of restructuring certain institutions, such as the Constitution and the electoral law, and although these goals included purging those Democrats who had been accused of crimes against the nation, the commanders specifically refrained from condemning civilian politicians as a group. Perhaps most important was a fourth reason: the country's democratic institutions quickly began to assert their continuing vitality. In response to considerable pressure from the remaining political parties and many other interests (complementing the commanders' own predispositions), this implicit confidence in democratic processes was made explicit in January 1961 when the NUC convened a Constituent Assembly which included representatives of the political parties. The NUC held a national referendum on the new Constitution, and elections took place in October, 1961, which inaugurated what some have termed Turkey's Second Republic.

The NUC period was important for Turkey in several ways. Certain necessary reforms were accomplished, including instituting the new Constitution, which contained significant new checks and balances (see chapter 8); a new election law which provided for proportional representation and for impartial administration; and the establishment of a State Planning Office. (Central planning had been fiercely resisted by the Menderes government during its entire tenure.) These steps undoubtedly constituted a positive legacy. Others were more debatable. One of these was the treatment of the overthrown Democrats. In October 1960, 592 former deputies, province governors, army officers and other officials who supported the DP's allegedly criminal activities (the charges included both political ones such as abridging political rights of citizens and criminal ones such as embezzlement) were put on trial on the island of Yassıada, a short distance from Istanbul in the Sea of Marmara. After eleven months of court sessions, 402 of the defendants were convicted, 133 acquitted. Three of the leading defendants, former Prime Minister Menderes and his finance and foreign ministers, were later executed.[8] While the trial was undoubtedly necessary to legitimize the May 27 coup, and while there is unanimous agreement that it was conducted with scrupulous fairness, it also served to keep the name of Menderes in the public eye and to give at least some credence to the implication that many of the actions charged to the DP were only little different from what had gone on during the period of single-party rule by the RPP. There are not a few who think that whatever the negative repercussions might have been, immediate execution of the DP leaders after the coup would have been preferable. The long trial did not prevent Menderes from becoming a popular martyr after his execution. (On the trials, see Weiker, 1963; chapter 2.)

But in important ways the NUC period was notable because it was also one of basic continuity with previous Turkish politics. Few major economic and social reforms were achieved during the armed forces' rule. Neither reform of the tax structure nor land reform was significant, partly because the time was too short for resolving problems of such great complexity, but also because the NUC became involved in political bargaining in its bid to have many of its ideas legitimized. Nor did the NUC have any success in lessening the popularity of the DP. The old resentments against the RPP and the favorable attitudes among the peasants and many provincial and business leaders toward DP social and economic policies were in no way mitigated by the revelations of the trials, and once the commanders made it clear that they were serious about handing power back to the political parties, few people took them seriously anymore. Of course, no one was tempted to directly defy the military rulers on important points of the junta's governance, but in the referendum on the Constitution in July 1961, those who campaigned against the new charter only thinly disguised their desire to discredit the NUC, and some 38 percent of the electorate voted in the negative. In the October election, two-thirds of the votes went to three parties (Justice, New Turkey, Republican Peasants Nation) which were all but openly aspiring to become successors to the DP in their social and economic programs. Immediate return of conservatives to power was prevented only because these three parties split the former DP votes. The RPP consequently became the largest single party in the Assembly, despite its vote declining to 36.7 percent from its 40.9 percent of 1957.

Between 1961 and 1965, Turkey was governed by a series of coalitions based on the RPP in combination with some of the smaller parties, some independents, and nonparty "technicians," most of these coalitions being under the Prime Ministership of Ismet Inonu. (For an account of these coalitions see Dodd 1969:55–103, and Ahmad, 1977:212–31.) The military's role remained relatively passive, though they were always in the background, to be sure. NUC leader Cemal Gursel was elected President of the Republic, and all former NUC members received *ex officio* lifetime Senatorships and for a while were very visible and vocal. The National Security Council, which contained the top commanders, met frequently, and while it often commented on public affairs, did not interfere directly in Assembly matters, even as the successive coalitions became progressively more conservative on social and economic matters. The military's most important specific action was to decisively put down two attempts by young military radicals at *coups d'etat,* in February 1962 and May 1963. This reaffirmation of adherence to democratic politics had the effect, among others, of emboldening the aspirants to DP succession. (On the attempted coups see Weiker, 1963a.)

By the time of the 1965 election there had been several other new developments. One was the success of the Justice party in consolidating the former DP votes so that it emerged with an absolute majority in both votes and Assembly seats, thus dealing the RPP a severe defeat. Second, there was the birth of Turkey's first avowedly socialist party, the Turkish Labor party, which received only 3 percent of the votes and fifteen seats but which quickly became highly visible via several capable and articulate leaders. This emergence of a radical leftist party was made possible in large part by one of the major changes of the NUC era: the insertion of firm guarantees of full freedom of expression into the new Constitution. In addition, most responsible Turkish political leaders were determined that the curtailing of political freedoms which had occurred under the DP would not be repeated. Also, over the years the nation has gained a sense of confidence in itself and in its political institutions and no longer had an inordinate fear of "internationalist" ideologies.

The 1960s also saw a quickening of social and economic change and growth. Urbanization continued at a very rapid pace, and extensive shanty-towns (*gecekondu* areas) grew up on the edges of almost every large Turkish city (see chapter 3). Concomitant with the continued high rate of population growth there emerged a large amount of unemployment, only partly alleviated by the beginning of migration of many Turkish workers to the labor markets of western Europe. In 1963 labor unions received the right to strike, and quickly became a major interest group. The expansion of education also continued, as did the growth of communications and transportation, integrating a steadily and rapidly increasing proportion of the population into the mainstream of national (and increasingly into international) life. All of this produced greater demands for economic and social benefits. It also made it harder and harder for traditional leaders who relied on issues which formerly had great appeal (such as religion) or who capitalized on resentful memories of bureaucratic or single-party authoritarian behavior, to maintain control.[9]

Economic growth took place at an even faster rate than during the 1950s, despite more difficult circumstances. After a period of hesitation following the 1960 Revolution, the private sector resumed its activity, and government efforts came under the guidance of a series of five-year development plans which sought to coordinate all sectors of public and private investment and development. On the darker side of the economic scene was continuing inflation (which had begun to affect larger and larger proportions of the population as national integration continued), and the beginnings of what were to become very large balance-of-payments deficits. Nevertheless, expansionist economic policies which were in many ways similar to those of the DP continued, though with more caution.

Another important phenomenon was the splintering of the political party system. On the left, the TLP was making itself even more visible, and was getting support from radical student groups which had sprung up simultaneously with similar groups around the world. On the more moderate left, the RPP underwent a major soul-searching. Just prior to the 1965 election, under the domination (though not yet formal leadership) of Bulent Ecevit, it adopted a position labeled "left-of-center." This move (which did not help the RPP in the 1965 election) soon (May 1967) precipitated a defection by some conservative deputies and Senators. Led by Turhan Feyzioğlu, they formed the Reliance party (*Güven Partısı*) and further weakened the opposition. (In 1969 the RPP's vote fell to an all-time low of 27.4 percent.) Justice party leader Suleyman Demirel, who had become Prime Minister in 1965 when his party succeeded in consolidating the DP-successor votes and vanquishing its rivals, also had his troubles. He had alienated several important factions within his party because of his relative moderation on some social issues, his allegedly excessive favoring of large entrepreneurs, and personal and family scandals, all of which led to the emergence of a series of new parties farther to the right. They included the neofascist National Action party of Colonel Türkeş in 1969, the fundamentalist religious National Order party of Necmettin Erbakan in 1970 and also his National Salvation party of 1973, and the Democratic party, based on a variety of complaints about DP leadership personnel and programs, in 1971. In the 1969 election, a revised election law benefited the two largest parties (the JP and RPP together received 74 percent of the votes—down from 81.5 percent in 1965—but 89 percent of the Assembly seats) and saved Turkey from another period of coalition governments. The combined leftist parties (RPP and TLP) received barely over 30 percent of the votes, and the JP continued to rule.

Thus as the 1970s opened and the Republic approached its golden anniversary, many saw cause for worry. The country was beset at once with a government challenged on many sides, a not very popular prime minister, vast urban problems, a high level of unemployment, severe inflation, and a balance-of-payments deficit which grew with every succeeding year and was kept manageable largely because of remittances sent home by Turkish workers in Europe who now numbered close to a million. Added to these problems was a rapidly escalating level of urban violence. Leftist students and other radicals, motivated by a variety of national, international, and student issues, were increasingly being answered by rightist "commandos," reportedly under the organization of the radical right-wing parties, particularly that of Türkeş. These factors led Turkish politics to two other important developments before the Republic's half-century mark was reached.

The first was in March 1971, when the armed forces once again attempted to intervene in Turkish politics, this time via a "memorandum" to Prime Minister Demirel strongly suggesting that his services were no longer required because he had failed to solve the problems of economic stability and urban violence. Demirel took the hint a month later, and for the ensuing two and one-half years Turkey was once more governed by "caretaker" cabinets. Under martial law, many extremists were dealt with harshly. The authorities went considerably further than many people thought necessary, particularly in acting against virtually anyone who could be at all considered a supporter of or sympathizer with the radical left. The TLP was closed by martial law authorities in 1972, and many of its members were given long prison sentences. Nevertheless, and of more long-range importance, the commanders did not take over the government *per se*, confining themselves, rather, to a "supervisory" role, and did not directly interfere even as successive "above-politics" cabinets grew steadily less inclined to make economic and social reforms which many (though not all) of the generals felt were needed. Once again the Turkish body politic asserted its strong preference for civilian politics, and the political parties resisted further military dominance, even though various reforms which the officers might have been able to accomplish if they had had a direct government role would probably have been to their interest. The RPP, for example, was sympathetic to economic and social reforms advocated by at least some of the officers, and the right-wing parties certainly stood to benefit from the armed forces' propensity for curbing leftist urban violence more harshly than violence from the right. It was clear to all that without the cooperation of important civilian groups the armed forces could not govern with any effectiveness, and even those factions whose strength in weapons might have tempted them to resort to more authoritarian methods seemed to realize that, for better or for worse, the political process was the only effective road to political dominance.

The second major development was the election of 1973, its results later confirmed by the election of 1977. On the basis of much social change and a vigorous campaign by Bulent Ecevit (who had taken over leadership of the RPP from octogenarian Inonu in 1972), the RPP emerged as the largest single party. Though it must also be pointed out that it was the sole left-wing party and received only 33.3 percent of the votes, it had at long last seemingly reversed the downward trend which had been its almost continuous direction during the multiparty period. Significant too was the fact that it drew a great many of its new votes from the urban lower classes, which were struggling with the conflicting pressures of modernity and tradition. A considerable portion of voters opted for modern economic and social reform rather than continuing to be greatly influenced by the traditional issues on which the DP and JP had based much of their appeal. The National Salvation party received 12 percent of the votes (and forty-eight seats). Although its showing alarmed many Turks, given the disarray of the right, the lackluster appeal of Prime Minister Demirel, and the potency of antisecularist issues in Turkey, it was rather significant that the NSP got as few votes as it did. (The election is discussed in greater detail in chapters 4 and 5.) The Justice party, for all its troubles, remained the strongest party on the right, in part because its conservative platform also contained a very strong emphasis on modern economic issues.

In 1973 Ecevit became Prime Minister, in coalition with the NSP on the basis of some common economic programs and the intense desire of both to come to power. The coalition was very uneasy, however. It was probably ready to collapse in any case when Ecevit, on the heels of the invasion of Cyprus, which had made him a national hero, resigned after only eight months in the hopes of winning a quick new election and a larger victory. This time, however, the conservative parties refused to acquiesce (under the Turkish system a new election can only be called by a majority vote in the Assembly), and in March 1975, after several months of caretaker government, Suleyman Demirel succeeded in returning to power at the head of a "National Front" government of four conservative parties with a parliamentary majority of three votes. Dependent on the support of both the National Salvation and National Action parties, he virtually gave up attempts to avoid moving further toward the extreme right, and his hair-thin majority made it all but impossible to take difficult decisions needed to stabilize the rapidly worsening economic situation. From 1975 on, the level of urban violence rose even higher, the country experienced ever more rapid inflation, skyrocketing unemployment and foreign indebtedness, and made little progress on major foreign policy issues (Cyprus, which flared anew in 1974, led to a major rift with the United States, and the Aegean dispute with Greece seriously strained NATO relations).[10]

In June 1977, after another vigorous campaign, the RPP emerged for the second time as the largest single party, though its 41.4 percent of the votes left it with only 214 seats, again short of a majority. An attempt to form a minority government failed, and after more protracted negotiations the "National Front" was reconstituted by the Justice party together with the two radical right-wing parties, National Salvation and National Action. (The National Salvation party had declined from 11.8 percent in 1973 to 8.6 percent, another sign that religion was losing its appeal as a political issue; but the National Action party increased its 3.4 percent of 1973 to 6.4 percent in 1977, a showing generally interpreted as an expression of considerable frustration among groups experiencing strains of rapid social change.) The

Demirel government was again not able to move far toward solution of either the economic or social problems, however, and in December 1977 the RPP succeeded in getting the Assembly to vote no confidence. Upon gaining the support of two splinter parties, several independents, and some ten deputies who defected from the Justice Party, Ecevit again became Prime Minister. But although his government exuded vigor and energy, and included many capable ministers, the combination of his very precarious majority and the seemingly ever-increasing intractability of Turkey's economic problems and domestic violence steadily eroded the RPP's popularity, and in October 1979 Ecevit, in turn, resigned following severe defeat in Assembly by-elections. He was succeeded again by Demirel and the Justice party, whose ineffectual minority government was in turn set aside by a military intervention in September 1980.

In sum, every decade since the beginning of the Republic has brought change to Turkey at a faster rate than in the preceding one on virtually every major indicator of "development"—economic activity, education, public finance, communication of all kinds, political participation and conflict, urbanization. Each succeeding decade appears also to have brought increasingly complex and difficult public problems. The following chapters will explore the effectiveness with which these changes have contributed to the construction of a firm foundation for "modernization" as defined in the introduction to this work. It remains to be seen whether the most recent military intervention can make structural changes that will restore the basic political vigor with which Turkey has addressed many problems in the Republic's first half-century. But as the conclusion will detail, there is considerable ground for optimism that important roots have indeed been planted for meeting the challenges of the decades to come.

TWO

The Development
of Modernizing Leaders

The effectiveness with which a society develops the leadership talents of its population is crucial. As modernization proceeds, the number, variety, and complexity of tasks undertaken in service of the society as a whole increases continually. The need for persons who can innovate, who can organize and administer technical and other large-scale operations increases apace, as does the need to mobilize the talents of the general population in order both to expand the size of the leadership groups and to draw on all available talent. It is also necessary to build strong new relationships between leaders and an increasingly integrated body of followers. The latter cannot remain merely subjects, with social horizons confined to those of small groups, such as lineages and villages. Rather, followers inevitably have to be made citizens of a nation, a larger entity with which they will have to take on a set of new relationships and for whose advancement their efforts and abilities will have to be harnessed in new ways.

In a modernizing situation both quantitative and qualitative aspects of leadership recruitment and performance are important. Quantitatively it is necessary simply to increase the number of individuals who are able to take leadership roles, including political, economic and social roles in both the public and private sectors. Success in this area can to some extent be measured by examining the spread of education and of technical qualifications. (See Table 2-1. The data indicate great educational advances, although the 1975 figure of less than 5 percent with lycee or higher education—vocational education not counted—is still far below what is needed.) The degree to which a society is mobilizing all of its potential leadership talent may also be measurable in part by consideration of the socioeconomic background of its leadership. Although it is an imperfect measure of social mobility, it can at least give us some notion as to whether potential talent found in the lower socioeconomic strata is being recognized and tapped.

It is harder, of course, to define and to assess quality of leadership. In the present context it should be considered from at least two separate perspectives: technical and political. The quality of technical leadership may be assessed by the degree of competence in one's field, be it science, administration, or whatever and, perhaps even more important, by leadership's creativity and propensity to innovate. Quality of political leadership is to be judged by the kinds of relationships built between leaders and followers. In a modernizing society, followers' demands for equality and participation (in addition to demands for material well-being) grow rapidly, and effective leadership should be measured in part by the degree to which leaders are able to meet these demands of their followers (as well as how well leaders contribute to the mobilization of the talents of nonelites). It is often difficult, to be sure, particularly in a society in which authoritarian habits have deep social and historical roots, for leadership groups to act in ways which might undermine their own power and status. One should also not expect that leaders should entirely cede influence to followers in such functions as defining issues, and formulating and outlining specific policies.

Hard as it is to define the characteristics of appropriate leader-follower relationships in specific and operational terms, it is even more difficult to find suitable data for measurement. The chief sources of data are attitude studies (of which there are, unfortunately, only a few and which have the weakness of being unable to indicate clearly the relationship between attitudes and actions) and the reports of outside observers of leaders' performance.

TABLE 2-1
Population by Last School Graduated

	1960	1965	1970	1975
Primary school	4,221,026	6,097,107	8,346,488	11,762,162
% graduates of population over 10 years old	22.7	28.9	34.7	40.1
Middle school	521,973	695,435	1,014,731	1,609,445
% graduates of population over 13 years old	3.1	3.7	4.6	6.1
Middle level vocational schools			32,382	36,730
% graduates of population over 13 years old			.015	.01
Lycee	187,373	275,097	423,101	733,402
% graduates of population over 16 years old	1.2	1.6	2.3	3.1
Lycee level vocational schools	184,048	269,682	340,655	540,747
% graduates of population over 16 years old	1.2	1.6	1.8	2.3
Higher	119,487	170,741	275,981	333,107
% graduates of population over 20 years old	.9	1.2	1.7	1.7

Source: DIE #s 580, 825.

The Ottoman Legacy

In important respects, the Ottoman legacy to the Republic was positive. Quantitatively, as Dankwart Rustow found, "of the trained public servants of the late empire, 85% of the administrators and 93% of the staff officers continued service in the Turkish Republic" adding that "in 1919 and 1920 the Turkish nationalist movement was led by Ottoman generals and colonels, the Arab nationalist movement around Sharif Faysal by Ottoman captains and lieutenants" (1973:109). As a result of the long history of Ottoman governing, military enterprise, and the political activity of the Tanzimat and Young Turk periods, there were also leaders with a wide variety of skills and experience, including officers, bureaucrats, writers and publicists, and politicians. The biggest single deficiency was probably in entrepreneurs, most industrial and commercial activity having been in the hands of the non-Muslim minorities. In qualitative terms, among the most technically competent groups were the officers, who had had the benefit of the best schools, training by European experts (both in Turkey and abroad) in connection with the "defensive modernization" of the nineteenth century, and who often had extensive leadership experience.

On a more negative note, the Ottoman legacy was one of centralization, elitism, and authoritarianism. This legacy was only partly counterbalanced by such things as the fact that a sizable number of the military and bureaucratic leaders had risen from lower- or lower-middle-class origins and might therefore have been expected to have leavened this elitist tendency, and that many had also been exposed to the idea that one of the bases of European superiority was nationalism and patriotism, i.e., the building of connections between leaders and followers. (Most analysts of the Turkish bureaucracy and other Turkish institutions relate current characteristics in large part to this historical Ottoman legacy. On leadership viewed in historical perspective see Mardin, 1962; Chambers, 1964; Weiker, 1968; Szyliowicz, 1975; Frey, 1975; Lewis, 1961; Davison, 1963, 1964.)

National Political Leaders

We have a good deal of data on the social backgrounds of members of the Turkish National Assembly. The data are relevant to the two important aspects of developing suitable leaders which we have noted above: educational-technical qualifications, and relationships between leaders and followers. The most striking showings of the data (summarized in Tables 2-2 and 2-3) are:

1. During the single party and early multiparty years, the distribution of occupational backgrounds of deputies underwent marked changes in conjunction with political changes. More recently, the change has been far less marked.

2. The social background distributions within the major parties have become, in general, strikingly similar. Even members of the minor (frequently

radical) parties show many characteristics similar to those of major party members, with, however, a few distinct differences.

TABLE 2-2
Social Backgrounds of Turkish Deputies
(by percent)

	1923	1935	1946	1950	1961	1965	1969	1973	1977
Occupations									
Official	*54*	*48*	*36*	*22*	*21*	*23*	*28*	*24*	*16*
Government	25	19	14	10				10	7
Military	20	18	11	6				4	3
Education	9	11	11	6				10	6
Professional	*20*	*24*	*35*	*45*	*42*	*43*	*37*	*44*	*47*
Law	12	12	19	26				28	27
Medicine (dentistry, pharmaceutical, veterinary)	7	11	14	15				7	6
Engineering	1	1	2	4				9	14
Economic	*14*	*19*	*24*	*29*	*27*	*23*	*23*	*23*	*27*
Agriculture	6	8	9	10				7	7
Commerce, Industry, Banking	8	11	15	19				16	20
Other and Unknown	*12*	*9*	*5*	*4*	*10*	*11*	*12*	*9*	*10*
Religion	*7*	*3*	*1*	*1*				*5*	*4*
Education (% with higher education)	68	77	73	73	73	88	70	67	75
Age (average, years)	43.2	51.8	52.8	47.8	42.5	44.6	45.2	45.4	46.1
Localism (born in constituency represented	60	35	57	60	69	62	75	74	72[a]

Sources: Frey, 1965: 181, 176, 170, 207; Tachau, 1973:Table 2; Tachau, 1977: Table II; Meclis Albümü, 1977.

[a]Would be 84 without Istanbul, Ankara, Izmir.

TABLE 2-3
Social Backgrounds of Deputies by Political Party
(by percent)

OCCUPATIONS	RPP	DP-JP	Others
1950 Official	35	19	
Professional	35	46	
Economic	25	29	

TABLE 2-3 *(continued)*

OCCUPATIONS *(continued)*	RPP	DP-JP	Others
1965 Official	23[a]	22	
Professional	52	46	
Economic	31	34	
1969 Official	30[a]	36	
Professional	51	46	
Economic	21	33	
1973 *Official*	26	24	
Government	10	12	
Military	3	5	
Education	13	7	
Professional	49	39	
Law	33	24	
Medicine	7	6	
Engineering	9	9	
Economic	16	30	
Agriculture	5	10	
Trade, industry, banking	11	20	
Other	9	7	
Religion	0.5	4	
1977 *Official*	18	12	23
Government	8	6	5
Military	2	3	9
Education	8	3	9
Professional	44	41	53
Law	29	26	21
Medicine	6	5	7
Engineering	9	10	25
Economic	22	32	9
Agriculture	8	8	4
Trade, industry, banking	14	24	5
Other	16	15	15
Religion	1	7	4

EDUCATION
% with higher education

	RPP	DP-JP	Others
1950	79	73	
1965	91	74	69
1969	74	69	66
1973	70	64	66
1977	75	70	80

TABLE 2-3 *(continued)*

AGE
Average age (years)

1950	52	47	
1965	46	44	44
1969	45	45	47
1973	44	48	45
1977	44	48	46

LOCALISM
% born in constituency represented

1950	63	59	
1965	65	61	50
1969	78	76	61
1973	76	78	67
1977	72	73	72

Source: Tachau, 1973: Table 2; Tachau, 1977: Table IX: Meclis Albümü, 1977.
[a]Multiple responses counted by Tachau.

3.   The assemblies have always contained a high percentage of members with higher education.

4.   There has been a steady rise in the percentage of members born in the constituency which they represent.

5.   Although there are few hard data, there are indications that an increasing number of deputies have had province or local political-party experience.

Let us examine some of the social characteristics used in the data.

Occupation. Occupation is important because it is often closely related to the political programs of particular leaders or parties. In Turkey, changes in the distribution of deputies' occupations from one assembly to another have often strikingly reflected political changes.

The assemblies of the single-party period reflected Ataturk's political aims. Up to 1943 about half the deputies in each assembly were drawn from the "official" sector, i.e., government and the military. Men from these groups were readily available, were in large part sympathetic to Ataturk's reforms, and capable of running the institutions which were to put them into effect. Many were persons whom Ataturk knew personally. Low representation of the "economic" sector was related to factors such as the dearth of Turkish commercial and industrial experience, and, in the 1930s, the dominance of the bureaucracy over economic development under the policy of *etatism*. The slow but steady increase in the third major occupational grouping, professionals, probably reflects both the increase in the number of professionals in Turkish society and the fact that many of them had begun to move into nongovernment employment and were no longer identified as "officials."

Major shifts appeared as soon as the multiparty period loomed. Officials dropped from 47 percent to 36 percent in 1946, and to 22 percent with the Democratic sweep of 1950 when only 69 RPP deputies remained as compared with 396 newcomers in the DP. The economic group, a mainstay of DP support, jumped from 16 percent in 1943 to 24 percent in 1946 and 29 percent in 1950, while the professionals increased even faster, making up almost half the deputies in the 1950 Assembly.

As the multiparty period continued, however, changes in reaction to shifts in political strength of the parties, and differences among the major parties, became increasingly less marked. Since the mid-1960s, professionals have made up about half the deputies in each party, those with economic backgrounds most often between one-fourth and one-third, while the official group has declined fairly steadily, in 1977 becoming distinctly the smallest. These shifts reflect, among other things, changes in the availability of persons with political leadership qualifications in the various categories (and, as will be discussed shortly in the section on students, changes in the prestige of various occupations) and freer opportunities generally for entry into politics.

Perhaps most significant is the decline in broad occupational cleavages between the two major parties. There are, of course, still differences within the major categories—e.g., the expected findings such as more deputies with industrial and commercial backgrounds in the JP, and that the RPP has fewer persons with religious occupations than do the other parties. A limitation of the data is that we are not able to distinguish within groupings well enough to see if there are possible class distinctions among the parties (e. g. the amount of wealth of the farmers). But on the whole, it seems justifiable to conclude that the occupational data support a major hypothesis of this study; i.e., that one strength of Turkish politics is that there are two major parties, *each* of which draws on a wide spectrum of groups and that at least some of the deep gulfs between groups are being bridged.

Age at election reflects the "modernity" of the Turkish polity. Seldom has it exceeded an average higher than the mid-forties for either major party. At the Assembly level at least, leadership age, a major factor sometimes used in categorizing a nation as "traditional" or "modern," would seem to disqualify Turkey for membership on the "traditional" category.[1]

Education. From the data, it appears that Turkey is likely to continue to be led by a preponderance of men with considerable formal education. In 1973 for only the first time since 1931 did the percentage of deputies with higher education fall slightly below 70 percent, and seldom has it been less than 65 percent for any party. In 1977, the percentages of members with higher education in the minor parties was NSP 75 percent, NAP 81 percent, GP 100 percent, independents 86 percent.

Local experience. There are few hard data on local government or political experience of Assembly members, but impressionistic evidence indicates that it is becoming more important as a stepping-stone to Assembly membership. Frey found that although local government experience was low among Assembly members as a whole, for the period 1920–57 it was more than twice as high for deputies with economic backgrounds than for those with official or professional ones. In other words, it was higher among those who were elected because of local power rather than intellectual or official status (1965:98). Tachau concludes from indirect evidence that "connection between local and national political experience is by no means absent" and notes that in his data there was "extensive under-reporting" of political experience, partly perhaps because it did not always take the form of formal office" (personal communication). Kili found that 88 out of 143 freshmen RPP deputies elected in 1969 "had had years of experience as leaders of province and district parties" (1976:255). More informally, in conversations one hears increasingly often about deputies with such experience. It appears clear that as the importance of local politics (and of localism among Assembly members) increases, so will the degree to which experience at that level is brought to bear on the outlook of parliamentarians, and it is likely that these influences will have an important impact on the political structure. (For more on this point see chapter 5 and the section on local government in chapter 8.)

Localism (being born in the constituency represented) has been profoundly affected in the multiparty period. From 60 percent in the 1923 Assembly it declined steadily to a low of 34 percent in 1935 and rose slowly to 42 percent in 1943. But in 1946 it jumped to 57 percent, a change soon formalized in a significant change in the RPP by-laws: after 1947 almost all of the candidates were selected by province party organizations rather than the National Council. The localism rate has been rising ever since. Each year since 1969 it has been over 70 percent. In 1977, if one excluded Istanbul, Ankara, and Izmir it would have been 83.8 percent. (Localism among Istanbul deputies was 22.7 percent, for Ankara, 37.9 percent, and for Izmir, 52.6 percent.)

Somewhat surprisingly, in many Assemblies since 1950 the RPP has had a higher localism rate than the DP or JP. This runs counter to the generally accepted picture of the RPP as the more "cosmopolitan" party, less rooted in the localism which characterizes the deputies with economic occupations.[2] It can only be partly accounted for by the role of local notables in the RPP organization, particularly in many eastern provinces. But since the RPP is not a very radical party, its rating on localism shows that it too recognizes the degree to which local identification is still a major basis for much electoral strength in even the more "modern" parts of Turkey. (This is one place in which the meaning of the findings is particularly unclear, however. The effects of the large amount of internal migration both from villages to towns and from one region to another is surprisingly absent, and thus it may well be that despite their relative youth and large amount of higher education, the deputies at the same time continue to represent to a significant degree the local elites which have long been dominant in many places. Many more data are needed.)

It is frequently believed that leaders having higher education, relative youth, and professional expertise will bring a high degree of intellectual and technical skill to policymaking and will evidence a degree of openness to new ideas. To the extent that this is accurate, it is particularly significant for Turkey that these characteristics are shared by the deputies of both the moderate conservative and moderate liberal parties, and that both groups share the characteristic of localism. (This state of affairs also, to be sure, serves to reemphasize the degree to which social background factors account only partially for differing political views.) As discussed elsewhere in this study, it may well be that it is the moderate or "modern" conservatives who are best able to build connection between the needs of Turkish development and the social values of most of the Turkish population and thus provide a measure of necessary stability to Turkish modernization (though others will contend that the slow pace of modernization may be too high a price to pay for stability and orderliness).

Local Political Leadership

How far down the political elite ladder do these characteristics go? To answer this question we can look at subnational political leaders (see Table 2–4). They are important partly in that it is at the levels of province parties and large city mayoralties that we are most likely to find candidates for the Assembly. Perhaps even more important, however, is the fact that given the limited number of deputyships available, the great majority of these leaders will remain at the subnational level in a period where the importance of that level is likely to become very rapidly more important.

We have two studies of party leaders at or near the province level. Tachau (1973) surveyed province party executive committees in fifteen provinces in 1964, and Özbudun (1977) examined party leaders in several districts of Izmir province in 1968. (Here we utilize his findings concerning the urban leaders of the two major parties.[3])

About 30 percent of both Tachau's and Özbudun's groups are in professional occupations, somewhat below the level of deputies, but higher than the rural mayors. The high percentage in economic categories puts them close to the latter but is distinctly different from that of their Assembly counterparts. Educationally, too, both groups are at a middle level, although we should note that in provincial cities the pool of the "educated" probably includes those who attended lycee as well as those with higher education, and hence the province party leaders are markedly among the select. It is also noteworthy that, as among the deputies, there is considerable similarity among the province leaders of the two major parties (with some differences, to be sure, including 35 percent professionals in the RPP compared to 23 percent in the JP, and a somewhat greater percentage of younger leaders in the RPP). The characteristics of national leaders are clearly filtering down the ladder.

Extending down another level, we have some data on mayors. (Some

TABLE 2-4
Social Backgrounds of Deputies and Local Political Leaders

	Deputies			Province Party Leaders *Tachau Özbudun*		Mayors, Towns Over 20,000			Mayors, Towns Under 20,000		
	1969	1973	1977	1964	1968[c]	1968	1973	1977	1968	1973	1977
OCCUPATIONS: Professional %	37	44	47	29	30	30	52.3[a]	4	24.7[b]	24.2[b]	
Official	28	24	16	6	15	14		15.4[a]	12	14.1[b]	14.8[b]
Economic	23	23	27	60	45	47		32.2[a]	76	52.8[b]	58.8[b]
(of which agriculture)		(7)	(7)	(7)	(zero)	(12)			(35)	(36.2)	(27.5)
EDUCATION: Higher	70	67	75	41	45	47	53	52			
Lycee				13	21	18	14	14			
Middle				24	18	14	10	16			
Primary				17		7	13	11			
Other or unknown				5							
LOCALISM: Born in constituency represented[d]	75	74	72	87	59		68	62		62	55
Mayors born in same province							16	9		31	26
AGE: Average age (yrs.)	45.2	45.4	46.1	42.4		50	44	42.3	38	41	43.5
% over age 45				37	34		44	32			40.5

SOURCE: Deputies: same as Table 2-2. Province party leaders: Özbudun 1977; Tachau 1973a. Mayors: Gökçeer, 1978, and my own calculations from *Belediye Başkanları Albümleri.*

[a] Province capitals (Gökçeer, 1978.)
[b] All mayors (Gökçeer, 1978.)
[c] Urban leaders of major parties in Izmir. See note 3 (of this chapter).
[d] Localism for deputies: born in same province. Localism for province party leaders 1964: born in same province or region. Localism for province party leaders 1968: current residence. Localism for mayors: born in same town unless otherwise indicated.

observers strongly insist that mayors, even more than province-level party officials, are merely fronts for traditional elites. There is some validity to this assertion, but it is clear that as penetration by the national government into local affairs increases, more and more dealings between national and local administrations are being conducted through the channel of the formally elected officials, and mayors should certainly not be automatically written off as unimportant though only further study will enable us to gauge their real significance.[4])

The social background information on mayors closely parallels the patterns found at higher levels. In each of the three years for which we have data in the form of albums compiled and published by the Turkish Municipalities Association *(Türk Belediyecilik Dernegi)*, (mayors elected in 1968, 1973 and 1977), the general similarity to national and province leaders in terms of occupation and education persists as far down as towns of twenty thousand. Only in cities below that size did the backgrounds of mayors more closely mirror that of the general population. Thus in cities over twenty thousand in 1968, the 30 percent who were in professional occupations resembles the groups mentioned, and although the published data for 1973 and 1977 unfortunately did not include occupations, an analysis done by Fikri Gökçeer found that for the sixty-seven province capitals over 50 percent of the mayors were professional, exceeding the percentage in this category even among deputies. He also found that (by taking all mayors together) in 1977 the difference between backgrounds of mayors of small and large communities was very distinct (1978:234–44), paralleling the present author's findings for the 1968 group. In education, the resemblance of the large city mayors to their province and national counterparts and their differences from small town mayors are even more clear. It is noteworthy that in localism the levels for both large and small city mayors is somewhat lower than for national and province leaders, reflecting the rapid urbanization of recent years. However, when those born in the same province are added to those born in the same city, the levels exceed those for deputies, and the short-distance migrations which this represents indicate that even the mayors who had moved to other communities probably had at least some past ties with the geographic areas in which they were serving as elected officials. And, once more, when the social characteristics of mayors of small cities are analyzed by political party affiliation, more similarities appear than do contrasts. If one can be cautiously optimistic that "modern" social characteristics may be associated with better policymaking, the findings about subnational leaders, as those about deputies, may bode well.

The Bureaucracy

Elected leaders are not the only ones who will shape Turkish society in the future. The civil bureaucracy has been an important element of Turkish leadership for many decades, and despite inroads by military and religious elites to varying degrees in Ottoman times, by provincial notables (among others) in the latter Ottoman period, and by elected political leaders and the private economic sector during the multi-party years of the Republic, it continues to play a very important role. (On the Ottoman bureaucracy see especially Chambers, 1964, and Weiker, 1968.)

In trying to assess the role which the bureaucracy is playing in Turkish modernization, we must look at it somewhat differently from the way we have been examining elected political leaders. The chief reason for this is the difference between the relationships of the political elites and the bureaucratic elites respectively to nonelites. Political leaders are to a large extent subject to some direct controls by their followers through the electoral process. Bureaucrats, in contrast, are subject only to very indirect popular control since supervision of administrators is generally channeled either through political leaders or through the bureaucracy's own hierarchy. Thus while some personal and social background characteristics of its members can give us a rough measure of the degree of utilization of nonelite talent, we must also look at the bureaucrats' technical competence and political responsiveness.

That the bureaucracy is seen by many as a problem is attested to in numerous official documents, as well as by general popular agreement. The State Planning Organization, for example, as one of the items in its "Strategy and Basic Targets of Long-Term Development in the Third Five-Year Plan" stated that "Public administration is unable to become an efficient instrument for development, because it is incapable of conducting its functions in required quality, speed, and productiveness. Lacking the characteristic of supporting development, the public administration grows steadily in volume, it does not regenerate itself, becomes more and more costly, and constitutes a rigid structural problem difficult to solve" (1973a:15). (For a more detailed criticism see Cohn, 1970:85–99.)

Numerous reasons have been given for this inadequacy of bureaucratic response to public needs. Amond the most frequently cited ones is the contention that in the past quarter century, i.e., during the multiparty period, the bureaucracy was subjected to severe pressures which eroded its former high quality, and that the demoralizating effect was especially great because this diminution followed a period of almost unprecedented power. There is some truth to this. In the single party period the bureaucracy was overwhelmingly dominant because it was the chief source from which Ataturk drew his agents of rapid reform, and because there were a large number of new tasks which the government undertook which were central to almost all aspects of national affairs, including law and general administration, and a large number of economic development projects which under the *etatist* policy were almost entirely carried on by the state. The bureaucracy grew from around 104,000 in the early 1930s to almost a quarter million in 1946. During the multiparty period, though it has continued to grow numerically, reaching 665,000 in 1970[5] and an estimated one million in 1978, in almost every other way it has indeed suffered. At least three specific sources of the decline can be distinguished.

First, bureaucratic salaries and emoluments underwent a serious relative decline as a result of both rapid inflation during much of the period since the 1950s and the general disfavor with which the Democrat and Justice party governments looked on civil servants, whom they considered prime competitors of the private enterpreneurs. Civil servants were also major targets of many socially conservative voters as a result of the bureaucratic domination of the single-party period (see chapter 5). Both the entrepreneurs and the former "victims" of the bureaucracy were major components of these governments' support. The situation of the bureaucrats was partly eased by sharply increased government saleries in the early 1970s, but these increases were not really sufficient to make salaries once again an important factor in attracting the best talent to public service. The personnel reforms of the mid-1960s also failed to remedy another major problem, the tight grip of seniority on promotion and financial rewards. As under the old laws, entry-level salaries continued to be "based on the amount of education received, with increases thereafter . . . largely based on seniority" (Bent, 1969:61–62). One result is that Turkish ministries and agencies have increasingly resorted to the "contract system" for recruiting strategic but scarce skills. In view of these scarcities, the risks which "contract employees" took because they were excluded from fringe benefits and received no guarantee of permanence were minimal, and a mid-1960s estimate found that the contract system was used to hire almost half of the high-level scientific and technical employees in some ministries (Bent, 1969). Similar hiring problems and practices exist today in provincial cities which are trying to upgrade their staffs. The internal friction and the reduced prospects of recruiting first-class administrators caused by contract hiring are clear.

Second, there has been a vast increase in alternative career possibilities for those who earlier would almost automatically have entered the civil service. The free professions and the rapidly growing private sector have been the chief competitors, both financially and in that their prestige has risen rapidly at the very time that the prestige of bureaucratic positions has been declining. (See the section on students, below.)

Third, still another problem has been the general tone of politics. After 1950 the general public took to its new power with enthusiasm, and carried its opportunities for defying the politicians over into defiance of the government's bureaucratic arm as well. Not that there was a sudden tidal wave of refusal to respect officials' directives or of arguing with them on a large scale, but practices such as attempting to invoke the intercession of one's Assembly deputy or party official began to catch on quickly[6] as soon as initial doubts that the outcome of the free elections of 1950 would be respected had passed.

Who Are the Bureaucrats?

Because bureaucratic careers had long carried high prestige and security in Turkish society, it is not surprising that members of the bureaucracy often sought to assure public positions for their sons. Despite some tendencies toward stress on merit and achievement in Ottoman times, and to a greater degree under the Republic, there has also been evident a "traditional tendency toward fixed career lines" (Chambers, 1964:306), to some extent through considerable favoritism in admission to special training programs, but more generally through a system of access to education which favored the sons and daughters of those already in the urban, educated class.

The extent to which these practices have been altered under the more open political system since 1950 is not fully clear. Unfortunately the data on the social background of bureaucrats are not as rich as we would like, and much of the information is quite old. But although the data are sufficient for only tentative generalizations, they are fairly consistent, and in general we can say that among the highest levels of government officials the trends seem to have been similar to many just noted among elected officials, i.e., new bureaucrats tend to be drawn increasingly from families with economic or professional backgrounds, with a decline in those from the official sector. Their origins also show a steadily widening geographic dispersal. On the other hand, the data indicate that in many ways this change came much more slowly to the bureaucracy, and that many characteristics of a rather narrow elite group were preserved for a long time (e.g., the bureaucrats at the higher levels were drawn from a very small number of schools).

To summarize some of the data, as early as 1950 Matthews' survey of junior and potential (still students) administrators found that the fathers of the juniors had considerably more education and were more likely to have economic occupations, and that more of the juniors came from major metropolitan centers (1955:passim). A 1957 study by Gorvine and Pay-aslıoğlu found that far more *valis* (province governors) than *kaymakams* (district governors) had been born in province capitals, and that in general the *kaymakams* showed "an interesting representation of sons of lower-level civil servants, small merchants and farmers." They attribute this at least in part to scholarships which enabled recruitment from a wider diversity of backgrounds for some schools of administration (1957:passim). In 1957 and 1964 Dodd found also that *valis* as compared to *kaymakams* came significantly more from official backgrounds, while the latter were far more often from lower-class origins (1969:Tables 14, 15). Contrary data, on the other hand, were found by Szyliowicz in his study of the Political Science Faculty (PSF) of Ankara University, the successor to the Ottoman *Mülkiye* (School of Administration) and still one of the central sources of Turkish bureaucrats. He concluded that at least up to 1961, about half the students continued to come from official backgrounds, and among the economic group there was a tendency for students to come from its wealthier rather than its poorer segments (1971:393). This may be partly due to the very great prestige which the PSF continues to have and may also be an indication that at the highest levels change in the character of the bureaucracy may not come so easily. But given its rapidly growing size, the increasing number of available persons with higher education, and the increasing diversity of schools from which they come, a more representative bureaucracy seems likely to emerge more and more rapidly.

What Do the Bureaucrats Think?

There are many difficulties in answering a generalized question like this, important as it is. The range of attitudes within the bureaucracy on political questions and on policies and philosophies of social change is fully as great as in Turkish society as a whole.[7] It is also conceptually difficult to define with much operational precision what constitutes "modern" or "democratic" behavior among bureaucrats. Further, there is often only slight correspondence between social backgrounds, attitudes, and behavior. The small amount of data and its weaknesses (questions in surveys have been diverse, only rarely rigorously comparable over time, and on many important matters no questions were asked at all) aggravate these problems, but even with these caveats we are able to draw at least tentative conclusions on several important points.

The available studies agree that the typical Turkish bureaucrat is relatively security-conscious, and not particularly innovative. Matthews found that his "emergent administrators" overwhelmingly (76 percent) preferred "maximum security; low salary," only 7 percent preferring "little security; high salary" and a mere 14 percent opting for even "moderate security; moderate salary" (1955:24). Bent, similarly, found that "when asked why they entered public service, the most frequent reason (given by his respondents in 1966) was economic. . . .less than ten percent gave a public service reason for entering government. . . .when asked what they liked most about government work and what was the best thing about public employment, 40 percent and then 60 percent mentioned security . . . what is perhaps most significant is that security was more frequently mentioned by the younger, and better educated, and those more exposed to western culture."[8] Corollary to this was his finding that "when contronted with a problem involving risk-taking the Turks were cautious—even more so than Berger found the Egyptians to be" (1969:51, citing Berger 1957).[9]

The reasons for this have considerably to do with the environment in which the bureaucrats often find themselves. In addition to factors mentioned earlier, specific problems have for some time now included a high level of bureaucratic unemployment and an inadequate level of salaries. There is also a system of elaborate internal controls which is designed far more to avoid mistakes (commendable as that may be) than to encourage creativity and innovation.[10] And on the most general level, numerous analysts have found Turkey to have a strong "socially required value of respect for authority" (Kağıtçibaşi 1977:31) which reinforces tendencies toward self-protection which are far more universal than they are uniquely Turkish.

There is also general agreement among analysts that much of this conservatism and insecurity is expressed by the bureaucrats taking an exceedingly domineering attitude toward the public. Among the reasons for this (in addition to the various factors just cited) we should add the political views which apparently continue to prevail among many bureaucrats, i.e., the seeming incapability of both the politicians and the general public to solve Turkey's problems. Heper's extensive research leads him to conclude that "The Turkish bureaucratic elite's longing for a 'tutelary bureaucracy' continues" (1976a:499), that "Turkish bureaucrats rank relatively low on tolerance for democratic political life" (1977:75), and that they are "surely status-discrepant" (1976a:499).[11]

There are, to be sure, scattered findings in some studies that indicate possible betterment of the situation. As noted earlier, the educational level of much of the bureaucracy is high, and Frey concluded that authoritarian values seem to decline as education increases (cited by Kazamias 1966:204). The Rooses found that "the level of trust seems fairly high among Turkish bureaucrats. . . .roughly similar to that reported by Almond and Verba for American and English respondents and considerably greater than the level of trust found in Germany, Italy and Mexico. . . .these data imply an overall level of trust which would seem to facilitate cooperation within the middle ranges of the administration" (1969:561–3). It is also true that there are presently province and district governors who make it a special point to meet the people and hear their views and to keep their office door open to the public. A populist government might well encourage such practices.

We must conclude, however, that the negative factors continue to prevail. Though the study is old, it is worth noting that McClelland found the n-Ach level of Turkish public bureaucrats to be *even lower than that for private entrepreneurs* (on whom more below). (Cited by Bent, 1969:48; my emphasis.) And the Rooses found that among 1956 and 1965 graduates of the Political Science Faculty there were increasing proportions who aspired to nonpublic and nonadministrative careers (1971). The competition for Turkey's best talent is intense. The advent of bureaucrats from the lower socioeconomic strata might bring in persons who are personally even less secure and so need even more to reinforce their own sense of status, even though they may also be more like their nonelite "clients" and thus more empathetic with their problems and needs. We must conclude that the contribution of the civil bureaucracy to the development of modernizing Turkish leadership, at least in the political sense defined above, remains rather limited.

The Economic Elite

A relatively new, but increasingly important group of leaders are the private entrepreneurs.[12] Though the "hard" data are again scarce, indications are that there is still a good deal of traditionalism among this group even as some of its members seem to be adopting more "modern" characteristics very rapidly.

The number of entrepreneurs is now increasing rapidly, even though entrepreneurship is still a relatively new occupation for Turks. Prior to World War I most of the industry and commerce was in the hands of the non-Muslim minorities, in part because these activities have long had low status in Islam. As Bernard Lewis observed, "The Turk still preferred the three professions of religion, government and war, and left commerce, with its degrading infidel associations, to the Christians and Jews" (1961:448). Another reason was the general state of underdevelopment of the empire's economy (see chapter 7).

The development of entrepreneurship was further retarded, as noted earlier, when, after a short period of encouragement of the private sector during the 1920s, the *etatist* policy of the 1930s began to stress industrialization via the public sector.[13] It was only with the beginning of the multiparty system that the business community received both encouragement and resources on a significant scale. Its rapid expansion during the 1950s and thereafter, however, would indicate that a sizable reservoir of both human and material resources had accumulated even during the *etatist* years, and as early as 1960 Bernard Lewis described the new businessmen and managers as "self-confident, self-reliant and ambitious" (1961:467). The number of private-sector manufacturing plants employing ten or more workers increased from 2,515 in 1950 to 3,012 in 1963, 4,820 in 1970 and 5,912 by 1975 (DIE #825:226). To the operators of these enterprises should also be added the directors of the more than 400 large state-owned factories (1975), many of whom are committed as fully to standards of manufacturing excellence as are the best private entrepreneurs.

Unfortunately, both of the only two surveys of the social backgrounds and characteristics of Turkish private entrepreneurs which we have date from the late 1950s. Alexander, in a study of 63 entrepreneurs in the Izmir area (1960) and Payaslıoğlu, in a more detailed study of 138 entrepreneurs in the Marmara region, agree that at least in that period, the initial years of rapid expansion, those who moved into industry were for the most part those who had already been in related occupations. Payaslıoğlu's study of their wives also led him to the conclusion that the entrepreneurs "form[ed] a fairly closed social group" and his data "reveal[ed] how much becoming an entrepreneur [was] influenced by family connections and by families as sources of capital" (1961:11).[14]

More recent (and "softer") data indicate that movement into the private manufacturing sector is still quite frequently from related economic occupations, but that this sector is also becoming increasingly attractive to bright young men from other areas. Student surveys (cited below) show that the private sector has risen significantly in prestige, and that in some of the best universities it is increasingly regarded as an attractive alternative to a traditional bureaucratic career. A study by the Rooses found that "the attitude of Political Science Faculty graduates showed little of the hostility towards [politicians and] businessmen suggested by comparative administration theorists and many commentators on the Turkish scene. . . . .Businessmen and politicians—the groups which most successfully challenged the traditional power and prestige of the Turkish official class—were the two groups seen as making the biggest contribution to the development of the Turkish state. Government administrators were ranked a poor third, and almost no one had a kind word to say for the military" (1971:160–1). It has also been reported that there is now direct entry into the private sector by many university graduates, whereas earlier the private sector recruited managers mainly from State Economic Enterprises. The number of students in the university faculties of management has also risen steadily, (from 548 in 1970–1971 to 989 in 1974–1975 at Istanbul University and 410 to 619 in the same period at Ataturk University) as has enrollment in the Economic and Commercial Sciences Academies and Higher Schools (31,642 in 1970–1971 to 45,960 in 1974–1975). (Most people agree, however, that the graduates of the latter institutions will most likely remain at lower levels and not become real entrepreneurs.)

In their attitudes, however, many Turkish entrepreneurs seem not yet to fully fit the "modern" mold. As will be discussed further in chapter 7, many are still not oriented to aggressive competition, competition which would entail more attention to activities such as advertising, marketing and quality control. Another "traditional" trait is the disinclination to form joint-stock companies.

The little "hard" data we have on this dimension are again old, but they tend to be confirmed by what we know about Turkey in general and about businessmen in other countries, and by informal impressions of numerous observers. Bradburn, in a 1958–1959 study of forty-nine junior executives attending a middle-management program at Istanbul University, found that in business management, as in Turkish family organization (and, as noted above, in the bureaucracy) there tended to be very centralized authority. Delegation of authority and responsibility was rare, in part because of the low general level of clerical skills and worker standards, and in part because of a "generalized unwillingness or psychological inability to take responsibility without the constant checking of a superior." Another cause of the problem was unwillingness to jeopardize superior-subordinate separation, which was seen as important to the functioning of the enterprise. Bradburn observed that Turkish managers agreed considerably more strongly than a counterpart American sample with the statement that "Workers should not be promoted to managerial jobs, even if they are qualified, because it would destroy the respect for authority which the workers must have toward management." The reason for this, Bradburn comments, "appears to lie in the conception of the good manager as one whose orders will be obeyed without question." He further noted that "the primary focus of role evaluation is thus placed on the ability to control others, rather than on the ability to achieve the goals of the organization (i.e., productivity or efficient operation)." He cites a number of examples where this attitude resulted in severe production bottlenecks (1963a:65–7).

McClelland, carrying Bradburn's data further, concluded that Turkey (in the late 1950s) drew many more of its businessmen from the upper and upper middle segments of the population than did the United States, Mexico, Italy, or Poland; that top businessmen in Turkey had considerably higher n-Ach scores than those at the middle levels, and that while n-Ach among Turkish businessmen was not generally lower than among businessmen in the other countries, men with high n-Ach were not being efficiently recruited for the lower ranks of business management;[15] that among the top level of businessmen, those from the upper class had lower n-Ach levels than those recruited from further down the social scale, and that on these grounds recruitment from the upper classes could be also termed "inefficient"; and that a vicious circle was involved in the sense that countries like Turkey "have to create a larger middle class before they can efficiently draw talent from it . . . [but] development is necessary to create a larger pool of middle-class entrepreneurial talent which makes development possible" (1967:261–4, 279–80).

Perhaps the middle class is now large enough so that this vicious circle is broken. New data are badly needed, but there is ample reason to believe that the total contribution, qualitative as well as quantitative, being made to Turkish modernization by the private entrepreneurs is still considerably below its potential.

The Military

The armed forces are likely to remain important politically. When Turkey's military officers act together or when they act in the name of other parts of Turkish society, their strength and organization can be decisive. But there are also reasons to believe that the relative contribution of the military to Turkey's modernizing leadership has been and will continue to be reduced. If so, this represents a major reversal of a strong Turkish tradition.

The military route has long been one of Turkey's most open channels of social mobility and a major source of recruitment of the nation's best talents. As Bernard Lewis has written,

> The army had always drawn its recruits from a wider circle than the religious hierarchy, with its entrenched dynasties of rank and wealth, or the bureaucracy, with its inevitable bias in favor of the capital and its insistence on traditional, formal education. The poor and the provincial, the low-born and the uneducated, all had their chance in the armed forces, and in the course of the nineteenth century the expanding, modernized army offered the most promising career open to talent (1961:457; see also Rustow, 1959:515).

In addition, the military had long enjoyed high prestige in Ottoman society. Soldiers individually and the armed forces as an organized group played important roles throughout Ottoman times, and military men were to a large degree the leaders in the Young Turk revolution, in the War of Independence, and in the founding of the Republic. Ataturk, himself probably the most prominent example of the opportunities for social mobility available through Turkey's system of military schools (which today still offer free education

TABLE 2-5

Social Backgrounds of Officers and Noncommissioned Officers
(in percentages)

	Officers (N-239)		NCOs (N-531)	
Father's Occupations				
Military (officers or NCOs)	11.7	⎰Official	2.2	⎰Official
Bureaucrats	34.7	⎱ 46.4	17.7	⎱ 19.9
Economic (merchant, entrepreneur, industrial)	7.9		2.6	
Free professions	12.9		6.2	
Farmers	14.2		37.8	
Workers	5.0		16.0	
Small esnaf and other	13.6		17.5	
Father's Education: Higher	18.4		None or only primary 85	
Lycee	16.7			
Officials w/higher educ.	16.3		Officials w/none or only primary 48	
Economic occupation, only primary or orta education:	68			
Economic occupation, higher education	7.9			
Grandfathers: Official	23.3			
Farmers	33.4		Farmers 69.8	
(other changes from father's occupations small.)			Workers 6.5 Small esnaf 9.9	
Continuities: 85% with farmer fathers also had farmer grandfathers. 58% of officer or NCO fathers had officer or bureaucrat grandfathers.				
Place of birth: Large city	23.8		5.8	
Village or small town	33		71	

SOURCE: Ahmet Taner. Kişlali, Yanki, #296.

beginning in middle school (*orta*) for those lucky enough to qualify), also saw to it that the "Gazi" (warrior hero) image was not lost.[16]

The status of the military, like that of the bureaucracy, declined during the 1950s concomitantly with the increased status of other elites under the rule of the Democrat party. The attractiveness of a military career was further lessened as material perquisites became relatively smaller because of inflation, government policies, and the rapid rise of business and professional groups. Its status rose again, at least in the eyes of much of the urban educated class, when the armed forces joined in the overthrow of the Menderes government in 1960, and the attractiveness of a military career was also undoubtedly enhanced anew when the military government of 1960–1961 took steps to restore previously lost material benefits.[17] In 1971 the more conservative groups of the population had reason to be pleased when the military "supervision" of civilian politicians included harsh treatment of Turkish leftists. On the other hand, the prestige of the military was again seriously tarnished when the armed forces during both of their periods of rule proved unable to effect (or to cause civilians to effect) social and economic reforms which the officers had announced as among their goals.

The few social background data which we have (the armed forces are extremely reluctant to let themselves be studied) support the general consensus that, as in the past, the officer corps is still indeed a channel for social mobility. "The Turkish officer corps is recruited, by and large, from the lower-middle and salaried middle class." Özbudun and Weiker both found that, in 1960, among the members of the National Unity Committee, "none . . . appeared to belong to the top political or economic elites," over half "apparently came from what may be broadly defined as middle class families," and "at least eleven out of the twenty-nine could safely be classified as belonging to lower or lower middle-class families."[18] However, analogous to other elite groups, it also contains significant elements of inbreeding (Özbudun 1966:28–9; Weiker, 1963:118).

Similarly, a 1971 survey of 239 officers by Ahmet Taner Kışlalı showed that while 46 percent of their fathers had been in "official" occupations, only 16.3 percent of that group had had higher education and that they were distinctly from the lower ranks of both the military and civil bureaucracies. The survey also showed that among the fathers who were merchants or entrepreneurs, 68 percent had not gone beyond *orta* education, a clear indication they were small merchants; that while over three generations there has been a distinct shift in occupational background (33.4 percent of the officers' grandfathers were farmers but only 14.2 percent of their fathers, 23 percent of their grandfathers were officials while among their fathers this figure rose to 46.4 percent), their class origins seemed not to have changed, and the military continues to be an important channel for making sizable upward moves. Kışlalı also found that becoming a noncommissioned officer is an even more widely used route of social mobility. Thirty-eight percent of his sample of 531 NCOs were the sons of farmers and 33 percent the sons of workers or *esnaf*.[19] One should add, though, that this aspect of social mobility is limited because NCOs almost never move through the ranks to become officers in the Turkish armed forces. The social distinction between the two categories remains very sharp.

There are a number of factors, however, which seem to limit the contribution of the military to Turkey's leadership. Among these are the far smaller size of the Military Academy (*Harbiye*) than is that of educational facilities for other career lines, though the quality of military education appears to be quite high;[20] the uneven opportunities for middle school education preparatory to taking *Harbiye* entrance examinations which makes the officer corps, like other parts of the elite, less than equally accessible to the lower classes; that despite the restored increase of prestige of a military career its attractiveness has still suffered a relative decline in comparison with other available careers; the rarity of promotion through the NCO ranks to officer status just mentioned; and, finally, the necessarily authoritarian nature of armed forces which makes them possibly the least effective of Turkish institutions in inculcating democratic attitudes in the men whom it channels to leadership.

Students

In the early 1960s, Kazamias calculated that of one hundred primary school students, fewer than three could expect to enter a lycee (1966:171). Considerable progress has been made since then. In 1972–3, 42.6 percent of primary school graduates entered a middle school the following year (13.0 percent more entered middle-level vocational-technical schools). In the same year the number of students entering lycees was about 64 percent of the number of middle school graduates of the previous year (DIE #676). Still, as was shown in Table 2-1, in 1975 less than 5 percent of all Turks age sixteen and over were lycee or higher education graduates (vocational-technical not included). Lycee graduates remain a very select group. Once a student has entered lycee, however, the chances that he or she will graduate and continue into higher education are high (even if that continuance is not immediate— the many lycee graduates who do not get into higher education the year they graduate are extremely persistent).

Background and Attitudes of Students. Analysis of the social backgrounds of students shows consistently that ascriptive criteria continue to be significant in determining the likelihood that a talented young person will be able to receive education and become trained to be a leader. Table 2-6 presents the most recent data, a survey of those who took University Entrance Examinations in 1973–74. Two sources of inequality are revealed: the distribution of those taking the examination is very different from the distribution of social backgrounds among the population as a whole in several major categories, and further differentiation takes place among those who pass the exams. The State Planning Organization has calculated that if chances of a farm child being able to enter the examination are 1, those for a worker are 2.8, artisans (*esnaf*) 4.7, professional 6.9, government employee

TABLE 2-6
1973–1974 University Entrance Examination Survey[a]

	Percent among students taking examination	Percent among students passing examination	Ratio of percent of students passing to percent of students taking examination
Father's occupation			
Professional	5.7%	8.9%	1.56
Bureaucrat	19.8	28.6	1.44
Entrepreneur	1.2	1.6	1.33
Commerce	7.1	8.8	1.24
Artisan	10.3	9.9	.96
Worker	11.7	10.1	.86
Farmer	23.7	13.5	.57
Other and unknown	20.5	18.6	—
Income			
Under 1,000 TL	16.6	9.5	.57
Under 2,000 TL	54.5	37.5	.72
Under 3,000 TL	75.9	63.4	.84
Under 4,000 TL	85.9	77.2	.90
Under 5,000 TL	90.1	84.9	.94
Under 6,000 TL	93.9	91.2	.97
Over 6,000 TL	3.8	6.8	1.79
Graduate of regular lycee	6.97	81.4	1.17
Graduate of lycee level school	30.3	18.6	.61
Urban	69.7	81.4	1.17
Rural	30.3	18.6	.61
Taking examination first time	56.1	51.9	.93
second time	27.2	30.6	1.12
3rd or 4th time	16.7	17.5	1.05
Boys	77.4	70.7	.91
Girls	22.6	29.3	1.30
Took special preparatory course	14.6	26.5	1.82
Regions			
I. Antalya	2.8	3.2	1.14
II. Western Black Sea	3.4	2.3	.68
III. Eastern Mediterranean	9.1	5.2	.39
IV. Eastern Anatolia	15.4	9.5	.57
V. Eastern Black Sea	9.6	7.5	.78
VI. Aegean	11.1	17.2	1.55
VII. Marmara	21.0	30.3	1.44
VIII. Central Anatolia	26.9	24.1	.90

SOURCE: DIE #734.

[a]Questionnaires were returned by 165,625, or 72% of those who took the exam, and 61.9% of those who passed the exam.

(*memur*) 8.4, merchant 9.9, and industrialist 34.3 (1978b:par.453). To take anther example, the success rate for students from public *orta* and lycees is under 70 percent, compared to over 90% for those from private ones.
Career aspirations of the students are dominated by three general areas: health sciences (chiefly medicine), engineering, and social sciences (chiefly law and business). These areas accounted for 68.5 percent of the career choices of the 1973–74 examinees. It is notable that they include two newly prestigious ones, engineering and business. (Unfortunately law, business, and public administration are not separated out in the statistics.) These data generally conform with earlier studies (see, for example, Helling, no date; R. Stone, 1973; Tinto, 1977). Altogether, the data support some additional observations:

1.   Every study since the mid-1950s has shown the free professions to be the most sought-after. This is true across regions, for both the high and low SES groups (such as in Tinto's analysis). It is also duplicated in the response to the 1968 Village Survey (see chapter 3).

2.   Choices of occupations reflect socioeconomic differences. Those in the lower SES groups and in the less developed regions were significantly more inclined to choose the occupations of elementary and secondary school teacher,[21] government official, military officer or religious leader. These are all, of course, public-sector positions which offer job security and are as well as longstanding channels of social mobility, so that the pattern here is not surprising. As Tinto observed, these choices are quite pragmatic, reflecting at least partly the students' expectations of what they will actually attain (1977:337).

3.   The greatest preference for business occupations, also not surprisingly, is found among students from the Marmara and Aegean regions where these occupational fields are well founded and carry a good deal of prestige.

4.   The growth in preferences for business and engineering (along with medicine and law) probably reflects the fact that these are fields in which the largest amounts of money are to be made. The SPO estimates, for example, that the current deficit between demand and supply of some 12,000 engineers and 39,000 technicians will grow to 27,000 and 118,000 respectively in 1983 (1978:175).

5.   A comparison of aspirations of the 1973–74 examinees with the distribution of enrollments in higher education leads one to suspect that there is some truth in the observation by one analyst that one cause of student unrest is that there are a large number of students who are frustrated at being forced to study areas considerably removed from their choices. This seems particularly true for the many who continue to compete fiercely for the small number of places in medical schools, although we do not know how many might have had a second choice other than free professions (engineering, law) or business and public administration in which there were more available places than there were first choices. More serious might be the fact that for many of those choosing professions, accommodation for University placement (in contrast with placement in Higher Schools and academies, whose prestige is much lower) could only be found in the field of education. The education system itself might, consequently, become plagued with a large number of teachers who would really rather be elsewhere.[22]

	Career choices of 1973–74 examines (in percentage)	Enrollment in higher education 1974–75 (in percentage)	
Health sciences	29.7	7.6	
Engineering	18.6	24.9	
Social sciences	20.2	29.1	(Law, 3.8 Soc. Sci., 24.6)
Agriculture	5.4	1.9	
Humanities	4.7	5.1	
Education	3.6	26.8	
Fine arts	.1	.8	
Natural sciences	1.8	4.5	
Unknown	15.9		

Source: DIE #734; and #825, p. 113.

Thus, whether the college-trained Turks of the future are able to help meet the country's manpower needs may well depend on their personal flexibility, though the situation can perhaps also be affected by adjustments in financial rewards, particularly for the sizable number of jobs opening in the public sector. For the other major occupational categories being chosen by college students, law and business, success may depend chiefly on the personal characteristic of initiative. In general, one can say that the extent to which this group of future Turkish leaders contributes to overall national development will be to a considerable degree in their own hands.

To what extent are the lycee and college graduates likely to be leaders in cultural and political change? That they will play a major role is certain— witness the predominance of college graduates among the leadership categories discussed earlier in this chapter. If one reviews the data on the group as a whole, however, the students emerge as certainly being more "modern" than the general population, but they do so to a surprisingly small degree. The data are somewhat dated, but despite the rapid change in many aspects of Turkish life, it is generally agreed that they remain basically valid.

In general cultural attitudes, the studies show, consistently and not surprisingly, that Turkish students are strongly secular[23] and nationalist— one comparative study showed that Turkish students are significantly more nationalist than their counterparts in virtually every part of the world.[24] They describe themselves overwhelmingly as Kemalist. In more social respects Abadan has characterized Turkish students as spending their leisure time rather "uncreatively," a great deal of it being devoted to "aimless strolling," a very high level of cinema attendance, and much general "socializing." Much of this is attributed to environmental factors, such as poor facilities for sports and recreation (to say nothing of reading and study space), to the dearth of part-time jobs, and to poor economic conditions (1963:84). Abadan found that they strongly preferred foreign to Turkish films—although this perhaps reflects the poor quality of the latter more than any political preference—and in musical tastes, "alaturka" music was the most preferred, but jazz and light western music were not very far behind, while both Turkish folk music and classical western music ranked significantly lower (1961:44, 50).

On the role of women and relations between the sexes, Turkish students seem significantly more "advanced" than the general Turkish population, but not yet as "emancipated" as many of their western counterparts. In this area there are also some of the greatest variations within the student group. For example, around 1960, 65 percent of the students at the Political Science Faculty who were of urban background would allow their wives or sisters to bathe at public beaches, but only 56 percent of the urban background students at the administrative sciences faculty of METU, 41 percent at the Ankara University law faculty, and 21 percent of the rural-background political science students would do so (Abadan, 1961:116). In contrast, 70 to 80 percent of the students at these latter three faculties agreed that it is possible to have "ties of true friendship" among persons of opposite sexes (Abadan, 1961:64), and only 50 to 60 percent of those at the two Ankara University schools (about one-third at METU) said that their marriage choices would be influenced by whether or not their future spouse had had a close friend of the opposite sex. Interestingly, on the latter question the urban and rural-background students scored quite similarly (Abadan, 1961:117.) Although no data exist on the attitudes of the general population on this particular question, one suspects that the majority of Turks are more conservative than these students.

In the general realm of cultural values, then, Turkish college students seem poised on a middle ground (as are many members of other elites) having moved somewhat away from traditional mores but not yet as far as most of their counterparts in other countries. And, as expected, the least change has occurred in the spheres of interpersonal relations.

As to political attitudes, interest in politics is high, and all observers agree that it is now even higher than the available studies indicate. There has, in fact, been a general increase in politicization of many sectors of Turkish society. It may also be that a significant generational gap is developing here: Özankaya found that even in the early 1960s 81 percent of the students discussed politics with their friends, but only about 57 percent of his sample from ten Ankara University faculties said they discussed political and social topics comfortably with older members of their families, and only 14 percent said they discussed these subjects with their families at all. Among the reasons may well be habits of respect for elders and reluctance to offer opinions contrary to theirs, but it is also notable that the students reported that 14 percent of their fathers had no interest in politics, 57 percent had "a little," and only 22 percent that their fathers were "much" interested (1966:II-26, II-24, III-28).

Turkish students would seem, however, to be more interested than active in politics. Observers unanimously conclude, for example, that the number of students actively involved (even in party work, not to speak of being active in campus rallies or guerrilla movements) with either radical or moderate parties is very small—the estimate was often no higher than 5–10 percent. Also, there continues to be considerable support for the right-wing parties even as left-wing ones are making gains. Few observers find reason to expect much change from Abadan's earlier finding that only 44 to 48 percent of students at Ankara University and METU felt that being active in student organizations should be considered an obligation of university students (1961:76) nor from Özankaya's data that while 19 percent of his sample belonged to non-political associations, only 3.8 percent belonged to political ones, and 78 percent belonged to neither kind. And even more strikingly, while the students who had a political party preference were for the most part for the RPP (47.7 percent), as expected, fully a third (32.2 percent) of the sample as a whole and 27.6 percent of those identified as student leaders answered the party preference question with "none" or "don't know"! (1966:II-46, 48). Also, despite the impression of many observers that Turkish female students tend to be less political than their male colleagues, Özankaya's data found the difference slight (1966: III-31, 33). He further noted a distinct personally instrumental cast to much student political activity, lower SES students being more politically active (in attending meetings and demonstrations as well as being in associations) both because such activity was prestigious and because association membership was of potential financial benefit (1966: 185–7). Lower SES groups are both more conservative and more populist in political and economic matters. Thus, while many student activists are likely to be militant in pursuit of the welfare of their own group, they are less likely to be militant about national political issues.

On some general political attitudes, the following findings of Özankaya are more or less typical of those of similar studies:

TABLE 2-7
Political Opinions of Sample of Students from Ten Faculties of Ankara University

Statement	Percent agreeing	
	All students	Student leaders
Favor government "by the people"	54.9	45.9
Favor government "for the people"	36.0	46.7
Socialism is more just and human	61.8	74.3
Foreign trade should be nationalized	70.7	78.9
Extremist solutions to social problems must be avoided (one should be middle of the road)	77.9	59.6
The state must support private enterprise	81.7	55.1
Statism opens the way to unproductiveness, laziness, and bureaucracy	49.8	34.9
There should be an equal vote for all, regardless of education	37.9	39.4
Upper SES (males only)	24.1	
Middle SES	33.1	
Lower SES	53.3	

Also interesting is that in a study of ten nations by Gillespie and Allport in the late 1950s which asked whether students favored government "by" the people, the less elitist choice received a far higher percentage of favorable responses in Turkey than in any other country (53 percent as compared to 47 percent for the United States and 18 percent for Italy), and Payaslıoğlu's finding that the percentage of METU graduates choosing the same answer in 1977 had risen to 76 percent (1977:66–7). The reasons for this attitude are not entirely clear, particularly in view of the populist though also anti-elitist nature of these opinions and the fact that many have reason to be disillusioned about Turkey's recent events. Perhaps the most persuasive is Abadan's observation that "growing experience seems to increase political realism" (1963:87).

It is also noteworthy that despite general adherence to socialist values, Turkish *etatism* appeared to half the students to have or have had at least some negative effects. Considering that *etatism* was one of the mainstays of Ataturk's policies of the 1930s, and that support for private enterprise and opposition to *etatism* was a central plank of the Democrat party's program of the 1950s which incurred so much hostility from the urban educated class, the willingness to criticize it (at least in regard to how it was applied) indicates that there may be a relatively independent dimension to student political opinion, and that students even in the mid-1960s were not averse to identifying at least in part with what was generally identified as the position of the moderate conservative parties.

In sum, the Turkish student elite, like the other elite groups we have examined in this chapter, appears to be steadily, if rather slowly, opening its ranks to the lower strata of the population. To fully "democratize" access to this future elite group will, however, require efforts far more deliberate than those made to date, and will have to include reforms all the way down to the primary school level. In some ways Turkish students have come to resemble many of their counterparts around the world (e.g., their aspirations and their assessment of prestige of various occupations conform quite closely to those found elsewhere), but on other dimensions including many social and political attitudes they resemble their own countrymen a good deal more than one might have expected. Although they certainly show concern for their nation, their major preoccupations are, understandably, their personal welfare and future. Frey's observation in reference to lower-level education that "the Turkish public school . . . does not act strongly or regularly upon the political opinions of its pupils" (1964:228) would seem to apply equally to Turkey's system of higher education.

Conclusion

Beyond doubt, Turkey will be led during the Republic's second half-century by men and women who are more "modern" than "traditional" in outlook. Those who are now in political office at almost every level have had the benefit of considerable formal education. Today's political leaders and administrators are increasingly the children of well-educated Turks. It also seems clear that the opportunities for social mobility, and thus the possibility of mobilizing the best talents of the Turkish people no matter where in the population they may be found, are increasing, albeit somewhat slowly and unevenly.

But while these things arc likely to bring increased technical, organizational, and intellectual abilities to bear on the solution of Turkey's public problems, the evidence presented in this chapter also indicates that Turkey's current leadership is unlikely to bring about a very radical social revolution. Despite whatever "modern" background characteristics they may have, leadership groups retain many "traditional" social and politicial attitudes— bureaucrats continue to display highly "elitist" attitudes, businessmen continue to a significant degree to draw associates and partners primarily from family connections, and students have a surprisingly high degree of conservative social and political opinions.

Perhaps the most apt description of these elite groups is that they are children of their own society rather than being among the vanguard of world-wide radical change. This state of affairs is not necessarily undesirable. There are changes aplenty in Turkey, and tradition has certainly not kept Turkey from rapid economic growth, ever-increasing integration with the modern world outside Turkey's borders, nor rapid increases in communications and transportation facilities. And as much of recent Turkish history shows, traditionalism among elites need not, in the long run, prevent a positive response to demands for a more democratic distribution of wealth and political power. Indeed, the fact that values and attitudes, be they traditional or modern, are shared across most of the leadership spectrum augurs that such distribution can be accomplished in due time and with a minimum of disorder.

Should more be expected? One might argue that it should not, on at least three grounds. One is that for many Turks the personal and psychological disruptions caused by the changes already made are great enough, without having to absorb very rapidly the shock of even more radical changes in values and lifestyles. A second is that if one looks at the history of most countries which have modernized, including those which did so in the eighteenth and nineteenth centuries, it is only rarely that elites have of their own volition become true democrats, acquiescing other than grudgingly in diminution of their own status. Turkey is no exception to this general rule. Third, it should not be overlooked that for a quarter century the Turkish electorate has freely chosen leaders whose socially conservative ways were in no way a secret.

Proponents of faster and more radical change can, of course, point to the many unsolved problems which Turkey still faces. But the ultimate test of Turkey's leadership is not merely how well or how quickly it inaugurates social change. It is also how well the nation's leadership is able to accommodate the pressures which come from below as inevitable by-products of development itself. Slow as some aspects of Turkey's social revolution might be, the Turkish elites have by and large succeeded in competently dealing with such pressures, at least so far.

THREE

The Modernization of
Turkish Followers

Modernization of the general population is of major and increasing importance in the development of the Turkish nation.[1] Pivotal as elites may be both in setting general and specific public policies and in influencing popular attitudes, Turkish "followers" are equally important to the country's development, and they have acquired a large role in determining public policy. This major role is partly a result of the firm implantation of multiparty electoral politics, but more generally it is a by-product of the integration of most of the general population into the mainstream of national life. This integration has given rise to numerous economic and social demands, and recognizing and meeting them is now important not only politically, but perhaps even more from a developmental perspective. The further that modernization of the nation advances, the more it will be necessary that the general population contribute to it by working efficiently, that they make wise political and economic choices, and that a large percentage of them become *agents* of development, not merely *objects* of it. Finally, the study of Turkish followers is rewarding because the changes in popular attitudes, ambitions, characteristics, and values which have taken place during the last quarter-century have come about in a relatively "free-choice" context (i.e., coercion has been used only rarely in getting followers to conform to the ideals of certain elites, in contrast to the situation in some other countries whose governments aim at rapid modernization).[2] Turkey, therefore, presents us with an important opportunity to study how "modern" and "traditional" traits interact and combine spontaneously, so to speak, in the modernization process and how these interactions and combinations may relate to national development.

Very little modernization of the general Turkish population took place during the Ottoman period. The overwhelming majority remained poor, isolated, uneducated and ruled by the most conservative elements of the nonlocal and local elites (though there were gradations in this general situation, to be sure, particularly among regions). There were several reasons for this state of affairs:

1. The *millet* system, which divided the population into religious communities, each of which had a great deal of autonomy in education, law, and internal social, political and economic organization. An important effect of this system was to enhance the power of religious and other traditional authorities. Their power did not, of course, come solely from this institutional arrangement, but the system did assure that there was less direct influence by the central government or other "outsiders" than there might have been, and less penetration of other influences which might have widened the horizons of the population beyond their essentially parochial view.[3]

2. Center-periphery relations, which has been called by one leading Turkish scholar "a key to Turkish politics" (Mardin, 1973). Not only was there a wide separation between the Ottoman elite and the general population, there was also a gulf between the central and provincial elites. These two elite groups were in more or less constant competition (though this is not to imply that there were two totally distinct and internally united forces clearly identifiable as "central" and "peripheral"). It is significant that this competition "occurred against a background of localism tolerated by the center, for Ottoman social engineering stopped before insurmountable organizational tasks" (Mardin, 1973:171). Even in periods when the Istanbul government was at its strongest, "the Ottomans dealt with new social institutions by giving the seal of legitimacy to local usages and by enforcing a system of decentralized accommodation toward ethnic, religious and regional particularisms" (Ibid). (This is not to say that locally focused communities are necessarily nonmodernizing. Research, however, suggests that local communities most often become modernizing entities only after *some* outside stimulation.)

3. In most cities and towns the occupations which most directly exposed persons to the modern world, commerce and industry, were predominantly in the hands of non-Muslim minorities. This was true not only in the western coastal cities such as Istanbul and Izmir, but also in many major interior centers such as Kayseri (Weiker, 1972:46) and Trabzon (Meeker, 1971). The Muslim working population of these centers consisted mostly of unskilled laborers and farmers who resided in towns. Many of the interior cities had the additional handicap of having connections primarily with lands to their east, rather than with influences from Europe as was the case with the Aegean and Mediterranean ports and Istanbul.

4. Most of the rural areas were also the victims of indifference to their economic development by the Ottoman government.[4] This was not because the Ottomans were uninterested in economic affairs, but their economic focus was elsewhere than on the rural population. Even during the Tanzimat period, military modernization, political stability, and export-import matters dominated Ottoman economic efforts. In any event, the government's extremely poor financial situation would hardly have permitted significant investments in rural areas. (Military modernization did result in some new rural infrastructure, such as roads and telegraph lines, but their effects on most of the population were small.) The government also found it impossible

to reform the tax structure, which might have increased both government revenues and incentives for peasants or landowners to raise production. Even further setbacks to modernization occurred when increased contact with the West led to the squeezing out of traditional local crafts, which eventually succumbed to the more efficiently produced European goods, and when the capitulations enabled the minorities to maintain their positions. (On this period see Sugar, 1964:149–60; Issawi, 1966:65–70; Lewis, 1961:32–34.)

The Young Turks were more attentive to development, but circumstances were also difficult for them and they accomplished relatively little in the rural areas or among the lower classes in towns and cities, though for the middle and upper classes there were some advances in education and the beginnings of political nationalism.

Under the Republic, policies for rural development were quickly inaugurated, but the effects of these policies on rural areas and the lower classes were to become manifest only later. As detailed in chapter 1, national self-awareness, which had been significantly increased as a result of the War of Independence (conducted largely from Anatolia) was given further impetus by improvements in transportation and communication, though such improvements were initially directed toward security needs and it was not until later that roads and railroads were extended beyond major cities and towns to serve the villages. Penetration of rural areas by social and administrative means, such as education and the provision of social services, also began, but initially it was what might be termed "negative" in that it emphasized the tearing down of rival power centers, such as religious institutions, and the imposition of other Ataturk reforms. In many areas of eastern Antolia traditional landowners and local notables were left in place, in tacit exchange for their support of the new regime. The departure of many members of minorities was a stimulus to opening nonagricultural occupations to Turks, but many of the activities of the minorities were taken over by Turkish migrants from the Balkans rather than by Turks indigenous to Anatolia.[5]

Although more vigorous efforts toward modernization were made during the 1930s, it remained for the multiparty period to provide the setting for the far-reaching changes which rural Turkey has since undergone.[6] In part the changes came about as a result of electoral competition, which at long last impelled governments to pay major attention to the rural areas. But after World War II, other pressures also came into operation, including the pressure of rapid population growth, which increasingly drove peasants into the cities. In addition, a quarter-century of Kemalist exhortation to greater ambition and participation in national life had begun to make itself felt. Perhaps the most important factor in the acceleration of change was the momentum induced by the changes themselves. It was a perceptive observer who asserted that possibly the most momentous single action one can take to bring peasants into national life is to build a road. Much else would follow, and in Turkey, it did.

Let us survey the changes which have taken place both in rural areas and among the urban lower strata. We shall look at their material existence and their social and political attitudes, and the implications of both for potential changes in the future.

Villagers

At the end of the Republic's first half-century, about 60 percent of the population still lived in localities officially classified as villages, and a third of the total population lived in communities of less than a thousand inhabitants (See Table 3-1). While the *percentage* of both the total village population and the total national population of Turkey who are living in places of less than a thousand has decreased markedly, the actual *number* of persons living there has increased by a quarter since 1935, and villages of this size still represent 86 percent of Turkey's more than 36,000 villages. Despite the fact that modernization of places so small is more difficult than for larger communities (e.g., the smaller ones are less able to support nonagricultural occupations, and health and education facilities and government services are less economical to run)[7], in many ways the conditions of villagers have been greatly improved. For example:

- By 1968, roads had been improved to the extent that three quarters of the villages were within two hours or less travel time to a district center (*ilçe*), and the same proportion of villages were within four hours of a province capital. (Nevertheless, roads were still cited by 81 percent of the village headmen (*muhtars*) as one of their most important problems, a figure matched only by water (84 percent), with the next highest being electricity, which was listed by 37 percent) (MTV:9, 12, 13).
- In 1968 about 88 percent of the villages had schools compared to 73 percent in 1960, and by 1972 virtually all were five-year rather than three-year schools. In 1968 the Village Survey found that three-quarters of the villages had had these schools for over ten years (MTV 134, 152, and DIE #676).
- By 1968 half the villagers read a newspaper at least once a week, and newspapers were available once a week or more in 60 percent of the villages (MTV 165, 263).
- Daily radio listening increased from 19 percent of the villagers in 1962 to 40 percent in 1968 (MTV 167), and the number of radios in villages more than doubled, from twenty-eight per thousand villagers in 1965 to fifty-eight in 1975 (DIE #670, 825).
- By 1968 half the villages had a hospital, health center or health clinic near them (defined as less than about fifty km.) (MTV 308).

There were also still many shortcomings, of course:

- In 1968 half the villages did *not* have easy access to health facilities.
- In only about half the villages did more than 80 percent of the houses have separate bathrooms, and in 37 percent of the villages, none had such a facility (MTV 222).
- 71 percent still reported a shortage of drinking water (MTV 184). (In 1978 the SPO found that despite progress there were still some 9.5 million rural Turks without adequate drinking water. (SPO 1978b: par. 256.)

TABLE 3-1

Rural Population by Size of Community

Village Size	1935	Cumulative	1945	Cumulative	1955	Cumulative	1965	Cumulative	1975	Cumulative
Under 500 # villages	28,110		25,490		23,121		21,028		20,888	
population	6,649,372		6,678,377		6,547,994		6,199,276		5,996,168	
% of rural population	54.1		47.5		38.2		30.1		25.5	
501–1000 # villages	5,497		6,818		8,814		10,441		10,243	
population	3,686,857		4,619,122		6,047,396		7,233,083		7,115,246	
% of rural population	30.0	84.1	32.8	80.3	35.3	73.5	35.1	65.2	30.3	55.8
1001–2000 # villages	1,098		1,635		2,400		3,366		3,571	
population	1,431,798		2,145,843		3,143,582		4,410,319		4,687,816	
% of rural population	11.6	95.7	15.2	95.5	18.3	91.8	21.4	86.6	20.0	75.8
Over 2,000	171		366		452		803		1,413	
	529,117		784,050		1,398,415		2,742,926		5,679,421	
	4.3	100.0	5.5	100.0	8.2	100.0	13.3	100.0	24.2	100.0
Average size of villages	353		413		492		578		650	
Total village population	12,297,224		14,073,472		17,137,420		20,585,604		23,478,651	
Village population as % of total population	76.1		74.9		71.2		65.6		58.2	
% of total population in communities under 1,000	64.0		60.0		52.3		42.8		32.5	

SOURCE: Yavuz 1963; DIE #568, #813.

- In only about a quarter of the villages was meat eaten more than about once in two weeks, though three quarters of the villagers had eggs, yoghurt, and milk twice a week or more (MTV 200, 220).
- In 1974–75 there were still 3,716 villages (10 percent of the total) without schools (DIE #812).
- A particularly troubling shortcoming is the continuing great disparity in living standards among regions (as will be detailed in chapter 8).

Despite these shortcomings, it is not overstating the case to say that a very high percentage of Turkish villagers are now to a significant degree materially integrated into the mainstream of the nation. What social and attitudinal changes have accompanied this material development? We have a number of early studies and assessments to help us answer this question.

In the 1930s, members of *Halkevi* village committees took frequent trips to become acquainted with and to help villagers, and a number of accounts of these visits were prepared. Almost universally they found villages to be in a deplorable state materially, but attitudinally the villagers were usually described as intelligent, eager to learn, and outgoing and friendly toward their city compatriots. Reflecting the buoyancy of those years, most visitors on such excursions came back full of optimism and enthusiasm.[8] There were also less pleasant reports, of course, of which the most famous is the 1950 account by Mahmut Makal entitled *A Village in Anatolia (Bızım Köy)*. Assigned as a teacher to a village of 700 people about 130 miles southeast of Ankara, the author encountered a great deal of hostility both to himself and to the education he wanted to bring to the village.[9] However, we also have reports from the Izmir region that as early as the 1930s urban merchants who went to buy villagers' crops found (much to their vexation) that they were faced with sellers who were shrewd, and well-informed on such matters as prices and sales conditions (Weiker, 1973:87). These early accounts must be taken with care, to be sure, and it is clear that, as Roos and Frey have remarked, "the [Turkish village] mass is no monolith" (1968b:22).

We can, however, supplement these reports with more scientific studies. Some aggregate data are shown in Table 3-2a. Most of these found that, whatever the attitudes held by many villagers before the intense penetration of modernizing influences which took place after World War II,[10] the typical Turkish peasant today is pragmatic, shrewd, cautious in dealing with outsiders. He is also aware of outside events to a very considerable degree, far from automatically averse to the acceptance of new things and new ways, increasingly mobile geographically, and has ambitions for himself and his children which in magnitude (how much improvement is sought) and direction (e.g., preferred occupations) are decidedly similar to those of his urban countrymen. Table 3-2b also indicates that while on some matters there is a clear linear progression from villager attitudes to attitudes in larger communities, on others it is only in the largest settlements that attitudes differ sharply from those of villagers (*namaz* [prayer] performance, scarves for women). However sharp distinctions may have been in the past, they are now considerably blurred, with villagers frequently leaning distinctly toward the

TABLE 3-2a
Values and Attitude Characteristics of Villagers

	Percentage	MTV location
Uses of savings:		
Kept in banks	42.2	Table 81
Kept in the house	10.8	
Used to purchase land	15.7	
Ages of muhtars:		
30–39	35.2	Table 112
40–49	34.7	
50 and older	17.6	
Conflict takes place between traditional and modern villagers (tradition defined as those who are faithful to the traditions, moderns as those who change and innovate).		
A great deal	44.6	
Some	19.3	
None	27.6	
Villagers who favor old or new (asked of those who have said there is either little or much conflict)		
New	74.2	Table 133
Old	19.7	
Respectful behavior of youth toward the aged compared to earlier period		Table 129
More	37.7	
Less	38.8	
Same	20.4	

Measures to be taken in response to improper act
by 10 to 15-year-old boy toward his father

	Men 16–25	25–50	50+	All men	All women	
Scold or beat	40.5%	34.9	31.7	34.8	48.5	Table 131
Give advice	39.5	44.7	44.1	43.7	27.1	

Villages in which less than 50% of adult males go to the mosque daily	55.0	Table 139
Villages in which less than 75% of males attend Friday prayers (according to imams)	54.7	Table 140

Tables 159,
161

	For boys		For girls	
Level of education desired	1962	1968	1962	1968
Higher	49.0	74.1	26.0	28.7
Vocational and teacher	3.0	7.6	6.0	12.3

Occupations desired for sons (male respondents)	*1962*	*1968*	Table 162
Professional (doctor, lawyer, engineer)	30.8	47.8	
Teacher	19.7	12.9	
Official (governor, district governor, army officer)	18.4	13.6	
Religious	1.1	6.8	

Wanting 4 or less children	*1962*	*1968*	Table 207
	58.0	65.1	

Percent of villages from which workers have gone to foreign countries		49.6	Table 89

Want to migrate to cities		77.8	Table 98
Intraregional		55.2	
Extraregional		22.6	

Reasons for families migrating to cities			
Poverty and landlessness		57.2	
Found job in city		19.1	

Age at first marriage	*Girls*	*Boys*	Table 103
14–15	31.1	8.0	
16–19	40.6	36.9	
20–24	13.5	36.1	

SOURCE: Srikantan, 1973: Table IV.

TABLE 3-2-b
Attitudes by size of community (by percentage)

	Over 2,000	2,000– 15,000	15,000– 50,000	Over 50,000	Metro- polises
Marriage registered legally	78	95	95	93	95
Marriage arranged by family	79	84	79	81	67
Unconditionally disapprove of family planning	35	25	18	23	14
Husband does not allow men and women to sit together while visiting	51	52	45	35	22
Husband does not allow fie to go out without a scarf	96	91	81	77	36
Husband generally makes decision about which friends to associate with	58	56	59	59	46

Husband generally makes decision about how to spend family income	59	54	61	64	51
Most important requirement for success in life is patronage and luck	45	36	45	35	34
Sometimes performs *namaz*	93	92	87	83	71
Performs *namaz* once or more daily	70	62	45	53	24
Ideal number of children for a family like hers (asked of women)	3.62	3.11	2.62	3.00	2.38

SOURCE: Srikantan, 1973: Table IV.

"modern." Regional differences (see chapter 8) become considerably smaller on most attitudinal dimensions than they do on statistical indicators of material growth.

Several matters warrant particular note here:

1. Despite the fact that 60 percent of the villagers reported that their personal wealth situation had improved, 40 percent asserted otherwise (MTV Table 80), even in 1968, which was shortly after general wealth in Turkey had increased spectacularly. There are probably several reasons for this, although we have no hard data. Certainly one is that rapid population increase has eaten up a good deal of the higher rural income. As villagers become increasingly integrated into the larger nation, they also become ever more affected by inflation. The fact that this report also comes in the context of what we know to have been a significant rise in rural consumption, however, leads to the belief that villagers' expectations are themselves rising, and that the phenomenon of an expectation-achievement gap will probably become increasingly serious. It is also likely that increasing integration will heighten feelings of inequality—as Manfred Halpern has observed, one of the new characteristics of poverty and inequality in the Middle East is that it has become so *visible*.[11]

2. Over 40 percent of villagers said that they had difficulty understanding the language spoken on the radio. This is understandable in the eastern provinces where there are a large number of Kurds, but the figures of 31 percent even in the "developed" regions of the Aegean and Marmara and 44 percent in the center of the country (MTV Table 171) lead to the conclusion that there remains a serious elite-mass gap in communication capabilities, certainly in language and probably in concepts as well.

3. As shown in Table 3-3, Turkey has foregone a major advantage for development by continuing to tolerate a low level of village literacy, one of the most significant facilitators of modernization. That overall 1975 literacy was, after a half-century of Republic educational reform, still only about 62 percent for the nation as a whole, with rural literacy markedly lower, is

certainly a great barrier to modernization, and a functional burden on the illiterate.

Literacy	Total		Men		Women	
	1970	*1975*	*1970*	*1975*	*1970*	*1975*
Total (by percentage)	57.2	61.9	70.3	75.1	41.8	48.3
Urban	71.6		82.6		58.9	
Rural	47.1		62.3		32.7	

Source: DIE #756, 825.

The Village Survey also concluded that efficiency of village education is very low. More than one-third of those interviewed who had attended school left before they graduated, and in 1968 only 26.9 percent of males (and 8.8 percent of females!) were primary school graduates. Even the graduates included many for whom only a three-grade primary school had been available.[12]

TABLE 3-3
VILLAGER CHARACTERISTICS BY LITERACY

	Literates	Illiterates	MTV Table
Percent whose Agricultural Bank credits were over 1000 TL	51	34	64
Use fertilizers	55.5	41.8	36
Use insecticides	62.2	50.4	36
Consult agricultural personnel	54.2	33.7	40
Annual household income over 5,000 TL	37.6	15.3	75
Annual household income under 2,000 TL	21.7	40.9	75
Report improved state of personal wealth			
Males	64.2	53.2	79
Females	72.4	51.5	
Leave the village once a week or more	56.2	37.0	87
Desire only primary education for their daughters	37.2	45.7	160
Desire professional occupations for their sons	50.4	32.2	163
Listen to news broadcasts on the radio	41.0	31.2	169
Would only "advise" child who behaved disrespectfully to father	43.8	29.9	174

4. On other dimensions, almost all (97.4 percent) of the villagers, literate and illiterate, male and female, said they "expect the future to bring pleasant events" (MTV 273). This is particularly interesting in that 45 percent stated that their personal problems at the time of the interviews were unbearable (there was a significant difference here between literates—35.4 percent—and illiterates—51.2 percent). The main causes of their problems were asserted to be poverty (about 50 percent), followed by health (14 percent). Perhaps one reason for this optimism about the future was that 84 percent of the villagers interviewed wanted to settle in a city if they could, and they generally anticipated that city life would be an improvement over their life in the village. The notion of the fatalistic villager is not borne out by these data. They do, however, point to the need for far greater efforts at rural development if there is to be any chance of reducing the constantly growing pressures on urban areas.

5. Nor is any marked tendency toward tradition shown by data on religious observance. Imams of 55 percent of the villages reported that less than half their male residents went to the mosque daily—to say nothing of performing the obligatory prayers five times per day—and in a similar percentage of villages less than 75 percent of the men attended even Friday prayers.

6. The data in Table 3-2a about respect for parents' wishes are also striking. The trend in modernizing situations is almost everywhere described as one of youth becoming less respectful of elders, yet the number of Turkish villagers who perceived their youths to be *more* respectful were as numerous as those who perceived it to be less; and almost half the men would only "give advice" rather than scold or beat a ten- to fifteen-year-old boy who showed disrespect to his father (though it is not clear whether this was because fathers felt that the more severe sanctions were unneeded, or because they felt they were unlikely to be effective). The Village Survey concludes that "according to villagers in developed regions there have been changes in what is considered respectful behavior. As a result of progress, that is, economic and social development, change has taken place in customs and traditions and this change is reflected in intergenerational relations. The parent villagers wish to rear their children in accordance with the expectations of the community...." (MTV 179). Asked to interpret this, SPO researchers replied that though respect is still expected by the old, villagers also increasingly agree that the young often do know more than their elders, and that if the young give reasonable justification for their "modern" behavior, the behavior is likely to be accepted. Recent findings by Stirling parallel this interpretation. In two villages near Kayseri he noted that fathers' control over their sons is clearly decreasing in such areas as marriage choices and financial contributions to the parental household, and that, for the most part, sons no longer want to follow in their fathers' footsteps. Stirling attributes this mainly to the sons' acquisition of literacy, which has opened up opportunities that have, in turn, changed the very nature of family relationships and of village life as a whole (1976:85–6).

In addition to aggregate data we have some studies of specific villages:

1. The Turkish sociologist Mübeccel Kıray, in a study of four villages in the Çukurova area around the fertile Mediterranean plain of Adana, found that one of the most profound impacts on village life was the emergence of wage workers, both those who stayed in their villages and those who migrated to towns and cities on either a permanent or seasonal basis.[13] Most significantly, she concluded that, far from being passive in accepting their lot, " . . . the villagers are not yet satisfied with the results they have obtained thus far, [and] one may easily expect them to try to *organize* and *take action* for more secure jobs, more incomes, and a more integrated social order" (1974:203; emphasis added. For the full study, see Kiray and Hinderink, 1970. For general summaries of social change in Turkish villages see also Kolars, 1973:182–202 and 1974:204–36).

2. Several studies have found that many villagers are not at all averse to using the modern legal norms and institutions of the Republic to counter traditional social and economic mores. Magnarella's review of some of these studies, as well as his own research, prompts him to conclude that "the social norms prescribed by Turkey's new family law (the Swiss family law) are gaining wide acceptance." A particularly significant development which he cited is that "many young Turkish women are utilizing the new law to free themselves from traditional confinement and to choose their own husbands," and that the earlier statement by Paul Stirling that "no girl would feel at all abashed to admit that her marriage is not registered with the State" would be invalid today (1973:113). Pool and Starr concluded, similarly, that "the Turkish legal revolution is a revolution in more than form. Rural Turks are using the courts—using them more than the government itself is. Their use extends to arenas formerly within the sanctum of religious law alone, and increasingly women, perhaps the most traditionally deprived group of all, are turning to the court to redress their grievances" (1974:552–3).

3. A study by Suna Kili of a village eighty kilometers from Ankara in an area of very rapid growth in mining found the villagers highly adaptable to new conditions, rapidly learning to be efficient, productive and innovative, and well able to use voting in a discerning, instrumental fashion (1978a).

4. Deniz Kandiyoti also pointed up the growing importance of both personal and contextual factors when she found the in a village ninety kilometers south of Ankara that "while modernity in the areas of education and mass media exposure was associated with high economic standing, and with younger age fore reasons of availability, changes in familial attitudes were found to rest largely on feelings of pessimism and insecurity about the village caused by structural changes in the economy and household composition" (1974:60. For a picture of changes over time which yielded findings parallel to those cited here, see the two studies of Hasanoğlan by Ibrahim Yasa, summarized in Yasa, 1969).

What are some of the possible implications of these situations for Turkey's future? While it is, of course, difficult to make such predictions with precision, a few conclusions seem warranted:

1. Large-scale migration from villages to urban centers is likely to continue, and urban problems will become more and more severe. The problems of village and rural development may be further aggravated if migration drains villages of their most development-minded people.

2. The rise in villagers' demand for consumption goods, which will probably rise a good deal faster than increases in available supply, will also be likely to continue.

3. There is not likely to be significant rise in rural standards of living in the immediate future, in part because of inflation and in part because of population increase. This situation is also related to a lack of significant increases in the productivity of small and medium-sized farms (as detailed in chapter 7).

4. Among the most important issues for the future is how Turkish villagers will respond in the area of politics. As early as the mid-1960s, Frey's large-scale survey of villagers concluded that some of them had changed their political attitudes only little, but that others, mostly in the more developed regions, seemed to be reacting to recent Turkish politics much as their urban compatriots were. All indications continue to be that social and economic development of Turkish villages will bring more active political orientations as well.

(a) "National identification" has significantly increased in rural areas and, as in urban areas, is strongly associated with sex, literacy, and region, as well as with mass media and education. (Cited in Özbudun, 1976:156. He also gives a detailed description of the Frey survey.)

(b) "Turkish peasants feel efficacious vis-a-vis their elected leaders," in part due to the fact that there is a strong sense of "downward" orientation among *muhtars*. These village officials "exhibited more similarities than differences in relation to the other villagers" (Frey, 1967:S-3 and Özbudun, 1976:156–7), more often than not taking the part of the villagers rather than attempting to be primarily responsive to the demands or opinions of government leaders at higher levels. (Özbudun concludes significantly, however, that "if the term 'local government' had been used to include municipal governments in the cities and towns, and especially the local agents of the national government, local political efficacy would probably have been much weaker." 1976:156. Most other analysts would agree.) A feeling of efficacy, vis-a-vis national officials on the other hand, was low both among *muhtars* and villagers in general. Fifty-seven percent and 69 percent respectively agreed that "if the national government were doing something deemed harmful or unjust, respondent would or could do nothing" (Frey, 1967:30). This contrast appears to be at least partly related to the fact that the gains of many villages have come as a result of contact with political parties, whereas the bureaucracy, the most visible representative of the national government, has more often remained unresponsive to village requests, oriented as it is to implementing general national policies. That a sense of political efficacy was found to be stronger in the least developed regions of the country, notably the southeast and northeast (Özbudun, 1976:157), may in part reflect lesser expectations of responsiveness in those regions, but the data are insufficient for one to be precise on this point.[14]

(c)   Although Frey found "very few signs of any increased propensity to make excessive demands upon government or even any increased desire for greater political participation associated with heightened national identification (1968:958), he also found that when villagers were asked if they preferred a strong and decisive headman (and national government) or one that stressed consultation, preference for the latter was found to be strongly associated with literacy and with living in a more developed region (Özbudun, 1976:157). These findings and others cited above, indicate that traditional norms seem to be fading, and that demands for a more open society probably cannot remain unanswered very much longer.

(d)   There is little separate data on rural voting, but a number of general studies indicate that it has, on the whole, followed nation-wide patterns. Voting participation has declined in general since the opening of the multi-party period (for national statistics see chapter 5), and has fallen further in the more developed regions than in the less advanced ones. Özbudun found fairly strong correlations between voter turnout and "the village establishments, development and mass media access," and weaker (though still significant) ones with several other developmental indicators. His conclusion, from his own work and from other studies which he reviewed, is that there is now a clear distinction between villagers in developed regions who are "voting" and those in more backward provinces who are "voted" by their landlords, ağas, etc. (1976:162). The more significant coming division in Turkish society may well be not an urban-rural one but a regional one, in that, like their urban counterparts, "Peasants in [developed area] villages, being better informed about and more attentive to national politics, may have more reasons to be disillusioned with particular outputs of the political system and more likely to express it by non-voting." (Ibid.)

(e)   Political party preferences of rural voters also appear to follow national trends. Through the early 1970s the Justice party did best in the more developed villages, but since about 1973 the RPP has made gains there, generally in conjunction with its improved urban performance. Özbudun concludes that "there appears to be room among the more modern sectors of the Turkish peasantry for an appeal based on an effective social reform program" (1976:175). Similarly, there has not been evidence of a greater degree of radicalism in villages than elsewhere (either to the right or to the left), and voting for minor parties has been "generally insignificant" (1976:175–79), except in particular local situations, and situations which reflect relationships to particular developmental indicators. The two large, moderate parties, though they "perform somewhat better in urban areas than in villages, still command impressive rural strength" (1976:179).[15]

What of future policy? Possibly the most important political lesson of Turkish experience to date with village modernization is that direct efforts at imposing change have had meager results. Initiatives during the single party period—for example, mandating a central role for teachers in village government (they were once appointed *ex officio* members of village councils)—usually had at least as many negative as positive effects. During the multiparty period, on the other hand, the parties generally sought to win over the existing village leaders, and it is significant that many of these older leaders have become quite politically capable and often continue to retain the confidence of their villagers.

Nor are imposed measures really needed in most Turkish villages.[16] What would seem potentially much more fruitful is to continue, but also to greatly expand, the work of providing villagers with facilities they can utilize to improve their *own* lot—in education, communications, technology, credit, etc. One of the most intriguing concepts of Frey's village research is his "Propensity to Innovate Index" (1967a). He found that a tendency to innovate was highly correlated with several "psychic measures," particularly literacy, media exposure, some cognitive dimensions, and "experience which lessens distrust of strangers coming into the village environment." He also concluded that propensity to innovate is more related "to an *individual's* want and desire than it is to the state of his village" (1967a: 7, 14; emphasis added) and, significantly, the influences of key importance are in the areas of social support. There was a positive correlation between individuals choosing the "modern" side and those saying that the "modern group" in their village usually won innovational conflicts. There was positive association also between an individual's "willingness to be the first person in his village to innovate, and his report that there are people in his village who frequently introduce new ways" (1967a:5).

Frey cautions, to be sure, that "many factors intervene between a generalized propensity to innovate and actual innovation" (1967a:16), and in this regard a crucial element is certainly the availability of material resources so that innovation can *succeed*. It is also clear that resources will have to be increased. All observers testify that the demand for credit and education is rising at very rapid rates, and that the expectation-achievement gap may be expected to grow rapidly as the stimuli for change continue to penetrate rural Turkey. And because, from the data reviewed in this section, there seems to be little doubt that even as many of the conservative ways which have successfully sustained peasant communities for many decades are maintained, the potential for modernizing Turkish villagers and making them significant contributors to development is indeed great and it would be foolish to fail to take advantage of this potential by not supplying its wherewithal. The need to subject development measures to the scrutiny of discerning recipients and to adapt them accordingly is perhaps one of the Turkish elite's greatest challenges, but also perhaps its greatest opportunity.

The Urban Lower Strata

Rapid urbanization is one of the most important—and certainly one of the most written-about—characteristics of "developing" countries. For many years now, a good deal of theorizing has been done about how modernization would affect these new societies. Our relative ignorance of the urbanization process is made clear by how much of this theorizing has already been discovered to be wrong.

Not too long ago, for example, it was thought that urban lower classes, increasingly exposed to tangible evidence of their inequality with elites, would rapidly become politically radical. More recent research leads us to speculate that the conservative social and political views of the newly urbanized are quite persistent. (For a brief summary of such theories and research findings, see Özbudun, 1976:183–6.) In the social-psychological realm, urbanization was generally considered so deeply uprooting and frustrating a process that adjustment to it would be very difficult for many new migrants, and that it would consequently lead to a great deal of social and psychological disturbance. But more recent research, while not denying the reality of such problems, has shown that new city dwellers have been able to adjust quite well to their new environment. They have quickly formed their own local institutions and associations to help one another and have displayed a good deal of vigor and initiative in many aspects of urban life. The forces of modernization change the new migrants, to be sure, but the degree to which mechanisms for stability exist is also impressive.

In Turkey, it is noteworthy that the Village Survey and numerous other studies have found that villagers have an almost unanimously optimistic view about city life, and that this is based not on wishful thinking but to a very great extent on reports from personal acquaintances who have already migrated there.[17] Thus it will be particularly interesting to see whether these views will be maintained in the face of new factors which could well lead to the degree of instability predicted earlier: the migration of immense numbers of workers to Europe and their eventual return to cities which might not be able to absorb them; much higher inflation in the cities than heretofore; the steadily worsening problem of urban unemployment (with which almost no developing country has been able to deal). The evidence is by no means all in, but we can examine the situation as it appears to date.

The percentage of Turkey's inahbitants who live in urban areas went from 16.3 percent in 1927 to only 18.5 percent in 1950, but it jumped to 35.8 percent in 1970 and to 41.4 percent in 1975 (Table 3-4).[18] Today Turkey may be said to be "more urbanized than . . . most other developing nations" (Keleş and Danielson, 1980b:270). The greatest growth has occurred in the twenty-seven cities which by 1975 had grown to over 100,000. The 1975 census showed that some 9,585,000 people, almost 25 percent of the population, had changed their permanent residence during 1970–75 (DIE #825: Table 28). A few special characteristics of Turkish urbanization are worthy of particular note.

- Provincial cities are often growing as fast, if not faster, than the five cities which are now labeled as "metropolises" (Istanbul, Ankara, Izmir, Adana, Bursa). Because migration is relatively short-distance (a Turkish geographer notes that

TABLE 3-4
Urban Population

Year	Total Population	Population in places 10,000 +	Percent	Percent in places 50–100,000	Percent in places 100,000–500,000	Percent in places 500,000+
1927	13,648,270	2,218,108	16.3			
1935	16,158,018	2,683,872	16.6	1.6	1.8	4.6
1940	17,820,950	3,215,962	18.0	2.2	1.9	4.5
1945	18,790,174	3,466,046	18.4	2.1	2.8	4.6
1950	20,947,188	3,923,852	18.5	1.9	3.7	4.7
1955	24,064,763	5,414,884	22.5	3.2	4.8	5.3
1960	27,754,820	7,189,122	25.9	4.4	4.5	7.6
1965	31,391,421	9,343,006	29.8	4.0	6.6	8.4
1970	35,605,176	12,734,761	35.8	4.0	8.4	10.9
1975	40,347,719	16,706,528	41.4	4.7	10.9	12.1

SOURCE: DIE #683, 672, 813.

"The main parts of the non-local population in all provinces . . . excluding Istanbul, Izmir and Ankara, are from the neighboring provinces." Tümertekin cited in Özbudun, 1976:190), the provincial cities experiencing rapid growth aré spread throughout the country and are becoming important "growth centers." (On the potential of two of the cities, see Weiker, 1972.)

• Industrialization has not kept up with urbanization. A very high percentage of the new urban residents who have found employment have done so in the service sector, many in low-paying jobs or in menial occupations presently over-supplied with workers. As Keleş has remarked, "Nothing is more noticeable than the abundance of shoe-shiners, porters, bellboys and janitors in cities such as Ankara and Istanbul" (1972a:13). Keleş also found that in 1967 only Istanbul and Ankara had a higher industrial growth rate than urbanization rate,[19] and in 1972, the province of Istanbul still contained 45 percent of Turkey's private manufacturing plants and employed 54 percent of all the workers in the private sector.

• Recent OECD estimates are that twenty percent of the nonagricultural labor force was unemployed in 1977 (OECD, 1978:31). (Eight percent of the agricultural labor force was also unemployed, thus supplying another "push" factor to urbanization.) This represents a major increase over a few years earlier and a significant difference from the 14.8 percent which the OECD estimated in 1974 would be the 1977 figure (1974:Table 2).[20] Projections indicate continuing increases for up to another fifteen years (Ibid). Even though Turkish urban migrants have often done well in coping with joblessness or low pay,[21] when it is noted that these unemployment percentages currently involve almost 1½ million workers (plus their families, of course) and that the number may become greater before long, the magnitude of the problem becomes very clear. A further increase in unemployment may come if a substantial number of the nearly one million Turkish workers currently in Europe are forced to return home.

• Virtually all Turkish cities have fallen far behind in their efforts to provide municipal services to new migrants. Perhaps the most prominent deficiency is in housing. The total number of dwelling units constructed with official permits increased from 59,000 in 1955 to 140,000 in 1970 and to 182,000 in 1975, but because of very rapid urbanization, the number of units per 1000 urban residents fell from 2.6 in 1965 to 1.2 in both 1970 and 1975 (Keleş 1978:137). As to separate housing units, an estimated 70,000 less than needed were built during the first plan period, 186,000 less in the second period, and 242,000 less in the third. The SPO predicts that the need during the fourth plan will be 341,000 annually. Only 196,000 were actually built during the third plan years (1978b:pars. 1707–11). The shortfall is due in part to a steadily falling availability of investment resources, but also to the fact that private capital has been more attracted to financing luxury housing, whose value has increased even more dramatically than the already high value of urban land and real estate resulting from rampant speculation.[22]

Housing needs have resulted, of course (as in virtually every Third World country), in rapid growth of shanty towns (gecekondus).[23] It has been estimated that in 1975 close to 4½ million Turks, or more than a quarter of the urban population, lived in squatter housing.[24] Figures cited by Karpat indicate that the Turkish cities in this respect rank among the highest in the world in percentage terms (1976:Table 1.3). Although the average number of occupants per room fell (from 2.05 in 1960 to 1.9 in 1970) and the percentage of families living in one or two-room residences decreased (from 63.8 percent in 1965 to 43 percent in 1975), the percentage of homes with separate kitchens fell from 61.5 percent in 1970 to 60.6 percent in 1975, and those with their own bathrooms from 49 percent in the former year to 45.1 percent in the latter (Keleş 1978:132–3).

As to utilities, the situation has also been steadily worsening. It has been estimated that in 1970, 39 percent of urban housing lacked electricity and that in 1975 the figure rose to 47.9 percent, and that where 33 percent were without city water in 1970, 56.7 percent lacked it in 1975 (Ibid.: 132). Schools are also inadequate (see chapter 6) as are health facilities. In Istanbul the rate of infectious diseases in 1966 for the city as a whole was 159 per 100,000, in the gecekondu areas 356 (Keleş, 1972b:126. For some similar figures in particular gecekondu areas in Istanbul, see Heper, 1978:88–91. There are, of course, variables to be considered: the age of the gecekondu areas, their location, etc.).

The people most intensely affected by these circumstances are, naturally, the new migrants and the urban poor. What are they like? What social and attitudinal changes have they undergone? What "traditional" traits have persisted? What social and political consequences might arise from these circumstances of rapid urbanization?

It is striking that gecekondu studies agree that on the whole there is little evidence to date of mass discontent. In the words of one observer, the recent migrants (residents of gecekondu areas), usually thought of as constituting the greatest concentration of the dislocated, are "far from a destitute mass" (Özbudun 1976:191). As Keleş asserts, the gecekondu areas are definitely not to be considered "slums" (1978:183–4). On the contrary, studies of urban lower class Turks almost unanimously find them quick to adjust to city life, possessed of a good deal of initiative, living in rather stable communities with (as yet?) little class consciousness. Material values are rapidly changing but many traditional social and cultural traits persist. As in other aspects of Turkish society discussed in this study, this combination of change and stability has, so far at least, had beneficial results and has helped make Turkish modernization orderly. The synthesis of old and new which is evolving here bears close watching.

The most important reasons for this situation would seem to be that (1) most of the urban migrants *think* they are better off than they were in their villages, (2) that this view is based on opportunities which they see for continuing improvement, and (3) that the social and cultural changes which they have had to undergo have not been as drastic as it was commonly believed they would be. Specifically:

1. All of the *gecekondu* studies found only a minuscule number of migrants who expressed a desire to return to their villages (e.g., Saran, 1974:359; Yasa 1966:85; Karpat 1976:106; Keleş and Danielson, 1980b: 281–83). Women, interestingly, were found even more loath to return to rural areas than were men, probably a reflection of the harsh life of many rural women. Keleş also notes that "overcrowding in villages is more serious than it is in urban areas, with almost 25 percent more persons per room" (1972b:182).

2. This generally optimistic attitude is based at least in part on positive experiences in urban areas:

(a) A quarter to a third of *gecekondu* household heads are skilled or semiskilled workers (Yasa found 27 percent, Hart 35.6 percent, Şenyapılı 22 percent), small businessmen, *esnaf* and shopkeepers (Yasa 17 percent, Hart 12 percent, Şenyapılı 18 percent), or government employees (14 percent, 17 percent, 14 percent respectively). That is, a high proportion have moved into urban occupations which are distinctly above the lowest level. (Classifications are quite inexact and not always strictly comparable. For a general summary, see Özbudun, 1976:191–4.)

(b) In Yasa's study, 70 percent of *gecekondu* family heads stated they had found their own first jobs, while only 17 percent stated that they had had the help of relatives, persons from the same village or region, or acquaintances (1966:120). Karpat's findings were somewhat different but not decisively so: 40 percent found jobs through their own efforts, 31 percent through friends, 29 percent through relatives (1976:91). Şenyapılı found some progression on this score over time: 59 percent of her sample who answered this question stated that they had found their first jobs with the help of friends and relatives, but only 31 percent had used such help in finding their second jobs (1978:151).

(c) When Yasa asked on whom they would rely for help in time of need, only 22 percent of his *gecekondu* respondents said relatives, acquaintances, or compatriots, 25 percent cited official agencies, unions, or insurances, and

45 percent said no one (1966:84). Karpat found that there was a significant increase in those trusting themselves more than they did relatives. Among those whom they found trustworthy and reliable, there was a sizable increase in the mentioning of "friends" (1976:116). Şenyapılı's parallel finding was that the percentage relying on relatives, acquaintances, or those from a common place of origin fell from 59 percent at the time help was first needed to 33 percent later, and to 2 percent at the time of her survey (1978:152). The findings take on added significance when we see that they are in the context of fairly close physical proximity to relatives. In Izmir, Kongar found that only about 15 percent of his sample had no close relatives anywhere in the city, and even in luxury areas 60 percent reported relatives close by or in adjoining neighborhoods. Between a quarter and a third in all categories reported exchanging visits with their relatives daily, but only 13 to 20 percent asserted that proximity of relatives was at least one reason they had chosen their residence (1972:passim). In Şenyapılı's survey, 83 percent had relatives living in the city of Istanbul, including 33 percent who had them living in the same district, but only 12 percent visited their relatives daily, 37 percent doing so but once or twice a month (1978:150).

The significance of these findings is not easy to interpret, and several researchers have sounded warnings against overoptimism. Kağıtçıbaşı puts stress on the continuance of "dependence on relatives and expectations of help from them. . . .even in the urban and semi-urban contexts" even though they are "at a lower level than in the traditional rural community" (1977:30). Karpat detected "an almost exaggerated sense of self-confidence and individualization" (1976:114). Perhaps the most disturbing finding is that of Şenyapılı. In her sample, not only did the percentage of those relying on "self" decline from an initial 27 percent to 23 percent at the time of her survey, but the percentage saying their problems are insoluble also rose from 1 percent initially to 18 percent later and 27 percent at the time of the survey (1978:152). If these findings are accurate, it is clear that *gecekondu* areas contain the seeds of considerable frustration should circumstances take too many turns for the worse.

(d) To return to the positive aspects, research also indicates a perception of opportunity for social mobility. Hart found that the question, Why do you want to educate your children? elicited "the belief that in Turkey there are two classes of people: the educated and the uneducated" (Saran, 1974:354) with the clear expectation that education will prove to be an open road for social mobility. He also noted that the advantage of urban living which *gecekondu* residents listed first was schools (1963:7). (For further discussion of Turkey's educational system see chapter 6). Şenyapılı reported quite rapid movement of migrants out of the "marginal sector" of the economy (i.e., occupations such as street peddler), that many *gecekondu* residents had ambitions to set up their own businesses or artisan shops (which in their eyes carry high prestige), and that they also had very high ambitions for their sons and expectations that these will be realized (1978:109–17, 122). Most studies have also found occupational mobility to be considerable, most often from the "unorganized" into the "organized" sector (e.g., factory work).[25]

(e) Income appears to rise steadily in relation to how long families have resided in the city (Yasa, 1966:141), and there is no doubt that incomes in absolute terms are higher than in the villages.[26] (But the degree to which this is a "relative" perception is particularly hard to appraise. There is to the present author's knowledge no income study which has also tried to compare rural and urban costs of living, or the relationship between the standard of living and the level of expectations—thus also the possible level of frustration. Keleş, for one, seems to have some doubts on this score, wondering whether the comparisons which the *gecekondu* families make with the standard of life in the villages may not be optimistic in part because they want to convince themselves that they are better off (1972b:192).

(f) Hart's and Karpat's studies also found that it did not take long for many of *gecekondu* residents to improve their houses, build second stories to rent out to increase their incomes, succeed in getting the government to provide utilities, and even to start small enterprises in the squatter areas (shops, repair shops, even small manufacturing facilities). Although the designation "squatter area" is still applied officially to all *gecekondu* areas, some of these areas are a good deal better off than others. Wise government policies can help this trend to continue.[27]

(g) The 1973 Hacettepe Population Survey found that 75.6 percent of migrants from villages were earning more than their expectations prior to migration, 12.1 percent earning as much, and only 12.5 percent earning less or uncertain about the matter (Danielson and Keleş, 1980b).

(h) Again, however, we must not overlook signs of more negative evaluations. Şenyapılı's sample found 64 percent saying that their income was insufficient for a "comfortable life," and of those, 43 percent said that there was nothing they could do to remedy it. Further, only 7 percent blamed personal inadequacy for their plight (1978:102–3). Another disturbing phenemenon is the growing degree to which urban extremist violence is becoming centered in *gecekondu* areas. It has been reported that some are virtually armed camps, and that in addition to political violence there has been an increasing incidence of robberies and other "economic" crimes. Clearly the potential for the kind of frustration-based dislocations and disorders predicted by some earlier social scientists is not to be taken lightly.

3. The still remarkable degree of stability found in the urban lower strata is at least partly due to the fact that in the midst of all of the physical, occupational, and material dislocation, there is a simultaneous social and cultural continuity, and that while social and cultural values are certainly changing, their rate of change seems to be moderate.

(a) Change from the extended to the nuclear family has not been as traumatic as a perusal of the social science literature on the subject might have led one to expect. Sociologist Serim Timur, in a major study on *Family Structure in Turkey*, found that the nuclear family is already the norm for the *entire* country. She also compiled persuasive evidence that it is economic conditions rather than urban vs. rural residence which is the chief variable in nuclear-family quantitative variation (1972:31–3).[28]

(b) Family size seems for the most part to respond to "modern" influences rather readily. Timur found it to rise linearly from 4.1 persons in the three largest cities to 4.9 in large and small cities, 5.6 in towns, and 6.1 in villages (1972:37). Kongar likewise found that family size in many *gecekondu* areas is becoming more similar to that of their urban surroundings than to that of their village origins (1975:Table 3), and Hart discovered a significant relationship between time and family size in that in Istanbul the "older gecekondu" area of Zeytinburnu had an average family size (4.7) quite close to the average for cities, but in a new squatter area (Yeşiltepe) family size was still significantly greater (5.25.) (Saran, 1974:347). Kağıtçıbaşı, determined that the value Turkish parents placed on having children responded quite readily to factors related to economic circum-

TABLE 3-5
Family Characteristics

		Istanbul= Ankara= Izmir	Large Cities	Small Cities	Towns	Villages	Turkey
3	Percent nuclear families	67.9	65.8	63.3	61.5	55.4	59.7
			Cities				
5	Average family size						
	Percent families nuclear from beginning	4.1	4.9		5.6	6.1	5.5
	Percent nuclear families after 1 year	47.2	28.8		21.0	19.7	24.2
	of marriage	50.4	41.1		17.4	9.3	20.4
	Percent nuclear families after 5–9 years of marriage	74.6	69.4		44.3	39.7	48.9
23	Women's marriage decisions						
	Percent "family decisions with own consent."	59.1	67.7		72.2	67.0	67.0
	Percent "own decision with family approval"	29.6	12.0		10.5	10.0	12.5
25	Who influences men's marriage choices? Percent "self only."	52.0	33.1		29.6	23.3	29.1
46	Percent having religious wedding	45.7	60.9		59.5	69.7	64.2
	Percent having reigious wedding only	5.1	5.6		4.8	21.3	15.0
50	Average age at marriage—girls	18.5	17.6		17.2	16.7	17.1
	Average age at marriage—boys	24.0	22.6		23.1	20.4	21.9
60	Family Modernization Index						
	Percent Modern	61.7	28.0		16.2	3.3	
	Transitional	27.9	41.3		32.4	24.3	
	Traditional	10.3	30.7		49.6	72.4	

SOURCE: Timur, *Türkiye'de Aile Yapisi.*

stances and ambitions for social mobility (1977). Timur found that the average age at marriage for both women and men rose in a fairly straight line as one moved from villages to cities, but that the slope of the line was rather mild (1972:Table 50).

(c) In contrast to the relative openness of the lower urban classes to new economic and material ways, there is also evidence of strong persistence of more "closed" attitudes, especially in relationships with those outside the family. The thrust of many of the findings is typified by a recent study in which Kağıtçıbaşı measured intergenerational and cross-sex comparisons within families in middle and lower class districts of Istanbul. Among her most interesting discoveries are a *lack* of difference between mothers and daughters on sex-role self-concepts and standards, and that on these topics women often had more traditional attitudes than men. She concludes that her findings "point to some inherent conflicts regarding modification of sex roles through social change. It appears that at a superficial level sex role standards regarding sex-typed behavior, rules of conduct, etc. change due to mass media exposure, diffusion of information, etc. However, insofar as definitions of sex-roles and self-perceptions regarding these roles do not change, the achieved changes are bound to remain on the surface" (1977:47–8. This study is particularly useful because it summarizes the results of most of the major studies of cultural values in Turkey). Some more specific items include:

(i) Similar to the findings of the villager studies presented above, Yasa's study found that 68 percent of *gecekondu* men disapproved of their wives going out without wearing a head-scarf, 72 percent felt the same way about women going out in short-sleeve clothes, 78 percent disapproved of their wives going without stockings.[29]

(ii) Timur found that a high percentage of urban women (59.3 percent in the three largest cities) continued to list as the basic way in which they would choose a husband "family decision with my own consent" (in the villages the percentage was 67.0). While this is a good deal less "traditional" that having a husband chosen *without* the wife's consent, only 29.6 percent chose the next less traditional answer, which contained an important change in emphasis: "my own decision with family consent."[30] For men, the situation was similar. In answer to the question of who influenced their choice of a marriage partner, in even the three largest cities only 52 percent cited "only myself," whereas 40 percent named mother and/or father or "other relatives." For cities other than the metropolises the answers closely resembled those given in small towns and villages, only a quarter to a third of the men responding "only myself" (1972:Table 25).

(iii) In matters internal to families, personal relationships seem to be less rigid. Timur has devised a "Family Modernization Index," composed of five items concerning family decision-making, five on the degree of husband-dominance, and five on husband-wife companionship and distinction of sex roles (allowing the wife to go alone to visit neighbors, friends, or relatives, or to parks, movies, and restaurants). Here she found a very distinct urban-rural difference indeed. Of the families in the three largest cities 61.7 percent came out "modern," twice the ratio for the smaller cities (28.0 percent, which in turn was almost twice that of towns (16.25 percent) and the rate for villages was only 3.3 percent (1972:181–4).

Another dimension is added by Kongar, who also measured changes in some family relationships. He found that they tend to change toward the "modern" more rapidly as income rises. Thus, 36 percent of those in the lowest income group in the Izmir study reported that there was more equality between husband and wife in their families than in their parents' families, but 57 percent of those in the highest income group reported such a change.[31]

It is not completely clear how to account for these changes in husband-wife relationships, given the persistence of tradition which we have been pointing out. It may most probably be accounted for by the fact that, in addition to decision-making being essentially a within-family matter, in urban areas it is simply more difficult to confine women to their homes or gardens than it is in villages (as well as the fact that men are often away from home at work during the times when shopping and related outside activities must be done).

(iv) Karpat summed up his findings with the observation that "the inferior position of women in the village resulting from division of labor and a hierarchy of values, although showing signs of change, seems to have been preserved in the gecekondu" (1976:130, also citing there Yasa, 1966:74, 217). And similarly to the findings of other studies cited above, he also found that "inside the family (however) women assumed more authority than men and appeared in general pleased to settle in the city and take advantage of urban educational and cultural facilities." (Karpat, 1976:130). But he also noted the beginnings of unrest, going so far as to say that "the sense of outrage and revolt among women in general, because of their low status, seemed to be acute and violent, indeed. This may become more evident if the level of social and political consciousness reaches an advanced stage," and he also found that "the difference in outlook, style of living, and level of aspiration showed much sharper variation among the gecekondu women than men" (1976:131).[32]

(v) Stirling's revisit to two villages near Kayseri found villagers maintaining that although both women who had migrated to town and those who were still in the village were "less submissive, want more comforts, consumer goods and personal freedom," and although "most villagers are eager to send their girls to school," they also asserted that village women resident in town were still closely restricted. His own conclusion was that "values regarding female modesty and purity have changed little" (1976:83, 85).

(d) In addition to the role played by persistence of "traditional" attitudes in social and cultural matters, potential psychological dislocation of new urbanites is kept down by urban settlement patterns. Turkish cities (like most others in developing and often in developed countries) contain numerous areas in which persons from particular regions, towns, or even villages live in close proximity to each other, a phenomenon to which John Kolars has given the name "shadow villages" (1967:69). For some specific data on this phenomenon, see Karpat, 1976:70–71). A kind of "landing place" for migrants, they provide initial shelter and guidance, and although we have as yet little information on whether groupings tend to be of more benefit (in terms of easing personal dislocation) or more hindrance (in that they slow down the integration of their members into the urban mainstream), most observers would now agree that there is an urban analogy to Suzuki's observation that ". . . the peasant's attachment to his most meaningful unit of social organization (the village)—deplored by the social scientist because it is felt to militate against socio-economic development is, in this case, operating to promote such development" (1960:891–2 and Kolars, 1967:69).

These communities are bolstered by other relationships which also resemble ones found in many villages. For example, the role of storekeeper is frequently a many-faceted one, including advisor and creditor, with the members of the "shadow village" providing him in turn with continuous and often exclusive patronage. Relatively few Turkish shoppers set out for the shopping area without knowing the specific shop (food, clothing, home furnishings, etc.) at which they will buy (see Kiray, 1964:43–4 and 61–3).

(e) A related major factor easing dislocation is the rapidly increasing number of urban local associations. A study by Yücekok in 1968 found there were over 28,000 "cultural" associations, most of them in cities and most of them at the neighborhood level. Their growth since the beginning of the multi-party period (when the Law of Associations was liberalized) has been one of the most spectacular developments of Turkish urban life.[33] Organized primarily in gecekondu areas where group solidarity tends to be high and dependence on government is great Danielson and Keleş, 1980b:298), they provide a comfortable haven. Membership is likely to be based on commonality of place of origin, and they are often centered around a mosque. They perform numerous social and informal acclimatizing services and they also frequently have direct instrumental functions, such as "liaison between *gecekondu* dwellers and the political parties, local authorities, and central government" (Ibid. See also Karpat, 1976:200 and 132–6). Many have had considerable success in winning government services for their members. (Full-scale studies of these organizations would be welcome.)

If there is considerable stability and social conservatism among the urban lower strata generally, what of a particular group in that stratum in which the potential for unrest may even be greater: industrial workers? Unfortunately, we have very little hard data on this subject, but it is the impression of observers that the situation here is volatile, that future economic and political developments will greatly affect the situation, and that conservative attitudes in this group may change quite rapidly. If there is currently still relatively little class consciousess among workers, this state of affairs is probably related to (among other things) the fact that most are still employed in small enterprises rather than in the large ones which are the most rapid breeding ground for discontent,[34] and to the continuing aspiration of many factory

TABLE 3-6

Growth of Voluntary Associations

	1950		1960		1968	
	Number	Percent	Number	Percent	Number	Percent
Economic						
Employer assns.	—	—	23	.1	190	.5
Agriculture assns.	49	2.3	272	1.6	683	1.9
Labor unions	91	4.2	408	2.4	995	2.6
Professional assns.	53	2.4	189	1.1	259	.7
White collar assns.	166	7.6	665	3.9	2,355	6.2
Artisans (esnaf)	253	11.7	2.745	15.9	3,670	9.7
Subtotal	612	28.2	4,302	25.0	8,152	21.3
Cultural						
Social welfare and charity	208	9.6	635	3.7	1,520	4.0
Sports	699	32.2	3,376	19.6	5,334	14.1
Religious-mosque-building and preservation	142	6.5	4,821	28.0	8,419	22.3
Other religious	12	.6	283	1.6	2,311	6.1
Culture	285	13.1	2,511	14.5	6,327	16.7
Beautification	102	4.7	853	5.0	4,644	12.3
Subtotal	1,448	66.7	12,479	72.4	28,555	75.5
Other						
Foreigners and minorities	75	3.5	218	1.3	290	.8
Miscellaneous	36	1.7	230	1.4	809	2.1
TOTAL	2,171		17,229		37,806	

SOURCE: Yücekok, 1972, following p. 149.

workers to leave those occupations and become self-employed. Other factors will include the future success of moderate institutions such as the conservative labor federation (*Türk-Iş*) as sponsors of material improvement.[35]

As with other groups, voting patterns provide a valuable guide to the political characteristics of the urban lower strata. Özbudun, fortunately, has included in his study of political participation an analysis of election returns in Istanbul, Ankara and Izmir by income level (1976: chap. 8). Though, again, the data are insufficient for definitive conclusions, they do indicate that voting activity as an expression of needs and demands by these groups should not be discounted by policymakers. Among his points are:

1. Voter turnout among the lower strata is high, though in most *gecekondu* areas it had already dropped by 1965 to a level closer to the urban averages than to the higher turnout found among rural voters. But he also found that most lower-strata members were *regular* voters, and "believed in

democracy" (1976:199–204). Several studies have also found that perhaps up to 14 percent of the urban lower group were also registered as political party members (Ibid.:204). It appears that politicization is likely to remain high among this group.

2. It is agreed by students of *gecekondu* areas that voting behavior is increasingly instrumental and responsive to factors of material performance, that the astuteness of urban political "machines" is a major factor in attracting *gecekondu* votes, and that *gecekondu* dwellers realize full well that they are particularly vulnerable to government reprisals as well as "highly dependent" on its favors (Özbudun, 1976:205 and Sayarı, 1975). Thus, in 1965 and 1969 there was strong support for the Justice party, in the early and mid-1970s the resurgence of the RPP had its base in many *gecekondu* districts—which also resisted blandishments by both left and right-wing radical parties—and it is widely predicted that should the RPP government fail to bring material improvements, the urban lower strata will not hesitate to return to their earlier JP preferences, despite either the ideological logic of supporting the RPP or in spite of the vicarious pleasure but uncertain benefits of strengthening the radicals.

3. On the other hand, the possibility of radicalism cannot be entirely ignored. In 1969, when the two major parties were somewhat weaker than in earlier times, the *gecekondu* and lower middle-class areas frequently (though not always) led most of the rest of the metropolises in returning to voting for minor (conservative) parties and for independents (Table 3-8). These groups, at least in some part, base their electoral decisions on either noninstrumental

TABLE 3-7
Voter Turnout by Type of Urban Area

		Percent voting		
		1965	1969	Change
Istanbul:	Entire city	63.6	51.7	−11.9
	Gecekondus	64.6	51.0	−13.6
Ankara:	Gecekondus	69.8	59.7	−10.1
	Lower middle class	68.5	55.7	−12.8
	Middle class	67.8	59.8	−8.0
	Upper middle class	69.5	60.0	−9.5
Izmir:	Gecekondus	69.4	58.7	−10.7
	Lower middle class	72.0	61.2	−10.8
	Middle class	71.2	59.3	−11.9
	Upper middle class	70.6	59.1	−11.5
Turkey:	Total	71.3	64.3	−7.0
	Urban	66.2	56.3	−9.9
	Rural	73.3	68.1	−5.2

SOURCE: Özbudun, 1976: 201–3.

TABLE 3-8
Voting Behavior by Type of Urban Area

1965		Left of Center			All Moderate Parties	Right of Center		
		Total	Radical	Moderate		Moderate	Radical	Total
Istanbul:	Gecekondus	71.1	8.7	62.4	81.5	19.1	8.4	27.5
	Entire city	58.2	6.2	52.0	82.4	30.4	8.5	38.9
Ankara:	Gecekondus	68.8	16.3	52.5	78.3	25.8	3.5	29.3
	Lower-middle	62.4	13.7	48.7	80.5	31.8	4.6	36.4
	Middle	34.4	7.0	27.4	80.5	53.1	10.6	63.7
	Upper-middle	33.4	6.6	26.8	80.9	54.1	9.7	63.8
Ismir:	Gecekondus	76.3	4.1	72.1	89.1	17.0	6.2	23.2
	Lower-middle	77.2	3.8	73.4	90.8	17.4	5.0	22.4
	Middle	69.2	3.3	65.9	91.5	25.6	4.9	30.5
	Upper-middle	57.1	3.0	54.1	90.6	36.5	6.4	42.9
All Turkey		65.1	12.2	52.9	81.6	28.7	3.0	31.7

| | Left of Center | | | | | | All Moderate Parties | | Right of Center | | | | | |
| | Total | | Radical | | Moderate | | | | Moderate | | Radical | | Total | |
1969	Total	Change from 1965	Radical	Change from 1965	Moderate	Change from 1965	All Moderate Parties	Change from 1965	Moderate	Change from 1965	Radical	Change from 1965	Total	Change from 1965
Istanbul: Gecekondus	69.1	−2.0	13.3	+4.6	53.8	−8.6	75.6	−5.9	21.8	+2.7	9.8	+1.4	31.6	+4.1
Entire city	57.6	− .6	11.3	+5.1	46.3	m5.7	81.2	−1.2	34.9	+4.5	6.1	−2.4	41.0	+2.1
Ankara: Gecekondus	66.2	−2.6	22.8	+6.5	43.4	−9.1	73.5	−4.8	30.1	+4.3	1.7	−1.8	31.8	+2.5
Lower-middle	63.2	+ .8	16.1	+2.4	47.1	−1.6	79.6	− .9	32.5	+ .7	2.0	−2.6	34.5	−1.9
Middle	34.1	− .3	9.3	+2.3	24.8	−2.6	85.2	+4.7	60.4	+7.3	4.7	−5.9	65.1	+1.4
Upper-middle	34.6	+1.2	8.8	+2.2	25.8	−1.0	85.9	+5.0	60.1	+6.0	4.7	−5.0	64.8	+1.0
Ismir: Gecekondus	70.5	−5.8	9.8	+5.7	60.7	−11.4	83.3	−5.8	22.6	+5.6	6.3	+ .1	28.9	+5.7
Lower-middle	68.6	−8.6	7.3	+3.5	61.3	−12.1	87.0	−3.8	25.7	+8.3	5.4	+ .4	31.1	+8.7
Middle	64.4	−4.8	5.5	+2.2	58.9	−7.0	91.2	− .3	32.3	+6.7	2.8	−2.1	35.1	+4.6
Upper-middle	52.3	−4.8	5.5	+2.5	46.8	−7.3	90.7	− .1	43.9	+7.4	3.2	−3.2	47.1	+4.2
All Turkey	64.3	− .8	17.8	+5.6	46.5	−6.4	73.9	−7.7	27.4	−1.3	2.7	− .3	30.1	−1.6

SOURCE: Özbudun 1976: Tables 8.2, 8.3, 8.4.
Note: Independents not included.
Left Radical = TIP, UP; Left Moderate = RPP; Right Moderate = JP; Right Radical = NP, NAP, NTP, RP.

(ideological) or personalistic grounds. Though Özbudun found evidence that for the most part migration to urban areas has indeed "changed the modal pattern of participation from mobilized to autonomous, from deferential or solidary to instrumental" (1976:213), the process is incomplete. In some important respects the *gecekondu* voters, at least to date, continue to indicate that if there is to be radicalization, it is more likely to be to the right than to the left.

Conclusion

One of the significant strengths of Turkish development is that to date the "followers" simultaneously display "modern" and "traditional" characteristics, that they are at once "stable" and "in motion." Their stability thus far has been a strength in that it has kept their demands on government relatively moderate and generalized and because the persistence of traditional attitudes (such as patience) and institutions (such as the communal and religious-based voluntary associations in lower-class urban areas) serve to help them accept the slowness with which economic improvement is likely to come and to ease the socio-psychological dislocations of modernization.

Their motion, on the other hand, is important because it is unlikely that pressure on governments for real social change and material improvement will disappear or will be easily muted. (For a disapproving critique of the effectiveness of government performance in improving conditions in *gecekondu* areas, see Heper, 1978:esp. 55–62.) And because the role of the followers is steadily becoming greater in many significant respects as they become economically, politically, and psychologically more integrated into the mainstream of national life, it is likely that their demands will include many things which up to now have been the prerogatives of elites. In addition to the greater material demands which will probably come on the heels of inflation and heightened material ambitions, Turkish followers will undoubtedly demand greater opportunities for social mobility, for participation in decision-making (at least electorally), and for the maintenance of conservative social values (even though the latter demand is becoming generally less important).

One major significance of this pattern of demands is that the demands are of a kind which the elites, heretofore in dominant positions, may be least prepared to meet. Bureaucrats do not easily become subservient to the wishes of their clients. Factory owners and managers do not easily adjust to diminution of their status relative to workers (albeit most of the demands of Turkish labor are unlikely to go so far as insisting upon something like worker participation in management). Not all children of upper-middle-class families will welcome measures to lessen the disadvantages which bright rural students have in competing for university admission. Highly trained persons whose services are badly needed in the less developed regions for more balanced development, are likely to balk at relocation. Many secularists are sure to remain frustrated when conservative governments devote resources to mosque-building. But the pressures from the "mass" will not disappear, and the demand will increasingly be for qualitative as well as quantitative change, for redistribution of wealth rather than only an increase of wealth, and for sharing in the right to define the nation's goals and aspirations.

One should not, of course, extol the role of the nonelites in modernization to the exclusion of the elites. Turkey *has* had many wise leaders, and many members of elite groups are truly devoted to the public good. Nor are followers necessarily any more willing than leaders to voluntarily make short-term sacrifices which might be necessary for long-term development (foregoing current consumption in favor of contributing to the country's ability to generate investment resources, for example, or subjecting oneself to far greater production discipline and quality control standards).

The setting into motion of Turkish followers has been a natural by-product of the first half-century of modernization. The relative stability with which this process has taken place to date is to a considerable degree due to the fact that Turkish governments have been willing to accept preservation of important traditions which might have been treated as expendable obstacles to progress. In return, the followers have shown considerable patience and fortitude. Now, however, "second-generation" problems (attaining far more equal distribution of material and nonmaterial resources, dealing with highly organized political followers at all points of the political spectrum, greatly increasing productivity to compete with the European Economic Community, etc.) may bring challenges even greater than heretofore. Whether the Turkish polity will be able to utilize its strength and its experience to creatively meet the new problems, of course remains to be seen.

Turkish Workers in Europe

We cannot conclude an analysis of Turkish followers without examining a new phenomenon—now no longer so new—of the Turkish workers in Europe (and, since the mid-1970s, in several countries of the Middle East). Of the estimated million currently in Europe, some 843,000 went under the auspices of the Turkish Employment Service between 1962 and the end of 1977 (T. C., 1978:148), while about 175,000 others went as "unofficial immigrants" (Hale, 1978:49 and Abadan-Unat, 1976a:8. All studies pretty much agree as to the general accuracy of the figures used in this section, but all also note the imprecision of the data. The sources cited in this section are selected as representative, not exhaustive). The number of Turks in Europe rose fairly steadily after 1962, varying in relation to the state of the European economies and the expansive or restrictive policies followed by the European states. During most of the 1970s Turkey was the highest among the six "sending" countries (Turkey, Yugoslavia, Italy, Greece, Spain, Portugal; Rist, 1978:66). Despite the fact that by 1976 the sending of new workers to Europe had almost completely stopped (and only a small amount of the slack has been taken up by workers hired for jobs in Middle East states, chiefly Libya and Saudi Arabia), the waiting list in Turkey is still estimated to be near a million.

The "export of workers," as Rist has called it, was considered by Turkey to be a useful policy for three reasons: to reduce unemployment, to give Turkish workers improved industrial training, and to generate foreign exchange from their remittances (1978:37–38). All of these aims have been fulfilled to some extent, but none to the degree that Turkish authorities had hoped. Let us review some of the characteristics of the workers and certain aspects of their experience.

TABLE 3-9

Workers Sent Abroad by Turkish Employment Service

Year	Total	Women	Percent Women	Percent Skilled	Number Abroad
1961–67	204,042	31,806	15.6	33.6[a]	—
1968	43,204	11,341	26.2	28.8	—
1969	103,975	20,765	20.0	24.5	—
1970	129,575	20,776	16.0	27.0	—
1971	88.442	14,200	16.1	35.5	—
1972	108,785	18,654	17.1	33.7	660,100
1973	135,820	27,035	19.9	42.0	766,800
1974	20,211	2,334	6.6	34.2	758,400
1975	4,419	402	9.1	51.3	710,700
1976	10,588[b]	372	8.0[c]	73.5	707,900
1977	19,084[b]	535	9.2[c]	72.8	710,880
1978	18,852[b]	485	64.4	—	

SOURCE: Abadan-Unat, 1976b; Hale, 1978; T. C., 1978, DIE #890.

[a]1964–67.

[b]Of the total, the following numbers went to Libya and Saudi Arabia: 1976: 5,930; 1977: 13,302; 1978: 7,863 (first 7 mo.).

[c]Percent of only workers going to Europe.

Origins and Characteristics

1. Since at least 1965, about 45 percent of the workers have been of rural origin. For many, the move to Europe was their second move following migration to a Turkish city, but is has also been estimated that some 18 to 27 percent have come directly from villages (Abadan-Unat, 1974:374; Rist, 1978:95–7).

2. Their places of origin include all regions of the country, though unevenly. The cities of Ankara, Izmir and Istanbul sent about 3.3 percent of their 1975 populations, and the city of Istanbul alone sent between 15 and 20 percent of all workers, Eastern Anatolia supplied only 0.86 percent of its population, and "the eight most rural and least developed districts of Turkey

together contributed on the average no more than 1 percent of the workers who eimigrated" (Hale, 1978:56; Rist, 1978:95; Abadan-Unat, et al., 1976b:17).

3. Two-thirds of the migrants were between the ages of 25 and 40, the mean age for those of both rural and urban origins being about 37. (Hale, 1978:58 and Abadan-Unat, 1974:376.)

4. In 1974, about 83 percent were primary school graduates or better (primary school is a minimum requirement for employment in Germany— Rist, 1978:93n). Only 53 percent of the total Turkish population has a primary school education or better. Sixty-nine percent of the migrants were primary school graduates only, compared to 40 percent in the general population, and an additional 13 percent were graduates of some post-primary education, compared to 13.4 percent in the general population (Hale 1978:59).

5. There was a steadily rising proportion of women among the workers. Whereas before 1964 they numbered under 10 percent, since 1965 they frequently made up a quarter of those going to Europe. A 1972–73 study found that 22 percent were unmarried (compared with 14 percent of the men) and that 32 percent were under the age of 25 (compared with 9 percent of the men (Hale, 1978:59, Kudat, 1974:6, Abadan-Unat, 1976:9).

6. Personal reasons for migration were overwhelmingly economic, i.e., the prospects of earning higher incomes and/or saving up money (Paine, 1974:Table A24).

Skill Levels

Up to 1972, between a quarter and a third of the workers sent to Europe by the TES were "skilled." After 1973 this percentage rose to include about half the workers sent in 1975 and three-fourths in 1976, as the European countries imposed greater restrictions in terms not only of numbers but of qualifications as well (Hale 1978:57). One effect of this was that Europe threatened to become not so much a training ground for Turkish workers as a competitor of Turkish employers for the relatively small pool of skilled labor. The extent of this problem has been an area of some disagreement. Hale has concluded that emigration was only a relatively small cause of the shortage of skilled workers for Turkish industry, varying among sectors such as metal and machinery workers, where the estimated emigration 1964–77 was about one-third the number of the deficit in supply estimated by the Ministry of Labor, to only about 2.5 percent for electricians (1978:63. He is of the opinion that a considerably more important cause was the shortage of training facilities). Aydınoğlu came to a similar general conclusion (though he does not arrive at as precise quantitative estimates). Turkish employers have nevertheless at various times complained about the effects of emigra-tion. Many apparently share the view of Rist, who described as "staggering" the fact that 33 to 35 percent of all Turkey's workers had gone abroad, and that the waiting list made the total of those who *wanted* to be elsewhere as high as 85 percent (1978:93–5). He also asserted that emigration "had had a considerable impact upon the ability of these countries to undertake their own development programs" (1978:93). In any case, it was widely recommended that the system of mandatory rotation, which has been a part of the policies of both the sending and receiving countries, be far more strictly enforced (1978:16; Aydınoğlu, 1976:132, Abadan-Unat, et al., 1976b:41).[36]

There is considerable disagreement among the analysts also about skill improvement during the workers' stays in Europe. A 1971 SPO survey found that whereas 54 percent of the workers were classified as unskilled during their first year abroad, only 16 percent were still in that category by the time of their fifth year in Europe. The percentage who were skilled rose from 15 percent during their first year to 30 percent in their fifth (Paine, 1974:204). Fifty-two percent of the workers surveyed had advanced at least one category, and only 6 percent had been demoted. Of those promoted, the rate among workers of urban origin (35 percent) was twice as high as for those from rural areas (17 percent) (Ibid.:205). Rist, however, citing 1976 data, found that while 28.4 percent of the migrants had been skilled workers or foremen in Turkey, only 18.0 percent found their first jobs in Germany at that level, and that not only did 80.4 percent hold their first jobs in Germany at the unskilled level but 69.8 percent were also in that category in their last jobs there.[37] The SPO survey also found that 69 percent held only one job during their entire stay (Paine, 1974:203). Although these data must be used with some care (e.g., the returnees in the surveys who supplied "last job" data may well have been the least successful), it seems clear that while some workers certainly came back better equipped, many others have not. As Abadan-Unat has asserted, "it is exaggerated to say that one of the indirect results of migration is the 'training of untapped industrial skilled manpower.' Such a contention seems to be much more wishful thinking and much more a convenient social and political myth than a quantitatively measurable assertion" (1976a:23).

Social Adjustment and Problems

Whereas in 1965 virtually no Turkish workers brought their wives with them, by 1976 about two-thirds had their families in Europe, and a considerable number of the wives were also employed.

Most of the studies conclude that there was a remarkably high degree of successful social adjustment. Apparently one important area of adjustment was intrafamily relationships, particularly increased status of wives. Reasons for this increased status included being away from kin, the large number of employed Turkish women in Germany, and familiarity with European women who enjoyed greater independence than their Turkish counterparts. One manifestation of this adjustment was that family decision-making in matters such as budgeting appears to have become more equal between the two spouses (Kıray, 1976:224). Kıray also found that Turkish women adjusted particularly well, something she attributed at least in part to Turkish women's "traditional upbringing in the family (which) is geared to prepare them to adjust to totally different environments," such as uprooting and movement into totally new circumstances at marriage (1976:224). Kudat, on the other hand, cautioned that the number of reported cases of serious conflict or frustration was also considerable, and appeared to be more severe when a family was first separated in Turkey and later reunited in Europe (1974:27ff.; 1974b;1975).

Their social situation is not without problems, of course. A major one which the Turkish migrants face is that they are often looked down on by their European hosts. The Turks, even more than workers from some of the other southern European countries, often live in the most squalid areas and conditions, and many Europeans shy away from social contact with them. (See, for example, "Die Türken Kommen—Rette Sich Wer Kann," in *Der Spiegel,* Nr. 31, 1973: 24–34, and Suzuki, 1976. On ghetto life see Mik and Verkoren-Hemelaar, 1976.) Other alienating factors include language difficulties, and differences in culture and religion. One manifestation of this (as well as of other sources of frustration) is that "the crime rate is higher for immigrants that for the indigenous population, and particularly so for Turks" (Paine, 1974:109, also Abadan-Unat, 1969:41).

Another social problem is inadequacy of educational and other facilities for Turkish children. The number of school age children had by 1973 risen to over 200,000, this in addition to preschool children who in 1975 numbered 167,000 (Hale, 1978:52; Abadan-Unat, 1976a:Table 11). Although exact figures are difficult to get, one estimate is that in West Germany and Holland only half of the children of foreign workers receive education (Kok, 1976:310). Beginning in 1973, the Turkish government made efforts to open Turkish-language schools, but the facilities are quantitatively and qualitatively inadequate. The choice for most Turks is to either stay away or be educated in German and in the Christian faith. Not surprisingly, many Turkish parents opt for the former (Paine, 1974:109).[38] (For a systematic discussion of this problem, see Bilmen, 1976:235–52.)

It is difficult to know how much psychological frustration arises from such problems. Apparently many of the workers do want to integrate into their host societies (Mik and Verkoren-Hemelaar, 1976:274). However, the financial attractions of foreign work undoubtedly help them to cope with the situation. When the SPO survey asked whether the workers were content with their overall situations, it was found that 46 percent were content, 44 percent were neutral, and only 10 percent were not content (Paine 1974:205). It is conceivable, however, that these attitudes were expressed partly so as to avoid the possibility of the discontented being identified and sent home. It is also notable that a high proportion did not want to return to Turkey, at least soon.

Returnees

Of those who returned to Turkey (in 1972 the number was about

600,000—Paine, 1974:183. I have been unable to find any reliable later figures) most did so reluctantly. The SPO survey found that only 5 percent considered their return permanent (Ibid.:183). Of those who returned, only 18 percent said they did so because they had saved enough money to set up work at home, while 44 percent did so because of family problems, 11 percent because of inability to adapt to their work surroundings, and 6 percent because of illness or unhappiness (Ibid.:208). Rist observed that several studies lead to the inference that a high percentage of returnees were "returnees of failure" (1978:49–50). The Boğazliyan study (Abadan-Unat, et al., 1976b:190–1) found over 50 percent in these categories, and of those who felt they could eventually solve their problems, 63 percent said they wanted to go abroad again. (As noted above, in order to maximize the learning benefits available to the future Turkish labor force many analysts have urged stricter enforcement of the policy of rotation, but it is not clear how long that period ought to be, since those who learn the most skills are the ones who stay abroad the longest, often five years or more.)

The experience of the Turks in factory work does not, however, appear to have had the effect of interesting them in continuing such work on their return. On the contrary, the SPO study found that only 13 percent wanted to become an "employee" on their return home, whereas 50 percent wanted to become employers, operating their own small businesses or shops, and a substantial portion wanted to become independent farmers (Paine, 1974:209, 111). Abadan-Unat similarly concluded that few wanted to stay in the secondary sector at all, but rather wanted to move into the tertiary one (1974:392). However, the SPO survey found only 2 percent who in fact became employers,[39] whereas 41 percent became wage-earners (none had listed this as their aspiration), and 47 percent had become self-employed, which probably meant either agriculture, artisanry or unemployment (Paine 1974:209). Thus, those who did stay in industrial occupations may well be those who have the lowest levels of skills or initiative for moving out, or those who had been the least able to accumulate savings for investment to start small businesses. Nor was much of the workers' savings invested in industry. Though few specific data are available, Keleş has concluded that most workers with savings give their first priority to real estate rather than commercial activities or manufacturing industries.[40]

Research on returnees is only beginning, so that we have as yet little in-depth knowledge of the social and psychological benefits and drawbacks of worker migration. The Abadan-Unat, et al., study, Migration and Development, The Effects of International Labor Migration on Boğazlıyan District, is hopefully only the first of many.

Remittances

Workers' remittances were for some years a major positive factor in the Turkish balance of payments. In 1972, 1973, and 1974, in fact, they were only slightly less than total Turkish export earnings, and in excess of the deficit in visible trade (Hale, 1978:Table 29). The average remittances per worker abroad grew at a decreasing rate after 1971, however, with absolute decreases in 1975 and 1976 (TUSIAD, 1977:161). Turkish workers today appear to be purchasing an increasing quantity of goods in Europe, which they will seek to import upon their return to Turkey. Their appetites for imported goods will likely remain stimulated.

All in all, there are many reasons for those who had placed great hopes in the benefits of worker migration to be severely disappointed.

FOUR

Groups and Forces

Among the most important determinants of the course of public affairs in any society are the political, economic, and social pressures of various interest groups and social forces. Some of these groups, such as trade unions, business associations, agricultural groups, and professional associations are organized specifically to pursue their particular interests, partly through interaction with government and partly through private means, such as collective bargaining. Other groups, such as the armed forces, may not be organized to promote specific policies, but they may nonetheless act in pursuit of particular interests. In addition to specific matters which deal with their own welfare, they may also pursue more general goals such as altering or preserving the nature of the nation's political, economic, or social structure. In another vein, pressures can arise by virtue of the pervasiveness in society of more general forces such as religion (which may, of course, also be sometimes represented by specific organizations). Finally, a specific issue may become a movement and a movement may become a force—for example, the role of women is now an issue in Turkish society and has the potential of taking on more organized form.

In a modern society, as noted earlier in this study, it is important that the views and wishes and needs of the general population be both articulated and responded to. For optimum contribution to the stability and development of a nation, the articulation of interests should be balanced (in that all groups and forces are heard, particularly those which might otherwise disrupt the society) and moderate (not making extreme demands whose fulfillment might do major harm to the interests of other groups). It is using these criteria that this chapter will examine some major groups and forces acting on Turkish public affairs.

Interest Groups

Turkey has changed a great deal since 1965 when Dankwart Rustow felt free to assert that "pressure groups are notably absent from the Turkish political scene" (1965:196). Today there is hardly any sector in Turkish society (except peasants and agricultural workers) which is not organized, active, and highly visible in pursuit of its interests.

Labor

The Turkish labor movement has grown rapidly in size, strength, interest in politics, and militancy. Figures on trade union membership are very unreliable[1] (official and/or generally accepted ones are given in Table 4-1), but one may more or less safely accept the estimate that close to 50 percent of nonagricultural wage and salaried workers are now organized (Ekin 1977:42). An estimated 70 to 75 percent belong to the oldest and politically moderate labor organization, the Turkish Confederation of Trade Unions (*Türk-İş*). Perhaps 20 to 25 percent belong to the newer and more radical Revolutionary Trade Unions Confederation (DISK), and the remainder to the conservative Nationalist Trade Unions Confederation (MISK) or to independent unions.

TABLE 4-1
Trade Union Activity

	Number of Unions	Number of Members	Number of Agreements	Number of Strikes	Number of workers Striking	Work-days Lost
1948	73	52,000				
1950	88	76,000				
1955	363	190,000				
1960	432	283,000				
1963	565	296,000	96	8	1,514	19,739
1965	668	360,000	871	46	6,593	336,836
1970	717	2,088,000	1,516	111	25,963	260,338
1975	781	3,329,000	1,893	90	25,389	1,102,682
1977	863	3,808,000	2,033	167	58,899	5,778,205
1978	879		1,870			

Source: TUSIAD, 1977, 1978; DIE #2 850, 825, 890; Ataöv, 1967; Ecevit, 1973.

Note: There are many and widely varying figures on these items. Those here are as far as possible official figures and/or ones that seem generally agreed on. For further comment see text.

Labor organization began in Turkey shortly after the Young Turk Revolution of 1908, but unions remained small because of the rudimentary level of industrialization and the unsympathetic attitudes of the CUP. During the Republic's first quarter-century the labor movement remained weak, although the number of industrial workers began to increase. Among the reasons for the failure of unions to grow was the basic doctrinal hostility of the Kemalists to any associations based on social class.[2] At the same time, workers were unilaterally granted many economic and social rights by the government, including improved wages and working conditions and "compulsory labor inspection and compulsory arbitration committees for disputes" (Lewis 1961:470). These and other benefits undoubtedly were instrumental in making potential labor leaders allies of the RPP, even though many of the benefits were more apparent than real.[3]

The opening of the multiparty period gave strong impetus to the formation of trade unions, as it did to other associations, including opposition parties. Unions grew only slowly, however, until 1950 when the Democrats came to power with the support of urban workers (and other groups).[4] During the 1950s the number of unions increased five-fold and the number of union members more than tripled. Union activity remained limited, however, because the 1947 Labor Law, while restricting the powers of employers and government vis-a-vis trade unions and giving the unions the right to make collective agreements, did not give them the right to strike. The Democrats, though advocating the right to strike in their 1949 program, did not write it into law during their decade in power.

An important milestone was reached in 1961 when the new Constitution obligated the State "to take necessary measures to protect the rights of the workers," and asserted that "Workers' Representation, Collective Bargaining, and Strike (were) accepted as essential rights" (Alpay, 1976:2n1). These provisions were translated into the Labor Laws (No. 274 and 275) of 1963, whereupon unions began to grow rapidly. A period of increasingly more militant collective bargaining and strike action was inaugurated which continues to this day. Labor militancy was given further impetus when DISK was organized in 1967.

Economic impact. Since unions received the right to strike there has been progressive improvement in the economic status of Turkish labor. During the decade 1965-74 average daily wages in manufacturing industry more than tripled, and average annual wage increases have exceeded the increase in the consumer price index every year since 1969 (Alpay, 1976: Tables 3 and 4, and OECD, 1978:11), though with great variations in the amount of improvement in real wages (for example, 1.19 percent in 1974, 14.79 percent in 1976). There have also been substantial improvements in fringe benefits, which now on the average add another 50 percent to total compensation (TUSIAD, 1977:221). As may be noted in Table 4-1 in reference to the number of collective bargaining agreements, strikes, and workdays lost, the unions have been quite active. It is difficult to know how much of the improvement was due to the economic bargaining strength of the unions, however, There is general agreement that a considerable amount of labor's success has come about because of the desire of both JP and RPP governments to win the support of the unions, which they often succeeded in doing, in large part by granting sizable pay increases to workers in the State Economic Enterprises. The private sector followed with relatively little resistance, also influenced by a factor not really attributable to union power, namely the ability of manufacturers to sell all they could produce and to pass along virtually all of the increased labor costs to consumers in the form of higher prices.

Political impact. The active political role of labor is also relatively new. As recently as the late 1950s there was general acceptance among most political and labor leaders that "one of the basic Turkish doctrines about trade unions is that they should concern themselves with social and economic, not political matters" (Dodd 1969:177). This philosophy had been expressed in the Labor Law of 1947, and supported throughout the 1950s by the Democrat government which saw to it that "the definition of what was political was kept wide" (Ibid.).[5]

The reasons for support of the idea that labor should be "nonpolitical" varied. For the RPP, even after the party itself had amended the Law of Associations in 1946, there was still lingering wariness of class-based associations, although this feeling gave way as early as 1953 to "generous promises" including the right to strike (Karpat, 1959:316). As for the Democrats, they could have enacted such laws, but there was little reason to do so. Not wishing to alienate their supporters in the business community, they were further fortunate in that the support of most urban workers for the DP was all but certain because of the high rate of economic growth and consequent employment opportunities, and the specific economic benefits previously mentioned. (For historical and social factors involved in this situation, see chapter 5.)[6] Radical ambitions of the unions were also dampened when both the RPP (between 1946 and 1950) and the Democrats (thereafter) did not hesitate to arrest labor leaders along with other persons during various crack-downs on leftist political parties and their sympathizers.

At the same time, however, both major political parties solicited support of the unions. When Türk-İş was formed in 1952 it was quickly integrated into the political mainstream, and labor was counted among the many who supported the DP as the sponsors of rapid economic growth and bringers of democracy. In the late 1950s the unions began to become more independent and to move toward supporting the opposition RPP, this in response to increasing inflation and urban unemployment, the DP's more pronounced pro-business position, and growing criticism that the unions were government "puppets." In the Constituent Assembly of 1961 labor received six seats (although the union leaders felt rather slighted when the universities, a group much smaller in numbers, received twelve). The Assembly strongly supported the increased rights for labor which were shortly afterward incorporated into the 1961 Constitution (Weiker, 1963:76–7). These successes and the continuation of generally conservative social attitudes of most Turkish workers were enough to keep most of the union movement moderate, although the level of activity increased significantly in the areas of organization and collective bargaining, and labor, like many other groups, also began to speak out on general political issues. (On this period see Karpat, 1963:271–75.)

Although Türk-İş, under its veteran leader Halil Tunç, continued to act as a nonparty pressure group, the 1960 Revolution also gave rise to the

beginnings of labor radicalism. Twelve labor leaders were among the founders of the Marxist Turkish Labor party (for details, see chapter 5).
Radicalism, however, did not get a great deal of support from most of the
labor movement, whose members for the most part were still socially
conservative as well as satisfied with the economic gains they were continuing to make. In fact, in the 1965 and 1969 elections the TLP drew more
votes from middle class precincts than from working class areas. But the TLP
did have the effect of making Türk-Iş more militant in regard to economic
and social demands for workers, and many benefits were won during the
1960s at least in part because of the desire of political and business leaders to
keep the majority of workers from becoming radicalized. Radicalization of
trade unions could not be completely prevented, though, and in 1967 a group
of labor leaders, dissatisfied with the moderate positions of Türk-Iş resigned
from that group and organized DISK.

Several reasons have been given by observers for the failure of DISK to
attract more than about a quarter of Turkey's organized workers (though
under the circumstances, it would also be easy to call that level an impressive
success). One important reason was Türk-Iş's continued success in improving the economic status of its members. Part of this success lay in the
fact that Türk-Iş contained (and still contains) all the unions in the public
sector. As mentioned above, there were strong political motivations to grant
the demands of public-sector unions. DISK, in contrast, was (and is) active
almost exclusively in the private sector, where bargaining is considerably
more difficult because of factors such as increasingly less ability and willingness of private industry to absorb sharply increased labor costs, the high level
of urban unemployment, and the unions' inability to organize the many small
factories which continue to dominate much of Turkish manufacturing. (One
DISK official admitted recently that the difference in the average daily wages
for public and private sector workers, which he estimated at the end of 1978
as 178 and 128 TL respectively, was a serious image problem.)

The political direction which labor will take in the future is by no means
certain. DISK officials assert that they will succeed in the long run as a result
of the far better job they are doing in political indoctrination and in focusing
on workers' rights over and above wages, but their task is formidable. For one
thing, the very structure of Turkish bargaining is likely to keep the focus on
economic issues, in which Türk-Iş's record is generally good. The labor law
forbids craft unions, so that organization is by branches, and although
industry-wide bargaining is permitted, almost all bargaining is at the factory
level, which help deemphasize the appeal of political issues. In addition, it is
likely that employers will continue to favor Türk-Iş with relatively good
settlements, if for no other reason than to inhibit the expansion of DISK.
Another factor is the continued political conservatism of many unions, even
in trying times. While all union leaders now accept the premise that it is no
longer useful to remain "above-party," when Türk-Iş met to formulate its
position for the 1977 election if found a substantial enough portion of its
constituent unions and federations supporting the Justice party so that it was

thought prudent not to take any overall confederation position.[7] In a move to change this situation, in 1978 the RPP government negotiated a "Social Contract" *(Toplumsal Anlaşma)* with Türk-Iş, outlining general guidelines for labor relations and economic matters.

In DISK's favor are that some of its major successes have come in the large private-sector factories where there is the greatest potential for militant class consciousness (see Dubetsky, 1976 and 1977, Makofsky, 1977, and chapter 3 above) which might well spread to the large public sector ones. In addition, DISK has led several dramatic and successful protests against what were very poorly disguised antilabor tactics by the Justice Party and National Front governments and by employers.[8] Also in its favor is the fact that the increasingly severe inflation of the late 1970s is heightening the level of worker dissatisfaction. On balance, the RPP and *Türk-Iş* have the potential to keep labor among the moderate forces now being brought to bear on Turkey's modernization. But is may not be easy.

Business and Industrial Groups

The growth of commercial and industrial interest groups has also become important. They have many strengths and considerable power, but also some important areas of weakness. As one leading Istanbul industrialist puts it:

> Everybody should know that the private sector in Turkey is not as influential and effective a pressure group as it is often thought. It is heterogeneous and intra-sector jealousies are all-pervasive. It is not well organized. Istanbul versus Anatolia competition persists. Large industry is always in conflict with small industry. Some of the chambers of industry do not view favorably the Turkish Association of Industrialists and Businessmen which they think is an exculsive club of big industrialists. There are no close ties between chambers of commerce and of industry. Only one third of the employers has been organized within the (Turkish) Confederation (of Employers' Associations). (Ertuğrul Soysal, "Hükümet ve Özel Kesim," *Milliyet,* Apr. 30, 1974, as cited by Heper, 1976:497.)

The Turkish commercial and industrial sector is represented by several organizations. The most important are The Confederation of Artisans' Associations *(Esnaf ve Sanatkar Derneği Konfederasyonu)*; Employers' Associations *(Işverenler Sendikaları)*; the Union of Chambers of Commerce and Industry; and the Turkish Industrialists and Businessmen's Association (TUSIAD). In 1976, these four, together with the Union of Chambers of Agriculture, formed the Free Enterprise Council *(Hür Teşebbüs Konseyi)* to be a general spokesman for Turkish employers. There have since been some public pronouncements from the council, but no move to form its constituent organizations into a more structured unit.

Esnaf. Representing the smallest scale segment of the business sector, but by no means the least influential, are the artisans' *(esnaf)* associations. Their economic importance is clear from the estimate of Mubeccel Kıray (in the study of Izmir) that although "70 percent of the total value added in Izmir during 1965 was created in large scale, organized industry . . . small manufacturing encompasses 60 percent of the total number of employees" (1973:7). (The large number of essentially handicraft shops can also be attested to by anyone who has ever visited a Turkish city.)

The degree of organization of the *esnaf* has increased rapidly since 1946, together with other associations as shown in Table 4-2. Long organized at the local level, broader association was authorized by Law #507 in 1965, and in 1978 the Confederation of Artisans and Craftsmen's Associations contained nine occupational federations, 68 province-wide associations (two in Istanbul), and some 4,000 local associations representing an estimated 50 percent of Turkey's approximately 3 million *esnaf*. (Estimates supplied by the confederation.) Membership is not compulsory as it is for a number of other business and professional groups.

TABLE 4-2
Business and Professional Associations

Year	Esnaf Associations	Employer Associations	Agricultural Associations	Professional Associations
1946	103	—	20	28
1950	253	—	49	53
1955	1,460	2	146	119
1960	2,745	23	272	189
1965	3,578	106 assns. (1,927 members)	570	260
1970	ca 4,000	120 assns. (10,760 members)		
1975		118 assns. (8,943 members)		
1979	ca 4,000	113 assns.		

SOURCE: Yücekok, 1972; Kili, 1976–7; TUSIAD, 1977; DIE #750, 825; information from the associations.

Esnaf guilds have long been active both politically and economically. Turkish and Middle East history abound with incidents of them actively pressing their interest. Sometimes their actions were direct, such as opposing the import policies of the Ottoman government which threatened the position of their own products. (On disruption caused in the Middle East by the incursion of Western competition see, for example, Issawi, 1965 and Costello, 1977.) Other times the *esnaf* associations were active in more general and political areas, such as opposing radical social reformers or showing displeasure at the display of certain types of social or political books in local shops. On many matters they have worked closely with other conservative groups to set the "social tone" of their communities. Carrying on this tradition, the confederation's newspaper, *Türkiye Esnaf,* and numerous pamphlets and occasional publications are currently among Turkey's most strident assailants of "communist anarchy."

In the Republican period their economic and political power, particularly at the local level, has been supplemented by the Turkish practice of giving semiofficial associations important formal roles in regulating the activities of their members. Thus, under Law 507 each craft association is given responsibilities such as supervising the licensing of taxi drivers or setting the number of establishments of a particular kind which can operate in a specific town or district. Authority is in the hands of each province association, and it is therefore not surprising that artisans and small merchants comprise the largest single group on the city councils of most of the communities on which we have studies. Significantly, this is true not only of older and more conservative centers, such as Kayseri, but also of newer ones, such as Eskişehir, Zonguldak and Izmit (a city which has grown extremely rapidly, almost wholly as a result of spillover of the burgeoning Istanbul and Marmara industrial region), and even of present-day Ankara! (See Weiker, 1972:38, 54; Tekeli, 1977:89; Keleş, and Danielson, 1980a:333; Tachau 1973a:288, Magnarella 1974:146.) There is little evidence as to whether the *esnaf* on the city councils are large or small operators. Magnarella notes that the RPP in Susurluk tended to contain the richer ones, but the present author's studies of Kayseri and Eskişehir found that most of the *esnaf* city council members of both political parties were owners of quite small enterprises. The associations also maintain strong ties to the political parties: Tekeli found that of some sixty *esnaf* guilds in the Ankara province federation, 21 had clear ties to one of the parties—for example, association officers also being party officials (1977:86–7)—and my studies in Kayseri and Eskişehir also found numerous such cases (Weiker, 1972:55).

Though interested in social and political matters, the *esnaf*'s pursuit of their interests is most frequently focused on their economic concerns. The instrumental rather than ideological character of this aspect of *esnaf* activity is reflected in the fact that as many local associations can sometimes be found affiliated with the RPP as with the right-wing parties.[9] Much effort has gone into the work of seeking government resources for the establishment and improvement of "small industry zones," of which some 55 have been completed and 57 more are under construction (see the confederation's Annual Activity Report for 1978, pp. 22–23). The *esnaf* have also been particularly active in mobilizing and organizing their own resources, such as the networks of loan-guarantee cooperatives (though a considerable part of the funding also comes from government sources). Unfortunately, the *esnaf* sector has not shown much as initiative in modernizing production, increasing efficiency, new technology, economy of scale, etc. Because such initiatives are vital to the economic development of the country as a whole, and although the *esnaf*'s record in economic activity is generally good, *esnaf* cannot be said to be in the forefront of development. But at the same time, conservative though the *esnaf* are politically and socially, describing them as "anti-modernization" would be doing them a considerable injustice.

Employer Associations. The Turkish Confederation of Employer Associations *(Türkiye Işveren Sendikalani Konfederasyonu)* was established in 1961. In 1971 it represented over 1000 large and medium-sized enterprises employing some 350,000 workers, plus about 100 associations of smaller enterprises in individual localities, according to confederation sources. (Four public sector associations left the Confederation in 1978 in conjunction with the "Social Contract" between *Turk-Iş* and the RPP government.) The confederation's chief function is cooperative action in collective bargaining to counter the strength of the trade unions. Toward that end, in 1977 the confederation established a "Mutual Support Fund" to which all members contribute in proportion to their number of employees and amount of sales (Annual Report, April 1978, pp. 18–19). It is also quite active in other spheres, including representation on numerous national and international bodies, and carries on programs of research, publications, and public relations. Designed to appeal to wide general audiences, the confederation's publications frequently appear in English as well as Turkish, and include annual analyses of the Turkish economic scene, critiques of labor relations and laws and regulations related to them, as well as vigorous statements of confederation views, which are, not surprisingly, quite conservative.

The membership of the confederation is composed in large part of small and medium manufacturers, who are among the bitterest opponents of what they describe as politically and ideologically (rather than economically) motivated strikes. They regularly make it a point to cite surveys they have taken on the reasons why businesses fail—usually excessive labor costs—and one of their bitterest areas of complaint is the elaborate system of seniority rights which have been given to labor through collective bargaining and government regulation. Their power as a unified force in collective bargaining is difficult to measure. As noted above, the high level of consumer demand has to date made it easy for many employers to pass along to their customers higher labor costs, so that there have as yet been relatively few real tests. In the long run, the power of the employers will also be affected in major ways by government policy, and confederation discussions of labor relations give prominent attention to such matters, including concern with strengthening the laws governing lockouts. Their future role will depend on numerous conditions both within and outside their control.

The Union of Chambers of Commerce and Industry and Commodity Exchanges is the oldest national organization in the private sector and in many ways is still the most prestigious, and certainly the most visible. It is a semiofficial organization to which all commercial and industrial employers with ten or more workers must belong, and is based on local chambers in every Turkish city and in many towns.

The Istanbul Chamber of Commerce dates back to the 19th century (see Hoell, 1973). By the 1920s there were some fifty local chambers, which the new government brought under its jurisdiction in the Chambers of Commerce and Industry Law of 1925. For some time they were generally inert, due chiefly to the weakness of the Turkish private sector. In the early 1940s, after some industrial development had begun, private entrepreneurs started to show more vigor, expressing dissatisfaction with various government policies and engaging in independent competition for scarce goods. As a result they were brought under tighter government supervision in 1943. Discontent and a desire for more independence surfaced again in 1948 with the advent of the multiparty period. Early in the DP era, the private sector was given authorization to form a "peak association," the present union (Law 5590, 6 February 1952. For a more detailed history see Öncü, 1980). In 1977 its membership totaled 50 Chambers of Commerce, 8 Chambers of Industry, 131 combined Chambers of Commerce and Industry, and 52 Commodity Exchanges, and the union's national headquarters had some 300 to 400 fulltime employees and a budget of 95 million TL (1977 Annual Report:11, 118).

Law 5590 has been a source of both strength and weakness for the Union. In the 1950s the union was perhaps the strongest business-interest association in the private sector, as a result of very close relations with the industrialization-bent DP government. Its importance was augmented when in 1958 its self-regulation powers were expanded to include the allocating of import quotas (within general parameters set by the government) both among commodity groups and among individual entrepreneurs. It also received the responsibility of certifying whether individual applicants were qualified. These close connections to government and the union's great concentration of power caused the opponents of strong private-sector authority to look for opportunities to "cut it down to size." After the 1960 revolution the government's role was considerably strengthened, but some power was left in the hands of the union, at least partly, in the words of one analyst, because the number of projects which received "investment encouragement licenses" was always considerably greater than the amount of available import quotas and the authorities preferred to leave to the union the problem of "how to distribute five dollars among fifty applicants" (Öncü, 1980:468. For details on the union's role in these processes see also Krueger, 1974:150–2 and Singer, 1977:259, 386). The 1965–71 JP governments were content to leave the union's authority alone, partly because the JP had the ability to control elections to the union's Board of Directors (Saybaşılı 1976:127). Still, one of the early actions of the above-party Erim government of 1971 was to transfer the union's import allocation functions to the Ministry of Commerce.

Law 5590 led to troubles for the union in another way as well, by institutionalizing some of the divisions already inherent within the private sector. A provision of the law permitted the establishment of separate Chambers of Industry, and industrialists in Istanbul and Izmir, who had lobbied vigorously for this provision, broke away to form their own organizations in 1952 and 1954 respectively (although it was not until the 1960s that others began to follow suit).[10] One major reason for this breakaway was that, despite the increasing divergence of interests, the commercial groups were able to remain dominant because of the law, which prescribed weighted voting but also prescribed an upper limit for any single chamber, so that the small Anatolian local units remained in a controlling majority. This situation led to additional divisiveness because within the commercial sector the larger centers (of which there are several in Anatolia), in which the strongest firms were located, were also being kept out of power, with the consequence that on significant matters like export and import facilitation they were being regularly outvoted.[11] The large chambers were in fact in many ways autonomous from the union because of their very economic strength (Öncü, 1980:458–60). These growing conflicts (the law prevented the formation of a separate *union* of Chambers of Industry even though it permitted the separate chambers themselves), were a major factor in the formation of TUSIAD in 1971.

Despite these difficulties the union continues to have considerable power, partly because in the pattern of Turkish administrative practice it retains important functions in areas such as credit, guidance of government investment in industrial parks, and supervision of firms' accounting procedures. Another source of influence is that it continues to represent a large number of powerful groups in the commercial and industrial sectors of most Turkish cities and towns. The union's ties to members of the political parties remain close, and, as is the case with other "peak associations," it is also represented on many national and international bodies. A third strength is the union's high visibility through its research and publications. In addition to its prestigious Annual Economic Report, the union, as well as many of its local chambers, regularly publishes analyses of economic matters in the national press, and its numerous seminars and meetings are well attended by national and international economic leaders.

TUSIAD, the Turkish Industrialists and Businessmen's Association *(Türk Sanayıcıler ve İş Adamları Derneği)* was founded in Istanbul in 1971 by several of Turkey's largest industrialists. A private association with individual membership, the twenty holding companies and conglomerates, sixty-five industrial companies, seven banks, and five insurance, brokerage, and publicity companies which sponsored TUSIAD's 1979 *Economic Survey* represents a very large proportion of the modern private sector. Its advisory council, headed by Vehbi Koç, consists of individuals with worldwide contacts and reputations. Although it has no semi-official status or regulatory functions, as has the Union of Chambers, TUSIAD is nevertheless becoming a major rival to the Union in its research, publication, and representation activities, and in its visibility. Its list of activities includes offering assistance in education, guiding and counseling enterprises, and efforts with direct policy implications such as "activities to channel the investments to the priorities of public interest and to the productive areas that give impetus to exports and earn foreign exchange. . . ." (*Ibid.,* inside back cover). Its increasing number of publications and analyses includes widely distributed English language editions. It is also making itself increasingly visible through frequent public statements on both economic and general policy and public problems, and its leaders and members frequent the highest political circles. It is not yet clear how its power will compare with that of the more Anatolian and locally based Union, whose members have interests which are often different from those of TUSIAD members.

In sum, business and commercial groups have come onto the political stage prominently in conjunction with their increased economic role since the 1950s. Their chief strengths are in their constantly growing numbers, in their base in local politics, and in their ability to contribute to economic development. Their most important weaknesses include growing disunity as the interests of various of its segments become more differentiated, and their very considerable dependence on government policies and resources in areas such as import allocations, credit and investment, and infrastructure. (On these matters see chapter 7 below.) The business and industrial community has a large stake in the question of which political parties come to power, but probably more important for their interests will be how effective *any* government is able to be in putting Turkey back on her economic feet.

Agricultural Organizations

There has also been considerable growth of agricultural organizations. On one level is the Union of Chambers of Agriculture, with many local branches, established by law in 1963 and semiofficially related to the Ministry of Agriculture. Its purposes are general ones designed to further agricultural development (see T. C. 1973:540. No membership figures nor other details are given). Their political role, not surprisingly, is quite conservative, as a result of their largely representing and being dominated by the wealthier farmers (Kili 1976–7:70; Erguder 1980:175; Tachau 1973a:313). As noted above, the UCA was one of the five national organizations which established the Free Enterprise Council, and a report of the Employers' Association Confederation describes the UCA as an "employer association."

On another level, there are the cooperatives. As shown in Table 4-3, their number and membership has increased very rapidly. However, as Kili has calculated, membership in village coöps in 1975 was only about 10 percent of its potential—i.e., of the economically active population in agriculture (1976–77:75). The 8,385 village coöps total less than a quarter of the number of villages. According to the Village Survey, in 1968 only about half

TABLE 4-3-a
Agricultural Cooperatives

	1950	1960	1965	1970	1977
Total	—	—	—	—	12,334
Village Development	—	—	686	—	6,642
Forest village development	—	—	—	—	755
Agricultural credit	900	1,572	1,734	2,023	2,071
Agricultural sales	143	214	209	631	721
Soil and water	—	—	40		1,394

TABLE 4-3-b
Agricultural Credit Cooperatives

	1950	1960	1965	1970	1975
Number of co-ops	900	1,572	1,734	2,023	2,055
% which are in villages	(27.1%)	(46.7)	(57.6)	(58.0)	(56.0)
Number of members	438,410	937,696	—	1,305,461	1,308,580
Number of new members	—	—	96,247	41,617	34,768
Percent of new members	—	—	(8.8)	(3.2)	(2.6)
Number members leaving	—	—	34,212	29,967	37,373
Percent members leaving	—	—	(3.1)	(2.3)	(2.8)
Number villages newly included	—	—	1,492	358	151
Number villages leaving	—	—	154	138	64
Percent of eligible village farmers who are co-op members	—	—	(50.52)	(46.20)	(38.62)
Assets (million TL)	—	—	413	638	1,140
Loan funds (million TL)	—	—	1,260	2,564	4,922
Credit outstanding to to members (million TL)	—	—	1,010	1,554	3,327
Number co-ops making a profit	—	—	1,437	1,119	830
Number co-ops losing money	—	—	379	902	1,225
Percent employes with middle school education or more	—	—		(9.3)	(29.0)

SOURCES: Kili 1977; 4th Five Year Plan; T. C. 1973; Türk Kooperatifçilik Kurumu.

the males in villages where there were coöps were members of them, and only about half of those who were members said that they participated in their administration. The latter fact is due at least in part to the rather rigid administrative rules laid down by the Cooperatives Law. Although most of those who were members of coöps felt that they derived some benefits from them, there were also a great many complaints, most often about inadequate capital and poor management (State Planning Orgnization: MTV Tables 62–65).[12] Turkish Cooperatives Association figures also show that although the number of coöps increased (partly because certain benefits, such as limited credit, are given only through organized bodies), since 1971 the number of persons listed as quitting agricultural credit coöps equalled or exceeded the number of new members. Association officials attribute this to reasons such as a large number of "passive" members who forgot to pay their dues but continued to be carried on the rolls.

The Turkish Cooperatives Association, organized in 1931, has made valiant efforts at improving the conditions of its members. It engages in extensive education activities, publishes a magazine, analyses, and manuals, and has worked with government authorities to improve policies of agricultural development. But it is also the first to admit serious shortcomings which still exist. Some of these difficulties are related to the sheer magnitude of the job of agricultural development and the almost total dependence on government resources. Programs to train cooperative leaders have been conducted since 1966 by the Association and by various ministries, but to date they have trained only some 5,000 persons (Kili 1976–7:71). Credit and other services are inadequate, to the extent that a major leader in the cooperative movement recently wrote that their development is "mostly numerical . . . and has not yet reached its objective, which is to organize small farms and to save them from the bad effects of middlemen, money-lenders and industrialists" (Mulayim 1977:203. This is also a good summary of the current situation).[13]

It cannot be said that the agricultural sector as a whole has fared badly in furthering its interests. As will be detailed in chapter 7, most Turkish farmers still do not pay any taxes, and they have benefited considerably (if unequally) from high price supports for numerous of their products. Much of this benefaction, while not directly due to organized pressure from the farmers and peasants themselves, did come as a result of competition for votes and the ability of the larger farmers to maintain their influence. Under current circumstances, it is not likely that the general strength of rural interests will decline. However, only major changes in the structure of Turkish agriculture are likely to bring change in the current distribution of power within rural Turkey.

Professional Organizations

All of the major professions are now organized. Most prominently, these include the Turkish Bar Association, the Medical Association, the Turkish Teachers Union (TÖB-DER), the Union of Chambers of Architects and Engineers, and various associations of journalists, pharmacists and veter-inarians. All are chartered by special laws, and have professional functions relating to the licensing and regulating of professional affairs as well as educational and technical functions. Barred from formal political activity, they are nevertheless highly visible. Their importance is often based on the social standing of their members and on the degree to which they study and take positions on major issues of public policy relating to their professional interests.

The Military

The political role of the military in Turkish society dates almost from the beginning of the Ottoman Empire, with the "Gazi" tradition and Sultans who were both military and political leaders. For most of the period of the Empire's glory professional soldiers were prominent among the highest officials of the government. At the beginning of the eighteenth century the armed forces became major beneficiaries of "defensive modernization," and quickly became one of the leading channels for upward mobility of men who not only possessed political as well as military leadership abilities, but whose exposure to Western political forms also made them potential reformers. Their strength was bolstered by the continuing high status of the military in Turkish culture (for a fuller summary see Rustow, 1964:353–61).

The first major incident in which reformist political action was directly identified with the armed forces was the Young Turk revolution of 1908. Two of the revolution's three principal instigators were active officers. Although not directly involved in this revolt, a number of career officers who were later to be major leaders of the Republic were on the edges of the stage, including Mustafa Kemal himself, Ali Fuad (Cebesoy), and Fethi (Okyar). A considerable part of the Young Turks' effectiveness stemmed from their organizational cohesion, which not only provided institutional channels for action but also a sense of common interest, as well as, of course, the physical resources with which to carry out the officers' aims.[14]

During the War of Independence, and subsequently as founders of the Republic, a large proportion of the chief political leaders were professional officers. Ataturk, on the eve of his move to abolish the Caliphate in 1924, went to the site of army maneuvers to check personally whether the officers were likely to support such a move (they did). During Ataturk's rule, one of the most important single actions affecting the political role of the armed forces *per se* was an Assembly ruling in late 1923 that barred individuals from being simultaneously members of the Assembly and active officers. Most of the important officers chose the Assembly. While this action did not, to be sure, lessen their identification with the institution in which they had spent most of their adult lives, nor reduce their sense of solidarity with the military or the public's identification of them as *Paşas*,[15] it was an important harbinger for the future (Rustow, 1959). Most analysts attribute much of the reluctance of most of the officer corps in 1960 to interfere in politics more deeply than they did to the tradition of political neutrality engendered by Ataturk.

During the single-party years there was little political visibility of the armed forces per se, although during the entire period between 14 percent and 20 percent of the deputies in the Assembly were men with military backgrounds. In 1950 this percentage dropped to 6 percent, due mainly to the election sweep which replaced most RPP deputies with Democrats (see Frey 1965:181). The percentage has remained very low since that time. A few ex-officers joined the DP. The most politically noteworthy action by an officer who had chosen to remain in active service was that of retired Chief of Staff Marshall Fevzi Çakmak, who in 1948 became one of the founders of the conservative, religious-oriented National party. He did not become a major political figure, however (see Karpat, 1959:431–5 and Tamkoç, 1976:321–2).

Although the military kept a low political profile, there was considerable behind-the-scenes concern with the course of national affairs, beginning as early as 1954 (Harris, 1965b). In part this concern grew out of the increasingly difficult situation into which the DP was getting the nation, out of the government's conservative social policies, and later out of restiveness at the political repression in which the government engaged. But in considerable degree it was also connected with the officers' concern over their own welfare, as they (along with the bureaucrats and intellectuals who had been main supporters of the RPP) saw their positions suffer economically from the high rate of inflation and shortages which were the result of DP economic policies and because of government restriction on their salaries, and also saw their social and political status decline through the steady transfer of power to the business and commercial sectors and to local and provincial leaders. There can be only speculation as to whether there would have been an attempt to intervene in politics to overcome these disabilities (and thus to act as a fully self-serving interest group) if the DP had not made the serious mistake of drawing the armed forces directly into politics by calling on them to put down the antigovernment demonstrations which began in the latter part of 1959.

The period of military rule between May 27, 1960, and October 25, 1961 (described in chapter 1) reveals much about the potential for government by armed forces in a modernizing nation like Turkey. It is particularly notable how limited the political potential of an essentially nonpolitical force has become in the modern Turkish nation. As the months passed, it became more and more difficult for the National Unity Committee to do anything except hand power back to the political parties.[16]

In part this was due to the values and perhaps to some tactical errors of the officers themselves. As noted earlier, the tradition of a professional and politically nonpartisan military was deeply imbedded in the ideology of Kemalism, and to this tradition the junta subscribed. Soon after the coup it declared its goals to be limited in scope and that they were to be achieved quickly—one month to draft a new constitution, two for trials of the fallen regime, and elections within three months (Weiker, 1963a:139). The officers also proceeded almost immediately to install a civilian cabinet made up predominantly of "technicians" who had not previously been identified with any political party. The cabinet promptly put forward a list of items which required urgent action, including important economic and social measures (Ibid.:21–2), and on that basis, during the eighteen months which eventually proved necessary for completing the structural changes just mentioned, the officers also debated and sought to enact a variety of policy reforms. Partly by design, but partly also because of the strength of the political elements in the country, however, the NUC enacted most new policies only after extensive consultation with, and often formal approval of the civilian political leaders. In January 1961 a Constituent Assembly was convened to approve the new Constitution and Election Law. Composed of representatives of many economic, professional, and other private groups and associations, as well as representatives of the political parties (the officers had not condemned politicians as a whole, but had confined their hostility to members of the Democratic party), the Assembly quickly became the main focus of public attention, particularly when it was given the tasks of passing the national budget and other policy laws (though the NUC retained the power to veto any Assembly actions). The Assembly was dominated by conservatives who successfully blocked any reforms which had "radical" potential. In July 1961, a highly visible sign of the weakness of the military as governors appeared: in the referendum on the new Constitution, for which the members of the NUC had campaigned vigorously throughout the country, some 38 percent of the voters openly showed their dissatisfaction at the overthrow of the Menderes regime by voting "no" (Weiker, 1963a:166). Shortly before the election the officers again sought to show their impartiality by authorizing parties of *all* views to organize and compete, a move to which the voters reacted by returning a majority of deputies from three parties which were all but openly competing for votes on much the same social and economic platform as the DP had offered (Ibid.: chapter 5).

In one area the officers did directly act as an interest group. During their period in power they provided for themselves and their comrades by significantly raising officers' salaries and establishing auxiliary benefits, including housing, commissaries, and other perquisites.[17] Since 1961 the officers have also made concerted efforts to protect their collective power by establishing several mechanisms to facilitate united action. One, whose existence has never been formally acknowledged, was an informal military "council" of high officers, reported to have often given instructions to the NUC, which the council members considered to be only the armed forces' "public face" (see Harris, 1965b, and Ipekçi, 1965). It appears that one of the aims of this "Şura" was to keep internal disputes out of the public eye, disputes which reportedly were frequently quite strident. As a result, for the sake of public unity the officers usually agreed to limit their governmental involvement to matters of law and order rather than venturing into economic and social policy areas, though they remained watchful that economic policy did not again go to the lengths of inflation and chaos that it had in the latter years of the Democrat regime. The second major mechanism set up to protect military interests, one which has assumed continuing importance, is the National Security Council. Commanders make up about half of its membership. It meets frequently, with considerable publicity given to meetings whenever there are particularly severe political tensions.[18]

It was not until March 1971, when urban guerrilla violence had reached very serious proportions, that the armed forces again moved publicly onto the political stage. This time their role was even smaller than in 1960–61, and it again was focused on issues of law and order rather than on substantive economic and political matters. In a "memorandum," the military strongly suggested that the government of Prime Minister Demirel resign, which demand was promptly complied with. It was followed by the imposition of martial law, but also by the continuance of civilian government, even though it was via a series of "above-party" cabinets. This formula was attractive for several reasons. One was that it provided means for combatting extremist violence, often centered among left-wing students but regularly answered by right-wing extremists. In action against the guerrillas, the political sympathies of at least the senior officers were revealed in that the reach of martial law authorities quickly extended into wider elements of the socialist left, even though these elements included many highly respected writers and professors, and even though the alleged connections between groups like the Turkish Labor party and the leftist student guerrillas were not proven. Of course this anti-left bias was also shared by most members of the general population, so that the crackdowns were relatively popular. A second reason why the officers were attracted to an indirect role was that it enabled them not to have to assume responsibility for continued economic and social difficulties, it being clear that solutions to the many problems in these areas were most elusive and would not be found in a set of simple orders, or in reforms which would be unpalatable to much of the nation. The 1973 election was held on schedule.[19] Despite the serious worsening of both economic problems and urban violence the same basic pattern continued during the late 1970s. The armed forces' role in public affairs was manifest as a result of several periods in which martial law was declared in order to assist regular security forces, and Security Council meetings increased in frequency, but other public actions by the officers were confined to relatively infrequent exhortations to the political parties to take action, pleas to which there was generally little response. In 1980, it was not until guerrilla violence between left and right extremists became so widespread that there was all but unanimous agreement among political as well as military observers that the breakdown in law and order was unbearable, that the officers acted again to repair some of the institutions of Turkish democracy so as to preserve them.

The role of the military, in sum, has become limited, in part because of the very circumstances of modernization, although it must be added that the legitimacy of at least some political role for the military is still generally accepted. And despite the erosion of the attractiveness of military careers, as discussed in chapter 2, the military profession continues to be a respected one for Turks generally. Today, too, the higher ranking officers live among and often work side-by-side with their civilian compatriots and are reported to have a considerably weaker sense of separate identity than was true in earlier periods. The high budgets for the armed forces during most of the last half-century have also minimized the degree to which the officers have had to organize as an interest group to compete for scarce resources (though as mentioned above, when their emoluments and prestige were directly reduced as in the late 1950s they did not hesitate to function as a pressure group and to restore them at the first opportunity).

Perhaps most important, however, is that events have shown that Turkey has become too complex to be governed by fiat. Major social and economic reforms can now only be promulgated with the agreement of the major social and political forces in Turkish society, or by authoritarian means which may well pose more difficulties for potential military rulers than they might have advantages. Among other things, for the armed forces to impose economic and social policies by force would imply that both civilian leaders and followers were either less than fully patriotic or unfit to make decisions, either of which implications would be serious indictments indeed of the Turkish polity. As long as extremes of policy and of social disorder are avoided, therefore, neither the officers nor the body politic as a whole appears ready for another plunge which would fundamentally disrupt the political process by which Turkey is governed.

Religion

To turn now to a more generalized social and political force, religion as a factor in modernization is of particular importance in Turkey. It has been a primary political issue since the very inauguration of the Republic. Secularization, as we have noted, was one of the central tenets of the Ataturk program. It was implemented through a series of decisive steps taken to disestablish Islam from a role in law and education, and as the official religion of the state,[20] and to generally reduce its influence among the Turkish people in favor of a "scientific mentality." In the multiparty period, many of the proscriptions were relaxed (although basic secularist policies were certainly maintained), and a general religious "revival" is said to have taken place. In the late 1960s, several political parties emerged which appealed openly to religious sentiments. Today it is generally agreed that "secularism" per se is no longer an issue, but debate continues on many related issues of religion vis-a-vis government policies.

Developments which eventually became important foundations of Ataturk secularist reforms can be traced back to Ottoman times. Niyazi Berkes in his definitive history dates "the glimmerings" from 1718 (1964:23). Despite the fact that many of the Tanzimat reformers continued to be personally religious and to believe that Islam must remain one of the pillars of the Ottoman state (on this see Mardin, 1962), they were also becoming increasingly dissatisfied with *ulema*-dominated educational and legal systems, and were recognizing the necessity of change and innovation (Berkes, 1964:30 ff.). The eighteenth and nineteenth centuries were times of frequent struggles between reformers and those favoring the status quo. Although the general population remained untouched by this turmoil, by the 1920s there was virtually no remaining resistance on the part of elite groups to the basic Ataturk religious reforms, including abolition of the Caliphate, the ending of the Şeriat courts, promulgation of new penal and commercial codes, state takeover of education, and nationalization of *vakifs* (pious foundations) (see Lewis, 1961: passim). While doctrinally there were some profound difficulties for many Turkish intellectuals in the creation of what would virtually become an entirely new ideology (see Mardin, 1971a), there was also broad agreement on steps intended to "modernize" Islam, in line with Ataturk's repeated insistence that his purpose was "to 'purify' Islam and to open the gate for a reformist Islamic thought" (Daver, 1967:55), to "liberate society from the hold of Islam, and to bring about a new type of free individual" (Ibid., 62), and to demonstrate, as Bernard Lewis has put it, that "the basis of Kemalist religious policy was laicism, not irreligion" (1961:406; see also Rustow, 1957:84 ff.). Measures to improve the quality of religious personnel included establishment of some training schools for *imams* and preachers, requiring minimum educational qualifications for them (although these could be enforced only to a minimal degree in most parts of the country), and the creation of a new Faculty of Divinity at Istanbul University "intended to serve as the centre of a new, modernized, and scientific form of religious instruction, more appropriate to a secular, Westernized republic" (Lewis, 1961:408. See also Reed, 1955 and 1957, and the source footnote in Weiker, 1973:249n1). The *tekkes* and *tarikats* (religious orders and brotherhoods), on the other hand, were closed completely, the government feeling that "their popular support, their radical traditions, their Masonic organization, all made them too little amenable to state control, too dangerous for experiment" (Lewis, 1961:407).

Most controversial were policies which touched directly on religious observance and customs. In 1928, for example, following a recommendation of a committee headed by the distinguished historian, Professor Fuad Köprülü (later one of the founders of the Democratic party), charged with examining the problem of reform and modernization of the Islamic religion, a project was begun to translate into Turkish the Koran and the Traditions of the Prophet, and later to prepare a translation of the mosque service as well. Both were abandoned in the face of opposition. And try as they might to allay suspicions, the policy of discouraging public displays of religious observance (such as forbidding the clergy to wear ecclesiastical garb outside of mosque grounds and discouraging prayer services, particularly those which could be described as impairing the efficiency of office and factory production) caused many Turks to believe that the militant Kemalists were out to destroy religion entirely.

Thus, it was partly for symbolic reasons, partly for political ones, that the role of religion became again a public issue as soon as the multiparty period opened. But another element must also be cited. It was not only "tradition" which was operating. For the lower classes and in the villages, the religious institutions served more than just a religious or spiritual function. As Şerif Mardin has put it, "there are . . . many dimensions of religion among the lower classes in Turkey which are more secular than religious" (1969:10).

> . . . the Ottoman equivalent of the parish was really the locus of administrative structure. I use the word "parish" intentionally; the local communities which took up the functions which, in the west, were those of the local gentry or later of the state, were in the Ottoman Empire organized on a religious basis. That is, it was the religious institution which was the center of the community and which actually provided the services. This is the reason why the dervish orders were so important in the Ottoman Empire: because, like the wider religious community, they provided many services for their members: conservatories, gymnasia, a second channel of upward mobility: if one can't make it at the Süleymaniye Mosque, one can go to a dervish order and learn over there: a second chance at success (1971b:12).

Religious institutions were also a barrier against officialdom (Mardin, 1971a:204–5). Thus, one of the reasons for the revived role of religious-based *institutions* (as distinct from the revival of *religion*) was simply that in large part the Republic had not yet succeeded in replacing those services. It is widely agreed that the large number of religious-based local associations which have been organized in all Turkish communities have at least as many community functions as theological ones. Of course, one of the problems is that these associations often also serve as vehicles for political influence for persons who have radically conservative orientations to social, economic and political issues. But on the other hand, their leaders are often fairly representative of the general social values of much of the Turkish people, and they may thus be able to serve as sources of stability and of easing the potential psychological dislocation of people who are undergoing rapid social change. (For another expression of this view and that religious-based associations are also used to ward off the growing power of "the dynamic forces of capitalist development" see Ergil, 1975.) As hypothesized in this study, such a situation may be functional for orderly Turkish development even though some other aspects of modernization may be slowed down as a result.

When the Democrats came to power and began to retreat from some of the stricter policies of secularization,[21] there was no consideration of repudiating fundamental tenets of secularism, such as *ulema* power over education and law, and nobody disputed the importance of continuing to develop a "scientific mentality" or of institutions like banking, or non-Islamic commercial codes which were the very foundation of the modern business community (which was a prime supporter of the DP). But other areas lent themselves readily to controversy. The reintroduction of the prayer call in Arabic, for example, which had been allowed only in Turkish since the mid-1920s, was one of the DP's first actions. Other controversies arose over the new government's policies of using state funds for direct support of religious activities, including construction of village mosques, opening more *imam-hatip* schools, and authorizing Koran courses.[22]

A particularly rich source of fuel for controversy has been the fact that once the reappraisal of specific secularist policies began, and as freedom of expression continued, it has proven more and more difficult to specify exactly when religious bases are being used for political aims (the prohibition of such use being one of the most basic points of Kemalist secularism). Certainly one of the most dramatic manifestations of this problem has come with the emergence of political parties with an openly religious identification, most prominently the Party for National Order in 1970 and the National Salvation party since 1973 (see chapter 5). Their role in the conflicts about secularization is difficult to assess with precision, however, One problem is that even though these parties phrase their appeals in terms of tradition, morality, and piety, their programs also include "legitimate" political issues, such as the NSP's opposition to most foreign-manufactured products and its advocacy of far greater emphasis on small and Anatolian-based development in the industrialization process. There is no direct evidence about the degree to which these "nonreligious" issues attracted voters to the NSP. On another dimension, it may be conceded that the increased demand for admission to *imam-hatip* schools is partly related to their religious orientation (and their very rapid expansion since 1975 is a direct result of the NSP's membership in the National Front coalition), but it is also in considerable part due to the fact that those schools provide cost-free education for those lucky enough to be accepted. It should also be noted that the NSP's demands for "moral education" in the public schools were usually carefully differentiated from demands for direct religious instruction, and that the party also carefully avoided any advocacy of an official role for religion in government and politics. Possibly the clearest basis on which to assess their role is the fact that the NSP's 8.6 percent of the votes in the 1977 election was a decline from its 11.8 percent in 1973, despite grave fears that the NSP might be the wave of the future.

Another area of importance for assessing the question of religion as a social force is personal religiosity. Data on village religious observances (presented in chapter 3) indicates that in at least the more formal aspects, there has been some erosion. On the urban scene, what is most striking is that religious practices, such as fasting during Ramadan, are observed in most Turkish cities not only by many of the recent lower-class migrants, but also by a substantial proportion of the educated middle class. There is no doubt that during the holy month, productivity of most offices and factories is considerably less than during the remainder of the year (a specific consequence of Ramadan observance which concerned Ataturk as much as the fast's symbolic importance did). A large number of Turks have also recently taken advantage of relaxed foreign exchange restrictions to go on the pilgrimage to Mecca. So far as the Turkish people are concerned secularization should by no means be equated with irreligiousness.

A related matter which deserves mention in a discussion of the role of religion in Turkey is that although the 1924 Constitution defined the concept "Turkish citizen" to be "without distinction of religion or race" (Article 88) and that equality is guaranteed without regard to religion or creed (*din ve mezhep*)[23] or to language, race, sex, and political or philosophical beliefs (1961 Constitution Article 12), the popular unofficial definition of "Turk" is still Muslim Turk. Traditional animosities among sects such as Sunnis and Alevis also continue to exist.

Religious issues are thus likely to retain at least some of their volatility. Although the major parties are reluctant to approach such issues directly, some smaller parties are less hesitant. The subject continues to have attraction for many seeking political position. In part this is because the line between religion as a personal and a political matter is so difficult to draw. Although it is clear that furthering or opposing religion as a function of government has become less important to voters in recent years as economic and other issues have come more to the fore, it is impossible to tell how much the *relative* importance of these issues has changed. It is also very difficult to distinguish between actions of political leaders or voters impelled by specifically

TABLE 4-4

Religious Education

	1951–2	1955–6	1960–1	1965–6	1970–1	1974–5	1976–7	1977–8
Orta Level Imam-Hatip								
Nr. schools	7	16	19	30	72	101	248	334
Nr. students	876	2,181	3,377	11,832	42,600	24,091[a]	86,053	108,309
Lycee Level Imam-Hatip								
Nr. schools		7	17	19	39	72	72	103
Nr. students		254	1,171	1,648	6,708	24,809	25,688	26,177
Yüksek Islam Enstitüsü[b]								
Nr. schools			1	3	5			
Nr. students			165	846	2,024	1,856 (1973–4)		
Ankara University Faculty of Theology								
Nr. students	79	83	230	447	518	515 (1973–4)		
Koran-Teacher Courses								
Nr. courses	170	235	643	1,083	1,298			
Nr. students	11,568	12,235	27,677	53,482	56,169 (1968–9)			

SOURCE: DIE #676, 715, 825, 850, 890.

[a] "Some Imam-Hatib Schools have been gradually closed, in others all the classes were converted to classical middle schools." (DIE #715.)

[b] High Islamic Institute, college level but not university.

religious motives, and actions impelled by one's conservative social values. To keep its credit at least moderately good with the more secularist elements, both the DP and JP governments have cracked down periodically on the more extreme sects such as the *Nurcular* (on these see Landau, 1974:183–86), but the radical right-wing press has generally not been molested by either JP or RPP governments even though some of its publications could justifiably be charged with "attacking the moral dignity of the state," which is a serious offense under the Turkish penal code.

On the other hand, several major aims of Kemalist secularization clearly have been largely accomplished. The formal power of religious functionaries is ended forever. As the usefulness of secular education is realized, as the understanding of the connections between science, technology, and economic improvement becomes greater, and as general integration into the modern world proceeds, there is no doubt that "scientific mentality" and secular thinking will characterize an ever-growing proportion of the Turkish population. If the Village Survey is any indication, for example, *imams* are not likely to regain much influence until they become able to assist with "modern" problems, which may well mean that there is now popular pressure for at least a measure of the "enlightened" Islam which was one of Ataturk's avowed aims. It is also important to note again that religion continues to be a value held by much of the Turkish *middle class* (in this sense they are little different from middle classes in many developed countries).

In sum, one may fairly safely conclude that the secularization process in Turkey has reached a satisfactory *modus vivendi*. Whether it was necessary for Ataturk to be as drastic as he was in disestablishing Islam is still debatable, though his policies were certainly a catalyst for drawing the issues sharply and for stimulating much thought about a major issue. But as with numerous other aspects of Turkish development cited in this study, it may not be too much to say that it is the modernization process itself which is most responsible for moving the role of religion in Turkey onto a more "modern" plane. The final outcome of Turkey's religious issue will largely depend on the prowess and perspicacity of both religious and political leaders. But there is no doubt that the group which will face the greatest difficulties is, as Rustow asserted two decades ago, "the Clericalists [who are] chiefly those who are caught between the wheels of social and cultural change" (1957:107).

The Role and Status of Women

Not surprisingly, Turkey displays most of the formal accoutrements of modernity for women. In reality, however, full emancipation of and equal opportunity for them are still to be achieved.

A few scattered demands for the emancipation of women took place during the nineteenth century, but only a few upper-class women experienced much change in their status. The frequency of such demands increased somewhat after the Young Turk revolution, but it was not until World War I that proponents became something more than vocal. During that struggle and in the War of Independence a number of things gave the movement impetus, including participation of women's groups in political demonstrations, and a considerable number of examples of female heroics in support of military actions. Particularly notable was Halide Edib, whose military exploits and leadership in expanding educational opportunities for women led to her becoming an inspiration for future generations of fighters for equal opportunities for women. (For a detailed account of this period, see Abadan-Unat, 1978b:2–11. For a brief summary from pre-Islamic times to post-1960, see Daver, 1969.)

Ataturk from the outset declared himself in favor of giving women greater equality, but because of strong resistance from conservatives and the press of other matters, few concrete steps were taken until the mid-1920s, when new legal codes were promulgated. At Ataturk's initiative, women were granted political rights, beginning with the right to vote in municipal elections in 1930 and in national elections in 1934. Seventeen women were included in the Fifth Assembly of 1935. Ataturk also made symbolic gestures designed to further women's rights, such as periodic statements against women wearing veils, and making public appearances with women in modern dress in his entourage. (For an example of such statements see Lewis, 1961:265.) A Women's League, made up of some Istanbul women in the professions, was formed in the 1920s, and the Turkish Women's Association (Türk Kadınlar Birliği) was formed in 1950. But there was little other feminist activity until the 1960s, when it became visible in conjunction with similar movements in many other countries. In recent years, women's voices have been raised increasingly through their own organizations. Some twenty-seven women's organizations sponsored a seminar in 1978 on "Women in Turkish Society," which brought together an impressive number of participants from numerous branches of Turkish public life. (The proceedings are published in Turkish in Abadan-Unat, 1979, and will be published in an English translation by E. J. Brill. A summary of the papers is Kandiyoti, 1978.)

Legal Reforms

Legal emancipation of Turkish women took place almost at the beginning of the Republic with the adoption of the Swiss Civil Code in 1926. The code's provisions included making polygamy illegal, giving the right of divorce to women as well as to men, making civil marriage obligatory, and abolishing differences between men and women in matters of inheritance. Even Ataturk was not willing to go too far formally, however, and as Abadan-Unat points out, although the very conservative French and German civil codes were rejected as models for Turkey, "The Turkish Civil Code, in line with its Swiss prototype, does not allow absolute equality between husband and wife. The husband is the head of the family, the wife must follow the husband, who alone is entitled to choose a domicile. . . .The wife is required to participate in the expenses of the household by assuming tasks in the household. In case the wife wants to exercise a profession, she has to obtain the open or tacit consent of her husband, in case of refusal she might apply for arbitration to court" (1978a:294).

The urban middle classes adopted the marriage and divorce provisions to a great extent, and the number of marriages registered has increased fairly steadily. In rural areas and in eastern Turkey there has been less change, and although the rates of marriage registration have gone up, the disparity between the eastern regions and the country as a whole is still considerable.[24] One stimulus to further change will be the increasing need for official documents and the desire to take advantage of government benefits for children, none of which are available without marriages being registered.[25] Similar, though weaker trends have taken place in the numbers of registered divorces. Several recent studies also indicate an increasing willingness of women in all parts of the country to use the courts to enforce their rights (see chapter 3).

Women in Politics

Every Assembly since 1935 has contained at least a few women. There are also a small number of women mayors and municipal council members. Women are active in the political parties to a considerable extent through women's branches, though the main structures of the general party organizations have also frequently included at least a few women. Women's organizations also regularly make statements on political issues. There are few data on female voting participation, though it is clear that while it has increased significantly it is still generally lower than that of men (although a study in four Istanbul precincts in 1973 and 1975 found that there it was only 13.5 percent lower, Sirin Tekeli, 1979:408), that it varies considerably among regions and social class, and that is significantly less "autonomous." The scattered data on women's interest in politics indicate that it is generally high.[26]

Education

As shown in Table 4-5, there has been considerable advance in the education of women. The enrollment of girls in both urban and rural primary schools has risen steadily and is now approaching 50 percent. There has been much less change at the post-primary levels, probably partly as a reflection of the continued tendency for a family to give preference to education of sons in cases where it is impossible to support schooling for all the children. It is notable that the rates of female enrollment between middle school and lycee does not decrease significantly, indicating that, similar to the situation with boys, it is likely that when the post-primary line is passed, a transition has been made into the urban educated class. That change is making inroads at earlier levels as well is indicated by the finding that the dropout rate for girls during primary school is only slightly higher than for boys, and by the fact

TABLE 4-5
Women's Education and Employment

LITERACY	1950	1960	1970	1975
Men	47.1	53.6	69.4	74.8
Women	20.1	24.8	40.8	48.1

SOURCE: DIE, #380, 490, 825.

EDUCATION Percent female enrollment	1942–43	1949–50	1959–60	1969–70	1974–5	1977–8
Elementary:						
Cities	28.4	40.4	41.9	45.0	46.3	46.6
Villages	27.0	35.4	33.9	40.0	43.1	43.8
Middle	28.6	27.1	25.1	27.1	28.4 (1973–4)	32.0
Lycee	22.4	20.5	25.8	28.3	31.7 (1973–4)	34.5
Higher	21.3	18.8	20.5	18.7		
Universities					21.2	25.1
Higher Schools					21.2	24.9

SOURCE: DIE, #676, 825, 890

Percent females in higher education	1973–4	1977–8
All institutions	20.2	24.9
Universities	20.6	25.1
Higher schools	19.8	24.9
Medical faculties:	34.2	34.5
Ankara University	19.7	
Istanbul University	15.9	
Hacettepe	23.3	
Izmir	18.2	
Bursa	9.3	
Erzurum	12.4	
Diyarbakir	5.6	
Other (Kayseri, Sivas, Eskişehir, Samsun, Trabzon)	26.3	
Sciences	27.0	32.5
Ankara	23.4	
Hacettepe	31.1	
Istanbul	19.7	
Erzurum	11.7	
Engineering	8.2	11.6
Hacettepe	6.6	
METU	10.7	
Bogaziçi	23.2	

Percent females in higher education	1973–4	1977–8
Istanbul Technical University (entire)	8.3	13.4
Law	17.6	19.5
Ankara	20.2	
Istanbul	16.7	
Boğaziçi University (entire)	33.2	37.6
(engineering, basic science, admin. science)		
Education	37.9	31.6
Ankara University	16.4	
Higher Teachers' Schools	31.0	
Education Institutes	37.5	
Political Science, Ankara University	15.2	
Economics and Commerce	17.0	17.9
Istanbul University	21.7	
Academies	12.5	
Journalism	28.1	
Literature	36.8	
Ankara University	41.1	
Istanbul	8.8	
Erzurum		

SOURCE: DIE #715, 890.

Percent Female Teachers	1973–4	1977–8
Level		
Primary schools: Total	36.9	41.2
Cities	50.1	43.5
Villages	29.4	47.0
Middle schools	34.9	32.6
Lycees	35.9	36.4
Vocational-technical	34.4	—
Higher: Universities	25.9	23.6
Academies & Higher Schools	24.4	25.1
Nursery schools	93.8	—

OCCUPATIONS

	32 Cities 1967		107 Cities 1969	
	Men	Women	Men	Women
Occupation	(%)	(%)	(%)	(%)
Technical, professional and related	7.4	16.8	6.6	15.1
Managerial, administrative, clerical, sales & related	18.3	24.6	11.5	16.8
Farmers, lumbermen, fishermen	2.8	2.1	12.3	29.2
Mining & quarrying	.3	—	.4	—

Occupations (continued)

Transportation & communication	8.0	1.1	8.9	.9
Craftsmen, production workers, repairmen	26.9	29.0	26.4	23.8
Unskilled workers	9.2	4.5	5.9	.8
Service workers	11.2	19.0	11.2	10.9
Unclassified or not reported	2.5	.1	1.6	.2
TOTAL	100.0	100.0	100.0	100.0

Source: DIE #710: Tables 147, 155.

LABOR FORCE PARTICIPATION OF WOMEN

	Active Females Out of Females Age 15+	Non-agric. Female Labor as % of Active Females	Active Females in Total Labor Force Age 15+
1950	81.5	3.5	47.0
1955	72.0	3.9	43.1
1960	65.3	4.7	40.3
1965	56.2	4.0	37.9
1970	45.3	10.0	37.5
1975	37.0	10.4	35.2

Source: Turkish Social Science; Assn., "Women in Turkish Society"; Seminar, Table 8.

that parental desire for educational levels for their daughters is considerable and extends downward to include parents in towns as small as 2,000 to 10,000 (Özbay 1979). The harder struggle which girls have is also probably one reason why the "success rate" for female students in both middle schools and lycees has been greater than that for boys in every year since 1955 (DIE #676:23). The continuing great disparity in male and female literacy rates is apparently largely a catch-up matter.

Employment

In employment, the expected patterns are found. In rural areas a high percentage of women are classified as economically active because they are agricultural workers, so that the national figure for women active in the labor force in 1965 in every age group between 15 and 64 was around 60 percent (DIE #710:Table 145), though it declined in 1975 to closer to 45 percent in the middle age groups (DIE #825:Table 145). Several surveys of urban women's labor force status found the percentages to be only 10 to 13 percent. Table 4-5 includes distribution of men and women by types of work. It is not surprising that women are significantly less prominent in "public" positions, such as sales. Also expected is the higher percentage of women who are in clerical positions, and the large number of women in administrative categories. The percentages undoubtedly reflect the inclusion of lower level jobs in the definition. That the percentage of women employed in technical and professional positions is more than twice as high as for men (even though in absolute numbers it is, of course, much less) is a pattern typically found in countries in which formal reforms precede social change (for example, the USSR). The somewhat higher percentage of women in larger cities than in smaller ones who are unskilled workers probably results from the types of employment available there, and the higher percentage of women who are service workers reflects at least in part the greater employment of domestics in larger communities. Unfortunately, none of the data gives an indication of the level of jobs which women hold, but observation indicates that there are very few women in higher positions (or, in the event that they are at supervisory levels, they most often supervise other women only). This again is not dissimilar to the situation in most countries. (For a detailed analysis, see G. Kazgan, 1979.)

The enrollment patterns of girls in various branches of higher education indicate that the trends can be expected to continue. The percentage of girls is highest in the humanities and in education, and the highest percentages of women in most of the professions normally dominated by men (engineering, sciences, commerce) are found in the universities which draw the most students from the upper and upper-middle classes.

Social Position

The social position of women is more difficult to assess quantitatively. The studies we have indicate that it is changing, but often slowly, with great difficulty,[27] and with much variation according to region and social class. The studies cited in chapter 3 indicate that the attitudes of men regarding the proper behavior of women in their families continue to be distinctly conservative, though in the more private setting of family decision-making this seems less the case. But in addition to the areas discussed earlier, there are also many signs of change in more informal ways. The generational transition is evident. For example, one may see on the streets groups of women representing three generations, the eldest in traditional village garb, her daughter in western clothes but also wearing a long-sleeved coat or dress and a head kerchief, and the granddaughter in the latest western style. Sleeveless dresses (as a symbol of the "modern") are now also found even in the more conservative cities such as Kayseri. On the other hand, coffee house attendance, even in the cities, is still totally male, and it remains relatively rare for unmarried women above college age, even those from the upper or upper-middle class, to go to public social functions (or even to the movies) alone or even in a mixed group. Even some Turkish women professionals contend that after five o'clock they still feel themselves distinctly subject to conservative social mores and that they, too, tend to be reluctant to violate popular social restrictions on women's behavior.

In sum, Turkish women have advanced in areas similar to the ones in which women have advanced in most countries, developed and developing. Much ado is made in Turkey (as it is in other countries) when a woman becomes a high official, but most Turkish women are still a considerable distance from complete equality and the opportunity to make a maximum contribution to Turkish development.[28]

FIVE

Political Parties in
Turkish Modernization

Political parties perform important functions in any society. They help recruit leaders as well as to mobilize followers by fostering the latter's participation in the political process. They also function as vehicles for articulation of both public and private interests. Smaller parties which are likely to be relatively strongly ideological and which may even be single-issue organizations, help articulate the special interests of particular groups within the society. Larger parties are more likely to represent an aggregate of interests, forging them into broad policy alternatives on which public policy can then be based. Finally, of course, large parties frequently perform the function of implementing public policies and running the nation's government.

The Turkish Republic has had a variety of political parties throughout its history, large and small, broad and narrow, ideological and pragmatic. In this chapter we will discuss the role of individual parties and the party system itself in moving Turkey toward modernization. We will argue (1) that Turkey's political parties have carried out their recruitment, mobilization, and articulation functions with great vigor and considerable effectiveness and that solid connections between the political process and the interests of the people have been established; (2) that the party system as it has developed in Turkey (domination by two major interest-aggregating parties) has been an important factor in strengthening a relatively pragmatic approach to the solution of the nation's problems and in weakening extremist ideologies; (3) that, however, even the relatively small amount of left-wing and right-wing radicalism discernible in Turkish politics is making it increasingly difficult for both major parties to maintain their moderate positions, and that there is, consequently, a danger that some of the deep cleavages which earlier plagued the Republic's first half-century may be reopened.

Organizations calling themselves political parties first emerged on the Turkish scene during the Tanzimat period, a time of relative political freedom leading up to the first Ottoman Parliament of 1877. Rustow dates them from 1865 (1966:113. See also Lewis, 1961:373ff. and Payashoğlu, 1964.), when for the first time, groups of individuals gathered to organize for the specific purpose of wielding political influence and to develop political programs (although, of course, groups and factions competing for power as such had never been absent from governmental circles). They operated primarily at the highest elite level: in the elections of 1877 the franchise was so restricted that there were no significant inputs from nonelites, and it is not likely that many people were brought into the process who had not previously been active. There was some articulation of interests, but the parties proved not very effective and the forces of reform were unable to sustain open politics. Sultan Abdulhamid had little trouble in restoring autocracy and suspending the Parliament, which did not reconvene until the Young Turk revolution of 1908. Probably the main effect of this period of party activity on Turkey's future was to give a few men some political training and to whet appetites for free politics.

"The Young Turk revolution . . . ushered in a phase of party proliferation" (Rustow, 1966:113), which continued for some five years until it was ended by the CUP in 1913. Participation in politics became more widespread, in part because there were now more groups and individuals ready for participation, among them many officers, bureaucrats, journalists, and intellectuals. Articulation and aggregation of interests also increased, with the parties putting forth extensive programs and with the frequent making and unmaking of coalitions. A similar and also short-lived period of competitive politics occurred in 1918–19. For the modernization process, again the most important role parties played was the training of future political leaders. (On these periods, see the summary in Weiker, 1973:37–44.)

When the Republic was established in 1923 and the RPP was created to be Ataturk's political vehicle, the party quickly set out to perform "modernizing" political functions. Among the most important was the recruitment of large numbers of new participants into the political process. One of the first of its activities toward that end was to enroll as many members as possible. Membership was not very selective. The major conditions for admission were simply that one not have had a record of antinationalist activity, that one be of a minimum age, and that one adhere to the party program and principles. The only real control over admission was the minimal one that an applicant had to be recommended by two persons who were already party members. Though information is scarce, there is no doubt that quite a high proportion of those on the party rolls were members in name only.

The role of the party as a vehicle for indoctrination became much more sharply focused after the Free party episode of 1930, when it was discovered how shallowly many of the Kemalist ideas had penetrated into the general population. As was detailed in chapter 1, the RPP began to elaborate a much clearer ideology, and tried to train its members to behave democratically, to listen to popular wishes, to debate constructively and tolerate criticism, and to spread party doctrines and party participation as widely as possible throughout the country. Party membership grew,[1] but there is little evidence that the efforts at qualitative improvement had much real effect. Party lectures were mostly attended by those already convinced, the People's

Houses for the most part were run by the inner circles of party leadership, and indications in the data we have on party leaders (see chapter 2) are that there were very few among the some 2,000 men (and a few women) who held deputyships between 1923 and 1946 whose qualifications included successful performance of work at the lower levels of the party.[2]

The most prominent function of the large parties in the multiparty period has been in the area of interest aggregation. They have also been intent on recruitment of new members and on mobilization of voters, to be sure, but it is not inaccurate to say that since 1945 the entry of ever larger numbers of the general population into the political process has been primarily due to the eagerness of the followers rather than to major efforts of the party leaders. Although the parties were certainly concerned with getting followers to join one party rather than another, they were not very concerned, nor did they need to be, with recruiting new members into the political process *per se.*

That interest aggregation became a major feature of Turkish party politics was due partly to the circumstances under which multiparty politics began. The Democrat party found itself in the very fortunate, yet potentially difficult situation of having support from a wide range of groups, ranging from much of the intelligentsia to peasants. In order to keep this disparate support, it had to appeal to a variety of interests and do so without alienating important blocs. It promised a retreat from drastic secularism and to curb the bureaucracy, but at the same time it pledged that there would be more rapid economic development, expansion of education, and other advances. In almost every area of policy, in fact, the policy best suited for gaining and keeping wide support was one of eschewing radicalism, either on the right or the left. The RPP was compelled, in turn, to do essentially the same thing. All of this had the additional effect of making rather short shrift of most of the power of radical parties and factions. The ability of essentially moderate parties to maintain domination was also facilitated by electoral systems which did not provide for proportional representation (see below) and by legal limitations on radical expression. In any case, by the time conditions developed which were to give impetus to political radicalism and factionalism, the pattern had been set. The two major parties, each drawing their support from a broad range of groups and classes, were to remain essentially moderate. Although this moderation appears to be becoming more and more difficult to maintain, as will be discussed shortly, the pattern continues to be one of the central features of Turkish politics and continues to function as an important source of stability (a function which may become even more important in the years to come).

The Republican People's Party

The RPP in the Ataturk era played a pivotal role in Turkish political modernization. At least partly because of that role, however, its situation during most of the multiparty period has been far from happy. Founded and led by Ataturk as the major political vehicle for his revolution, it was kept out of power, by a combination of circumstances for almost an entire quarter-century, and although it now appears to be regaining popularity, its future power is by no means assured. One important cause of the RPP's woes was the unpopularity of some of its visible reforms, even though the basic thrust of Kemalist modernizing policies found widespread acceptance by most groups among the elites and, increasingly, in the nation as a whole. In addition, the RPP became saddled with the legacy of having been strongly authoritarian, and of having concentrated power in the hands of particular groups (intellectuals, the central bureaucracy, the military) to the exclusion of others (such as local leaders[3] and, later, the rising group of private entrepreneurs). It may be said that the party brought its later troubles on itself: there is still controversy as to whether it was necessary to impose the reforms with as authoritarian means as were employed, or whether the party might have been more conciliatory, even if that had meant accepting a slower rate of change. Given the experience of many countries in which a single party has had a monopoly of power, however, it would have been surprising (and probably unprecedented) if the RPP had policed itself more effectively, even if it had not been convinced that exclusively *its* program and *its* methods were in the best interests of the nation.

It is significant that the party recognized almost immediately what some of the problems were. In 1946, as the opposition Democrats showed more and more signs of strength (including the capture of sixty-four Assembly seats in the election of 1946 despite many pressures on the voters from strong RPP organizations as well as from the bureaucracy) the RPP made concessions in both program and structure. For example, religious instruction was allowed to be resumed in the schools (though in a quite restrictive way in that a parent had to specifically request it. The DP followed suit in 1950 with the modification that religious lessons were to be given to all children unless parents specifically requested that their children be excluded. See Rustow, 1957:94 ff.). Among the structural changes were amendment of the stringent police laws, which, among other things, defined political offenses rather loosely, and a new electoral law ending the practice of "open voting—secret counting." In addition, there were major steps to democratize and at long last decentralize the party itself, including such changes as electing a party chairman at every convention instead of having one elected for life (as had been done for Ataturk and for Inonu; Kili, 1976:19 and Karpat, 1959:397). Greatly expanded roles were also given to province party organizations in the nomination of Assembly candidates.[4]

But these things were too little and too late, and the DP victory in 1950 was very decisive. It left the RPP resentful and demoralized, although Karpat speculates that the longer-run effects were beneficial in that "after 1946, since membership in the party was no longer a privilege but a responsibility, many members resigned, leaving behind those determined to stay with and in the party, and this in a way strengthened it" (1959:402). The RPP became even more strident defenders of the reforms, and the party's conviction that a militant role was needed was reinforced by DP actions which RPP leaders viewed more and more as concessions to "reaction." For the 1954 election a few program changes were made which gave the RPP a more liberal economic and social tone, but they had little effect, and the former ruling party went down to an even more severe defeat (see election-results in Table 5-4). The party's showing was better in 1957, but this was due more to DP political and socioeconomic errors than to what the RPP did or did not do.

The Republicans' star seemed to be rising again late in the 1950s as the Democrats became more repressive and as the government also encountered increased economic troubles. The RPP became identified with the often violent protests which led to the 1960 revolution (although as an organization it never had any connection with either the demonstrations or the post-1960 military regime), but again it was unable to consolidate its position. On the contrary, the generally good record of the DP, as well as its skill in using the government budget to reward its supporters, added to the RPP's burden. The 1960 revolution was also regarded by many Turks as one which would allow the military to turn power back to the RPP. Vigorous denials by the National Unity Committee of any such intention were met with skepticism. Voter resentment at the ouster of the popular Menderes could not do other than heighten anti-RPP feelings among many voters. Finally, because the revolution had been largely sparked by upper middle class students, the general image of the RPP as an urban-based, militant reformist, secularist, and intellectual-bureaucrat party was, if anything, reinforced.

The 1961 election sponsored by the armed forces resulted in the RPP emerging as the largest single party, but only because the conservative successors to the Democrats were split into three rival parties. The RPP in fact polled only 36.7 percent of the votes, four percentage points below its showing in 1957. Additional elements were added to its woes when three RPP-led coalitions between 1961 and 1965 produced little progress on major social and economic problems, and when the ambitions of a new and younger group were effectively restrained as the party continued to be dominated by the leadership of the Inonu group, which had been in place for many years. The party made poor showings in local elections and by-elections, and in early 1965 the Justice party, by now clearly the leader among the Democrat successors, received a major boost from the armed forces. The military accepted its leader, Suleyman Demirel (a moderate who had succeeded in gaining the upper hand over more conservative elements of the party), as a deputy prime minister in a caretaker coalition. This all but assured JP victory in the 1965 election. It became the legitimate heir to the DP mantle, and impelled the RPP to make its first major new policy initiative since the advent of *etatism* in 1931. The RPP entered the 1965 election with a new slogan and thrust, "left of center" *(Ortanın Solu)*, which had been advocated by the young but veteran party worker and leader, Bülent Ecevit.[5]

Actually, it was the only way to go. Staying the same was clearly unproductive. Trying to capture more of the political center by endorsing some of the politically successful policies of the JP was not only unlikely to bring success (the JP was extremely well entrenched) but a move to the right would also have been viewed by many of the RPP's strongest supporters as vitiating its very *raison d'etre*. Moving toward the extreme left also had multiple dangers, including the likelihood of antagonizing the party's strong core of more conservative leaders (which happened anyway), and a backlash against ideas which were clearly too close to socialism and "internationalist" movements for most Turks (despite the relatively good showing which the leftist Turkish Labor party appeared to be making in certain urban circles).

The main focus of the new emphasis was economic and social, and revolved around promises to continue the rapid growth which had characterized the DP era, but also to correct the injustices which, the RPP charged, had been done in the decade of DP rule. For the peasants, the RPP promised continued attention to rural areas, with stress on social justice implemented in part by a strong land reform law, though because similar laws had been proposed a number of times, including 1945 and during the coalition government period of 1961–65, but not passed, it is not likely that many believed in this RPP promise. For the urban areas, there was to be a continued high rate of investment, as under the DP, though returns were to be used for the "general good" rather than as profits for private entrepreneurs. A more restrictive policy on the importation of foreign capital was envisioned, which displeased many industrialists but was attractive to certain smaller entrepreneurs whose competition would be reduced. Greater restrictions were also to be placed on the operation of foreign companies in Turkey, particularly through nationalization of mining and petroleum operations. Extensive tax reforms were proposed. Finally, in foreign policy, the RPP insisted that foreign aid would be accepted only if it were without strings, and that greater independence was needed in defense policy, but there was no suggestion of leaving the system of Western alliances which had been the foundation of Turkish foreign policy since shortly after World War II. (On the 1965 campaign and the left-of-center policies, see Abadan, 1966a and 1966b; Szyliowicz, 1966; Dodd, 1969:135–40; Ahmad, 1977:passim. On the emergence and content of the program, see Kili, 1976:211–21.)

However, the party's combination of handicaps was too much to overcome quickly, and in the 1965 election the RPP fell to another new low of 28.7 percent. Then in 1967, almost one-third of the party's senators and deputies resigned to form the Reliance party, partly in protest against the new leftward movement, partly in reaction to Ecevit's victory over Turhan Feyzioğlu for the office of party Secretary-General.[6] This substantial reduction in the RPP's legislative strength was serious, even though it still remained the major opposition party by a sizable margin. Perhaps even more serious was the loss of numerous local organizations and cadres. On the other hand, the defection did remove some major obstacles to Ecevit in his efforts to begin to reorganize the party, and it was not long before he began to bring likeminded and younger colleagues into major party offices.[7] In Ankara they were drawn mainly from the universities and the trade unions. In the provinces those who had been performing well in organizing, campaigning, and in attracting young people were vigorously sought out.

In the 1969 election, the RPP fell to still another new low, dropping 1.3 percent from its 1965 total to 27.4 percent. It was a bitter disappointment, even though the drop could have been explained at least in part by a number of short-term factors, such as the 6.6 percent polled by the Reliance party and the 2.8 percent by the newly formed Unity Party, which appealed largely to the Alevis in several north central Anatolian provinces. (On the 1969 election see Weiker, 1969 and Hyland, 1970.) But a far more heartening development was that the party had begun to shift its electoral base. As Özbudun has shown, in the 1950s "the DP vote was positively associated with provincial modernity, while the RPP displayed differential support from the more backward provinces." The RPP vote "did not correlate significantly with . . . developmental indicators." The DP-JP achievements continued to attract strong support in the more developed regions in 1961 and 1965, but in 1969 "correlations betwee the RPP vote and modernization indicators were all positive, and some were rather strong" (1976:135, 136. The larger significance of this trend is analyzed in this chapter).

During the following four years there were several important political events which did not involve long-term social trends, including the retirement of Inonu and Ecevit's election as party chairman in 1972; the 1971 closing of the Turkish Labor party by the Constitutional Court; the inability of the Justice party to settle its internal differences, leading to the defection of many members of its conservative and anti-Demirel wing into the Democratic party; and the JP government's inability to control urban violence or to solve serious economic problems, failures which led to the armed forces' "warning" of March 1971 and another series of "above-party" cabinets. But two long-term factors were more important in accounting for the RPP emerging from the 1973 election with a significant 6 percent increase over 1969 and becoming the largest single party. One was the rise of Ecevit as a extremely effective campaigner and the advent with him of a new cadre built around young, fresh personalities. The second was social change itself. As Özbudun has observed, the 1973 election "provided clear confirmation for the fact that the apparent anomalies observed in 1969 were not merely minor and accidental fluctuations, but that they signified a turning point in Turkish politics" (1976:214). The rise in the RPP's urban popularity continued, even in areas such as the Aegean and Marmara regions which had been the most firmly entrenched strongholds of the Democrats. Two months later there was further confirmation of these trends when the RPP scored decisive gains in municipal elections, winning the mayoralties in a large number of cities, most for the first time in the entire multiparty period.

In January 1974, after 100 days of negotiations, the RPP formed a coalition with the religion-based but also strongly populist and nationalist National Salvation party, with Ecevit as Prime Minister. For the RPP it involved significant concessions on social and cultural points, but these were outweighed by the fact that the new coalition shared emphasis on programs such as lessening the role of foreign capital, basing development more heavily on the public than on the private sector, coolness toward big business, and loosening the still very strong foreign policy ties with the Western powers (primarily the United States). There was also, of course, the attractiveness of power. The coalition was constantly strained, but it lasted until fall, when Ecevit resigned in the hope that there would be a quick election in which he could ride the crest of his Cyprus heroism to an even greater victory at the polls.[8] It was precisely because such a thing was conceivable, however, that the conservative parties in the Assembly refused to agree to its dissolution, and after long negotiations, four conservative parties (JP, RPP, NSP, NAP) formed a government, again led by Suleyman Demirel.

It was not only tactical considerations which had led the RPP government to seek to strengthen itself, however. More significant was that the party quickly found that there were limits to the degree to which it was willing to aggregate its interests with those of other elements. The rifts with the NSP had grown rapidly. On social matters, the NSP took every opportunity to pull the RPP further to the right in areas such as education (one demand to which the RPP acceded was the addition of "moral education" to the curricula of the public schools), and in tightening control over Turkish Radio and Television to curb alleged "leftist" programming. The NSP also wanted far stronger restraints on foreign private capital than the RPP could accept, the NSP asserting somewhat incongruously that economic development would in fact be quickened by shifting the emphasis of industrialization to local (and necessarily small) producers. Finally, in foreign policy Ecevit was willing to use the Cyprus issue to wrest concessions from the United States and the NATO allies, but was not at all willing to embrace the NSP's position which would have Turkey all but completely withdraw from its ties to the West unless virtually all Turkish demands were granted.

On the other hand, pressures from the party's left wing were also building up. They came from several sources. One such was the older leaders who were still disturbed at alleged compromises of Kemalist principles. A second was various younger leaders, including some who had been active in the Turkish Labor party before its closing and were ideologically motivated, and others who insisted that tactically it was fruitless to continue to try to compete with the JP for the middle ground and who viewed the electorate as moving rapidly toward the left. Ecevit, while on one hand encouraging the moderate rather than the radical trade unions, on the other hand also took the RPP into the Socialist International, and while not generally using revolutionary language familiar to Marxists, did give the RPP's populism a distinctly militant tone: "We are not revolutionaries (reformers) who come down from high, but 'people's reformers' " (Biz tepeden inmeci değil, halk devrimcileriyiz. Milliyet, May 3, 1976).

In 1976 the left wing launched a major offensive to capture the party machinery, and although they failed to win enough positions to control the party's executive council, the margin of victory for the older leaders was narrow. The party's improved showing in 1977 in the urban areas encouraged them, even though it could be argued that one thing that helped the party retain its voters was that the party did *not* move further to the left, and that factors outside the party were of major importance, including the continued poor record of the JP-led governments and a further splintering of the right with the growth of the National Salvation and National Action parties. Even though the RPP again emerged as the largest single party, it was still short of a majority, and was able to come to power in January, 1978, only after another period of failure by the right-wing coalition government, and by enlisting the aid of several deputies which the RPP was able to detach from the JP by giving them cabinet positions. At the party Congress in May 1979, the left wing renewed its bid for control, and again lost, but by only a narrow margin. As mentioned earlier, the RPP government resigned after being defeated in by-elections in October 1979. At a special party congress in November the moderates retained control of the party machinery yet again by a narrow margin, but at this writing a process of self-examination has begun which shows signs of being as important as that of a decade and a half earlier.

Whether the RPP is the party of Turkey's future, as some insist, remains to be seen. There are some positive signs that it may be. A sharp contrast to earlier times, for example, is the finding of one study that of the eighty-eight RPP deputies who entered the Assembly for the first time in 1969, "almost all had had years of experience as officers of province and district party organizations" (Kili, 1976:255). The RPP also appears to be able to recruit some of Turkey's best young talent, and a number of the ministers in the recent government were unusually capable. But while it is certainly important that there is a trend toward social change which is making more groups among the population less conservative (labor, for example) it remains the case that much of the RPP's recovery has been related to positive factors not of its own making, such as poor performance by its opponents. The same became a factor in the RPP's most recent fall from power.

More fundamentally, however, it remains problematic whether the RPP can continue to make progress toward overcoming the legacies of its past. Its largest base continues to be in upper-middle-class institutions such as the universities and the bureaucracy. There is major potential for expansion, such as among important leaders of the business community who favor RPP policies like tax reform, a larger government role in export and foreign exchange guidance, and better economic planning, and among urban workers, who seek extension of many of the RPP's pro-labor policies and are at least partly attuned to the RPP's portrayal of the Justice party as too pro-business. At the same time, the Turkish historical memory is long, and the conservative parties hammer away at the theme of the RPP's elitism, at its past authoritarian nature, and continually recall for the voters that, despite current difficulties, the Democrat and Justice parties have in fact been the sponsors of a great deal of economic growth. Invoking the spectre of the RPP being associated with international communism also has potency, in Ankara and Istanbul as well as in the more conservative provincial areas.

Perhaps one of the most unfortunate aspects of the RPP's return to power is that it came in circumstances which particularly heighten the intensity of mutual recrimination between the two major parties. One factor of significance is that the RPP had only a razor-thin margin in the Assembly, and that it obtained its majority only by detaching several members from the JP. Another is that the extreme difficulty of social and economic problems has made it unusually tempting for both sides to blame the other for their own inabilities to make progress toward solutions. The resulting return to ideological language on both sides, as well as the reappearance of intense personal enmities and the severe interelite conflict which characterized the 1950s indicates some of the strains which the Turkish party system is still undergoing.[9] How the parties react is especially significant in light of the voting data to be discussed below which lead one to suspect that the leaders of both major parties reflect considerably more ideological fervor than the general public has. It is not implausible to conclude that perhaps the RPP's greatest opportunity continues to be in attempting to mobilize support from a large and diverse number of groups and to compete for the broad middle ground which most voters still occupy.

The Democrat and Justice Parties

The Democrat Party

The role of the Democrat party in Turkish modernization remains highly controversial. On the positive side, there is no doubt that the DP was the vehicle through which large numbers of lower class Turks were brought into connection with Turkish political life. In large part this was because the DP sponsored very rapid social and economic growth, which greatly increased national integration and also gave Turks, for perhaps the first time, a truly responsive government. The Democrats also benefited from being the government through which a variety of groups began to articulate their interests. In response to these groups, for much of its tenure in office the DP made real efforts at aggregating interests and at resisting pressures from radical forces (for details, see Simpson, 1965, and Ahmad, 1977:chapters 2–5). On the negative side, the charge is made that under DP policies rural Turks were incorporated into the system in ways which in the long run retarded true development (i.e., that many resources were used for projects which would gather short-run electoral support for the DP but which stressed consumption and neglected more basic investment needs). In addition, villagers were given the idea that they could get anything they wanted from the government merely by giving the ruling party political support, thus inhibiting their self-development. There is also still spirited argument about the functionality for long-term modernization of policies such as relaxed secularism and conservative public education and the party's great emphasis on economic development via the private sector.

As noted in chapter 1, the DP began its existence with a considerable amount of support from political elites. Its founders had for some years been respected members of the RPP, making it difficult to assail their origins or their political training.[10] More importantly, many groups found appeal in various aspects of the DP program which stressed relaxation of *etatism* and militant social and cultural reforms but which, while differing from the RPP program in emphasis and tone, remained similar in direction.[11] At least as important was that even many members of the ruling RPP welcomed a situation in which there would be greater freedom of expression (even if often only to be better able to criticize their own party leaders).

On coming to power in 1950 the DP immediately moved to consolidate its popularity among all groups of the population available to it. The most important of these groups in terms of voter strength was the peasants, who were courted on cultural, political, and economic terms. Culturally, the most dramatic changes were seen in the relaxation of some aspects of secularism. As noted previously, the DP did not retreat in the fundamental areas of control over law and education, or a direct *ulema* role in politics, but it did place mosques high on the list of public works projects, restored Koran-reading on the state radio, and sent numerous other signals that the attitude of the new government would be a great contrast to the alleged "antireligious" attitude of its predecessor. Politically, the DP strengthened the power of local leaders through such methods as politicizing the distribution of public works projects, and by generally encouraging intervention by party leaders and members in dealings between citizens and the bureaucracy. One Turkish analyst has described the DP as "a rural political machine" (Sayarı, 1975:127). In the economic sphere, the Democrats began to put large amounts of resources into rural development, including roads, utilities, im-ports of farm machinery,[12] and high price supports for agricultural products.[13]

The widespread support generated by these policies led to an even more decisive DP election victory in 1954, an election also notable for the fact that 88.6 percent of the eligible voters went to the polls, only a slight drop from the 89.3 percent in 1950. With 490 of the 535 Assembly seats in their hands, the DP, however, like some of their RPP predecessors who had earlier found themselves in positions of unchecked power, found temptation very hard to resist, and it was not long before the Democrats started to make moves which began to severely polarize the political atmosphere. Some were economic. The tendency to use political considerations as a major criterion for allocating public works projects grew greatly. As resources available for distribution began to dwindle (poor crop weather beginning in 1954 quickly cut down the real growth rate, which had been very high in the immediately preceding years; see Tansky, 1969:chapter 3), the DP leaders engaged in more and more deficit financing, and larger and larger borrowing from abroad. This in turn led to severe inflation and shortages which—in contrast to earlier periods—not only displeased urban voters, but also began to affect the rural population, which was being rapidly integrated into the national economy—a byproduct of the very development programs which the DP was carrying out.[14]

These setbacks were in part responsible for the DP's electoral decline in 1957, the voters already having become attentive to economic issues as well as to social and cultural ones. Although they still held 419 seats compared to 183 for all the opposition parties combines, the Democrats intensified their militancy in a second sphere, the political. Their action in this area involved the urban elites more than it did the lower urban strata or the peasants, and was one of the major causes of the 1960 revolution. The status of the armed forces, bureaucracy, and intellectuals had been seriously reduced both politically and materially, leading to a return of much of this group to the RPP and increasing their complaints about what were now being called programmatic betrayals of Kemalism. A revolt in the DP's own ranks had taken place in 1955 when some thirty deputies founded the Freedom Party, and although its showing was poor (3.8 percent of the votes in 1957 and only four Assembly seats) it was worrisome both as a sign of internal party trouble, and because sympathy for the defectors among the general Ankara elite was clearly strong (Karpat, 1959:437). All these disturbing events led to repression of both the press and parliamentary opposition,[15] and the Republic's first period of multiparty politics came to an end.

Still, there had been significant political development. The mobilization of voters (followers) remained very strong (even though voting turnout in 1957 dropped to 76.6 percent), and the connection between political support and rewards was made very clear. The improved performance of the RPP in 1957 (rising to 40.6 percent from its 34.8 percent in 1954) was an indication that the electorate would also be discerning, though it is difficult to determine the degree to which the voters were judging the DP on economic, political, or cultural grounds. Recruitment of leaders, on the other hand, was not particularly significant in that the DP tended to rely on leaders who had earlier been prominent, with relatively few persons brought to political office who were essentially newcomers. There was little important development of new interest groups or other voluntary organizations during the DP period, though those which existed became much more active. But, as in the single-party period, important foundations were being laid for further development. The effects of both the successes and the failures of the DP period would be strongly felt in the post-1960 years.

For the political party system, among the most important results of the 1960 revolution was an enhanced new awareness of the importance to major political parties of remaining moderate in many policy areas, and the corollary development of conditions which could potentially change the two-party system into a multiparty one. In regard to the former, it became clear that the armed forces, intellectuals, and other elite groups would not tolerate political repression. Second, important elements among the electorate had begun (as in the 1957 election) to indicate that they expected solid performance in such areas as the economy, and that if development were accompanied by, for example, rapid inflation, it would not be to the benefit of the party in power, no matter what its cultural appeals were. Regarding the party system, the conditions for its fragmentation were created in the collapse of the DP machine, in the widened freedom of political expression which enabled a socialist party to be organized for the first time in 1961, a largely religion-based party in 1969, and in the growth of some of the frustrations of rapid modernization leading to a strong neo-fascist party in the 1970s. It is instructive in view of these factors, that what has in fact happened is the continuance of a system which is dominant two-party. The reasons for this are quite significant, and will be explored through an examination of the post-1960 parties.

The Justice Party

As one of three parties which all but openly competed to be successors to the Democrats,[16] the Justice party won only 35 percent of the votes in the 1961 election. During the next four years, however, abler leadership, plus being clearly the most promising of the competitors and therefore attracting those who sought a vehicle to gain power, propelled the JP upward so that in 1965 it gained an absolute majority, with 52.8 percent of the votes, and formed a government under the leadership of an engineer, Suleyman Demirel. In 1969, the JP's vote declined somewhat because of the appearance of several new small parties, but the vagaries of the electoral system enabled it to retain its absolute majority in the Assembly. It continued in power until the Demirel government was "persuaded" by the armed forces to resign in March 1971. In 1973, the JP faced more formidable electoral challenges with the appearance for the first time in the history of the Republic of a party which appealed to the radical right directly and ably (the National Salvation party), as well as a major defection from the JP's own ranks (the Democrat party) which took with it some prominent personalities and to a considerable degree weakened the JP's local party organizations. Although its votes declined by fully one-third (from 46.5 percent to 29.8 percent), the JP remained the dominant party of the moderate right, and returned to power after the short-lived RPP-NSP coalition of 1973–4. The challenges were much weaker in 1977, and the JP rebounded with 36.9 percent, enough to dominate but not to govern alone. A series of Demirel-led coalitions with radical right-wing parties, known as the "National Front," governed until its ouster by the RPP in January 1978. As already mentioned, in late 1979 Demirel returned to power, this time as head of a JP-only minority government whose performance is being watched with great interest.

The JP's strength has come from a combination of new and old factors. Its program strongly emphasized economic matters, stressing rural development in more "progressive" terms than the Democrats had, such as apportioning more investment to industry and agriculture and less to construction, and taking advantage of the fact that by the time of the 1965 campaign the religious issue had declined in importance.[17] It also promised continuing industrial growth through a freer economy, continued encouragement of the private sector, and further attraction of foreign capital, which had been important in the expansion of the 1950s.[18] Other features attractive to former DP voters included administrative reforms, and educational expansion concentrated on village schools and technical training (Szyliowicz, 1966b:488).

It also appealed to older interests. One such appeal was the promise of strong government, in contrast to the weak coalitions of 1961–1965. Another was specific projects and benefits to virtually every community in which Demirel campaigned, which is, of course, in the tradition of politicians universally. In social policy, no doubt was left that the conservative "tone" of the DP period would continue. Also of great importance was the fact that the JP was able to capture many of the old local organizations of the DP, and it was the skill of the party at this level which was in large part responsible for its routing of the NTP and the RPNP between the elections of 1961 and 1965.[19]

On the other hand, one of the early attractions of the JP was an appeal reflecting a key difference between it and the DP, a difference personified in the contrast between the leaders of the two parties. Adnan Menderes and Celal Bayar had been veterans of the single-party period and were representatives of the old families and landed wealth of the Aegean and Marmara regions. They also harbored deep personal as well as political hostility toward the leaders of the RPP. Suleyman Demirel, who won control of the JP at the end of 1964 by ousting the right wing under the leadership of retired General Ragip Gümüşpala (who was one of the large number of officers retired by the National Unity Committee in its "rejuvenation" of the armed forces in 1960), is an American-trained engineer from the west-central Anatolian province of Isparta, a graduate of Istanbul Technical University, and an official of the State Water Works before entering politics. One observer has noted that while Demirel "obviously resembles Menderes more than [Ataturk or Inonu, he] is basically a modern, pragmatic executive and organizer, rather than an inspired leader possessed of a special kind of personalism" (Sherwood, 1967:54). Demirel's connections were primarily with the industrialists, and it was the contrasts between Demirel and Menderes (and similar contrast between Demirel and several competitors within the JP) which very much helped make him acceptable to the military in 1965.

That the Justice party continued in power for so many years is not surprising. A number of factors help explain both its successes and failures and are instructive to an understanding of recent Turkish politics.

1. The JP was able to remain in power as long as it did partly because it had a "natural constituency" inherited from the Democrat decade. Resentment against the RPP was deep and durable, particularly in conjunction with the efforts which the DP had made to be responsive to popular demands in specific as well as general terms. For many voters, the economic gains of the

1950s and early 1960s still outweighed current economic difficulties, such as inflation. The public also remained responsive to the conservative social tone of the government, even as this issue was declining in relative importance. The JP's return to power after 1973 was also a boost, in that it could be interpreted as a defiance of the armed forces, who had earlier forced the resignation of the Demirel government and who, while curbing the leftists—always a fairly popular thing for many Turks—had also installed a series of governments between 1971 and 1973 with a distinct bias toward the left in social policies (see Ahmad, 1977:chapter 11).

2. The JP's attractiveness was further enhanced by its ability to remain the largest party on the right, and therefore the one with the most promise of power for its supporters. In the competition for dominance of the moderate right, the JP was also helped by the dearth of attractive personalities among its competitors. Within the JP itself, Demirel's political flair has made him so dominant a party symbol as to discourage potential competitors. His leadership has seldom been seriously threatened.

3. The JP's decline, on the other hand, is due mainly to factors which are increasingly coming to the fore in current Turkey:

(a) The continuing economic crisis, which has resulted in the extremely severe inflation and shortages of recent years.

(b) The shift of the predominance of voters to the urban areas and the more developed regions, where economic problems are felt more severely and where the influence of established local notables is less.

(c) The nature of the competition has also contributed to the JP's decline. On the right, freedom and frustration have combined to take both votes and publicity away from the moderate right. On the left, the RPP has succeeded in at least partially rehabilitating itself and is thus able to bring pressure on its opponents.

One observer has called the Justice party "Turkey's new Jacksonians" (Sherwood, 1967:65). There is now less reason to be as sanguine, and while the JP continues to have many opportunities for contributing constructively to development and stability, it also has formidable challenges. Perhaps its greatest asset for its most recent return to power was that the RPP government had little more success in solving the country's short-run problems than the JP had. Other assets include the fact that even out of power it remains big enough to be the major opposition party; that it has within it some very capable people; that in combination with other right-wing parties there is enough strength to have made the existence of the RPP government constantly precarious; that its organization at the province and local levels remains viable; and that it remains the chief spokesman of the brand of right-wing moderateness which has the potential of support by many groups which are no longer very conservative socially but which are also not ready to move to a party clearly identified as "left-of-center."

It is precisely this combination of assets which presents the JP with a significant opportunity to contribute to continued Turkish progress. If there is a single major lesson to be drawn from the recent situations of the two major parties, it is that the continuance of the dominant two-party system based on moderate policies has the potential to be a spur to development and to simultaneously fulfill the wishes of most of the Turkish electorate that many values from the past be maintained. The dominant two-party system also has provided a framework in which it is possible to accommodate the increasing attention of a great many voters to issues rather than to ideology. That neither of the major parties has been able to solve some of Turkey's serious short-run problems is unfortunate, but not attributable to the nature of the parties or the party system. Thus it may be considered to be all the more unfortunate that JP leaders (and some RPP leaders as well) have chosen to become increasingly strident and to markedly heighten the level of partisan rhetoric in discussion of public affairs. The JP in 1978–79 appeared to be succumbing to pressures from some of the more conservative deputies who have remained in it rather than joining one of the minor parties. Perhaps even more disturbing is the apparent readiness of the JP to make major concessions to the right-wing radical parties, a tendency which may have been understandable when it was required to do so in order to remain in power during the years 1973–1977, but which was far less so when the JP was in opposition. It took many years for the conditions to develop wherein the RPP was returned to a position from which it can now competently make an optimum contribution to the needs of contemporary Turkey. It is to be hoped that the JP will not now miss its chance to continue to do likewise.

Minor Parties

Many minor parties have been present at one time or another on the Turkish political stage, particularly since 1961. Two general types can be identified. One type is represented by those which began as factions in major parties and then broke away from the parties. Their major common characteristic has been that they have frequently been able to remain important because they were able to call on continuing "traditional" sources of strength arising from local loyalties to particular individuals or groups. But when they have had to stand for election on bases other than this, the dominant two-party nature of the Turkish party system has quickly reasserted itself and overwhelmed them. The record and prospects of the second type of minor parties, the radical ones on both right and left, are less clear. The radical parties are more dependent on developments in the nation as a whole than on the kind of nonprogrammatic factors that are important to the factions.

The *Progressive Republican Party* of 1924 was formed by a group of prominent leaders who were also political and personal rivals of Ataturk. Among their chief points of dissatisfaction were the lack of internal party democracy and concentration of all powers in the Assembly, and what they thought was the undesirably fast pace of some of the reforms (particularly the social ones) although they were undoubtedly generally supporters of the reforms themselves. Ataturk was unwilling to tolerate challenges on either of these points, and had little trouble dissolving the party after about seven months of activity. It was the last group to publicly take a conservative position until 1946.* (See Weiker, 1973:44–51; Karpat, 1959:46–8; Tunaya, 1952:606 ff., Rustow, 1959:547–49.)

The *Freedom Party (Hürriyet Partisi)* was formed in late 1955 by about thirty liberal and intellectual dissidents from the Democrat party. They had some generalized criticisms of the party's economic policies, but their chief complaints about the DP were over the waning of internal party democracy, its domination by personalities, its lack of focus on programs, and constraints being imposed by the DP government on the press and the opposition. Although it included some able men, the Freedom party had no outstanding personalities to help it win electoral popularity. It was also lacking in the local bases required to establish country-wide organization sufficient to rival the DP. In the Assembly it remained small because few deputies were inclined to give up the power they enjoyed as members of the ruling party, and probably also because most DP deputies shared the prevailing DP views on most program items. In the 1957 election the Freedom party won in only one province and returned four deputies. Most of its members joined the RPP shortly afterward (see Karpat, 1959:435–7; and Ahmad 1977).

The *Reliance Party (Güven Partisi)* was formed in 1967 by some fifty-two senators and deputies who accompanied Turhan Feyzioğlu in rebellion against the RPP's move to left-of-center, and who made their move in reaction to the accompanying election of Bülent Ecevit as RPP Secretary-General (an office to which the veteran Feyzioğlu had also aspired). The Reliance party had a considerably stronger potential base than the Freedom party had had. The RP included a number of members with strong personal followings and local bases.[21] Also, the RPP contained a sizable conservative wing on which to draw (in contrast to the Freedom party's having had to appeal to the DP's more liberal elements). In addition, the defectors to the RP did not have to confront the obstacle that they might be foregoing access to power, for few people saw any realistic chance that the RPP would be forming a government in the near future.

But despite these advantages, the pull of the major parties proved too strong, and in its first electoral test (1969), the RP lost over half its deputies. The only members who survived the 1969 election were those who had strong personal local followings.[22] The party was able to maintain its visibility only because its fifteen deputies numbered above the minimum (ten) which qualify a party in the Turkish Assembly to form a "group" and to have the privilege of presenting official party statements in debates. In 1973 the RP was able to avoid additional large losses chiefly because it had by then combined with still another group of conservative defectors from the RPP (who for a brief time operated as the Republicanist [*Cumhuriyetçi*] party; see Kili, 1976:341). The RP was later also helped by being one of the small parties which the Justice party needed to maintain a majority to remain in power during the National Front cabinets of 1975–1977. Feyzioğlu served

*The *Free Party* of 1930 was discussed in chapter 1.

as a deputy premier. But the inevitable attrition process reduced the party to only three stalwarts after the 1977 election, and as a political force it is undoubtedly destined for extinction.

The *Democratic Party* (not to be confused with the Democrat party of the 1950s) suffered an even quicker and more ignominious decline. Formed in 1970 by some forty defectors from the Justice party whose primary shared characteristic was their personal hostility to JP leader Demirel (though despite heterogeneous political views they were all also in the more conservative wing of the JP), it was able to capitalize on the fact that, like the Reliance party, it included a number of deputies with strong enough local bases to take their organizations with them. The DP was able to profit as well from some of the very real dissatisfaction with Demirel's leadership. Thus, in its first electoral venture (1973) the DP managed to return forty-five deputies. But it soon became caught between conflicting pressures, including the attractiveness of power which the JP was able to hold out to its members (the DP pointedly declined to join any Demirel-led coalition even though it shared many of the JP's political views), competition from the further right in the form of the new National Salvation party, and the reputation which the DP quickly acquired as being a personal vehicle for the ambitions of its leader, former Assembly speaker Ferruh Bozbeyli.[23] Offering little that was new or attractive, and having defections of its own, only one DP deputy survived the 1977 election. He, instructively, was Faruk Sukan, who had a strong and longtime personal following in Konya. The DP has all but passed out of existence.

In contrast to the above minor parties, minor parties with distinctly different programs from those of the major parties have usually been better able to appeal to particular social groups, and have had a good deal better record of survival.

The *Nation Party*[24] has been the longest lived, drawing on elements more socially conservative than those in the Democrat or Justice parties. It drew scattered support but won seats only in the province of Kırşehir, where NP leader Osman Bölükbaşı had his home base. Its longevity (1948–1977) was a presage, however, of the potency of parties with similarly distinctive programs, a corresponding social base, and dynamic leadership (see Ahmad, 1977:passim; and Karpat, 1959:219–21 and 431–35).

The *Turkish Labor Party,* the first radical party of significance to come on the scene and the only radical-left party of any importance, emerged almost as soon as socialism was legalized as a vehicle of political expression in 1961.[25] Its initial founders were mostly intellectuals, many of whom had been involved in earlier leftist activities. They were soon joined by some young Istanbul trade union leaders (Landau, 1974:123, Karpat, 1967:165). Despite the dynamism and attractiveness of many of these leaders, it was not surprising that most workers "were wary of the new party, whose theorizing was often highbrow and too complicated for their understanding" (Landau, 1974:125). Many were also deterred because joining the TLP would have required them to overcome long-standing conservative social values and political taboos. Nevertheless, by the time of the 1965 election the TLP had established "quite a few branches" in towns and districts (Landau, 1974:126) and was able to run candidates in fifty-one of Turkey's sixty-seven provinces (Karpat, 1967:167). It won fifteen seats on the basis of some 3 percent of the votes (267,000), largely from support in the upper-middle-class districts[26] of Istanbul, Ankara, and Izmir (and through the "national remainder" system, without which only two TLP deputies would have been successful[27]).

The party's program was strongly flavored with Marxist ideology, though it used relatively mild language in expressing the need for "both land reforms and deep-rooted agricultural reforms." It strongly favored nationalization of large industries, mining, and particularly the petroleum industry. It advocated drastic tax reform, and in foreign policy "continually stressed the need for Turkey to regain its complete independence from US domination" (Szyliowicz, 1966:487), though it also, somewhat pragmatically, "favored taking advantage of foreign capital and credits as long as they did not threaten Turkey's independence." (Ibid.:488.)

Though the TLP's spokesmen in the Assembly were articulate and for the most part responsible, and though its supporters and organizers were only rather infrequently extreme and/or violent, the party encountered several problems which led to a decline of about 13 percent in its votes in the 1969 election, despite the growth of the social classes among which it expected support (intellectuals, and skilled and organized workers[28]). The reasons for the decline included the continued leftward movement of the RPP and its ability to capture some of the TLP's less securely attached supporters, intensive attacks against it by the right-wing parties, severe internal splintering, and the beginning of urban guerrilla activities, which were naturally quickly attributed to the TLP. (On these factors see Onulduran, 1974:75 and Landau, 1974:29–44 and 122–31.) It was only a *coup de grace,* then (though deplorable nevertheless from the point of view of political freedom), when in 1971 (shortly after the armed forces obtained the resignation of the Demirel government and declared martial law in the face of major urban guerrilla violence), the Constitutional Court ordered the TLP closed on the basis of a variety of charges of subversion. Most of the party's leaders were tried and jailed. Only small and relatively cautious revivals of radical leftist political party activity have taken place since the influence of the military lessened after the 1973 election. A smaller successor version of the TLP did not significantly compete in the 1977 election.[29]

On balance, despite the TLP's weak electoral showings, some of its contributions have been important. Perhaps the most significant is that for the first time since the *Kadro* movement of the early 1930s (see Weiker, 1973:222–7 and Karpat, 1959:70–73) the breadth of debate widened, and many of the leaders of the TLP in the Assembly demonstrated that radicals could also be responsible critics. That the activity of TLP supporters was also one factor in arousing right-wing extremism and terrorism is, of course, unfortunate, but it was probably unavoidable. Another effect, one which may be of more comfort to TLP stalwarts, is that they constituted one of the factors pulling the RPP toward its left-of-center position, which serves to help realize some of the TLP's goals and to sharpen the issues, though, as previously noted, many RPP leaders realize that their own role in Turkish politics may be maximized by not moving too far to the left.

Radical parties will probably continue to be present in Turkish politics. Those on the left are likely most of the time to be in a precarious position in a polity which is both generally conservative and constantly being pulled institutionally toward the center. On the right, the prospects of radical parties may be more favorable.

The *National Salvation Party.* Until the end of the 1960s, what may be called the "Islamic right" had been significantly represented in politics only by the small and lackluster Nation party and by a few nonparty associations and publications (on these, see Landau, 1974:171–87). This was due in part to the DP's success in capturing the right wing of the electorate, in part to the absence of any outstanding personalities to lead the radical right. The former factor was removed in 1969 when Necmettin Erbakan[30] ran successfully as an independent from the conservative province of Konya. For sixteen months in 1970–1971 he headed the Party for National Order *(Millî Nizam Partisi),* until it was closed by the Constitutional Court on the grounds that it was calling for "Revolutionary Religion" (Landau, 1974:188 and Ahmad, 1977:317), a slogan which provided a basis for charging the party with violating the secularist basis of the Republic and with advocating violence.

Shortly before the 1973 election, Erbakan returned to politics by organizing the National Salvation party *(Millî Selamet Partisi)* on a platform which combined "morals and virtue" with populist economic and social programs. Among the latter were expulsion of pretty much all foreign-owned industry in favor of domestic production, and emphasis on helping small provincial manufacturers (though not in all branches of industry) as against supporting large industrialists, even if the latter were Turks. (For a detailed summary of the original NSP program, see Landau, 1976:8–11, and a long interview with Oğuzhan Asıltürk in *Milliyet,* January 21, 1974.) More recently, Erbakan has somewhat changed the latter position to one of support for heavy industry as well, as long as it is Turkish-owned and Anatolia-based.

It should not have been a surprise (though it did cause considerable dismay) when in 1973 the NSP gained some 12 percent of the votes, and forty-eight Assembly seats, making it the third largest party. Its support came somewhat disproportionally from the less-developed regions of the country (but was not skewed very severely in that direction), from religious-minded groups in the larger urban areas, and from groups such as *esnaf* in several cities who felt threatened by big business (see Landau, 1976:21 ff.; Tachau and Özbudun, 1975; Turan, 1978:4). It *was* surprising to most people, however, that the NSP joined with the RPP to form a coalition government in January 1974 after protracted bargaining, even though on reflection it was realized that the two parties had some significant common interests. In addition to convergence on major principles of populism and nationalism (even if they approached these principles differently and frequently had wide differences in program specifics), there was also the common interest of coming to power. Erbakan soon became a highly visible deputy premier whose activities included holding prayer services in the Assembly building and going on the *hajj*. Relations between the coalition partners were always strained, however, and, as mentioned, they broke apart over the Cyprus question, on which the NSP was extremely militant, and which gave Bülent Ecevit the opportunity to try to strengthen himself and become able to govern without the NSP.[31] The NSP's vote in the partial Senate election of 1975 declined to 8.5 percent, though this was still a good showing. In March 1975 the NSP again got a share of power, joining the four-party "National Front" coalition headed by JP leader Demirel, with Erbakan again as a deputy premier. Again Erbakan made himself very visible, taking full advantage of his balance-of-power position to pull government policies in his direction. In the 1977 election the NSP vote declined from 11.8 percent to 8.6 percent and its number of seats from forty-eight to twenty-four, but even this showing enabled it to continue to be important in the balance of power, and Erbakan continued his radical rightist pressures as part of the coalition that remained in office until January, 1978.

A review of the NSP's assets and liabilities leads to the conclusion that while the radical right as a whole will be prominent on the Turkish political scene for some time to come, the NSP's place in it may be only a minor one, and that the most impressive thing about even the 1973 election was not that the party got so many votes, but that it got so few. Among the party's assets are a colorful leader, and the fact that religion continues to be an important social factor in Turkish life. On the liability side, the greatest one is certainly the very obverse: the NSP's rival on the radical right, the National Action party, has a powerful and colorful leader of its own. But a far more important problem for the NSP is the steadily lessening potency of religion as a *political* issue. These things have worked against the NSP in two ways. One is that the party's loss of support in 1977 was general rather than specific or localized. The twenty-four seats which were lost were distributed in twenty-four different provinces, which were also scattered regionally, including eleven in the east and southeast, five in the Aegean and Marmara, and seven in central and western Anatolia. The second is that nine of the thirteen seats by which the National Action Party increased its strength were won in provinces where the NSP lost seats, so that if the frustrations of modernization are likely to help the radical right as a whole to maintain its support, it seems likely it will be expressed in votes for secular rather than religion-based radicalism.

In one important sense it is a positive development that an avowed religious force in Turkish politics gives signs of waning, but before completing this discussion of the role of minor parties we shall look at one whose future may be bright enough to make it an exception to the general pattern of limited success which we have seen in the others.

The *National Action Party (Millî Hareket Partisi)* of former NUC leader Alparslan Türkeş[32] was the only minor party which increased its vote over the previous election in both 1973 and 1977. Founded shortly before the 1969 election out of the Republican Peasants Nation party which Türkeş had taken over in 1965, it is radically right-wing in both its program, which emphasizes anticommunism, nationalism which frequently borders on pan-Turkism, populism, and morality, and in its tactics, which are described by many as fascistic. Casting itself in the role of militant enforcers of "the concept that the morals of Turks should conform to Turkish traditions, spirit and to the beliefs of the Turkish nation" (Landau, 1974:224), its most prominent activity has been urban guerrilla "commandos" organized through a network of *Ülkü Ocaklan* ("Homes of Ideals"), whose members have been in frequent violent action against leftist groups of all sorts. Although the NAP was a member of the National Front coalition governments, Türkeş's attempts to pull the other members further to the right and into supporting even greater repression of the left were, for the most part, unsuccessful.

The NAP, like the NSP, is likely to remain on the Turkish scene for some time, even though its chief role may well be more one of satisfying the needs of its individual members than of being a force actually influencing government policy (unless, as was the coincidental case in 1973–1977, it also holds part of the balance of power when neither of the major parties has a parliamentary majority). Basically a party of the "lumpenproletariat," its appeal has largely been based on supplying people who are having difficulty adjusting to modern urban life with a means of vicariously expressing their frustrations. The NAP differs from the NSP in the important respect that the latter has a fundamental anchor in religion, though in other respects the NAP has a great number of assets (attractive leader, etc.) similar to those of the NSP. An additional weakness of the NAP, however, is that many of the key aspects of its program—very strong repression of the left, nationalism approaching the extreme—are unlikely to be realized, this in contrast to some of the points of the NSP program which have been implemented with relatively little difficulty (moral education, etc.). In this sense it is conceivable that the NAP will settle down into being chiefly a nuisance factor, though a serious one because the curbing of the urban guerrillas for which the NAP is generally held responsible will not be an easy task for any government. It probably will not be until potential NAP followers become successfully integrated into Turkish urban society that such a phenomenon (so familiar in many countries) will disappear altogether.[33]

Party Activity, Organization, and the Party System

Participation in party activities takes place within the general framework of the Political Parties Law #648 of 1965, as amended, which covers most aspects of party organization, financing, and internal operation. While the formal provisions are of course only part of the picture, the fact that much of the law's thrust is toward democratization of party operations has had some important effects on participation in the political process. Its major features directed toward that end include (1) detailing provisions for voting by all party members for nominees for public office, (2) giving the final power in the nomination of most candidates for the National Assembly to the province party organizations and limiting the number of candidates which the national organization can "impose" on province tickets to 5 percent of the total number of deputyships in the country, (3) specifying provisions for members' participation in choosing party officials at all levels and for the apportioning of delegates at all levels of party congresses, (4) placing maximum limits (quite low) both on mandatory assessments and on individual gifts,[34] (5) mandating that all records, financial and otherwise, be subject to examination by the Constitutional Court. (For a detailed summary of the law before 1973 amendments which tightened it but did not change its basic thrust, see Dodd, 1969:130–35.)

On the other hand, the law also provides for party control over participation, most importantly through its provision for disciplinary committees at all levels. This has been a prominent feature of Turkish party organization from the beginning of the Republic, and although Law 648 provides for the democratic election of committee members and for elaborate channels for appealing their decisions, their mandatory nature helps reinforce the sense of hierarchy and conformity which informs so much of Turkish society. The actions and activities of disciplinary committees are widely reported in the press.

In quantitative terms, there is no doubt that the number of participants in the periodic act of voting has increased greatly and that parties have become to a very great degree the focal point for the articulation of the interests of those who seek to influence government policy. Unfortunately we have little direct evidence of whether or not the single periodic act of voting has had significant spillover into increased participation in other party activities. There are several indications, however, that this impact is relatively small. The accordion-like nature of expansion of participation during campaigns and contraction at nonelection times is clearly visible. For example, in several Anatolian cities visited by this observer in 1970, party activity in the province branches of both major parties was all but nowhere in evidence, unless the parties or their branches also doubled as youth groups, sport clubs, etc., or were involved in a factional dispute. In some provincial capitals, in fact, it was only with considerable diligence that many of the party officials could be located at all (for a similar picture, see Mansur, 1972:88 ff.). Similarly, Sayarı, in a study of several province and local party organizations, found that for most members, the notion of party "remains extremely vague. All the parties claim an unspecified number of registered members but concede that they do not maintain membership records, and that the annual payment of dues is an exception rather than the rule" (1976:189).

It is also clear that while party structures have increasingly become arenas for political conflicts, they also continue to be used as vehicles for older and more traditional rivalries which are seldom based on ideologies or party programs. Many private associations are "politicized" in the sense that some of their leaders may simultaneously hold party office (e.g., in one

Anatolian city the province JP leader was also the head of the Union of Craft Guilds, and both organizations operated, in fact if not officially, out of the same room). One is often told that the bulk of the members of a given private association belong to one party or faction, almost as if the two memberships were virtual correlates. Similarly, while there is a general correspondence between party and occupational group (e.g., economic groups tend more strongly to affiliate with the JP), in most places one can find, for example, many *esnaf* groups in the RPP as well, and on closer investigation it usually turns out that party alignments have taken place because one group's adherence to one party had come about mainly because a traditional rival adhered to another. In the Anatolian cities observed in 1970, even members of directly partisan bodies, such as city councils, frequently displayed much more interest in and identification with social, religious, or economic associations than with the political party in whose name they carried out their public functions.

On the village level as well, virtually all studies of local communities in Turkey agree that party branches are often little more than new forms for expression of older group solidarities (see, for example, Stirling, 1965; Szyliowicz, 1966a; Magnarella, 1974; Weiker, 1972). Factional bitterness became the basis of party competition to such a degree during the 1950s, in fact, that the National Unity Committee felt it necessary to abolish all local and county branches.[35] The weakness of party attachments is also evident in frequent newspaper reports of mass enrollment in a party in some village or town or the switch of the total community from one party to another. Parties have also become a significant arena for expressions of center vs. periphery disputes. The province party organizations are usually very adamant in guarding their authority to nominate Assembly candidates, and attempts by the national organization to place even some of the most popular party leaders on province tickets have frequently met with vehement protests, especially if such actions were seen as interfering with local political considerations (for some examples, see Kili, 1976:369).

Despite such instances of falling short of the "ideal" of political party activity as one in which citizens are stimulated to participate in politics on the basis of considerations of competing programs—an ideal which is nowhere achieved fully, of course—party activity in Turkey has made important contributions to national development. At least some formal connection has now been established between local, nonprogrammatic political disputes and the larger national picture with which the national parties are primarily occupied. Further, in Turkish election campaigns the main focus is in fact on issues of national party programs and the effectiveness of national leaders. In part, this is a result of the separation of national elections from local ones. Also important, however, is the overwhelmingly dominant role of the national government in so many areas of public policy (an element further discussed in chapter 8) and national predominance in campaigns by virtue of the fact that virtually all preparation of compaign materials, programs, etc., is done by the national organizations, on which the poorly equipped province and local branches become all but totally dependent. As a result, party leaders who are spokesmen for factions or local issues in one context, in fact become representatives of national, program-oriented organizations in another.

Turkish Voting Behavior

Tables 5-1 through 5-4 and Figure 5-1 present voting data for the eight elections of the multiparty period. They show a number of significant nationwide and regional trends which reflect the dynamics of Turkish politics in terms of the interrelationships between "traditional" and "modern" traits and attitudes in Turkey's body politic.

Participation

Voting participation (Table 5-1) dropped sharply during the 1960s from its initial levels of the 1950s, but began rising again in the 1970s, and at an increasing rate. While there are some differences regionally, the small size of the variations from the national average is a most striking feature. There are several likely explanations:

1. Certainly the attraction of elections as a "novel" phenomenon has passed. Some observers also suggest that too frequent elections (considering national and local ones together) may be a factor. There also seems to be some association between turnout and the excitement of a particular election or the degree to which its outcome is seen as being undecided. The increases in turnout over the previous election which took place in 1961 and 1977 are cases in point, whereas in 1957, 1965, and 1969 the results appeared all but predictable before the voting took place.

2. That voting in the eastern regions has tended to be slightly higher than in the country as a whole in the most recent elections may likely be, as Özbudun has hypothesized, an effect of the fact that voting there is a less autonomous and therefore a more public and community act than in urban areas and more developed regions, and also that in the eastern areas voting is more under the watchful eye of local notables (1976:133 ff.). It may also be that voting is to a greater degree the chief form of political participation for the residents of these regions.

3. For the more developed areas and the cities, the reverse may hold true. In the urban areas there is a great deal of interest in politics, as well as dependence on government for many services, but many of the relations between people and government continue to be carried on through factional patron-client relationships and through local associations and groups. It is likely that alternative forms of participation are thought to be more effective by residents of the middle-class areas, and also that *gecekondu* dwellers tend to remain more similar to rural residents (and therefore to have higher voting rates), at least for the early years of their residence.

There seems, in short, to be a decidedly pragmatic, instrumental flavor to much Turkish voting, and that once it is shown that political participation may bring concrete results to party adherents, the electorate can indeed be mobilized.

TABLE 5-1

Regional variations in voter turn-out

(Percent of eligible voters)

Year	1950	1954	1957	1961	1965	1969	1973	1977	Change 1950– 1977
National voting turn-out	89.3	88.6	76.6	81.4	71.3	64.3	66.8	72.4	−16.9
Region	*Variations from national average*								
Marmara	−2.1	−3.8	−4.7	−1.8	−1.6	−5.7	−3.4	−5.0	−19.8
Aegean	+.2	+ .3	+3.4	+1.7	−.2	− .7	−1.6	+7.0	−10.1
Mediterranean	− .2	+2.5	+ .3	+1.1	+ .0	+1.7	+ .9	−1.0	−17.7
North Central	+1.8	+ .6	− .2	+1.5	+ .8	− .3	− .8	+ .9	−17.8
South Central	+ .2	− .2	− .9	+ .1	− .6	−3.2	−3.4	−2.5	−19.6
Black Sea	+ .2	−1.3	− .4	− .8	+1.4	+1.5	−1.6	−2.6	−19.7
East Central	+1.6	+3.3	+3.4	+ .2	− .2	+3.5	+1.9	+1.7	−16.8
North East	−1.3	+1.2	+1.6	− .9	+ .5	+3.4	+2.4	+3.3	−12.3
South East	−1.0	+ .9	− .8	−3.0	− .5	−7.2	+4.9	+1.9	−14.0

SOURCES: Özbudun 1976; Özbudun and Tachau 1975; DIE #817.

Preferences

The general patterns of preferences show some striking consistencies over the years and among regions. (This is not to denigrate the importance of changes, which will be discussed in a moment and which may also signify significant trends.)

1. As seen in Table 5-2, the political right continues, despite important gains by the RPP in 1977, to maintain a solid majority of votes, even though these votes may not always have a direct effect on the number of Assembly seats (the RPP was able to come close to a parliamentary majority in 1977 despite having gotten only 41 percent of the votes). It is noteworthy, however, that in the 1977 election some of the voters who abandoned the Justice party appear for the first time to have gone toward the moderate left more than to the radical right.

2. As shown in Figure 5-1, the general and regional trends of party preferences have most often been similar in both direction and in magnitude. Not only have the differences among regions in left-of-center voting (the base point for this analysis) been, with only a few exceptions, fairly small (8 to 13 percent), but it is also notable that there have been only very few instances in which the direction of change in any region has been contrary to that of the nation as a whole. The degree to which the slopes of the 1973–1977 lines are parallel is particularly striking. It is not unjustified to conclude that despite significant regional variations and local factors, there is an important degree of nationwide penetration by the major parties and by national issues.

TABLE TABLE 5-2
Left-Right and Moderate-Radical Voting
(in percent)

	Percent of Voter Turnout	Radical Left		Moderate Left			Moderate Right				Radical Right				Indep.	Summary Left		Left Total	Summary Right		Right Total
		TLP	UP	RPP	FP	DP	JP	NTP	RP	Dem P	PRPNP	NP	NSP	NAP		Rad.	Mod.		Mod.	Rad.	
1950	89.3			39.9		53.3					3.3				4.8		39.9	39.9	53.3	3.3	56.6
1954	86.6			34.8	.6	56.6					4.9				1.5		35.4	35.4	56.6	4.9	61.5
1957	76.6			40.6	3.8	47.3					7.2				0.1		44.4	44.4	47.3	7.2	54.5
1961	81.4			36.7			34.8	13.7			14.0				0.8		36.7	36.7	48.5	14.0	62.5
1965	71.3	3.0		28.7			52.9	3.7			2.2	6.2			3.2	3.0	28.7	31.7	56.6	8.4	65.0
1969	64.3	2.7	2.8	27.4			46.5	2.2	6.6			3.2			5.6	5.5	27.4	32.9	55.3	3.2	58.5
1973	66.8		1.1	33.3			29.8		5.3	11.9		0.6	11.8	3.4	2.8	1.1	33.3	34.4	47.0	15.8	62.8
1977	72.4	.1	.4	41.4			36.9		1.9	1.9			8.6	6.4	2.5	.5	41.4	41.9	40.7	15.0	44.7

SOURCE: Özbudun, 1976; Özbudun-Tachau, 1975; Weiker, 1969; DIE #817.

145

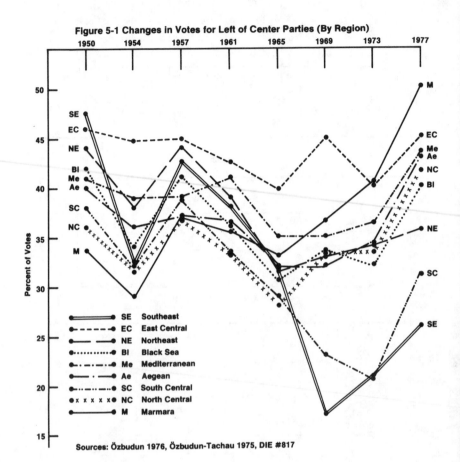

Figure 5-1 Changes in Votes for Left of Center Parties (By Region)

Sources: Özbudun 1976, Özbudun-Tachau 1975, DIE #817

Minor Parties

Minor parties and independents continue to do better in general in the less developed regions (Table 5-3) and to some extent in the *gecekondu* and lower-middle class areas of cities (see chapter 3, Table 3-3). That this is true for splinter parties and independents confirms Özbudun and Tachau's earlier hypothesis (1975:475–78) that institutionalization of parties is more signifi-cant in the developed regions, whereas less developed areas are more susceptible to appeals based on personal status and popularity. In recent elections both the Reliance and Democratic parties polled the largest portion of their votes in areas where they had candidates with strong personal followings, and in 1977 the thirteen provinces in which independents got sizable votes were all in the three least-developed regions.

That support for radical minor parties is also associated with lower levels of development is likewise important. As seen in Table 5-3, it is notable that

Minor Party and Independent Voting

	1965			1969			1973			1977			
	Total	Radical	Splinter & Indep.	Total	Radical	Splinter & Indep.	Total	Radical	Splinter & Indep.	Total	Radical	Splinter & Indep.	
All Turkey	18.3	11.4	6.9	26.1	11.7	14.4	36.9	16.9	20.0	21.7	15.5	6.3	
Marmara	14.2	11.6	2.7 L	17.2 L	10.6	6.5 LL	24.2 LL	10.6 LL	11.5 LL	12.8 LL	10.0 L	2.8 L	Most highly developed
Aegean	8.4 LL	7.0 L	1.5 L	13.4 LL	6.9 L	6.4 LL	24.6 LL	7.7 LL	15.6 L	10.1 LL	6.8 L	3.3 L	
Mediterranean	12.0 L	8.5 L	3.6 L	27.5	12.0	15.5	38.6	15.8	20.7	20.2	17.2	3.0 L	
N C	23.3 H	20.4 HH	2.9 L	25.2	17.4 H	7.8 LL	37.5	20.8 H	16.6 L	30.1 HH	26.6 HH	3.5	Intermediate level of development
SC	19.5	15.1 H	4.4	28.5	10.8	17.7 H	56.5 HH	22.4 H	33.4 HH	26.0	25.0 HH	1.0 L	
Black Sea	15.1	10.3	4.8	23.0	9.9	13.1	37.3	17.2	19.9	18.7	14.1	4.6	
EC	23.6 H	11.6	12.0 H	42.6 HH	22.9 HH	19.7 H	44.6 H	29.4 HH	15.3 L	31.1 H	25.4 HH	5.7	Least developed
NE	26.2 H	8.3 L	17.9 HH	25.8	11.0	14.8	46.2 H	21.5 H	24.6 HH	33.5 HH	20.9 H	12.6 HH	
SE	42.4 HH	7.2 L	35.2 HH	54.0 HH	4.6 LL	49.4 HHHH	55.5 H	14.9	40.7 HHHH	50.5 HHHH	23.0 HH	27.0 HHHH	

SOURCE: Özbudun-Tachau, 1975; DIE #817.

Totals may not add to 100% due to rounding.

Radical: NSP, NAP, TLP, UP, NP. Splinters: DemP, RP, NTP, Independents.

L = 5–10% below national average; LL = 10–20% below national average; LLL = Over 20% below national average; H = 3–6% above national average; HH = 12% above national average; HHH = Over 12% above national average.

the dividing line tends to put both the least developed and the intermediate provinces into contradistinction with the most highly developed ones. (For similar findings on the basis of ten deciles of socioeconomic development and four categories combining urban and rural development in the 1973 election, see Özbudun and Tachau, 1975: Tables 7 and 8.) One must conclude that tendencies toward the moderate political views which are vital to Turkish stability and orderly modernization, seem from these data to be emerging only at a fairly advanced stage of development, so that the potential for more radical political expression of dislocation and frustration in some regions remains considerable. On the other hand, rapid urbanization and westward migration in contemporary Turkey may have positive effects in this respect in the nation as a whole.[36]

The Left

The 1977 election showed continuation of the decided shift to the moderate left in the more developed parts of the country (for a general summary of the 1977 election, see also Kili, 1978b). As seen in Table 5-4, while in 1965 the least developed regions (L) were the best vote-producers for the moderate left RPP, in 1969 and again in 1973 and 1977 this changed dramatically, so that all three of the most developed regions (D) were in the upper half of the table. The increasingly positive correlations in both 1969 and 1973 between socioeconomic levels and voting behavior has already been noted above. It is worth repeating, however, that the size of the spread between the more and the less developed regions has also been increasing, and was particularly notable in 1977, and that, similarly, the RPP vote in *gecekondu* areas of Istanbul, Ankara, and Izmir rose in all cases between 1965 and 1969 and again between 1969 and 1973, but that, at the same time, the spread between the RPP's percentage in the *gecekondu* vs. the higher class areas also grew (Özbudun-Tachau 1975:473). It is not clear without further data whether we have here a case of increased class-voting, or one of general disenchantment with the Justice party, and we also need to know a good deal more about what has been happening in voting trends within the cities recently. It is quite conceivable that the RPP is becoming a more popular alternative, and if this development is occurring on the basis of its *not* becoming more of a class party, this should again be seen as a healthy development leading away from class polarization.

Conclusions

The voting patterns discussed above indicate that major changes have occurred in the Turkish party system since the 1950s and 1960s, but that important traditional features continue to be operative. The system is more fragmented than it was earlier, as a result of the rise of radical parties on the right and the resurgence of militant and relatively radical factions within the predominant party of the left. At the same time, however, the system is still

TABLE 5-4
Regional Voting for RPP, By Levels of Development

	1950		1954		1957		1961		1965		1969		1973		1977	
Best Region	SE 47.7	L	EC 44.8	L	EC 50.2	L	EC 42.6	L	EC 35.4	L	Mar 30.8	D	Mar 40.8	D	Mar 51.1	D
	EC 46.0	L	Med 39.0	D	Med 47.1	D	Med 41.0	D	Med 31.9	D	Bl Sea 30.7	M	Med 36.6	D	Med 43.9	D
	NE 43.4	L	NE 37.8	L	NE 44.2	L	NE 39.3	L	NE 29.1	L	Med 29.3	D	EC 35.4	L	EC 43.8	L
	Bl Sea 41.9	M	Aeg 36.0	D	SE 42.7	L	SE 38.1	L	Bl Sea 29.1	M	Aeg 29.1	D	Aeg 35.0	D	Aeg 42.4	D
	Med 40.9	D	Bl Sea 33.7	M	Bl Sea 41.0	M	Aeg 36.4	D	Mar 28.0	D	EC 27.7	L	NE 32.7	L	NC 40.8	M
	Aeg 40.2	D	SE 32.6	L	SC 38.9	M	Mar 35.7	D	SE 28.7	L	NE 27.4	L	NC 32.0	M	Bl Sea 40.1	M
	SC 37.7	M	SC 32.0	M	Aeg 37.3	D	Bl Sea 35.5	M	Aeg 27.9	D	NC 26.8	M	Bl Sea 31.4	M	NE 35.1	L
	NC 36.2	M	NC 31.9	M	NC 37.0	M	SC 33.6	M	NC 26.0	M	SC 21.0	M	SE 21.4	L	SC 31.1	M
Worst Region	Mar 33.7	D	Mar 29.4	D	Mar 36.7	D	NC 33.5	M	SC 25.9	M	SE 16.1	L	SC 21.3	M	SE 25.3	L

SOURCE: Özbudun, 1976; Özbudun-Tachau 1975; DIE #817.

[a]Categories of development level: D = Developed; M = Middle; L = Least Developed.

149

primarily a two-party one, and its dominant elements are essentially moderate. In part this is due to the fact that the issues which most concern the voters have become increasingly pragmatic and material rather than social and ideological. Although leaders of many of the parties are speaking in distinctly more ideological terms, they have apparently not as yet succeeded in similarly polarizing the electorate as a whole. On the whole, these developments give considerable cause for optimism about the future. (For a generally similar description but a rather less optimistic conclusion, see Sayari, 1978).

It is clear from the 1977 election that the two major parties remain viable, that both have considerable assets, and that both maintain the potential for drawing votes from a wide spectrum of social groups. It is also clear, however, that Turkish voters are continuing to become increasingly discerning, so that while the prospects for the moderate center in general are good, the prospects for the individual parties within it should not be taken for granted by any political leaders. The likelihood is that voter approval will continue to alternate between the large, moderate parties. If there is a danger of large-scale splintering, it probably comes more from within the major parties than from outside. The failure of either major party to obtain a solid majority in the 1970s has served to heighten the enmity between them and to stimulate militant rhetoric by their partisans. Many observers feel that the most important need is that one of the parties (some say that it almost does not matter which one) should emerge from the next election with sufficient strength to govern effectively. Should that happen, few think the radical minor parties would long survive with any significant strength. The history of Turkish electoral behavior indicates that if the majority parties perform well and hold to a reasonably moderate position on social issues, these "center parties" will continue to prosper. If the major parties veer from their moderate positions, the lessons of recent Turkish history may prove to have been poorly learned.

It is also clear that party activity in Turkey has made important contributions to national integration, to nonelite participation in national decision-making, and to articulation of the major issues of societal concern. It is further apparent that the nature of party activity and the party system itself have been as much shaped by modernization as modernization has been shaped by politics. Present political leaders now have the opportunity to fashion programs and strategies which can enhance moderation in politics and help resolve the numerous and often contradictory problems and pressures with which the Turkish polity is faced in areas such as economic growth, social values, and distribution of power. One can at least be cautiously hopeful that the legacy of political moderation from the Republic's first half-century, particularly through the presence of two major interest-aggregating parties competing for power, will not be squandered in the Republic's second fifty years.

SIX

Socialization and Integration: Education, Communications, and the Arts

One of the central phenomena of modernization is rapidly increasing national integration not only in the economic and political areas, but in the cultural sphere as well. One of the chief effects of cultural modernization is the refocusing of the horizons of large numbers of people so that they become psychological and intellectual participants in the life of the nation as a whole, as well as economic and political actors.[1] Among the major avenues for nationalization of a society's culture are the education system, communications, and the arts. Integration occurs as a result of deliberate efforts by national leaders toward this end and as a general byproduct of the spread of literacy, the growth of mass media, and the momentum of development in general.

Education

A nation's education system may function in several related but also separable ways as an impetus to modernization. It fosters the acquisition of needed skills, including literacy, skill in mathematics, general academic knowledge, and vocational training. It acculturates students by encouraging concepts such as critical thinking, innovation, initiative, and scientific reasoning. It widens intellectual and social horizons and thus helps focus attention away from parochial concerns and toward identification with the state as the embodiment of national pride and progress. The Turkish Republic's education system has been used to serve all these modernizing functions.

The education system which the Turkish Republic inherited was extremely inadequate in both quantity and quality. In 1923 there were officially 4,894 secular elementary schools and 10,238 teachers serving some 342,000 pupils in a total population (1927 census) of about 13 million. In actuality, there were probably considerably fewer (Başgöz and Wilson, 1968:39 and Appendix, and DIE #683). Literacy was 17.6 percent for males and 4.8 percent for females (Ibid.). Almost all the schools were in urban areas, and most were of poor quality, even though some efforts at educational reform had been taking place after the Tanzimat period. During the nineteenth century a small number of high-quality secondary and higher schools had been established, mostly in Istanbul, including some military schools and several foreign-run lycees, such as Galatasaray and the American Protestant Robert College, both of which produced many of those who were to become Republican Turkey's important leaders (Lewis 1961:120).

In establishing modern education for the Republic, Turkish political and educational leaders were immediately faced with a number of major policy choices. There was no doubt that first priority had to be the nationalization and secularization of education, and control of all schools was transferred to the government in 1924.[2] There was also agreement that the overall educational goal would be universal academic education, but that it would contain a strong practical component as well, particularly for villagers.[3] A number of Turkish education theorists, such as Ismail Hakkı Baltacıoğlu, stressed the importance of connections between classrooms and practical life (Başgöz & Wilson, 1968:60 ff.). A number of foreign consultants on education were brought in, including John Dewey who visited Turkey in 1924 and who presented a long series of recommendations including planning for schools to be centers of community activity as well as pedagogic institutions. (On this and later reports see Ibid.:63 ff.)

The 1920s were spent largely in gearing up an administrative system, devising curricula, and preparing textbooks. Initial expansion took place mostly in the cities and towns, where at least some educational facilities already existed and where, it was felt, expansion of secondary education could more quickly achieve one of the Republic's chief goals: the development of a modernizing leadership cadre (Erder, 1973:8–9). Thus while the number of primary school students increased 43 percent between 1923 and 1930, those in orta (middle) schools and lycees grew almost four-fold (see Table 6-1).

This development was followed in the late 1920s and in the 1930s by what has been called a period of "educational vitality" (Başgöz and Wilson, 1968:chapter 6). While quantitative progress continued to be rather slow because of financial and personnel stringencies, important foundations were laid for future expansion. Among notable innovational efforts was an experimental Village Teachers' School in 1925–1928, designed to train teachers qualified in both academic and "practical" subjects. This became a forerunner of a much larger venture in 1940, when a network of Village Institutes was set up in rural areas for the specific purpose of training students drawn directly from the villages themselves, and to make them a combination of village teachers and "multipurpose development agents" (Erder, 1973:10 and Başgöz and Wilson, 1968:58,133). The Village Institutes produced a corps of at least 25,000 effective and strongly motivated teachers before they were closed in 1954 in favor of regular teacher-training colleges.[4] Another early experiment was the training of recently discharged noncommissioned officers, whose leadership qualities were con-

TABLE 6-1
Education

Year	Public Primary				Orta (Middle)				Lycee				Secondary Voc-Tech	
	Number of schools	% incr.	Number of students	% incr.	Number of schools	% incr.	Number of students	% incr.	Number of schools	% incr.	Number of students	% incr.	Number of students	% incr.
1923	4,333		342,000		72		5,905		23		1,241		6,547	
1930 6,598	6,598	35	489,000	72	82	14	25,398	330	22	–5	5,099	459	8,150	24
1940 Total	9,418	43	905,000	85	34	285	92,308	263	82	372	24,862	336	14,310	76
Villages	8,037		534,000											
Cities	1,381		371,000											
1950 Total	17,106	82	1,591,000	76	381	62	65,168	–30	88	7	22,169	–11	55,522	288
Villages	15,505	93	1,134,000	112										
Cities	1,601	10	457,000	23										
1960 Total	21,429	25	2,515,000	58	715	88	254,966	291	194	120	75,632	241	98,010	77
Villages	19,157	24	1,563,000	38										
Cities	2,272	42	951,000	108										
1970 Total	37,171	73	4,907,000	95	1,629	128	708,950	175	518	167	253,742	235	217,332	117
Villages	33,729	76	3,177,000	117										
Cities	3,442	51	1,730,000	82										
1974–5 Total	41,060	10.4	5,354,593	9.1	2,480	52	946,000	33	768	48	339,000	34	312,000	44
Villages	37,310	10.6	3,273,158	3.0										
Cities	3,750	8.9	2,081,435	20.3										
1977–8 Total	43,116	5.0	5,432,355	1.5	3,305	33	1,105,189	17	979	27	454,402	34	469,000	50
Villages	39,001	4.5	3,124,847	–4.5										
Cities	4,115	9.7	2,307,508	10.9										

SOURCE: DIE #676, 683, 825, 850, 890.

sidered to have already been proven. Over 8,000 of these men provided schooling for over 200,000 villagers during the peak year of the use of these *eğitmenleri* in the mid-1940s. Without them many more villagers would have been without any teachers at all (Başgöz and Wilson, 1968:142–3 and DIE #676).[5]

Attention to economic development during the *etatist* period of the 1930s was accompanied by increased emphasis on vocational-technical education and adult education. A number of vocational schools were opened, though again financial restrictions and shortages of teachers impeded these efforts. The adoption of the Latin alphabet for the Turkish language in 1928 impelled the opening of "Nation Schools" for adults, from which close to 600,000 persons graduated in the peak year of 1928–1929, and over 1,350,000 altogether, although one study found that these schools seemed to have lost their energy and fervor in only a few years (Ibid.:119–20, 175–82). In part, the gap was filled by the *Halkevleri* and by some government schools and private efforts, which together awarded nearly one and three quarter million literacy certificates between 1929 and 1950 (Weiker, 1973:175n5. Adult education has always fallen far short of its goals, however. As shown in Table 6-2, literacy even after a half-century of the Republic remains far below what is needed). Also among the more dramatic education reforms of the 1930s was the wholesale reorganization of Istanbul University, which had been severely criticized by foreign consultants for antiquated teaching, almost total disinterest in scientific research, and resistance to the incorporation of many modern subjects into its curricula. A large percentage of the faculty was dismissed, and replaced in part by German professors available as refugees from the Nazis (see Fermi, 1968). A new University of Ankara was also established.

TABLE 6-2

Literacy

(percent of population 6 years of age and older)

	Total	Male	Female	Urban	Rural
1935	20.4	31.0	10.5		
(7 years & older)					
1940					
1945	30.2	43.7	16.8		
(7 years & older)					
1950	32.4	45.3	19.4		
(5 years & older)					
1955	40.9	55.8	25.5		
1960	39.5	53.6	24.8		
1965	48.7	64.0	32.8	59.1	39.5
1970	54.7	69.0	40.0	82.6	52.8
1975	61.7[a]	74.8[a]	48.1[a]		

Source: DIE, #683, 825.

[a]Estimate—1975 Census 1% sampling results.

Greater quantitative increases took place after World War II with the beginning of rapid urbanization, economic growth, and "the realization of the now more visible links between education and the opportunities for urban modern sector employment" (Erder, 1973:11). During the 1950s, more than a million children were added to the primary school rosters, almost 2½ million more during the 1960s, and 1.6 million more by 1977. Enrollment in secondary schools during the multiparty period has grown almost twenty-fold. This growth was often characterized, however, by a dearth of planning. In the words of one analyst, "Turkey . . . entered the stage where the expansion of education was determined by social demand" (Ibid.). Among the consequences of all this was that vocational secondary enrollment grew far more slowly than did enrollment in conventional academic middle schools and lycees, and that the rate of increase in village primary education was considerably slower than in the cities. (It should be added, however, that there is as much reason to assure all city children of primary education as there is to assure it to village children. It is also true that, in financial and administrative terms, it is possible to achieve increases in urban education with greater ease than in rural areas. That Turkish education has sometimes taken the path of least resistance should not necessarily be interpreted as a negative observation.[6])

Despite many achievements, however, there is virtually no observer, Turkish or foreign, who has much praise for the educational system as a whole. Karpat has described it as "one of the most obsolete, uncreative and unproductive institutions of Turkey" (1973:79). Necat Erder, former chief of the Social Planning Division of the SPO, has asserted that Turkey "faces an educational crisis" with a system that is "unresponsive to economic needs, highly wasteful, and elitist" (1973:14–15). Edwin Cohn listed the education system among the "major constraints" to Turkish development, and gave numerous examples (1970:99–115). Criticisms of education stated in the second, third and fourth five-year plans are extensive, running the full range from technical to sociopolitical and from quantitative to qualitative shortcomings. In general, such criticisms can be grouped into three major problem areas of (1) distribution and priorities, (2) quality and (3) social and political content.

Distribution and Priorities

The number of students in primary schools reached close to the Republic's total number of children aged six to ten by 1975, though the scholarization rate reported by the SPO for 1977–1978 was only 87.5 percent because many of the students were repeaters or above normal primary school age. In 1975 some 3,116 villages were reported to be without schools, and the Fourth Plan estimated that one million primary school age children (urban as well as rural) were "without means to become literate" (1978:par. 454). The goal is for 100 percent scholarization by 1983–1984. Given the continuing serious shortages of funds and personnel, it seems doubtful this goal will be

TABLE 6-3

Scholarization

	Primary	Middle	Lycee	Number of Boys per Girl, Primary Schools
1925–26				3.4
1930–31				2.6
1935–36	34	6.3	3.3	1.9
1940–41	39	9.1	4.0	2.2
1945–6	57	6.7	4.2	1.8
1950–51	69	6.5	3.7	1.7
1955–56	74	12.1	4.9	1.7
1960–61	81	17.7	10.6	1.7
1965–66	94	21.6	12.9	1.5
1970–71[a]	86	31.8	10.0	
1975–76[a]	90	33.3	12.4	
1977–78	87.5	39.7	14.6	

SOURCE: 1925–66 Cohn, 1970: 181-3; 1970–71 and 1975–6, DIE #825; 1977–78, 4th Five-Year Plan ¶ 454.

[a]My calculations. Primary: percent of students minus 10 percent allowance for students above normal primary age, divided by percent of children aged 6–10. Middle: percent of students as percent of children aged 11–13. Lycee: same with ages 14–16.

attained, though there are high hopes that quicker progress can be made through implementation of a plan for "central villages" *(köy-kent)* in which facilities for several small settlements will be concentrated in a central locality.

There has also been a serious shortfall in an area extremely important to the long-term effects of education in the Republic (and one which the SPO identifies as critical for increasing the supply of skilled labor; 1978b:pars. 74–5): continuation into secondary schools. As shown in chapter 2, although such continuance has been steadily increasing, in 1973–1974 only slightly more than half the graduates of five-year elementary schools went on to *any* kind of secondary education. The SPO estimate also reflects a great disparity in distribution, in that whereas in recent years about 75 percent of the graduates of urban primary schools went on to middle school, opportunities for continued education (including vocational-technical) were available to only a quarter of those in rural areas (1978b:par. 455). The smaller dropout rates after middle school have been discussed in chapter 2. While a considerable part of the shortfalls is undoubtedly due to economic conditions (children who must work to supplement their family income) and in some part to social circumstances (reluctance to educate girls beyond primary school continues in many places, even though this reluctance has in general dropped sharply), it is related as well to a severe teacher shortage at the middle school level. The number of middle schools increased by 51 percent during the third plan period but enrollment increased only by 18.3 percent, a development ascribed by the SPO to an "inclination to a too quick and a planless school-opening" (1978b:pa. 458).

It is significant, too, that the great majority of those who do continue past primary school, including those students who do so in rural areas, go into *academic* middle schools. This is certainly to the long-run benefit both of the students and of the country as a whole, but the obverse result is evident in the fact that in almost every category of vocational-technical education, not only were the goals of the development plans not attained, but as has been pointed out, even if they had been, this would not have been sufficient to meet manpower needs (for example, SPO 1973:745 ff. See also Szyliowicz, 1973:334 ff., and Robinson, 1967).Some of the shortcoming is ameliorated by the fact that after middle school the opportunities for continuing in an academic lycee are not available to all the middle school graduates who are intent on continuing their education. Consequently, middle-school graduates are increasingly enrolling in lycee-level vocational-technical schools. A sizable number of middle school graduates are apparently intent on returning to academic schools even after interruption of their education, however (the number of new enrollees in lycee-level schools in 1973–1974 was greater than the number of middle-school graduates the previous year!) and the SPO has asserted that, in consequence, virtually all lycees are understaffed and underequipped, with a consequent sharp drop in their quality (1978b:pars. 459–60).

Pressure is even greater at the college level. In 1978 some 378,000 students took the entrance examination for 70,000 places in the universities, including 196,000 who were graduates of lycee-level schools in earlier years and who had probably been taking the exams year after year for some time.[7] Demonstrations by students who could not be accommodated have been regular occurrences in recent years. There are several reasons for this pressure. One is simply the fact that the number of lycee graduates has risen so rapidly. Another, as discussed in chapter 2, is that most students who have crossed the line of post-primary education see themselves as having taken the first step, but *only* the first step, toward middle-class status. Continuation into higher education is considered a natural progression toward that goal, virtually a right. A third is structural, in that only university graduates can become reserve officers when they do their military service, and civil service personnel laws base job classifications and promotion heavily on categories of completion of formal education: primary, middle, or higher. (For a discussion of the latter point see the article by Nuri Tortop in *Milliyet,* April 8, 1974, p. 2.)

There have been several responses to pressures for college-level education. University enrollments were increased by about 40 percent between 1969 and 1976–1977 (from about 69,000 to about 98,000), and since 1973, ten new universities have been authorized, of which nine are operating with one or more faculties.[8] Another response has been the rapid expansion of the Higher Schools and Academies *(Yüksek Okullar),* which enrolled 132,000 in 1976–1977.[9] They do not as yet have the quality or the prestige of the universities, and while pressure to grant them equal status has been resisted to date, it may not be possible to delay such a step much longer.[10] Finally, there has been inauguration of correspondence courses *(Yaygin Eğitim)*. They began with an enrollment of some 47,000 students in 1974–1975, but they quickly became plagued with extremely low success and continuation rates and seem to hold little promise for long-term effectiveness in their present form.[11]

In addition to problems of quantity, there are problems of balance. Distribution of students in higher education among specific fields has been discussed in chapter 2, and regional imbalances in distribution will be discussed in chapter 8. In addition there is an important imbalance in levels of vocational-technical skills. The SPO has noted that there is a major deficiency in the number of support personnel for high-level professionals—laboratory technicians and agricultural technicians, for example (1973:761 ff. and 1978b:par. 75. One observer has noted that in some fields, professionals were found to outnumber subprofessionals by almost two to one. Cohn, 1970:103).

Educational Quality and Efficiency

A useful measure is what may be called educational productivity. In addition to the dropout rate being high, there is also a very high rate of failure to progress through the system in the normal time. At the primary level, the SPO has estimated that during the period 1963–1973 an average of only about 289 out of each thousand primary school students graduated five years after they had first enrolled, and notes that the pass rates for primary school students dropped steadily between 1965–1966 and 1969–1970, from 92.9 percent to 82.6 percent in cities, and from 93.0 percent to 75.5 percent in villages (1973:pars. 1508–9). There are various reasons for this. Some are byproducts of structural factors: for example, when there is an increasing proportion of students from the poorest groups there is also an increasing number who must work (seasonally if not continually) to supplement family incomes. In addition, study facilities may also be in short supply. Other factors are, at least in part, more amenable to policy changes. For example, double and triple sessions in most urban primary schools[12] result in pupils being given a great percentage of their work in the form of homework, for which the necessary supervision (both in terms of discipline and of academic help) is seldom available to lower-class children. In villages, although most observers agree that the connection between education and economic and social gains is now clearly recognized, in practice that connection is often more apparent than real. The centrally set curricula frequently lack relevance to village economic and social concerns[13] (see Kazamias, 1966:141 ff.; Szyliowicz, 1973:354; SPO, 1969:177–80).

At the secondary level, though the dropout rate is lower, educational productivity appears little better. In 1971 only some 56 percent of male students and 60 percent of females were successful in graduating on time from middle school, 52 percent and 62 percent respectively from lycee (DIE #676:23). Statistics for higher education are spotty, but all indicate low productivity. Szyliowicz found that, in 1958 at the Law Faculty of Ankara University, only some 8 percent completed their course of study within five years, and that even in the elite Political Science Faculty, the percentage going through without delay dropped from more than 75 percent in 1955 to less than half in 1964 (1973:342). On the average, between 1965–1966 and 1975–1976 about 11 to 14 percent of students enrolled in Turkish higher education graduated each year (Table 6-4) and a high percentage of those were successful only by dint of taking examinations several times.[14] The causes of low pass rates at the post-primary levels are less in socioeconomic factors (some selectivity has already taken place) and correspondingly more in structural ones, for example that students were required (until recently) to repeat the entire year even if they had failed in only a small number of subjects. In addition, many students who probably are unqualified to be in higher schools stay there nonetheless, because student status qualifies them for reduced charges for public transportation, movies, etc., as well as, of course, for better jobs merely by virtue of having obtained a diploma.

The training of students who do complete their formal education proves all too often to have been inadequate as well. This is most clearly seen in two areas, literacy and vocational-technical training. There appears to be a high degree of lapse in functional literacy in Turkish villages, a lapse not completely reflected in official figures because the official definition of literacy is set at a very low level (often simply the ability to read and write the most elementary words and phrases). Those villagers who are literate often lack incentives to maintain literary skills. Available materials are scant and likely to be low level. Reading is not normally part of village leisure patterns. In recent years, however, the availability of newspapers in villages has increased substantially, a development which is likely to continue.

In the vocational-technical areas, the SPO notes the inadequacy of graduates' skills in almost every branch. For example, it criticizes the failure of the schools to train qualified management employees and technical experts for the State Economic Enterprises (1978b:par. 93). In part this failure is due to poor facilities, a problem which plagues academic secondary schools as well, particularly in the science areas. In 1971–1972 literature, geography, history, and methematics courses in Turkish lycees had teacher-student ratios of about 1 to 34, but for physics the ratio was 1 to 75, and for chemistry, 1 to 184 (SPO 1973:Table 570). Howard Reed has pointed out a similar situation in higher education. Since in the Universities only professors and docents are allowed by law to teach regularly, many junior faculty can teach only with special permission, which is only seldom sought and granted, "the ratio of students to regular, full-time teachers in 1970–71 was 51:1 instead of the alleged ratio of 18:1 in official figures in which all academic staff were considered to be teaching" (1975:210). Equipment shortages also abound.

There has also been what might be called a "technology lag," the failure of

TABLE 6-4
Higher Education

	Number of students		% in Higher School	Total	% Girls	Number Graduates	% graduates of Total Enrollment	No. Lycee Graduates Previous Year
	Universities	Higher Schools						
1942–3	12,888	3,057	21.2	15,945	21.2	1,485	9.3	4,857
1950–1	19,871	4,944	19.6	24,815	19.6	3,107	12.5	5,645
1955–6	29,076	7,922	21.4	36,998	16.8	3,124	8.4	9,056
1960–1	44,461	20,836	31.9	65,297	19.9	6,025	9.2	10,913
1965–6	55,561	41,748	42.9	97,309	20.9	10,611	10.9	23,227
1970–1	76,739	93,054	54.8	169,793	18.9	22,856	13.5	40,808
1975–6	93,706	138,384	59.6	232,090	23.0	(9,965 Univ.) (20,857 H.S.)	(10.6)	80,000[a]
1977–8	108,216	191,339	63.9	299,555	24.9		(10.9)	

SOURCE: DIE, #676, 683, 850.

[a]Preliminary estimate.

teachers to update their own skills and standards in the face of the rapidly increasing complexity of today's industrial needs. Both teachers and the curricula have been described as showing strong tendencies to consider levels of expertise which were satisfactory at the time they were being prepared, as good enough still. A final cause is the inclination of teachers not to impose very strict standards on their students, this being particularly visible in areas such as training for service occupations like commerce, and, perhaps more seriously, health (SPO 1973:pars. 1564–70).

It is likely that pressures for improvement in these aspects of education will have to come mostly from outside the education system itself—for example, from the need for improved productivity and quality in Turkish industry as competition increases with further integration into the European Common Market; from the increasingly stringent demands of businesses which must remain competitive in today's market; or from public dissatisfaction with the quality of health services. As with many other aspects of Turkish modernization discussed in this study, the development process itself is likely to provide the main stimuli to change. The process may be painful to many in the educational "establishment" however.

The Education System and Direct Socialization

Who gets to school, and what happens to them after they leave in terms of their success in finding employment, are important matters in a developing society, to be sure. But equally vital is what happens to values and attitudes during the educational process. Research on political and general socialization leaves no doubt that schools are extremely important agencies for the inculcation of values and attitudes as well as specific knowledge and skills. This is particularly important in a society such as Turkey's, where the confrontation of "tradition" and "modernity" in the political and social spheres is intense.

Education under the Republic has always had a strong political flavor. From the very beginning of the Ataturk period the curricula at all levels contained required study of Turkish history. As time progressed Turkish leaders felt that large doses of nationalism and patriotism were required in the schools to sustain the principles of the revolution. This kind of indoctrination continues today, though with less intensity now that a sense of Turkish nationalism and pride in the nation has been fully established. On the other hand, there is little evidence during the multiparty period of attempts on the part of education officials directly to propagate partisan political opinions through school curricula, although some attempts were made to politicize students through subsidizing student organizations which were sympathetic to the views of the party in power (see Szyliowicz, 1972). The fact that many teachers are highly politicized (the major teachers' association, TÖB-DER, is quite radical and militant) is relevant. We do not know, however, to what degree association members deliberately indoctrinate students, assuming they do so at all.

A more important matter is indirect politicization of education through determination of what general values should be stressed. Some aspects of the controversy are specific, such as whether religion and "morality" should be taught. But the more crucial point is in the realm of what we might call the cultural and social "tone" of education. Does it encourage or discourage innovation and criticism?[15] In reference to this aspect of education, the Turkish system is profoundly conservative. This is most directly manifested in its traditional teaching methods, which emphasize rote learning and memorization (even at the higher levels) and give little attention to creativity and original thinking.[16] There is a strong emphasis on discipline at all levels, enforced structurally by control from the central Ministry of Education (for details, see Szyliowicz, 1973:362), which constantly monitors teachers' strict adherence to centrally prescribed lesson plans and methods. Disciplining teachers is frequently a basis for their assignment, transfer, or lack of promotion. The Ministry of Education is considered to be one of the worst bureaucratic units in a generally stultifying civil bureaucracy.

There are few pressures for change. Turkish students have protested frequently for better facilities and more lenient conditions, but few, if any, have joined in the protests of more "radical" teachers for more "creative" teaching, perhaps understandably because it is certainly easier for students if they are responsible for only a limited and clearly designated body of factual material than it is to have to make the more strenuous efforts of criticism and analysis.[17] Nor is there evidence that demand for reform in the "tone" of education has come from other segments of the society, such as parents. Social conservatism continues to permeate most elements of Turkish society. Whether pressure for change will arise from groups such as the employers of graduates in the sciences remains to be seen. (As noted in chapter 2, many members of groups which one might expect to value innovation, such as industrialists, fail to exhibit that they do so very strongly.) It seems clear, at least for the moment, that the majority of the Turkish public is unprepared to forego what it believes to be the conservative social benefits of the education system by altering what still a relatively few critics (in proportion to Turkish society as a whole) say is a stultifying educational environment which will soon evidence serious consequences for future development. That reform in the social and cultural tone of education is needed is something which the dissenters have still to demonstrate to the Turkish public. It may not be an easy task.

Conclusions

There can be no doubt that the Turkish education system has achieved a great deal in its contributions to Turkey's modernization and development. If the above analysis seems to give more attention to the system's shortcomings, it is because the question of how well the first half-century has prepared the Turkish Republic for its second one is a central focus of this study, and the educational system remains caught in a web of situational factors—financial, political, and social—which impede its ability to give optimum future service to the Turkish nation. The educational system in Turkey today poses a familiar problem for its leaders: Turkish society in general desires that its educational system be such as to reflect conservative values in the interests of social and political stability. Yet that same society also wants development and modernization to continue, and toward these ends encouragement of innovation and criticism is necessary. How this paradox is unraveled is to be watched with interest.

Communications and Modernization

How a nation's communication system is used can both directly and indirectly influence social change. Information flows both downward and upward, and its movement in both directions is required to enable people to participate more effectively in the political, community, and economic life of the nation. Downward communication can be used for direct indoctrination and propaganda, as was done by Ataturk during the single-party period in the cause of his revolution. Indirectly, it can help increase national identification among the general population, nurture new lifestyles, and provide technical and vocational information for furthering the modernization process. The upward flow of information from followers to leaders is as important as the downward flow, for it encompasses the aspirations and demands of the populace, matters which leaders of any nation—particularly leaders of a developing one—can ignore only at their peril.

Communications systems are not isolated from other developments in the society. They act upon these developments and are in turn acted upon by them, with sometimes paradoxical effects. For example, increased information can bring about tolerance of the needs and awareness of the rights of others. This widening of horizons can also, however, simultaneously lead to demand for greater and faster satisfactions than the economy can supply, to the detriment of such things as accumulation of funds for long-term investment. To take another illustration, increased communication may sharpen awareness of inequalities and increase dissatisfaction which in turn may lead either to greater militancy or to greater efforts at self-development. We shall take as our basic assumption that communications systems can best serve democracy and modernity by providing opportunities and incentives for understanding political, social, and economic problems, and for pursuing enlightened self-interest to the general good of the nation.

The Mass Media

The mass media began to become instruments of change in the nineteenth century, when a group of nationalist publicists emerged from among the so-called Young Ottomans. The wider circulation of their newspapers and periodicals enabled people other than the ruling elites to become informed on public affairs, and through patriotic theatrical presentations and other forms of literary propaganda they helped fuel the revolutionary movements which were to come to fruition in 1908 and thereafter. Although important in the capital and a few other large cities, their efforts were limited in the nation as a whole by many factors, including the low rate of literacy among the population (on their activities, see Mardin, 1962; Karpat, 1964: 257-67; Lewis, 1961: passim). At their height (around 1872, before the reimposition of repressive rule by Abdulhamid, which lasted until 1908) "the total number of Turkish newspapers and periodicals . . . amounted to only nine, while foreign language journals numbered thirty" (Karpat, 1964:262). The approximately twenty-four papers published in the provinces in 1874 played but a very small role as instruments of change. They merely "expressed the townsmen's practical outlook and discussed agriculture and trade, thereby incurring the scorn of the journals in Istanbul." Average circulation of the Istanbul papers was a few thousand. During the Young Turk period from 1908 to about 1912, the press expanded rapidly. In 1911 there were 9 Turkish dailies in Istanbul, 113 Turkish newspapers in the provinces, and some 32 magazines in Istanbul. The newspapers were "profoundly political," and their popularity rose accordingly, one opposition paper reaching a circulation of 26,000 around 1909 and as high as 50,000 on special occasions, such as the Italian war, though its circulation declined thereafter. Newspapers also began to reach the urban lower classes about this time (Ibid.: 262-68).

From the very beginning of the Republic, "Mustafa Kemal used all communications media intensively to win over the public. 'Indoctrination and information,' in his view, 'was very important, as important as the question of the army, and even more important than the army.' " Oral communication was also widely used, as well as such things as "pamphlets and brochures . . . including epics in the folk style glorifying the movement and Mustafa Kemal," which were distributed "to be read to the public in towns and villages" (Karpat, 1964: 270). The government began publishing its own newspaper, *Hakimiyet-i Milliye* or National Sovereignty, as early as 1919. A number of factors limited the mass media's political role, however. One was the continuing low literacy rate, which among other things meant that interpretation of printed materials was often filtered through local leaders before it got to ordinary villagers. (For an even later example of this kind of situation, see Lerner, 1958: chapter 1.) Another limiting factor was technical. The provinces in most instances did not have capacity for producing more than the most rudimentary newspapers. Urban newspapers had very poor distribution systems. Radio was only in its infancy. In addition, the press, not very inclined toward analysis and criticism in any case, lacked autonomy. The emergence of a number of newspapers strongly supporting the Free party in 1930 led the following year to a stringent press law which was designed, if not to forbid all criticism, at least to give strong inducement to both the newspapers and to individual journalists to emphasize their "educational" function (Weiker, 1973: 278-82; Karpat, 1964: 273). Government-sponsored communications activities included at least fifty-five periodicals published by the *Halkevleri,* containing historical, sociological, and practical articles as well as interpretations of the reforms. They also provided opportunities for budding local writers, and helped popularize the new Latin script. Another attempt at mass communication was a series of special "wall newspapers" prepared for villagers and distributed as widely as possible (Karpat, 1964: 274-76).

The situation changed, of course, with the multiparty period. The number of newspapers and periodicals jumped between 1945 and 1950 from 154 to 477, rose to 787 by 1955, and continued to rise rapidly until 1970, after which the number of publications leveled off, although their circulation has continued to increase. The Directorate of Press and Publications estimated that daily circulation of Turkish newspapers at the end of 1978 was about 2½ million (information supplied by Dr. Oya Tokgöz of the Basın ve Yayın Okulu of Ankara University). The number of books published has also increased steadily, though since 1973 there has been some decrease due to the high price of paper (newspapers and periodicals have been able to purchase paper at reduced prices; SPO, 1978b: par. 473). The number of radios has increased phenomenally, and television sets even more so since transmissions began in 1972. Though there are the usual regional variations (see chapter 8) the number of Turks who do not have frequent access to at least one element of the mass media has declined very markedly.

Newspapers and Periodicals

The major Istanbul dailies are overwhelmingly dominant throughout most of the nation.[18] For the last decade or so, they have been available in almost all cities and towns the same day they are published (official figures are shown in Table 6-6). The Directorate of Press and Publications estimates that the four leading Istanbul dailies account for about 75 percent of the sales of all Turkish newspapers.

Newspaper content is dominated by political and economic news, with considerable space also devoted to a variety of "human interest" features. All papers have numerous columnists, many of whom have achieved considerable prominence as trendsetters and opinion makers whose writings are widely discussed in provincial cities and towns. In addition to current events, the newspapers contain sizable cultural sections, running the full range from modern fashions to the serialization of traditional folk epics and books on Turkish history. They are also particularly attentive to the doings of "celebrities," both Turkish and foreign, and all devote at least one entire page per day to sports. Observation in both homes and public places makes it clear that all of these sections are read widely, and that the newspapers are major educational channels.

In other ways, the newspapers vary widely. The largest consistent seller over the last decade has been *Hürriyet*, written at a popular level and read by both the middle and lower-middle class. It is agreed that at least part of its appeal (as even its critics concede) is that it has succeeded in remaining an accurate mirror of the day's news. (See, for example, a summary by Metin

TABLE 6-5
Newspapers, Periodicals, Radio, Television

	Newspapers and Periodicals					Registered Radios			Television Sets		
	Total	Daily News-papers	Other News-papers	Peri-odicals	Newspaper Circulation	Total	In Cities	In Villages	Total	In Vities	In Villages
1935	349	49	78	222	149,000	29,000					
1940	281	60	63	158	338,000	78,000		(1946)			
1945	441	75	79	287	336,000	176,000		15,712			
1950		131	346		647,000	362,000		22,397			
1955		278	509			999,000					
1960		506	1,152		1,658,000 (1963)	1,341,000					
1965	1,890[a]				1,722,000	2,345,000	1,761,000	584,000			
1970	2,470[a]					3,120,000	2,072,000	1,048,000	3,146	3,146	
1973	2,331[a]					4,010,000	2,615,000	1,396,000	222,924	211,573	11,351
1975	2,362[a]					4,120,000	2,777,000	1,345,000	639,348	599,961	39,387
1976	2,413[a]					4,198,000	2,850,000	1,348,000	1,313,523	1,195,544	117,979
1977	2,352[a]					4,251,000	2,850,000	1,401,000	2,019,282	1,775,745	243,537
1978	2,256[a]	800	600		2,500,000	4,279,000	2,908,000	1,371,000	2,531,541	2,194,211	337,330

SOURCE: Karpat, 1964; Karpat, 1973; DIE, #380, 683, 710, 850, 890. For 1978: Directorate of Press and Publications, courtesy of Prof. Oya Tokgöz.

[a]Statistics after 1965 only give newspaper and periodicals as one total. Figure here is for "general" category.

TABLE 6-6
Circulation of Leading Daily Newspapers

	1968	1970	1972	1974	1976	1978	Percent increase 1978/1968
Günaydın	201,594 (1969)	272,585	264,544	434,929	465,282	581,279	288 (1969)
Hürriyet	533,081	501,319	460,111	514,780	529,208	544,516	102
Tercüman	203,601	265,510	260,306	350,272	311,568	447,503	220
Milliyet	205,832	169,830	199,731	285,859	249,348	246,386	120
Cumhuriyet	131,897	90,508	63,395	80,504	105,643	96,822	73
Yeni Asir (Izmir)	47,747	48,465	42,245	58,658	46,157	53,935	113
TOTAL	1,323,752	1,347,758	1,290,332	1,725,002	1,707,206	1,970,501	149

SOURCE: Basın ve İlan Kurumu.

167

Toker in *Yanki*, #395, 9-15 October 1978, p. 36.) Over the years it has also raised its level of sophistication along with the general rise of sophistication among the reading public. It is now increasingly read by the upper-middle class, at least in part to keep a check on what the general public is learning. On the other hand, it is easy for Turkish readers to find newspapers which serve other purposes. Two newspapers have doubled their circulation in the last decade: *Günaydın* which is little more than a sensationalist, entertainment daily, and *Tercüman*, which is frankly and openly a vehicle for the Justice party. *Milliyet* is pro-RPP, but relatively mildly so, and is by no means "ideological." It is Turkey's most intellectual and "quality" daily.[19]

Much of the future role of the future role of the Istanbul press lies in the hands of its publishers and readers. The readers have an opportunity to choose among newspapers whose degrees of partisanship and seriousness vary widely. They can "vote" their wants and needs via circulation figures. (The comparative rates of growth among newspapers shown in Table 6-6 are instructive.) Simultaneously, the great influence of the major dailies gives their publishers an opportunity to support causes for the good of the nation and to set much of the tone of Turkish public life.

The four dominant dailies are complemented by numerous smaller ones. With the exception of a few venerable ones, like the now radically leftist *Cumhuriyet*, which was long the spokesman for Ataturk and edited by Yunus Nadi, one of his closest colleagues, they more often than not appeal mostly to particular political or social groups. There are also a considerable number of fly-by-night sheets which appear whenever there is sensational news which might sell papers. The number of these appearing in the first few days after the 1960 revolution and disappearing soon thereafter, for example, was truly amazing. The Directorate of Press and Publications estimates that in addition to the eight hundred newspapers throughout the country which are eligible for official advertising,[20] the so-called "pirate" newspapers just mentioned total about six hundred.

Salutary to modernization as the growth of national newspapers has been, there are also some drawbacks. One is its effect on the growth of the provincial press. In numbers, the latter has grown very much, and there is no Turkish city (or town of any great size) which does not now have at least one daily of its own (as well as others appearing less frequently). The major provincial cities usually have several. There were 588 provincial papers being published at the beginning of 1979 outside of Istanbul, Ankara, and Izmir. Only Hakkarı province did not have its own newspaper. More than fifteen were being published in each of twenty-five provinces (figures courtesy of Dr. Tokgöz). They are often staffed by able journalists. But their role as instruments of change is small, and their inability to compete with the major Istanbul dailies is undoubtedly a major cause of their weakness. Most are not over two to four pages in size. They are burdened with old equipment, and are unable even to cover local affairs to any extensive degree. Financially they are often merely adjuncts of print shops, through which their owners are able to subsidize them. They seldom reach far beyond government offices and businesses (for a content analysis of some of them, see Weiker, 1972: 35). The transmission of local news is still mostly done by informal means.

A matter which is both a positive feature of and a limitation upon the role of newspapers is their relationship to villagers. On the positive side is the steadily growing exposure which villagers have to the press. The 1968 Village Survey reported that of literate villagers, 48 percent read a newspaper once a week or more, and when we add this to the number of illiterates who sometimes listen to a newspaper being read, the percentage "in contact with daily newspapers" rises to 59.4 percent, a significant improvement over the 1962 "in contact" rate of 48 percent. On the other hand, while wide regional disparities are not surprising given both literacy and availability as major variables, only 60 percent of the villages reported that newspapers were brought there once a week or more. It is notable that even in the "developed" areas (Marmara and Aegean) the rate was only 66.9 percent, and that 25.2 percent and 15.9 percent of literates in those two regions respectively said that they *never* read one. All signs, however, are that increased literacy and availability do have significant effects on the usefuness of newspapers as media as disseminators of information as well as political and general news, and that their potential for expansion is great.[21]

Thus it is all the mȯre unfortunate that there is so little in many of the newspapers which is of direct concern or usefulness to villagers. What practical information there is, is very much oriented to middle class and to urban interests, which given the economics of the newspaper industry is understandable, but regrettable nonetheless. There have been only few and feeble attempts since the "wall newspapers" of the 1920s to provide newspapers specifically directed to the concerns of villagers, papers which contain village-oriented "practical" information, present news in language understandable to villagers and in such a way as to be meaningful to persons who are not likely to have the time, inclination, or even the ability to follow events day by day. (Turkish news articles very seldom give background information for those who may have missed the previous day's or week's issues.) It is to be hoped that the potential from increased newspaper contacts can be taken advantage of. It is likely, however, that this will entail government financial aid, a circumstance which may bring with it its own social and political perils.

The political periodical press is not of great significance. From time to time there have been magazine-style political weeklies, but only a few have lasted more than several months.[22] The weekly or monthly format is used more extensively by radical ideological groups on both the right and left, and a few singular ones have appeared, such as the satirical *Akbaba*, which effectively threw barbs at all sides for half a century before it ceased publication in 1977. There are also a number of nonpolitical popular periodicals aimed at women or children, or using chiefly pictorial formats, and there is a very large number of professional, literary, commercial and other specialized publications.

In sum, the Turkish press is lively, frequently very partisan (but in large part also quite responsible), largely urban-oriented, of some "practical"

TABLE 6-7

Periodicals By Subject

	1951	1955	1960	1965	1970	1975	1978
General			1,076	1,106	1,443	1,243	1,012
Specialized							
Philosophy, ethics			3	4	9	5	11
Religion, theology			5	19	18	19	22
Social sciences			290	365	507	653	806
Philology			5	4	8	4	9
Basic sciences			7	9	31	30	32
Applied sciences			131	188	237	216	183
Fine arts, sports, tourism			38	82	121	118	101
Literature			82	95	70	59	58
History, geography, biography			11	18	26	15	22
TOTAL		551	979	1,658	1,890	2,470	2,362	2,256

SOURCES: DIE #380, 580, 825, 850, 890.

usefulness, circulating to all parts of the country quickly, and serving as a significant means of spreading national information to a large part of the population. For a press which is privately owned and operates in an atmosphere of intense political controversy, the record is on the whole quite respectable.

Radio

As shown in Table 6-5, the number of radios in Turkey has grown rapidly, with recent growth greatest in villages. It is acknowledged that even the official figures significantly underreport the situation in both cities and villages, particularly since the advent of inexpensive portable transistors. (Turkey's second plan estimated that in 1968 there were about 2½ million registered radios, and at least 1½ million unregistered ones.) Until the late 1960s the role of radio for some parts of the country, mostly the east, was limited in that it was not until 1967-1969 that the power of transmitters in Erzurum, Adana, and Diyarbakir was raised to the point where Turkish radio could dominate those regions. Previously, the field had been left largely to Turkish-language broadcasts from Soviet bloc and Arab countries.[23]

The political role of Turkish radio has always been controversial. In the single-party period, as noted above, there was strong emphasis on the "educational" function of the media, stressing nationalism, patriotism, and secularism during the years when leaders felt that sozializing the population to "national identification" was a primary need. The DP period was one of all but open use of the state radio for partisan propaganda, which practice became a contributing cause of the 1960 revolution. One of the resulting reforms was that TRT (Turkish Radio and Television) was made an "autonomous institution" in the 1961 Constitution (Article 121), with particularly stringent rules to assure equal access of all parties to radio during election campaigns. In recognition of the great importance of radio as a medium of influence, however, the Constitution was amended in 1971 to restrict TRT's autonomy, though the institution is still supposed to be "neutral." (The stringency of controls during election campaigns was not changed.) While there are no longer strong grounds for charges of direct partisan propaganda via the state radio, there is vigorous debate about general bias, ideological distortion, etc., and both Justice party and RPP governments have regularly become embroiled in attempts to change TRT personnel and have gotten into numerous and spirited conflicts with the Constitutional Court.

In content, Turkish radio attempts to serve both an information and an entertainment function, and to appeal to both rural and urban audiences. There are some regional variations in content among radio stations, but all appear to try to reach the entire spectrum of their audiences. About a quarter of the broadcast time is taken up with news, educational, and cultural programs, a ratio to total broadcast time fairly consistent in all the regions. Almost all of the rest is music, about a third of which is, interestingly, popular or Western classical music. Even the easternmost stations devote about 16 to 20 percent of their time to Western music (DIE #750:289). (It is not clear whether this pattern is because of audience preference, or because of a continued effort at "Westernization.") The educational and informational programs, particularly on the regional stations, also contain a sizable amount of "village" material.

While the impact of radio is difficult to measure with precision, there is no doubt that it is widely felt. In the cities the sound of radio is everywhere, audible from numerous windows as one walks throught the streets (particularly at news time), and transistor-carrying young people are frequently seen. While much of radio's role is entertainment, there is frequent discussion in public places about particularly political or cultural programs, and persons who have appeared on radio programs are often amazed at the number of persons from whom they receive comment on their performance.

For village listening we have some quantitative data. At least a third of Turkish rural families have their own radios. (The 1977 DIE figure of 1,400,000 radios among the approximately four million village families is probably low in view of the large number of unregistered transistors just mentioned, and in relation to the Village Survey finding, p. 265, that 39.4 percent had radios in 1968.) The percentage of villagers found by the Village Survey to listen to the radio daily rose from 19.0 percent in 1962 to 42.4 percent in 1968 (p. 264). Other findings were that 20.5 percent of men but 51.2 percent of women never listened, that 43.8 percent of men but only 27.2 percent of women listened outside their own homes, and that 80 percent of literates but only 45.2 percent of illiterates listened once a week or more. These data point up the continuing importance of information "filters" in the modernization process, mentioned in chapter 3.

In terms of program preferences, the Village Survey found that among categories listened to most frequently, news was named by 36.9 percent and music and folk songs by 34.8 percent. Abisel and Kocabaşoğlu found in addition that "programs in the evening and in the early morning dealing with farming and village affairs are especially popular," that women's programs are becoming increasingly so, that "listeners write in with specific questions on social subjects, health, and legal problems, asking for advice on general and personal matters," and that "the programs growing out of these questions are well accepted and increase the villagers' confidence in the radio" (1978:9). It is also notable that religious programs were named first by only 5.8 percent of village listeners, and that in all of the program categories, regional variations in preferences were only minor. Perhaps one of the most important findings, however, was that 43.2 percent of the villagers answered "yes" when asked if they found the language spoken on the radio difficult to understand, and that while the 53.6 percent figure for the eastern provinces is hardly surprising, the 31.2 percent in the "developed" regions should certainly give those responsible for operating TRT cause for concern. For all these reasons, we can conclude that while it is true that the use of radio as a widespread educational medium is expanding very rapidly (SPO, MTV:269) its full potential is still to be realized.

Television

Television was a late starter in Turkey. Broadcasts on other than an experimental basis did not begin until 1972, it having been decided by successive governments that investment in television facilities was of low priority. Since then, however, the number of television sets has risen astronomically. Observation indicates that a large number of families now have their television sets turned on almost all of each evening, and the influx of television is given as one of the most important reasons not only for a steep decline in theater attendance, but also for the return of availability of cinema tickets without the long waits which characterized Turkey up to the early 1970s (see also SPO, 1978b:par. 478).

On the air nightly for some 5½ hours (more on weekends), television is a combination of education and entertainment. That the latter is preferred is apparent from a 1976 viewer survey (Abisel and Kocabaşoğlu, 1978:9–10) and from the shifts in emphasis of Turkish television between the beginning and today, as shown in Table 6–8. Taking into consideration the limited amount of program time, however, it is likely that the educational and cultural programs also have sizable viewing audiences. Most of the programs, except for news, are imported, though efforts are being made to expand domestic production facilities. As television spreads, particularly to villages and lower-class urban areas, the potential of this medium as an aid in development will become correspondingly greater.

TABLE 6-8

Television Programming

(percent of total airtime by category)

	1972	1977	Change
News	18.2	15.8	−2.4
News-related	30.4	24.4	−6.0
Sub-total	48.6	40.2	−8.4
Cultural and educational	16.8	11.8	−5.0
Theatre	4.8	3.6	−1.2
Children's	6.5	7.5	+1.0
Sub-Total	28.1	22.9	−5.2
Music and amusement	17.5	22.0	+4.5
Sports	5.8	15.8	+10.0
Sub-Total	23.3	37.8	+14.5

SOURCE: 4th Five-Year Plan, Appendix Table 48.

Literature and the Arts

Literature and the arts are information media of a different kind in that their message is not as a rule directly political, though at times they may be so nationalistic or populist in tone as to be almost so. Their "modernizing" message is often indirect, particularly in such forms as architecture or the pictorial arts. Quantitatively, their impact is likely to be considerably less widespread than other channels of information in that their reach tends to be confined more to urban areas and to the upper echelons of society. They are by no means unimportant, however.

Literature

Literature directed at popular audiences is relatively new to Turkey. During most of the Ottoman period Turkish writers produced mainly "divan" literature, i.e., court poetry and romances, which were complex and "fancy" in style and language and which concerned themselves with court heroes and similar romantic topics. The situation began to change in the mid-nineteenth century when some of the Young Ottomans started producing nationalist and patriotic works which soon found eager audiences outside court circles, but which were still read mostly by a relatively small number of people in the major cities.[24] The influence of the *Tanzimat* writers waned as efforts to unseat Abdulhamid II foundered, but they were followed near the turn of the century and in the Young Turk period by another generation of writers who began to focus more on the middle and lower classes.[25]

The Republic brought new literary ventures. Some were early novels, such as Yakub Kadri Karaosmanoğlu's *Yaban* (The Stranger) which dealt with Turkish introspection in rapidly changing times. During the 1930s and 1940s, an average of about 2,000 titles were published annually, of which between 300 and 500 could be classified as "literature." Most were folklore, poetry, and translations of foreign literary works, chiefly Western classics, close to 1,000 of which had been prepared by the Ministry of Education by the 1970s. All of these were published in inexpensive editions and given wide circulation. Their popularity and accessibility was aided to some extent by the *Halkevleri*, most of which had libraries.[26] Also important were the Republic's language reform measures which facilitated a faster rise in the rate of literacy, led to simplification of the language, and encouraged abandonment of the Ottoman style and vocabulary in favor of *"Öz Türkçe"* ("pure Turkish") as well as discarding of many Persian and Arabic words which had pervaded Ottoman vocabulary (see Weiker, 1973:231–3 and the source footnotes there). Indirectly, increased contact with villagers also took place through projects such as competitions among *Halkevleri* to gather large numbers of Turkish words and expressions for incorporation into the new language. The mandated conversion to the Latin alphabet had the additional effect of very much narrowing the selection of literature available to the new generation, and helped give the government a large measure of control over its selection. Of course, interest in folk and patriotic-nationalistic materials was also heightened by the general efforts to induce pride in Turkish accomplishments which characterized the Ataturk period. (For an interesting analysis of village literature in this period, see Rathbun, 1972.)

The post-World War II period has been one of great flowering of Turkish literature. Quantitatively, the number of books published annually passed 3,000 in 1952, exceeded 6,000 for the first time in 1971, and rose to over 7,000 in 1973. Of these, some 421 in 1952 and over 1,000 in each year since 1971 were classified as "literature." Turkish books still include numerous works of poetry, heroic and folk epics, and foreign translations.[27] The number of works by Turkish writers on contemporary subjects has, however, now become significant. Talat Halman has written of the vigorous development of Turkish literature in the 1960s which "reflected not only the turmoil of Turkish society but also its pluralistic culture. Turkish literature was never (during a lifetime of at least twelve centuries) more extensive, varied, inclusive. All of its own heritage and most of its external orientations were dynamically at work" (1972:387–402).

The emergence of village literature has also been a significant development. The first village book to gain widespread attention was an account of the experiences of a village teacher, Mahmu Makal's *Bizim Köy* (1950, translated into English as *A Village in Anatolia* in 1954.) Outside Turkey the best known novelist continues to be Yaşar Kemal, whose *Ince Mehmed* (1955, translated as *Mehmed My Hawk*, 1961) is a realistic portrayal of life in a remote Taurus mountain village near Adana and describes the exploitation of villagers by powerful *agas* in extremely stark terms. Numerous

TABLE 6-9
Books Published
(and categories in percentages)

	Total	Philosophy, morals, religion, theology	Social science, history, geography, biography	Basic & applied sciences	Literature	General & other language, fine arts, sports)
1928–38	16,046	423 (2.6)	7,998 (49.8)	3,665 (22.8)	2,629 (16.4)	1,327 (8.3)
1940	2,370	73 (3.1)	742 (31.3)	407 (17.1)	298 (12.6)	850 (35.9)
1945	2,621	86 (3.3)	641 (24.5)	450 (17.2)	625 (23.8)	819 (31.2)
1950	2,363	131 (5.5)	973 (41.1)	564 (23.9)	352 (14.9)	343 (14.5)
1955	3,250	146 (4.5)	1,294 (39.8)	642 (19.8)	863 (26.6)	305 (9.4)
1960	4,195	269 (6.4)	1,482 (35.3)	750 (17.9)	899 (21.4)	795 (19.0)
1965	5,442	327 (6.0)	2,177 (40.0)	1,252 (23.0)	863 (15.9)	823 (15.1)
1970	5,854	385 (6.6)	2,234 (38.1)	1,418 (24.2)	935 (16.0)	882 (15.1)
1973	7,479	344 (4.6)	2,316 (31.0)	1,787 (23.9)	1,373 (18.4)	1,659 (22.1)
1975	6,645	469 (7.1)	2,472 (37.2)	1,596 (24.0)	1,100 (16.5)	1,008 (15.1)
1977	6,830	523 (7.7)	2,641 (38.7)	1,515 (22.2)	950 (13.9)	1,201 (17.6)
1978	5,033	433 (8.6)	2,086 (41.4)	965 (19.2)	717 (14.2)	832 (16.5)

SOURCE: DIE #683, 825, 850, 890.

other village writers, such as Orhan Kemal, Kemal Tahir, and Aziz Nesin, are widely read.

The precise impact of village novels is hard to measure. Quantitatively, a recent estimate is that their average sale is in the 3,000 to 15,000 range, though the most popular novels by important novelists can easily reach 50,000, and sales of *Ince Mehmed* were reported to have passed the quarter million mark in 1978. The works of major poets have been reported as selling up to 10,000 copies (Prof. Talat Halman, private communication). For the urban educated class, who seem to read them ravenously, their principal impact may be in reinforcing liberal predispositions which some of this group already hold. (Many of the writers of "village novels" are prominent in left-wing politics.) For the growing number of readers among the lower class urban residents and even villagers, there is probably an attraction in the realism in which their lot is often portrayed. Some of the novels also romanticize village life and stress the noble characteristics of villagers, an obverse attraction. For this group, folk tales and heroic epics also help to increase their pride in the Turkish nation, of which many have only relatively recently become an integral part. It is, of course, difficult to attribute specific significant political actions and socio-cultural attitudes directly to literature, though that it has some role in this respect cannot be doubted.

Cinema

Even for villagers, the movies are becoming rapidly more accessible. The Village Survey found that in 1968 50.8 percent of villagers (74.9 percent of the men and 26.5 percent of the women) had attended a cinema showing, compared to 43.0 percent in 1962. There were the usual large regional variations. For urban Turks, the movies are a major form of entertainment, despite the impact of television. In 1970, movies played to over 246 million spectators, or an average of seven visits per year for every man, woman and child. The number of Turkish films being produced had risen from an annual average of about 55 during the 1950s to over 200 by 1965 and was close to 300 by 1972, ranking it among the highest in the world (Talat Halman, private communication).

Most critics agree that the content of most Turkish movies is deplorable. While there have certainly been some excellent Turkish films, and some which have won international prizes, for the most part they are geared to the low common denominator of mass audiences. In part this is attributable to the pattern established in the early days of the Turkish film industry when there was money to make only cheap films and priority was given to attraction of the mass audiences at any price, including loss of quality.[28] Film-industry personnel who were potentially the most creative often found themselves in fierce competition for audiences with those who were content to appeal only to viewing groups with the least discriminating tastes.

Whether Turkish cinema today can be called harmful to Turkish development is not an easy question of answer. There is little if any evidence that it has led to anti-social behavior, despite the predominance of violence, debauchery, and "anti-traditional" topics, though analysts in some countries have concluded that the link between movie and television content and behavior, particularly crime patterns, is demonstrable.[29]

On the other hand, one might doubt that the positive impact of more creative and artistic films or more realistic presentations of Turkish life and general human problems would have much measurable political and socio-cultural impact on cinema audiences. As noted above, the emergence of village literature may have aroused the sympathies and pricked the consciences of its middle class readers, but it is difficult to argue that much concrete political and social policy can be directly attributed to village literature. The sentiments, for example, of most RPP supporters in favor of the "masses" and redistribution of development resources can be attributed to political motives at least as much as to normative or altruistic ones. If this is true for literature, it would seem all the more so for the cinema, whose audiences are likely to be even less responsive to such messages. There may, of course, be lesser effects, such as giving villagers and townsmen a false impression of city life. But, if this is so, certainly it has been no deterrence to urbanization, and it is unlikely that many migrants come to town with unrealistic expectations gleaned from movies and are then disappointed and frustrated, with subsequent harmful effects for society. Of course, wrong impressions, simply because they *are* wrong, do have ill effects. For example, if Turkish cinema-goers were to judge America only on the basis of popular film imports from the United States, they could emerge with a picture that America is populated by few others than gangsters and cowboys.

Yet despite the likelihood that the effects of cinema may be marginal and indirect, given the addiction to movies which many Turks have, it is regrettable that Turkish films are not better than they are. Turkish cinema receives no state subsidy. Perhaps such a subsidy would help the industry break out of its predominant mold.

Other Communication Media

Theater was a growing art form when, in the mid-1970s, it had the misfortune of being afflicted by the advent of television, urban transportation problems, urban street violence, and inflation. Attendance has since dropped sharply. The 1970 audiences of about 666,000 in state theaters (T. C., 1973:451) fell to about 360,000 in 1972–1973 and 318,000 in 1976–1977 (DIE # 850). Attendance at privately operated theaters is said to have suffered similarly. This is all the more unfortunate in that there are numerous excellent Turkish playwrights as well as actors and directors, and plays of great artistic merit have been produced (for a translation of five such plays, see Halman, 1976). The State Theaters have in the last few years presented an average of about thirty works per season, of which in most recent years more than half have been translations, indicating a strong Western influence which is probably a result both of the preferences of the artists and the demands of urban upper-middle-class audiences. In total number of performances, however, original Turkish plays have had the edge (DIE #710,850). A State Conservatory for training actors, actresses, opera singers, and ballet dancers has been in existence since 1936.

Music is of social and political importance in any society in that it both reflects and influences popular attitudes and mores. It is also among the most pervasive of the arts. "Among all the arts," one analyst has observed, "music was of pre-eminent concern to Ataturk" (And, 1973:2). In pursuit of Westernization and Turkification, he began the Republic's musical development along several lines:

Western classical music was introduced via the Presidential Symphony Orchestra[30] (founded in 1924) and the State Opera (1949), and was fostered by sending young musicians abroad and inviting prominent European musicians to Turkey. Both the symphony and the opera give regular performances in various Turkish cities, though as in most other countries they attract largely upper-middle-class audiences.

Young Turkish musicians began gathering folk tunes from traditional sources as early as 1926. This interest in folk music resulted in two related musical genres: Performances of folk music per se, plus frequent performance of folk dances both in Turkey and by Turkish ensembles traveling abroad; and classical works based on folk melodies, often performed in Western style. The most prominent of these in terms of popular appeal are several works for voices and orchestra, such as Adnan Saygun's *Köroğlu* and his masterful oratorio *Yunus Emre* (Turkey's famous fourteenth century folk poet). The number of Turkish musicians working in these areas is steadily increasing, the quality of their work is often excellent, and they are played to ever-growing audiences.

Both Western and Turkish "pop" music have found great favor with Turkey's mass audience. Turkish radio stations devote an average of 15 to 20 percent of their broadcast time to Western pop music alone (DIE 1973:324) with only small regional variations. Some stations in Ankara, Istanbul, and Izmir II are devoted entirely to Western music, about half classical, half pop. Western pop records and tapes are also very good sellers among urban youth. An off-shoot of this has been the emergence of numerous Turkish musical groups who have created Turkish versions of Western rock music by adapting Turkish songs to rock formats. All this disturbs Turkish music critics considerably. In social terms it probably performs little more than an entertainment function. Indirectly, however, it is quite possible that it strengthens identification of urban Turkish youth with their western counterparts. It may also help inculcate desire for a more "glamorous" life than is generally acceptable in traditional Turkish communities, thus increasing the gap between the older and younger generations even further than it already is.

In general, *architecture, painting,* and *sculpture* play modest roles as agents of change. The main role of Turkish architecture, for example, has probably been in its retention of traditional Turkish styles and design, thus helping to heighten a sense of identification with Turkish history. Or, to take a more obvious example, monumental architectural and sculptural styles may possibly have contributed to Turkish patriotism and pride.

Conclusions

Though the social and political effects are very hard to measure with any precision, there is no doubt that the communication media, press, radio, television, and to a lesser extent the arts, have played a significant part in Turkish modernization. They have helped increase national unity and identification with the nation. They have widened and reoriented the horizons of both elite and lower-class Turks. International recognition of Turkish artists (as well as Islamic art in general) has probably helped overcome feelings of inferiority vis-a-vis the West. The conflicting pulls of modern and traditional Turkish forms have been eased by the successful blending of the two in many forms of art and music. Turkey's free flow of information may have increased generational conflict, but there is little direct evidence that this has happened, or to what degree generational conflict might have grown anyway, given the general urbanization which has taken place.

One is led to the conclusion that in social and political terms the net contribution of communications and the arts has been positive. There are, of course, criticisms of the "low-brow" nature of much of Turkish popular culture, but these again are little different from dissatisfaction expressed by critics in many countries, including the "developed" ones. But if it is true, as Metin And has asserted, that "a sense of the traditional *and modern* can persist and express itself more powerfully in the maintenance of traditional forms" (1973:26, emphasis added), Turkish communicators have the potential to make important contributions.

SEVEN

Economic Development

Without doubt, among the most insistent demands in modernizing societies are those for an improved material standard of living. In a country such as Turkey, as national integration increases and as public participation in politics grows, numerous pressures arise in the economic area. Among the most important is the seemingly continual demand for increases in the absolute standard of living—i.e., wage increases over and above increases in the cost of living. A second and related pressure arises from the changing composition of material demands as the general standard of living rises, necessitating increasing diversification of production as well as overall quantitative increases, with special stress on durable and industrial goods. This usually also entails increasing need both to import and export, thus subjecting the economy to influences from the international scene which are often very difficult to control. A third pressure, increasingly seen in Turkey as elsewhere, is demand for redistribution of wealth. While this is in some part a matter of "social justice," it also has important economic implications for such economic matters as propensity to consume vs. propensity to save or invest.

General Overview

The Turkish economy is presently in deep trouble. Inflation since the late 1970s has been 50 to 80 percent per year. GNP growth began falling significantly in 1977, and was only about 1 percent in 1979. The country's foreign debt is estimated at between 14 and 17 billion dollars, much of it short-term, and it is only because many governments, international agencies, and private banks have agreed to rescheduling that Turkey has been able to avoid bankruptcy. The balance of payments has for some time shown a very large deficit. Stagnant exports at a time when workers' remittances are also falling has made for inability to fund raw material and capital goods imports, a major factor in Turkish industry's operating at far below capacity. Shortages of consumer goods are frequent, as is also true for energy supplies.

Negotiations for association with the European Economic Community are going badly. Some of these difficulties are inherent in the situation itself: Turkey has arrived at a stage of "advanced development" but is not yet fully "developed." Another reason is failure to make certain major long-term structural reforms in industry, taxation, and finance. Political factors which have worsened many economic problems include the fact that successive governments have projected too rapid a pace of growth, from which commitments they now find it difficult to retreat. In addition, there is the public resistance against imposing major austerity measures, encountered by all governments subject to electoral pressures.

Yet numerous observers on all points of the political spectrum agree that many of these problems are essentially short-term, and that the performance and growth of the Turkish economy over the fifty-year period of the Republic has been highly respectable and that a "take-off" stage to further economic development has been reached. In some ways, Turkey's economic performance has indeed been excellent. Gross National Product has grown at an average rate of 6.6 percent annually from 1950 to 1976, one of the highest of the OECD countries, though real per capita income has grown more slowly due to inflation and rapid population growth.[1] Among the reasons for this growth in the Republic's first half-century have been the very large increase in production of almost all goods and services; major structural changes in the composition of production, from an essentially agrarian economy to one with sizable industrialization; acquisition of infrastructure (transportation, communication, utilities, education, etc.), which has literally transformed the face of much of the country; and, during most of the period, a steadily rising standard of living for most, if not all, of the nation's citizens. The rates of growth in many sectors compare favorably with those of many other countries both in the "developed" and the "developing" world. Also noteworthy is that the rates of growth of many lines of production and many aspects of structural change have in general increased continually over the fifty-year period. It is further impressive that this development has been strong enough to enable Turkey to survive numerous "crises" in which it was widely predicted (similarly to 1979) that Turkey would be the first country in the world to go bankrupt.

Economic problems have always been high on the agendas of policy-makers of the Turkish Republic. In addition to reflecting economic circumstances, economic policies have also usually been closely linked to social and political objectives of successive governments. In the Republic's first quarter-century, as one analyst has put it, the chief object of government policy was nationalism and general self-sufficiency. These objectives led to coolness toward foreign capital, stringent pay-as-you-go discipline in government budgets, emphasis on state-run industry, and stress on infrastructure.[2] As a result, although production in certain sectors of both agriculture and industry began to rise, there was little increase in per capita income and in the general standard of living, though it must be stressed that important bases for future growth were laid during the single-party period, in transportation and communication, education, the establishment of investment banks, some major State Economic Enterprises, etc. (These are discussed in the sections below on the various branches of the economy.) The economic situation was politically tolerable in part because of the relatively low level of overt public expression of demands in the single-party context, and in part because the majority of the population was not as yet integrated into the national economy.

All this had changed considerably by the time of the inauguration of the multiparty period. Popular impatience was growing, in part because of severe wartime stringencies. However, Turkey was poised to enter a period of rapid economic growth both in production and consumption. The economy was stimulated at first to a considerable extent by a regime intent on attracting votes and willing to use economic policies to get them, including large-scale expansionist financing and major attempts to attract foreign capital. Such policies were quite the opposite of those of the single-party period, starting what may be called the Keynesian era of Turkish economic policy. It was not long before this stimulation was also supplemented from below by rapidly mushrooming public demand for goods and services as the population began to undergo changes including rapid numerical increase, urbanization, and integration—with the concomitant realization that demands on govern-ment could be made effective. Growth in all sectors was rapid and included the emergence of a vigorous private sector, agricultural mechanization, vast public works, and the stimulation of agriculture through an extensive system of price supports. The Menderes period has been characterized as one of "rapid growth, inflation, uncoordinated development and almost unlimited sums of foreign assistance and borrowing" (Tansky, 1967:39).

The severe inflation and shortages which were by-products of these policies (and which led to the imposition of severe deflationary measures after insistence in 1958 on a major "stabilization" program by Turkey's creditors, led by the World Bank) were contributing causes of the 1960 revolution. Economic growth was only briefly interrupted, however. The period of uncertainty, which impelled both domestic and foreign elements to hesitate to continue further economic expansion, was short because of several factors. One was the basic momentum which the economy had already acquired, with growing demand and growing resources and a vigorous private sector determined to meet these needs. A second factor was the 1963 advent of a consortium of OECD nations to supply aid from abroad (on which talks had begun in 1961). Both foreign and domestic investors were further encouraged by one of the chief reforms promulgated by the military regime, economic planning, this in contrast to the aversion which the DP had had to that concept.

The Five-Year Plans, of which the fourth is now in effect, are part of a long-range strategy projected to 1995, by which time full integration with the EEC is to be negotiated. The plans are comprehensive, covering social as well as economic matters. Among the social areas (but also, of course, with economic implications) that are included are the problem of scattered, small villages, unbalanced distribution of income, and problems of education, health, and public administration. The overall thrust of the plans is toward rapid growth in all sectors of finance, income, and production and toward both freedom and social justice, and thus toward a mixed economy, and the enhancement of Turkey's status in the world.[3]

More specifically, the targets include a four-fold increase in per capita income by 1995, a similar increase in GNP, and structural changes to reduce the share of agriculture in Gross Domestic Product to around 10 percent (it was about 48 percent in 1950 and fell to about 27 percent in 1976), and to raise that of industry to 40 percent (from about 13 percent in 1950 and 22.4 percent in 1976), and the share of services to 50 percent. Average yearly growth of GNP is projected at 7 percent. Specific growth targets are set for all sectors of the economy. Full employment is envisioned in 1995, with 25 percent of the labor force to be in agriculture (it was 77 percent in 1962, 59 percent in 1976), 23 percent in industry (8.3 percent in 1962, 13 percent in 1976) and 52 percent in services. Targets are also set for health, education, urbanization, and other areas (TUSIAD, 1977:Tables 3, 41; SPO, 1973a: pars. 5.2, 5.6).

Performance in the first three Plan periods was generally positive, though very uneven. (It is summarized in Table 7-1.) Quantitatively, since the 1960s the Turkish economy has shown a generally increasing rate of growth until the current crisis. Economic shortcomings have been in areas which are important partly because they are the ones envisaged as supplying the basis for development in the future. (The will be detailed later in this chapter.) Problems have also arisen in that despite high rates of growth in production, demand has grown even faster. Thus, for example, while overall growth targets have been frequently attained, the share of industry in GNP continues to lag, while that of services remains higher than hoped for. Exports have increased, as has the proportion of exports made up of other than agricultural goods and raw materials, but imports have increased even faster. Inflation has been high. There have been lags in investment capital, a key factor for future growth. Continuing rapid urbanization has led to high urban unemployment. Rural unemployment has also increased as a result of population growth and agricultural mechanization. (The latter is a positive factor, to be sure, from the point of view of agricultural efficiency.) Important regional imbalances continue. This not only causes political problems, but also interferes with optimum mobilization of the talents and resources of the population to participate in development and growth (see chapter 8).

Industry

Industrialization has been the foundation of Turkish economic development strategy from the Republic's beginning, and the growth of the industrial sector has been very great. Quantitatively, production in a great many of the products which Turkey manufactures has increased rapidly and steadily, as

TABLE 7-1

Macroeconomic Targets and Achievements of the Development Plans

	1st Plan Target	1963–1967 Actual	2nd Plan Target	1968–1972 Actual	3rd Plan Target	1973–1977 Actual
Sectoral Growth Rates						
Agriculture	4.2	3.7	4.1	3.6	3.7	3.3
Industry	12.3	10.6	12.0	9.9	11.4	9.9
Services	6.2	7.5	6.3	7.7	6.8	7.9
GDP	6.9	6.5	6.6	6.6	7.6	6.9
GNP	7.0	6.7	7.0	7.1	7.4	6.5
Fixed Capital Investments						
Sectoral Distribution						
Agriculture	17.7	13.9	15.2	11.1	11.7	11.8
Mining	5.4	5.6	3.7	3.3	5.8	3.7
Manufacturing	16.9	20.4	22.4	26.8	31.1	28.2
Energy	8.6	6.5	8.0	9.0	8.5	7.4
Transport	13.7	15.6	16.1	16.0	14.5	20.6
Tourism	1.4	1.3	2.3	2.1	1.6	1.0
Housing	20.3	22.4	17.9	20.1	15.7	16.9
Education	7.1	6.6	6.7	4.7	5.0	3.3
Health	2.3	1.8	1.8	1.5	1.4	1.1
Other Services	6.6	5.9	5.9	5.4	4.7	6.0
TOTAL	100.0	100.0	100.0	100.0	100.0	100.0
Ownership (%)						
Public	59.9	53.6	52.6	52.9	56.4	51.1
Private	40.1	46.4	47.4	47.1	43.6	48.9
TOTAL	100.0	100.0	100.0	100.0	100.0	100.0
As % of GNP (Average in Plan Period)	18.3	15.3	21.3	17.8	23.4	20.2
Consumption Growth (%)						
Public	8.7	7.7	8.8	12.3	8.9	10.4
Private	5.4	4.8	5.1	5.5	4.8	6.2
TOTAL	5.7	5.2	5.8	6.6	5.4	6.8
National Savings						
Annual Growth (%)	13.4	16.2	12.2	9.1	13.6	6.3
As % of GNP (Average of Plan period)	14.8	15.7	20.8	18.3	21.9	17.9

Source: TUSIAD, *The Turkish Economy 1979*, page 101, used by permission.

indicated in Table 7-2. The share of GNP contributed by industry has also increased steadily since 1950, as has the nonagricultural percentage of Turkish exports. On the other hand, growth in certain industries has often not reached plan targets; industry remains highly uneven geographically; many

TABLE 7-2
Selected Industrial Production

	1930	1940	1950	1960	1970	1977	1978
Pig iron (000 tons)		8	59	83	132	367	258
Steel ingots (000 tons)				265	1,312	1,397	1,628
Coke (000 tons)		96	315	739	1,594	1,751	1,865
		(1939)					
Cement (000 tons)	73	284	296	2,038	6,374	13,833	15,344
Paper products (000 tons)		8	18	56	126	339	304
				(1962)			
Glassware products (000 tons)		6	8	34	161	271	273
Nitrogen industry products (000 tons)				184	208	653	688
				(1963)			
Livestock fodder (000 tons)				2	54	284	492
Cotton textiles (000 meters)	4	47	101	156	220	179	209
Sugar (000 tons)	13	95	137	644	518	1,080	1,090
Salt (000 tons)		234	310	445	648	777	
Alcoholic Beverages (000 litres)		19	36	54	102	144	
Sunflower Oil (000 tons)					8	79	77
Macaroni (000 tons)					62	95	105
Tea (dry) (000 tons)					33	78	86
Margarine (000 tons)					121	225	252
Domestic refrigerators (000)					126		755
Motor vehicle tires (000)					1,242	2,447	3,069
Light bulbs (000)					22,306	58,235	31,157
Vacuum cleaners (000)					23	167	101

SOURCE: DIE publications; Hershlag, 1968.

sectors are still far from attaining optimum efficiency; and the quality of goods all too often remains poor. Many important decisions remain to be made on matters such as the allocation of resources to the public vs. the private sector, the degree of international integration which will be allowed, and selectivity in stimulation of various branches of manufacturing.

Although economic development and industrialization were given major attention almost as soon as the Republic was launched—the declaration emerging from the Izmir Economic Congress of 1923 stressed that the "principal aim" of Turkish economic policy was "the industrialization of the country" (Hershlag, 1958:40)—industrial development began slowly. The major causes of the slow pace included the fact that the Republic had inherited almost no industrial base;[4] that it had suffered extensive damage during World War I and the War of Independence to its transportation and communication systems and to its agricultural areas and in its loss of

TABLE 7-3

Sectoral Origin of GNP

(Constant 1968 producers' prices, in percent)

	1948	1953	1958	1963	1968	1970	1977
Agriculture	46.3	44.6	40.8	36.6	29.6	27.9	21.8
Manufacturing	13.3	13.5	16.9	18.2	23.0	23.7	25.7
Construction	4.5	6.7	6.5	6.3	7.0	7.0	5.9
Commerce	7.2	8.5	8.4	10.0	11.4	11.5	13.8
Transportation and Communication	5.1	5.8	6.5	7.0	7.9	8.2	9.6
Dwelling	8.7						
Ownership	5.3	6.8	6.6	6.0	5.4	5.4	4.8
Private Services		5.3	5.3	5.3	5.3	5.3	5.2
Government	8.9						
Services		8.2	8.3	9.6	9.4	9.6	8.7

SOURCE: DIE Publications.

manpower; that it was burdened by restrictive provisions of the Treaty of Lausanne;[5] and that during the 1920s it chose the strategy of encouraging private enterprise.[6] Although with the help of the 1927 Law for the Encouragement of Industry the number of industrial firms rose from 470 in 1927 to 1,255 in 1930 and 1,473 in 1932 (Iren, 1975:5), the effect on production was not very great because most of the firms were small, used little technology, were concentrated in a few areas, such as food processing, textiles and mining, and were not supported by proper infrastructure or entrepreneurial and labor skills (Hershlag 1958:62 ff.).

This lackluster record combined with the impact of a worldwide depression made economic performance a major issue during the Free party episode of 1930 and led in 1931 to the policy of *etatism* (see chapter 1 above and Sarç, 1948). Under the aegis of two five-year plans, over a hundred State Economic Enterprises (SEEs) were established by 1950, eventually employing some 76,000 workers. About a third were in food, beverages and tobacco, a third in textiles, wood and paper, and a third in heavier industry, chemicals, mining equipment, machinery, transport, including the Karabük Iron and Steel facility which was established in 1926. Also important was that the SEEs were geographically dispersed, almost all being outside the Aegean and Marmara regions, in which private plants were (and are still) heavily concentrated.[7] What may be called a negative aspect of all this was that although the doctrine of *etatism* insisted that the SEEs would only be a supplement to the growth of the private sector,[8] the development of the latter, in fact, was inhibited[9] (although it is impossible, of course, to estimate how much it might have grown had it had more favorable circumstances).

On balance, however, the results of the *etatist* period were favorable, and few if any observers disagree with the conclusion that using the large public sector to assure quick growth was both economically and politically the only realistic option. Large increases in production and industrial employment began to be recorded in 1935 (see DIE #683:167–75) and continued until the interruptions and unavoidable stringencies of World War II. (For a detailed analysis, see also Singer, 1977:chapters 1, 2.)

After a period of readjustment in the late 1940s, growth resumed, coincidentally with the accession to power of the Democrat party. One of the new government's major policy innovations in the economic sphere was large-scale stimulation of the private sector, although, contrary to its own professed intentions, the DP also continued the expansion of public enterprises. The number of so-called "large plants" (the DIE definition of these is 10 or more workers) grew from 660 in 1951 to 1,159 in 1953, and 5,284 in 1960. On other dimensions, growth was far less spectacular. The average number of workers per plant, for example, rose only from twenty-five to thirty-three (DIE #683:206,210). The more dramatic growth which later characterized Turkish industry did not begin until the 1960s, stimulated by factors such as the 1958 stabilization program, the beginning of planning and other measures which restored investor certainty, and, probably, simply the fact that the economy had begun to mature, that enough time had elapsed since the beginning of large-scale investments for them to start to bear fruit. Also, entrepreneurs had gotten more on-the-job experience. Whereas industrial production had roughly doubled during the 1950s, it more than tripled between 1962 and 1973, and increased by half again by 1977. The OECD index, in which 1962 equals 100, showed 300.9 in 1973 and 435.2 for 1977 (1978:51). Structural changes accelerated: the share of consumer goods in industrial production fell from 62.3 percent in 1962 to 47.7 percent in 1976, while intermediate goods rose from 27.8 percent to 36.2 percent, and investment goods from 9.9 percent to 16.1 percent (TUSIAD, 1977:83). The share of manufactured goods among exports rose from 13 percent in 1960 to over 35 percent in 1975 (Ibid.:90). Another key economic factor, productivity, increased 4 percent in 1952–1958 and 16 percent in 1962–1968 (Gülten Kazgan, 1972:366–7).

Rapid industrialization continues to be one of the fundamental elements in Turkish economic planning. As the economy develops, economic decisions become increasingly more complex. High among such issues are the merits of a policy of import-substitution vs. a more international orientation; the precise combination of social and economic objectives which the public sector is to meet; and the role of foreign capital. Many of these problems, as noted earlier, are connected with the Turkish intention to move to integration with the EEC, a subject which we will consider at the conclusion of this chapter.

Strengths and Weaknesses of the Private Sector

The growth of the private sector in the last quarter-century has been little short of spectacular. Much of its growth has been related to specific and general government encouragement,[10] but in recent years there has also been increasing initiative on the part of the entrepreneurs themselves. In many of the years for which targets have been set by the development plans, the private sector has met them. Although in some areas expansion has been less than was envisioned, in others there is now excess capacity. The private sector is also imbalanced in another way in that while in some geographical areas private establishments are quite large, in others they are very numerous but very small (and very "traditional"). It is also only recently that significant geographic dispersal has even begun to occur. These conditions and problems arise in part because of the nature and pattern of the private sector itself, partly because of factors arising from government policies and the general financial and economic conditions of the nation. In view of the pivotal role envisioned for the private sector in the plans, it would seem to be vital that these weaknesses be corrected quickly.

As noted earlier, the initial policy of the Republican government in the 1920s was to emphasize the role of private industry, but the Law for the Encouragement of Industry had only minimal success. The increased number of enterprises was almost all in "very small firms which . . . engaged in throat-cutting competition."[11] During the *etatist* period the private sector continued some slow growth but experienced little "development," remaining dominated by small and relatively primitive firms. The 1930 five-year plan paid only the slightest attention to a role for private industry, and its stimulation was mostly a byproduct of spillover from the growth of the public sector (such as the need for sub-contractors).

When the period of strong encouragement of private industry began in 1950, therefore, many Turkish entrepreneurs were eager to enter the field, but poorly equipped to do so. In part this was due to absence of facilities, including ready financing for large-scale enterprises. There was neither actual nor psychological readiness to raise funds in the capital market, and although laws were passed providing for government credits, tax incentives, etc., their implementation was often stalled by bureaucratic red tape (and would probably have been so even with the best of intentions on all sides, which, of course, did not always exist). Another obstacle was the dearth of infrastructure, which began to be alleviated only during the late 1950s. Still other causes lay in the characteristics of the potential entrepreneurs themselves, including a "traditional" lack of trust of outsiders, so that most firms continued to be individual proprietorships or small partnerships. The merely rudimentary level of technology and managerial skills which most firms had reached was an obstacle as well. "Under these conditions the private sector could not be expected to accelerate economic development, and in fact between 1950 and 1960 the major part of investments belonged to the public sector, even though official economic policy for rapid development was based on the private sector" (Iren, 1979:369).

An important external factor encouraging "growth" without real "modernization" arose during the 1950s. Balance of payments deficits (to a considerable extent the result of a sharp decline in agricultural production and export due to bad weather) led to shortages of imported raw materials and capital equipment, and thus to factories operating at far below their capacities, "this in turn increasing the cost of production and creating cost inflation in addition to demand inflation" and leading to restriction of imports which provided "limitless protection" for domestic industry (Iren, 1979:371). It was only in the late 1950s that remedial steps (including a major currency devaluation) were taken as a part of the general stabilization program insisted on by the International Monetary Fund and Turkey's other creditors. Nevertheless, as Iren has concluded, the private sector on the whole showed "great dynamism" during the DP decade, and many entrepreneurs were quick to respond to the opportunities for expansion which became gradually more available, so that by 1960 one could consider the private sector as "established," the way the public sector had been during the years 1930–1950 (Iren, 1979:374).

Thus in many ways the private sector was ripe for a prominent developmental role when the period of economic planning opened after 1961, and the rates of growth began to increase more rapidly. In addition to the general maturation which had taken place both within the private sector and in its environment (e.g., more infrastructure) it was helped by the general strategy of the Plans, which emphasized import-substitution rather than export orientation. The rationale for this was that export capability was judged to be able to increase only slowly, so that reducing the balance of payments deficit could be better done by reducing the need for imports rather than by trying to earn additional foreign exchange through exports (Okyar, 1975:12). The economic validity of this strategy is still a matter of vigorous dispute among Turkish (and world) economists and planners. Its effect in the context of the thesis of the present discussion was to continue protection of traditional economic traits and concepts and leave development and modernization largely to the initiatives of the entrepreneurs themselves. Their response has frequently been vigorous, but again highly uneven. It is no longer really possible to discuss the private sector without noting how varied are the levels of "development" within it.

The strong and weak aspects of the private sector today reflect familiar themes:

1. A considerable number of large, modern plants have been established, but for the most part the private sector continues to be made up of very small firms. The 1970 Census of Manufactures listed some 175,000 "large" firms, but 93 percent of these employed four or fewer persons and were so classified only because they used fifty or more horsepower of mechanical equipment (DIE #782:2).[12]

2. The number of new joint-stock companies or corporations has also increased, from 210 formed in 1968 to 470 in 1973, and 1,584 in 1977 (SPO, 1978b:Table 13). A sizable number of firms also organized as partnerships of 300 or more (Ibid.:par. 1182), and efforts were made to deflect the savings of Turkish workers being remitted from abroad into manufacturing industry. The RPP government also began organizing to

implement its plan for an economic "People's Sector," with subscription of funds from the public for investment in manufacturing industry stocks and bonds. But no legislative measures were passed to establish the basic organizational structure for a stock market. Among many entrepreneurs "tradition" still persists. One analyst found that, even now, most joint-stock companies "are either family-controlled or owned by a small number of shareholders" (Hershlag, 1973:20). In even so major an Anatolian industrial center as Kayseri partnerships of even as few as five to eight are disliked by many because of the possibility of arguments over policies, to say nothing of trusting others with one's money (Weiker, 1972:48 and note 21).

3. The private sector has begun to spread outside the established Aegean and Marmara regions in a major way, but a very high proportion of the new enterprises and investment are still located in these areas, for understandable reasons.[13]

4. As noted, the share of Turkish exports which are industrial goods has risen steadily, and about 86 percent of all Turkish manufactured exports in 1972–1976 were made by the private sector, though this represents a small decline from the 89 percent of 1961–1965 (TUSIAD, 1977:160–61). There are also signs of long-term weakness. Industrial exports are largely to other "developing" countries, so that although many pay in hard currencies, the balance of trade with the crucial European nations is not much improved. The obstacles of insufficient raw materials, lack of skilled personnel, and energy shortages are such that even in an industry like cement, utilized capacity was only 90 percent in 1976 "although there were cement shortages on the local market, and the possibility of exporting the commodity was open throughout the year" (TUSIAD, 1977:48).

Still other problems result from government policy, acts of either commission or omission. (Deficiencies in the tax structure and the banking system will be discussed below, and the bureaucracy was considered in chapter 2.) Even in this period of economic planning there is reported to be a lack of sufficient direction, so that there is excess capacity in some areas, shortages in others. The very serious lack of foreign exchange, with the result that Turkish industry currently operates far below capacity due to inability to import raw materials, equipment, and spare parts, is most often attributed to governments having projected too great a rate of growth, in response to political rather than economic conditions. The great degree of protection mentioned earlier also continues, but is now being subject to more and more criticism.

One can only speculate, of course, about whether with more favorable conditions the Turkish private sector would have "modernized" faster, or whether some of its "traditional" aspects would have persisted even so. It cannot be denied that a sizable number of Turkish entrepreneurs *did* modernize. A great many members of the Istanbul business community, among others, show energy, innovativeness, and managerial abilities equal to those in any comparable country, and in numerous product-lines, Turkish goods are competitive and attractive. But how to spread these modern characteristics to the remainder of the economy remains one of the major challenges which Turkish leaders currently face.

Strengths and Weaknesses of the State Economic Enterprises

The mixed economy has been accepted in Turkey during the entire period of the Republic, sometimes somewhat reluctantly in principle but never so in practice. The State Economic Enterprises have been used by all the Republic's governments to pursue economic, social, and political ends. Currently, despite the great growth of the private sector, the public sector continues to operate plants which are generally closer to optimum size,[14] which make better use of technology than many plants in the private sector, and which often (though certainly not always) produce better quality goods than comparable private firms. On the other hand, there continues to be major disagreement about the degree to which they should pursue various objectives, such as profitability, maximizing of efficiency, and subsidizing consumers through low prices.[15]

Some aspects of the growth of the SEEs are shown in Table 7-4. In 1975 there were 405 state-owned manufacturing plants,[16] of which about 184 were in foods and beverages, tobacco, textiles, wood, stone and paper products, and 63 in metal products, machinery and transportation equipment. In 1975 the SEEs employed about 35 percent of all Turkish workers in "large" plants, paid about 41 percent of their wages, took about 32 percent of the

TABLE 7-4
Public and Private Manufacturing Plants

	1950	1963	1970	1974	1976
Number of plants	1,905	3,012	4,820	5,952	6,143
Public sector (SEEs)	103	237	254	385	406
Private sector (10 or more workers)	1,802	2,775	4,566	5,567	5,737
Annual average employees	147,825	298,965	504,054	666,110	737,919
Public	76,033	134,383	185,444	228,891	259,943
Percent	51.4	44.9	36.8	34.4	35.2
Private	71,792	164,582	318,610	437,219	477,976
Percent	48.6	55.1	63.2	65.6	64.8
Average plant size					
Public	738	567	730	595	640
Private (10 or more workers)	40	59	70	79	83

SOURCE: DIE.

inputs, and accounted for 37.5 percent of the outputs and 37.9 percent of the sales, small private industry excluded (DIE #825:212–19). Most of these figures represented only fairly small declines from the 1950s. Structurally, the SEEs somewhat reduced their share in the production of consumer goods, maintained their level in intermediate goods industries, and, in the most important change, reflecting allocation of tasks between the public and private sectors, reduced their percentage of investment goods from about 85 percent in 1950 to about 25 percent in 1974 (TUSIAD, 1977:19).

A major problem in operating the public sector in any country, of course, is choosing the economic and social ends this sector is intended to serve. In 1978 this problem became highlighted in very stark terms when it was revealed that the SEEs had lost some 30 billion TL in 1977, 48 billion in 1978, and that the projected loss for 1979 with the continuance of current policies would be 70 billion (Yankı #412:18, statement by Minister of Management Kenan Bulutoğlu). The entire 1977 government budget was about 225 billion lira. The major blame for these huge losses was put on the maintenance of very low prices for SEE goods, great overemployment, and the history of the willingness of the state to finance the losses. The difficult nature of setting objectives in the public sector that are socially, economically, and politically justifiable can be seen in the history of Turkey's SEEs.

The objectives set for the SEEs during the initial years of *etatism* were many and varied. They included rapid increases in industrial production, general stimulation of the economy, increasing Turkish independence from foreign influences, and domestic political objectives such as demonstrating that the Republican government could be of real material benefit to the Turkish people. Thus, under the aegis of two 1930s five-year plans, over one hundred manufacturing plants were established in various key fields, as noted above. The objective of increased production began to be met by 1935, from which time significant increases were recorded. Stimulation of other areas of the economy took place through such policies as the geographic dispersal of plants (strategic and defense considerations were also important in location decisions) and through establishing relations with farmers, which included not only opening up markets for their goods (such as sugar beets) but also extension and educational activities, the extensive use of local subcontractors, and encouragement of industries which would use domestic raw materials, such as metal ores. Efforts at increasing Turkish economic independence included ventures into heavier industry, including the Karabük iron and steel complex, and an abortive airplane engine manufacturing plant in Kayseri. Other social objectives were met by heavy price subsidization. The goal of "modernization" was addressed by establishing plants which were relatively large and which tried to use modern technology, the latter giving the public sector a start on achieving the relatively high productivity (in relation to the Turkish economy as a whole) which it still maintains today (even though overemployment sometimes tends to offset this advantage).

The RPP governments were not, of course, immune to the temptation to fulfill political objectives through the SEEs, and there were frequent charges during the single-party period of partisan favoritism in plant location, of using the SEEs to enhance the power of the bureaucracy, and of catering to the ideological biases against private enterprise held by policymakers who were attracted to the Soviet economic model. Some of these charges were undoubtedly true, and there is little disagreement that some errors in economic judgment were made. But for the most part, the SEEs contributed positively to the later development of the economy.

Not surprisingly, many of the policies established during the single-party period have continued after 1950. Alongside growth of the private sector, there was continued expansion of the SEEs. In part this was due to the Democrats being no more willing than the RPP had been to forego the opportunities for political gain from the control of such great resources. Also important, though, was the realization that the public sector could continue to be a very major source of the economic growth to which the DP was committed. Innovations in the public sector under the DP included joint ventures both with Turkish private capital and with foreign investors and entrepreneurs, policies which were especially useful in that the private sector was not as yet able to generate adequate resources to establish modern facilities and technology and thus take advantage of economy of scale.

The advent of economic planning after 1961 settled some issues regarding the SEEs, but left others unresolved. Of those which have been settled, the most important is the firm acceptance of the principle that a mixed economy is *economically* desirable, and for the first time direct attention was given to the matter of the public and private sectors as complementary elements of the economy (an issue not really very relevant during the single-party period, when the private sector was all but nonexistent and largely ignored during the DP years of government aversion to planning). As a result, since the mid-1960s there has been considerable adherence to the often-stated criterion that public enterprise should only tread where the private sector will not or can not; i.e., that public investment should be concentrated in intermediate goods, and that the private sector's greatest expansion should be in consumer and investment goods. Public investment should be in areas "in which great fixed capital investments are necessary," including petroleum and chemicals, iron and steel, paper, and nitrogen soil fertilizers" (Manisali, 1979:528).

It has proven impossible, however, to arrive at definite conclusions as to which goals are appropriate today (though the rapidly increasing deficits have newly put the problem into stark perspective) or about the validity of specific criticisms made against the SEEs.[17] There are numerous causes of low profitability, all involving social as well as economic factors. In addition to administered low prices, some industries frequently keep larger inventories than are necessary, under "a policy of employment providing a steady and secure income to the people of the region where the SEE is established (e.g., the Turkish Coal Industry)" (Haydar Kazgan, 1972:131). The SEEs also maintain a large number of auxiliary social facilities, such as housing, which, for example, is considered "essential in employing technical personnel in

Anatolia at the prevailing salary levels (Nitrogen Industry Co.)" (Ibid.:122). In the fertilizer industry, where subsidization is particularly high, Kazgan wonders if it might make for a truer picture if the profitability ratios for the industry were combined with the "profitability ratios obtained by the farmers who use the fertilizers produced by the firm" (Ibid.:123). The general tendency of the SEEs to be very lenient in granting wage increases was noted in chapter 4.

Equally difficult to assess is the contention of the State Planning Organization that much of the problem is due to the nature of public enterprise per se:

> The lack of responsibility associated with ownership, failure to establish a clear relationship between the risks and rewards of the undertaking and the deficiencies of the direct interference of the state in economic life. The absence of dynamism peculiar to private enterprise in the economic activities of the state causes bottlenecks in communication and an increase in red tape which reduces administrative efficiency (1969:111).

This contention would seem to be at least in part disputable in that the private sector has for some time recruited managers who have gotten much of their training and experience in the public enterprises. On the other hand, one observer has noted that political factors in appointing top SEE management have often resulted in the choice of men who, while not incompetent, are lacking in knowledge of nontraditional aspects of management, such as marketing (Kerwin, 1979:73–4). Most economists appear to be of the opinion that it is now necessary to give primary attention to efficiency and profitability (Hiç, private communication; Iren, 1979; Poroy, 1972), but the issue is likely to remain controversial for some time, and guidelines are likely to remain obscure. (A major component of a set of reforms introduced by the JP government in early 1980 was ending subsidies to the SEEs and letting the prices of their products rise sharply.)

Agriculture

Agriculture was the occupation of the overwhelming majority of Turks at the beginning of the Republic. In 1962 it still occupied 75 percent of the labor force, in 1975, 64 percent (DIE #850:76). Government attention to agriculture has been uneven, frequently controversial, and often geared more to short-run than to long-run development. Although the overall growth of the farming sector has been impressive, it is also generally agreed that it remains far below its potential and seriously inadequate to many of the country's needs.

At its outset, the Republic gave considerable attention to agriculture, including education, credit, improved seed and extension services, introduction of new crops such as tea and sugar beets, and legislation on land tenure. As a result, agricultural production in the period 1923–1932 increased by about half (Hershlag, 1958:54–59) even though rural Turkey remained on the whole poor and traditional. In the 1930s, the situation remained all but static as the attention of the country shifted to *etatism* and industrialization. "The development of agriculture was not even included in the first Five-Year Plan," and "the second Plan only envisaged the encouragement of agricultural exports" (Ibid.:143). The increase of 20 percent in real value in agriculture during the 1930s came almost wholly from expansion of cultivated land rather than from improved yields (Ibid.:150). Little basic reform took place. Steps toward mechanization were halted in the face of rising rural unemployment; the cooperative movement faltered because of insufficient capitalization and organizing skills; and the fact that state investment went almost entirely to industry meant that ambitious schemes like irrigation remained on paper. Some antidepression measures were taken to enable farmers to avoid disaster, and some particular attention was paid to crops like tobacco, which were important for export. But government preoccupation was elsewhere (Ibid.:chapter 12). There was, however, continued great sympathy for the peasants, whom Ataturk had often called "the backbone of the nation" (on this period, see also Sarç, 1948:438–51).

During World War II agricultural production fell sharply, due to mobilization and other wartime emergencies (Hershlag, 1958:216) and to poor weather. At the end of the war, the agricultural revival of competing countries dampened export demand which might have stimulated Turkish agriculture, and government attempts to rectify the situation through land reform and additional tax relief fell short of their marks.

The Democrat party after 1950 became more active in the agricultural area. Partly in order to continue to win peasant votes but also because an important sector of the economy was lagging badly, the DP sponsored a greatly increased amount of stimulation of the rural economy. Policies included large-scale mechanization, greatly accelerated distribution of state lands (but not land reform), which included efforts to increase the amount of land owned by the average farm family so as to at least somewhat increase efficiency, more credit, and, most importantly, a policy of very high price supports. Other, more indirect, stimulants included high world wheat prices and increased demand resulting from the Korean War, unusually good growing weather during several years of the early 1950s, improvement of infrastructure, and the growth of demand for agricultural products because of the rapid population increase and an increase in national disposable income. Production increased rapidly, but, as was the case with industry, it was not always accompanied by "development." Much of the increase in agricultural production was a result merely of an increase in cultivated area.

In the 1960s and 1970s the same general policies remained in effect. There has been more "development," in part because the limits of expansion of area had been reached[18] so that "intensification" was the only alternative (Dewdney 1976:94). In addition, development was assisted by the progress of the modernization process itself. Increased education enabled better use of modern technology and farming methods. More and better fertilizers were introduced, as were new varieties of grains, largely from abroad (see Aresvik,

1975:esp. chapters 12, 13). There was also continued government financing of irrigation projects, and special stimuli to export crops (such as fruits and nuts) and to industrial crops which could replace the need for imported raw materials (such as sugar beets).

The results of agricultural policies during the Republic's first half-century can be appraised from a number of points of view.

Production

In aggregate, production of most crops has grown a great deal since the end of World War II. As seen in Table 7-5, wheat production nearly tripled, and vegetables, fruits, and several industrial crops went up far more. Much of the increase in production of basic crops such as grains took place in the early postwar years, however, and the more recent rate of increase has been a good deal slower. In terms of per capita production, the situation seems not to be as good. Aresvik has calculated that for some time the increases have only barely kept up with increases in population, and that per capita food production in 1970 was only 108 as compared with an index of 105 in 1961 (1975:Table 1.2. For similar conclusions see Dewdney, 1976:98). Good weather and improved technology led to some improvement in the situation after 1975.

TABLE 7-5
Agricultural Production—Selected Major Crops
(Thousand tons)

	1948	1960	1970	1975	1978
Wheat	4,380	7,605	9,000	13,275	13,483
Barley	2,167	3,500	3,250	4,500	4,750
Tobacco	89	139	138	193	297
Sugar beets	726	4,385	4,254	6,948	8,837
Cotton (lint)	157	474	1,086	1,248	
Cotton Seed	114	306	640	768	760
Onions	161	400	680	670	880
Potatoes	454	1,400	1,915	2,490	2,750
Hazelnuts	51	58	295	317	310
Citrus fruits (oranges, lemons, tangerines)	56	280	530	935	1,049
Tea (wet leaves)	0.6	26	153	262	449
Poultry (hens & roosters) (million)	19	27	32	39	52
Eggs (million)	852	1,322	1,914	2,597	4,179
Meat	355	424	474	699	
Milk	2,152	2,536	2,849	4,273	5,157

SOURCE: Varlier, 1978; DIE; TUSIAD, 1979.

Productivity

In general, there have been good increases in the productivity of Turkish agriculture as measured by yields,[19] though it has varied considerably among different crops, as shown in Table 7-6. In general, yields per hectare for grains have moved generally upward but with continued wide fluctuations according to weather conditions (though Dewdney's five-year running means analysis has led him to the conclusion that the upward trend of wheat production is now secular. 1976:Figure 9). On the other hand tobacco, for example, has shown a general downward trend for much of the period since 1950, apparently in large part because of expansion of production for some time into considerably more marginal soils.

TABLE 7-6
Agricultural Productivity—Selected Major Crops
(kilograms per hectare)

	1948	1960	1970	1975	1977	1975 Index (1948 = 100)
Wheat	1,086	1,097	1,163	1,595	1,787	147
Barley	1,186	1,304	1,255	1,731	1,813	146
Tobacco	783	734	456	838	881	107
Sugar beets	14,806	21,608	34,348	32,389	36,133	219
Cotton (lint)	195	282	758	716	740	367
Potatoes	6,909	8,750	12,355	13,911		201
Vegetables	1,214 (1951)	1,648	1,907	1,641	135	(1951 = 100)
Onions	3,703	7,017	9,714	11,167		302
Hazelnuts (kg./tree)	30	36	131	130		433
Tea	211	1,507	5,902	5,206		2,399
Oranges (kg./tree)	12	33	48	56		518
Lemons (kg./tree)	31	84	81	107		345

SOURCE: Varlier, 1978; DIE.

Livestock

Livestock is a particularly important sector in that demand for meat and milk products as replacements for grains is one of the most rapidly increasing effects of changes in consumer demands resulting from rising incomes. Even though milk, meat, and chicken production approximately doubled between 1948 and 1975 and egg production tripled, meat and meat products output has fallen seriously behind demand, both in quantity and quality. It is generally agreed that the meat industry has far from realized its potential to date (see, for example, USAID, 1973a:49 ff.).

There are various reasons for this situation. Room for the expansion of grazing area which existed earlier has largely disappeared, partly as a result of the absence of price supports for animal raising, which led to the conversion of about half the former pasturage areas into crop land (DIE 683:116). Aresvik calculated that the grazing limit for available pasture land was approached in the mid-1960s, after which time the number of animals also began to level off (1975:55). He adds, however, that in recent years the rate of decrease in feed resources has also slowed down, because of such factors as greater grain production and increased mechanization, which has reduced the need for feed for draft animals. The most significant failures appear to have been in not improving breeds,[20] not making use of high-nutrient feeds, and poor control of disease and parasites. Reportedly, large-scale smuggling of meat into Iran, Iraq and Syria has also cut down potential export earnings. In sum, errors of omission more than commission appear to be the blame for the troubles in the livestock area. Certainly this area is now ripe for rapid development.[21] Favorable factors for expansion include the fact that meat-industry technology is well developed and highly transferable from more advanced countries (although animal husbandry also requires a relatively high level of skill), that the labor-intensive meat industry can particularly benefit from the relative cheapness of Turkish labor, and that both domestic and export demand and prices are usually highly favorable (Aresvik, 1975:56). There is also the growing realization that it is necessary to increase protein ratios in the average Turk's diet.

TABLE 7-7

Agricultural Technology

	1950	1960	1970	1975	1977	1978
Number Tractors	16,585	42,136	105,865	243,066	325,225	370,259
% of crop area worked	9	14	33	75	—	—
Fertilizer used (000 tons)	42	107	2,217	3,692	6,577	7,474
% acreage fertilized	0.04	0.07	—	34.00	—	—
Hectares irrigated (000)	800	1,177	2,100 (1973)	2,232	2,587	
% acreage irrigated	0.6	5.1	8.4	9.5	—	
Pesticides used (000 tons)	9.5	23.4	—	62 (1973)	—	

SOURCE: Varlier, 1978; DIE #850; TUSIAD, 1979.

Exports

Agricultural exports fluctuate particularly widely because of variations in weather and in internal demand. In general, the percentage of Turkish exports (by value) which are agricultural products has declined during the past twenty years, from about 81 percent in 1961 to about 75 percent in 1970 and 60 percent in 1977 (DIE 683, 850). But in 1978 and 1979 it was a sharp increase in agricultural exports, possibly because of unusually favorable weather, which kept the balance of trade from being far worse than it might have been. About 85 percent of Turkey's agricultural exports are fruits, vegetables, and industrial crops, with cotton, tobacco, and hazelnuts alone accounting for about half. This is a favorable situation since it is these crops which will likely be in most demand by Turkey's major customers. Potential for production increases in these crops is also particularly great.

There are other general reasons why Turkish agricultural development remains far below its potential, despite growth in many areas. Among them are insufficient credit,[22] weaknesses in organization (the weaknesses of cooperatives were discussed in chapter 4), shortages of agricultural extension personnel, insufficient investments in fertilizers and pest control, and regional imbalances which are in part due to very great differences in soil quality and climate, but which also result in the failure to tap important resources. (The latter topic will be discussed more fully in chapter 8.) In addition, there is the matter of land reform.

The Paradox of Land Reform

One of the notable aspects of Turkish reform policies is that they have not included large-scale land reform (though it was often envisioned). The Turkish situation raises some important questions about the functionality of land reform in modernization of the agricultural sector and its role in the larger process of economic development. While there is no doubt that from the viewpoint of social justice land reform is highly desirable, it is more difficult to assert that land reform—by which is meant here better distribution of land and movement toward universal ownership by farmers of the land which they work—is necessary or functional from an economic standpoint i.e., that it would lead to better land use or to greater and more efficient production.

Land reform legislation has been passed periodically. Laws in the 1920s and 1930s and in 1945, 1964, and 1973 authorized a variety of measures. Many were implemented, including ending of most taxation of agricultural products, expropriating vakif(pious foundation) lands, and distributing public lands to immigrants and to some landless and sharecropping families. Some progress was also made toward better establishment of land titles. There was not, however, action on the redistribution of land owned by wealthy landowners and local notables, in part because of the political support from the latter on which RPP, DP, and JP governments all relied at various times. Other reasons for this situation may be termed technical, including the absence of cadastral surveys, lack of personnel to carry out complex policies, and shortages of funds for compensating those whose land would be expropriated. In addition, pressures for land reform could be relieved through a variety of other economic and political factors, including the availability of new land and of public land for distribution,[23] the increase of nonagricultural employment in rural areas, the partial relief of rural overpopulation through urbanization and, to some extent, migration abroad, and the ability of many farmers to improve their situation through agricultural modernization. The situation today has both negative and positive aspects for the health of the agricultural sector. On the negative side, there seems no doubt that income inequality within the rural sector has increased, and it is estimated that "about 70 percent of agricultural households (are) below 'subsistence' income level" (Özbudun and Ulusan, 1980:11). There are a number of causes for this. In 1973 about 13.3 percent of all Turkish farm families were landless (Varlıer, 1978:28, 37). Of landowning families, 44.6 percent owned less than 20 dönüms, 25 percent less than 10, and 13 percent less than 5 (Ibid.:29). In 1970, it was reported that only 21.6 percent of farms consisted of one plot, whereas 50 percent were made up of four or more separate parcels (Aresvik, 1975:Table 3-3). The situation has worsened during the last quarter century in all of these respects as a result of population growth, inheritance practices, and the ability of richer farmers to buy out poorer ones.

While there is also no doubt that income inequalities have widened because the richer farmers were better able to take advantage of improved technology and credit (see Ulusan, 1980:127–32), it is also noteworthy that the use of some elements of technology on small holdings appears not to be significantly less than on large ones. Varlıer shows, for example, that for farms as a whole, 67 percent used fertilizers, and that the percentage that did so on holdings of all size-categories under 500 dönüms was at or close to that level. Similarly, pesticides were used by 58 percent of Turkish farmers as a whole, and by 54 percent of those whose farms were smaller than 20 dönüms (1978:Table VI-18-1). There were, of course, major differences among regions, and in all regions there were large differences between small and large farms on other factors, such as tractor use, the efficiency of which is directly tied to land size. Unfortunately, figures on the relative productivity of different farm-size categories are apparently not available, but the data would lead one to suspect that the large income differences within rural Turkey are due to factors such as the rent paid by sharecroppers, larger size of families of small farmers, and the ability of the richer farmers to take better advantage of improvements. But it is plausible to speculate that the small farmers have access to certain items which help improve productivity (fertilizers, pesticides, etc.) either through government sources or from landowners whose property the small farmers are cultivating.

Thus whether land reform, meaning an increase in the percentage of families owning their land, would bring major increases in total agricultural output is speculative. It may be that the key factor is farm size, and in this regard the picture is also unclear. Several analysts who have tried to calculate at what size there is a significant improvement in productivity have in general concluded that the increase in average farm size would have to be quite great to bring much improvement, possibly considerably greater than is possible unless the number of farm families declines sharply.[24] Most appear to agree, on the other hand, that from the productivity point of view "the most important problem . . . [is] the continued use of traditional methods of farming in many places" (Namik Ziya Aral, as quoted by the Careys, 1972:57n4). All optimistically note, though, that there is little evidence any longer to support earlier assertions that peasant attitudes are hostile to change if and when "modernization" is made available in proper form. (An example of a largely successful extension effort is given in Aresvik, 1975:161–2.)

One can only speculate also as to whether early land reform would have been economically beneficial and whether or not it would have had positive effects such as reducing the number of persons who migrated to rural areas and contributed to the intense pressure on city facilities. As in so many other areas of Turkish modernization, the benefits and drawbacks of land reform have not been easy to estimate.

Infrastructure

Among the significant factors affecting and reflecting the ability of the Turkish economy to reach its potential is its infrastructure. In general, much of the basic infrastructure is now in place in quantitative terms. What is now most important may be termed "refinements," though these also involve quantitative increases, and certainly can be at least as expensive as were the basic road networks, electricity grids, etc. For example, improvement is needed in the quality of services such as telephones, in feeder roads to more remote villages, and to forestry areas, in extension of water supply to individual homes and industries, and in upgrading the quality of personnel and of maintenance.

Transportation

Prior to World War II, primary emphasis was put on development of the railroad system, partly because of security needs. Since the war an extensive road network has been developed. Between 1927 and 1960, the length of national and province roads approximately tripled, and the basic highway network is now pretty well complete. Since the mid-1960s the emphasis has shifted to improving the quality of roads (paving, grading, and shortening circuitous routes, the latter improvement accounting for the fact that in recent years the total length of asphalt roads has stayed roughly the same). There has also been a start on constructing all-weather feeder roads to villages, and some 50,000 km. of village roads were improved by at least one grade between 1963 and 1972.[25] Concurrently, there has been a near-astronomic increase in the number of motor vehicles (Table 7-9), considerably in excess of Plan targets (SPO, 1978b:Table 220). As shown in Table 7-10, almost all passenger traffic and over three quarters of the freight now moves by road (despite recent increases in railroad capacity), which among other things makes Turkey all the more vulnerable to the recent sharp increases in world oil prices.[26] Other difficulties include insufficient preventive maintenance of railroads, roads, and vehicles (although it must be added that Turkish mechanics are often amazingly ingenious at making makeshift repairs).[27] Maintenance will become even more important if Turkey continues to be a major transit route to other parts of the Middle East.

Marketing and Distribution

Facilities for marketing and distribution require storage areas, specialized equipment such as refrigerator trucks, and assurances of regularly maintained delivery schedules. Skilled personnel and capital investment are vitally needed here. They are particularly important for perishable agricultural products like fruits and vegetables, which have such great potential for export. To date, deficiencies in this area have been quite serious.

TABLE 7-8

Road Quality and Network
(in kilometers)

	1950	1963	1967	1972 (est.)	1975	1978
National Roads						
Hard surfaced	1,322	9,926	13,090	18,879	31,895	30,551
Loose surfaced	4,126	19,577	15,910	13,116	11,111[a]	—
Graded	3,070	2,519	1,890	930	555	534
Unimproved	15,788	2,514	1,850	1,020	1,312	1,144
Total	24,306	34,536	32,740	33,945	33,762	32,229
Province Roads						
Paved	302	14,649	15,300	16,810	19,644	22,124
Graded	5,955	4,313	7,060	3,950	2,333	2,538
Unimproved	16,517	4,953	3,260	2,400	3,300	2,827
Total	22,774	23,915	25,620	23,160	25,307	27,489
Village Roads						
Paved (1st Class)	—	—	4,110	27,389		
Paved (2nd Class)	—	13,888	28,776	45,592		
Graded	—	13,873	18,509	29,694		
Unimproved	—	20,230	98,605[b]	59,380		
Total	—	48,081	150,000	162,055		

SOURCE: 1950, 1975–77: DIE; 1963–72: SPO, 3rd Five-Year Plan.

[a]DIE and SPO use somewhat different classifications.

[b]Not previously incorporated into official road network.

TABLE 7-9
Transportation and Mail Volume

Year	Road				Railroad			Domestic Air		Domestic Mail
	Kilometers of Roads	Number of Cars	Number of Trucks	Number of Buses	Kilometers	Thousand Passenger/km	Million Ton/Km Freight	Million Passenger/km	Million Ton/km Freight	Million letters and Cards
1927	22,053	—	—	—	3,756 (1923)	224 (1925)	192 (1925)	—	—	—
1930	39,583	5,056	2,579	204	6,639	630 (1934)	653	—	—	—
1935										
1940	41,582	—	—	—	7,381	2,113	2,005	—	—	—
1945	43,511	3,406	4,479	988	—	1,545	1,356	—	—	—
1950	47,080	10,071	13,201	3,185	7,671	2,516	3,078	—	—	118.9
1955	55,008	28,599	30,250	6,671	—	3,917	4,366	64	59.9	143.2
1960	61,542	45,767	57,460	10,981	7,895	4,396	4,632	—	—	177.2
1965	58,385ª	87,584	79,121	22,169	—	4,075	5,735	163	15.3	255.4
1970	59,451	137,771	122,882	36,896	7,985	5,561	6,092	308	25.0	432.7
1973	59,279	234,577	159,356	51,463	8,141	5,215	7,222	685	53.9	354.7
1974	59,069	303,845	175,010	55,808	—	5,753	7,039	582	46.5	400.4
1976	59,615	471,456	236,499	71,156	8,138	4,615	7,932	887	70.0	455.5
1978	59,718	597,530	289,279	85,234	8,139	5,600	6,649	807	63.5	455.9

SOURCE: DIE Publications.

ªReflects emphasis on improvement of road quality and shortening of old, circuitous routes.

TABLE 7-10
Percentage of Transportation by Road and Rail
(remainders by sea or air.)

	Passenger/km.		Freight (ton)/km.	
	Road	*Rail*	*Road*	*Rail*
1950	47.2	45.7	22.3	71.6
1960	69.3	28.0	43.4	54.7
1972	92.5	5.7	64.5	24.6
1977	95.7	2.7	76.4	13.9

SOURCE: T.C., 1962: Tables 33, 34; SPO, 1978b: Tables 216, 218, par. 1490.

Utilities

Another area of serious bottlenecks is in utilities. Both production and consumption of energy have risen rapidly from about 53 kwh per person in 1953 to 135 in 1963, 390 in 1975 (TUSIAD, 1977:80) and to 510 in 1977 (SPO, 1978b:Table 206). The demand, however, is steadily growing, and it was estimated that in 1978 the shortfall would be some 1.5 billion kwh (about 9 percent), a sharp increase from the 271 million kwh shortfall in 1975. The shortages appear largely attributable to construction delays (Uras, 1977:11). It was recently forecast that if all planned development were completed, it would have been possible to meet electric energy demand by 1980 (SPO), 1978a:68). The composition of electric energy production has shifted in the last few years so that there has been a decline in the percentage generated from oil (from 45.5 percent in 1972 to 34.5 percent in 1977). In 1976 Turkey produced only about 18 percent of its oil needs (TUSIAD 1977:79). Its hydraulic energy output was up from 28.5 percent in 1972 to 41.8 percent in 1977. (SPO 1978b:Table 207.) Much of the latter was a result of the Keban dam project. The remainder came from coal and lignite. The fourth plan reported, however, that during the third plan period, targets were not achieved in water power, and coal resources were not sufficiently exploited (SPO 1978b:par. 35). The price increases for imported oil since 1973 have also caused extremely serious motor-fuel shortages. Other areas of major difficulties include the need to maintain long delivery lines (the sources of production are far from the centers of consumption), and insufficient and for the most part very old facilities for extension of services to industrial users and individual homes.[28] Frequent voltage reductions and service interruptions are not only annoying to the general population, they also cause unnecessary wear and tear on many types of machinery.

Virtually every large Turkish city also has a very serious water supply problem, with Istanbul and Ankara users often being supplied for a limited number of hours per day. The limited amount of water now available for tapping, and the age and inadequacy of water mains, means that a very large amount of investment will be necessary to improve the situation.

It should also be noted that public transportation, a key utility enabling, among other things, efficient utilization of workers, is generally very inadequate in most Turkish cities.

Communications

There are few things about which there are more complaints than the telephone system, despite recent improvements in the quantity of equipment and installation of direct intercity dialing. One result of piecemeal development of the system has been that many different types and makes of equipment are now in use, presenting difficulties in connections and maintenance. Estimates of projected demand far exceed foreseeable supply. The mail system, on the other hand, is relatively good, and there may still be excess capacity in the telegraph system (SPO 1969:631).

Credit

Credit is made available though a large number of public and private banks, and increasingly by financial institutions such as insurance companies. Despite large increases in the amount of funds available in recent years, the total is still quite inadequate to the demand. Because of this shortage, there is also a variety of credit restrictions which further inhibit expansion of the economy. For business, one of the chief obstacles lies in the conservative practices of Turkish banks. Loans for construction (in housing almost more so than industry) are in great demand, and banks prefer them to loans for industrial production, partly because of their greater security. A very high proportion of loans continue to require real estate as security, and collateral up to 200 percent is often demanded. In addition, interest and service charges frequently amount to at least 17.5 percent (SPO, 1969:57 and TUSIAD, 1976:68), and as a result "until recently the commercial banks seldom if ever provided medium or long-term credits to enterprises other than those in which they themselves were shareholders" (TUSIAD, 1976:66). Some measures to improve this situation have been taken by public banks, including a requirement in 1973 that commercial banks set aside 20 percent of their resources for industrial development, but the credit situation remains more of an obstacle than an incentive for entrepreneurs.

Capital Formation

Although capital formation has been described as "the most rapidly growing component of GNP" since 1950 (Krueger, 1974:13), at a 1974 seminar conducted by the prestigious Economic and Social Studies Conference Board, the consumption-investment ratio (and the failure to obtain large amounts of foreign investment) was called one of the most serious and important problems of contemporary Turkey (*Milliyet*, 22 January 1974).

Quantitatively, over the period since 1950 it has shown both bright and dark spots, though more of the latter. General government consumption has risen, from a fairly steady level of about 10 to 12 percent in 1963–1975 to 14 percent in 1977, of which a significant portion is in defense expenditures. Private consumption, on the other hand, even with "rampant consumerism," has fallen in relative terms, from about 74 percent in 1963 to about 71 percent in 1972 and 68.6 percent in 1977 (SPO, 1978a:Table 4). Total domestic savings, a major capital source, have fluctuated between 17 percent and 20 percent since 1972, after standing at about 15 percent in the mid-1960s. The rate of overall savings growth has declined, however, because while private saving until recently has grown at about 9 percent per year (1973–1977), public savings have dropped precipitously, from 9.6 percent in the 1963–1972 period to 3.3 percent in 1973–1977 (Ibid.). The large increases in money supply and credit have been the result of high volume of new loans from the Central Bank, which only quite recently has begun to practice more discipline on this score. Plan targets for marginal domestic savings were met during the first plan (target 27 percent, actual 32 percent), but fell far short in both the second (target 34 percent, actual 19 percent) and third (target 38 percent, actual 12 percent) (SPO, 1978b).

The "inability to generate an adequate amount of domestic savings" (OECD, 1974:27) is rooted in factors both numerous and difficult to remedy. Contextual ones include periodic political uncertainty, rapid inflation (which is both a cause and an effect), and the frequently marginal level of living of much of the population, which leads to low propensity to save, which propensity might decrease even further if income distribution becomes more equal and "consumerism" spreads. Factors more directly related to structural aspects of the economy include the fact that "the capital market is inadequately developed as an institution" (OECD, 1974:36) and that "disparity between official and economic interest rates . . . not only impedes the flow of savings to financial intermediary institutions, but also weakens the effect of the interest rate to direct economic activity to more productive areas" (Yürükoğlu, 1975:4). Another weakness is that a very high proportion of capital formation is generated by the construction sector. While there are positive aspects to this (construction is labor-intensive, uses little or no foreign exchange, and is very much in demand), it also reduces the amount of investment channeled into new resource-generating (industrial) expansion (Krueger, 1974:14. She notes that this is at least in part due to strong encouragement of new building under Turkish tax laws). It should also be noted that much of the capital has come from foreign sources other than export earnings. These sources, which cannot be considered permanent elements in the economy, include large amounts of foreign aid, and, more recently, remittances from Turkish workers in Europe, which, as earlier noted, have already declined considerably.

Taxation

Taxation has, of course, economic, social, and political consequences.

The problems of the Turkish tax system stem from and have a serious impact on all of these areas. It is generally agreed that Turkey's tax system is not only regressive, but that it also fails to yield the amount of revenue it should yield. In addition to policy failures, there are inadequate collection procedures and widespread tax evasion and avoidance.

Much of the problem stems from the tax system's historical evolution. In the 1920s and 1930s, despite the pressing concern for social justice which led among other things to abolition of the tithe and other burdens on the agricultural population, there was a desperate need for public revenue, from whatever sources happened to be available. The aversion to deficit financing, and the small potential of direct taxes led to considerable reliance on indirect taxes, including excise and customs levies, which fell proportionately most heavily on the lower income groups.[29] A progressive income tax was introduced in the tax reform of 1949, and, as Oktay Yenal has written, "eventually as the economy developed, a prospering middle class started to bear the major burden of the taxes, relieving some of the burden on the poorest sections" (1973:10). But the effects were slight in terms of either increasing the amount of revenue or of spreading the burden more equitably, since there was still no tax on agricultural income. There was also a great deal of tax evasion. Rates were progressive but not very steeply so. *Esnaf* and small traders were exempted from income tax (on the grounds that many did not keep books and taxes were thus difficult to calculate). Instead, they were made to pay a "small-business levy" based on such things as rent paid, and on vaguer criteria such as "estimated" or "assumed" earnings.[30] The Hirsches' conclusion that "During most of Turkey's history taxes have been levied in accord with the ability to collect" (1966:339) would not be disputed by most observers.

After the 1960 revolution, a report by Finance Minister Kemal Kurdaş showed that 66 percent of all direct taxes collected in Turkey were paid by salary and wage earners (Weiker, 1963:151). The National Unity Committee sought to bring about some reforms. They were only partially successful. A tax was levied on agricultural income, but the NUC became involved in disputes over rates and settled for low ones which affected only a few of the richest farmers. There was also some upward revision in building and land taxes to take account of skyrocketing values of land and real estate, but it was far from what many thought was equitable, justifiable, or collectible. In other areas, there was either no change, or complex and more or less unworkable formulas were worked out to take account of numerous political interests. A final reform was the Declaration of Wealth, to be formally filed with the government by those other than salary or wage earners, in order to reduce tax evasion. Collection from government employees, salary and wage earners is done by withholding, and is still by far the most efficient part of the tax system. In 1977 some 52 percent of tax revenues came from income taxes and the remainder from indirect levies, still quite a regressive pattern (OECD, 1978:21).[31]

The degree to which the tax system fails to yield its potential has not been

TABLE 7-11

Government Finances

(million $ at 1977 prices)

	1963	1967	1972	1974	1976	1977
Total Public Sector						
Disposable Income	3,319	4,658	6,821	6,892	9,056	9,994
Of which Tax Revenues	2,652	3,756	5,551	5,733	8,108	9,552
% of revenues	79.9	80.6	81.4	83.2	89.5	95.6
Direct taxes	991	1,298	2,275	2,709	3,912	5,223
% of taxes	37.4	34.6	41.0	47.3	48.2	54.7
Indirect taxes	1,661	2,458	3,276	3,024	4,196	4,329
% of taxes	62.6	65.4	59.0	52.7	51.8	45.3
Expenditures						
Current expenditures	2,015	2,777	3,850	3,996	5,412	6,499
Investment	1,566	2,142	2,882	4,281	5,652	6,052
DEFICIT	−262	−261	89	−1,385	−2,008	−2,557
% of disposable income	7.9	5.6	1.3	20.1	22.2	25.6

Source: SPO, 1978a: Table 5.

measured, nor, probably, is it really measurable, because calculations of potential yield would have to be based on policy assumptions and preferences.[32] As has been frequently demonstrated, however, changes in the tax structure are approached by all government leaders with the greatest caution—the tax reform bills introduced by the RPP government since 1978 are moderate, yet many of its sections are doubtful of passage—and the conviction on the part of virtually all Turks that tax evasion is extremely widespread can only encourage others to join in that activity. The question asked several years ago in the title of an article by Nicholas Kaldor, "When Will the Developing Nations Learn to Tax?" remains very relevant for Turkey today (1961; for a summary of some of the problems of producing specific effects in developing countries through a tax structure, see also Goode, 1963).

Foreign Sources of Financing

Foreign Private Capital

It is only relatively recently that foreign private capital has played a significant role in the Turkish economy. During the 1920s there were a number of foreign firms which had operated in Ottoman times and later formed joint-stock companies with Turkish entrepreneurs.[33] Little new investment, however, took place. In the *etatist* period there was also little new foreign private capital, partly because of Turkish coolness toward it and partly because of the scarcity of capital generally during the world depression. In 1947 the RPP government somewhat liberalized its policies in areas such as repatriation of profits, and the Democrat government sponsored additional favorable conditions in 1950–1951. When mild measures attracted only about $6 million in three years (Iren, 1979:403), an even more liberal Law for the Encouragement of Foreign Capital (#6224) was enacted which "cancelled almost all previous restrictions" (Göymen-Tüzün, 1976:61).

As a result, foreign private investment began to increase around 1956 (for figures see Manisalı, 1979:551), though the increases were disappointingly small (Tanksy, 1967:49–50) and the share of foreign capital within total gross investment remained only about 3 percent (Ibid.:44). The government's desire for rapid industrialization and import-substitution were factors leading to the entry of foreign firms into Turkey as assembly industries in areas including automotives, electronics, electrical home applicances, elevators, chemicals, and pharmaceuticals. Many were joint ventures with Turkish capital. There was also sizable foreign investment in petroleum when, in 1954, the law was repealed which had reserved that sector exclusively to the state since 1924. When the period of economic planning began after 1961, criticism of the lack of controls led to more deliberate efforts to channel foreign private capital (FPC) into the more productive sectors, reduce waste and idle capacity, increase the percentage of domestic capital in what were considered some key industries, and to impose price controls on commodities such as pharmaceuticals, fertilizers, and pesticides. The general encouragement of assembly-type industries continued, however. The Justice party period of 1965–1967 has been described by Hiç as one relatively well-balanced between encouragement of FPC and the maintenance of controls.[34] The amount of new FPC during the 1960s was significantly higher than in the previous decade.

TABLE 7-12

Foreign Financing
(millions of dollars)

	1963	1967	1973	1975	1977
Private Foreign Capital	21	17	27	153	67
Project Credits	81	83	328	382	499
Imports with Waiver	5	12	50	98	102
Program Credits	197	162	135	5	4
Total	304[a]	274	540	638	672
Foreign Debt Payments	−119	−99	−107	−118	−214

SOURCE: SPO, 1978a: Table 8.

[a]$88 million food imports under PL 480 not counted in this total.

Another quantum increase began in 1970 in conjunction with a continuing increase in Turkey's economic momentum. Although the number of foreign firms decreased, the proportion of authorized investment which was realized increased (SPO, 1978b:par. 200). Average new investment in 1970–1973 rose to $49 million as compared to $21 million for 1963–1969, and increases brought the amount to $67 million in 1977 (SPO, 1978a:Table 35). FPC in 1976 financed production accounting for 11.7 percent of gross sales of manufacturing industry, and 6.3 percent of manufacturing employment (TUSIAD, 1977:182). "Most of the 109 firms under Law 6224 are concentrated in chemicals, metal goods and electronics" (Ibid.:183) and, since 1951, two-thirds of the FPC invested under Law 6224 has come from the United States, West Germany, Switzerland, France, and Italy (USAID, 1973:37 and SPO, 1978b:126).

The proper role of FPC in Turkish economic development remains controversial in two broad areas. One may be termed general-political; the other concerns specific ways in which FPC is used in the overall economy (for general analyses of both domestic and foreign policy implications of FPC, see also Tuncer, 1973 and 1975, and Manisalı, 1975). Opinions in the latter area are, of course, tied to the general industrialization strategy which various analysts advocate.

In general-political terms, the major parties accept the idea of FPC (the fourth plan states that subject to proper controls and channeling to meet Turkish needs, FPC will be encouraged, particularly by simplifying and speeding up bureaucratic decisions; SPO, 1978b:pars. 813–28), but there is still hostility to it from both political extremes. The radical left continues to regard FPC as an agent of neocolonialism and as strengthening the control which the Turkish private sector exercises over the economy. They also argue that given its profit motive, FPC will never agree to enter Turkey on terms under which the economic costs (excessive profit transfers, producing items with high profits but low priorities for Turkish development, etc.) and the political costs (compromising Turkish sovereignty, etc.) will outweigh benefits to Turkey. The radical right, in addition to asserting many of these same points, also stresses the undermining of Turkish nationalism and the squeezing out of small Turkish industry, particularly in the Anatolian heartland. Those on both sides (and many others) also are critical of the fact that so much of FPC has gone into assembly industries which fail to make use of Turkish raw materials, subcontractors, and worker skills.

The second category of disagreement concerns use of FPC for specific economic benefits. One is balance-of-payments effects, about which Hiç has calculated that as of 1974, 74.8 percent of the FPC which entered Turkey between 1963 and 1974 had been repatriated as profit transfers, so that there has been no major permanent addition to capital stock. Thus there has not been great permanent benefit from FPC as a foreign-exchange source, although at several critical times it was quite important. It is also contended by some that since FPC assembly industry has used components manufactured by the multinational corporations themselves, Turkey has been forced to maintain a high level of imports simply to keep some of these industries going. There is some validity to this, and the importance of the matter has grown in that targets for increasing the percentage of domestic private capital in many industries have not been achieved in recent years, while these very industries (such as automotives) have expanded rapidly in response to strong public demand. In sum, while there may have been many benefits from FPC, it would be hard to argue that balance of payments benefits have been prominent among them. Whether or not they have actually been negative, in that some of the goods for which parts have been imported might have been produced domestically in their entirety had not FPC assembly industries provided such strong disincentives for potential domestic producers, must of course remain speculative.

In other areas, positive aspects are clearer. 85 to 90 percent of FPC has gone into manufacturing, with only 11 to 15 percent to services and about 1 percent to mining and agriculture (SPO, 1978b:125). FPC has been estimated to be responsible for the jobs of 75,000 Turkish workers. Hiç also found productivity of FPC higher than average, the same 6.3 percent of the workers producing 11.7 percent of manufacturing industry's gross sales in 1973. Critics maintain that technology transfer has been unsatisfactory in that foreign firms have not used their most modern technology, that, in fact, they have "dumped" onto Turkish industry their own outmoded equipment and thus locked Turkey into it (see Göymen-Tüzün, 1976:75,78, also citing work of Gülten Kazgan, though these sources do warn that the data must be used with a great deal of caution). While there is undoubtedly some truth to this, and some cases of transferring obsolete technology appear to have occurred, it could hardly be expected that foreign companies would transfer to potential competitors their latest techniques. Firms with large shares of FPC are, however, generally more capital-intensive than most of their Turkish counterparts. As to plant size, often another key factor in productivity, the average size of firms with foreign capital was 458 workers, compared to 76 for private manufacturing firms as a whole (Ibid.:72).

The future role of FPC in Turkey remains unclear. The various factors involved might lead either to predictions of increase or decrease. Factors leading one to predict that expansion will be only modest include continuing pressures of radicals in Turkish politics; continuing bureaucratic obstacles; the likelihood of continuing balance of payments deficits, which can hamper the establishment of assembly industries and make it uncertain that other industries will have reliable sources of imported raw materials and equipment; general political instability, even though it is unlikely that even in the event of something like another military intervention there would be drastic changes in policy toward FPC; and, on the international scene, increased competition for FPC from several countries which are already further along the road toward association with the EEC than Turkey is (Spain, Portugal, Greece). On the other hand, positive factors include the general dynamism of the economy; its continued level of very high demand for manufactured goods; continuing inflation, with the prospect of high profits in relation to the less-inflated costs of capital from abroad; and the continued "opening up" of the economy to FPC as association with the EEC comes nearer. That FPC is reluctant to be discouraged was demonstrated when a decline in new FPC as a result of stringent controls in 1974 was more than offset after moderate policies were inaugurated in 1975 (Hiç). Careful government policy in this sphere would appear to be of great importance to maximize the potentially very beneficial contribution of FPC.

Foreign Assistance

Since the late 1940s Turkey has been the recipient of large amounts of foreign aid. (For a general overview of the external financing mechanisms of the Turkish economy, see Tuncer, 1967.) Begun by the United States under the Truman Doctrine, foreign aid has been carried on since the early 1960s in large part by an OECD consortium in which the United States and the major European nations take part. International agencies have also made major contributions, and in recent years Turkey has also received credits from the Soviet Union and some other East bloc countries. While the majority of the aid has been in "project credits," there has also been a substantial amount in direct grants, military aid, and commodity shipments under U.S. Public Law 480.

The exact amounts are difficult to specify because of the numerous different categories and because the major analyses all cover different time periods. The major category, project credits, has brought Turkey some 5,594 million dollars between 1958 and 1977 (SPO, 1978a:43), of which about half came in 1960–1970 (Başak, 1977:70) and half in 1971–1977 (Tuncer's figures are similar; 1975:215). About 36 percent came from the OECD countries (including 17.8 percent from the United States and 7.5 percent from Germany); 38 percent from international organizations (of which 23 percent from the IBRD); and 26 percent from bilateral agreements outside the consortium (of which 21 percent was from East bloc countries, including 12.5 percent from the Soviet Union, and 3.5 percent from Japan, SPO, 1978a:43). Total American aid for the years 1949–1973 was $2.7 billion, of which $958 million was in grants, $1,041 million in loans, and some $586 million in shipment of agricultural commodities (AID 1973:58). The credits have gone to a wide variety of sectors: "those by the Consortium were oriented mostly towards infrastructure projects, namely to the transportation, communication and energy sectors, whereas the credits provided by international institutions have been mostly allocated for the . . . agriculture, energy and services sectors. The credits from other countries . . . were directed in general towards the basic metals, energy, mining and petroleum refining" (SPO, 1978a:42). The latter included Soviet financing of Turkey's third iron and steel complex at Iskenderun.

Foreign aid issues are both economic and political. There is little disagreement that foreign aid has enabled Turkey to survive a number of potentially very difficult economic crises, and that it has fostered considerably more rapid economic growth in several periods than might otherwise have been possible. Tuncer has calculated that "the ratio between (external resource) transfers and the foreign exchange earnings has been strikingly high. It started from a level of forty five percent in the early 1950s, went up to nearly seventy per cent in the first half of the 1960's, and was approximately fifty per cent in more recent years" (up to 1969, the end of his analysis; 1975:220). Several leading Turkish students of the subject (Tuncer; Başak, 1977; Bulutoğlu, 1970), however, have serious questions about both the economic and political consequences of aid. Economically, two difficulties are pointed out: indirectly, the reliance on foreign transfers has frequently enabled Turkish policymakers to avoid or postpone basic internal structural reforms which might have been useful in increasing foreign exchange earnings. Directly, Turkey is today saddled with an extremely large foreign debt, estimated at the end of 1978 at some $13.5 billion (*New York Times*, March 4, 1979). An OECD estimate was that the amount of money which would be needed for debt repayment in 1978 would be $667 million, which would have been about 32 percent of total Turkish export earnings that year (1978:Table 9).

This situation leads, of course, to political dependency, about which there is great concern. In some respects, dependency has been direct, most vividly in the American aid embargo of the mid-1970s because of the 1974 Turkish invasion of Cyprus. But the instances of direct links between aid and foreign policy have been infrequent. More troublesome to Turks is the degree to which outside nations and institutions have acquired influence in Turkey's internal policies for economic development. For example, there was the Stabilization Program forced on the Menderes government by Turkey's bilateral and multilateral creditors in 1958. In 1978–1979 the political debate on this issue was far more serious because the problem was of much greater magnitude. In desperate need of new credits, estimated as "at least $8 to 10 billion in the next five years" (Vehbi Koç, as quoted in the *New York Times*, May 31, 1979), the International Monetary Fund and other potential creditors insisted that conditions for the aid include major devaluation, austerity measures, and internal reforms. Turkish governments resisted these conditions for some months, insisting, among other things, that the internal decision-making process could not be interfered with to such an extent, though many of the conditions were eventually adopted, if indirectly and in compromise form. But the problem had been made starkly clear. Of course, offering aid is also very much in the security interests of Turkey's allies. For example, Turkey became more important than ever as a member of NATO following the Iranian collapse of 1979. They also have a stake in Turkey's economic potential for future trade and for integration into the EEC. But the problem of proper policy choices by all parties in the area of foreign aid continues to be delicate.

Balance of Trade and Balance of Payments

Certainly some of Turkey's most serious economic problems of the coming few decades will involve the balances of trade and payments, both because of the important role which imports do and will continue to have in fueling Turkish economic development, and because of Turkey's avowed aim of joining the EEC. Turkey's balance of trade has been in constant and ever-increasing deficit since 1947 (for early figures, see Herschlag, 1958:245, 248 and Singer, 1977:392). In 1977 Turkish exports were only 30 percent of imports, an alltime low. The balance of payments has been periodically rescued only by large amounts of foreign aid and credits, remittances from Turkish workers in Europe, and in 1978 by drastic import cuts forced by the shortage of foreign exchange and by a large increase in cereal exports made possible by good weather. All of these are highly unreliable as continuing bases of support.[35]

As is true of most "developing" economies in advanced stages, Turkish economic growth has resulted in a steady and rapidly increasing demand for imports, particularly raw materials, capital goods, and component machinery parts. Since the most rapid growth period began, in about 1960, about two-thirds of Turkish imports have consisted of equipment (machinery), minerals, and petroleum products. During the first and second plan periods even these high ratios were generally not up ·to planned targets. In addition to the extremely rapid rise in demand, causes of balance of payments difficulties have included lower-than-anticipated availability of investment funds to

TABLE 7-13

Balance of Payments, 1950–1978

(millions of $)

	1950	1960	1970	1975	1976	1977	1978
Imports	−286	−468	−948	−4,739	−5,128	−5,796	−4,599
Exports	263	321	588	1,401	1,960	1,753	2,288
Balance of Trade	−23	−147	−360	−3,338	−3,168	−4,043	−2,311
Invisible Transactions	−27	−44	+181	+1,435	+854	+646	893
Current Accounts Balance	−50	−139	−171	−1,880	−2,300	−3,385	−1,418
External Debt Repayment	−15	−65	−158	−118	−119	−214	−256
Financing Requirements	−65	−204	−329	−1,998	−2,419	−3,599	−1,674
Financing Requirements as percent of Imports & Debt Repayment	21.6	38.3	29.7	41.1	46.1	59.9	34.5
Financing Requirements as percent of Exports and Invisible Balance	27.5	73.6	42.8	70.5	86.0	150.0	52.6

SOURCE: TUSIAD, *The Turkish Economy 1979*, page 206, used by permission.

finance domestic substitutes for imports, failure of exports to meet their targets, and the rapid worldwide inflation of the 1970s (for a summary of these factors, see SPO, 1978b:par. 170). In general, discipline in limiting the import of consumer goods (achieved in part by very high customs duties on selected products) appears to have been relatively good. There was some help from major devaluations in 1959, 1970, 1976, 1977, 1978, and 1979. Some economists have asserted, however, that some of the devaluations could have been even more helpful if they had been larger—despite unfavorable domestic consequences—and better coordinated with other measures such as foreign credits and strong, immediate export efforts, and if there had not been other obstacles, such as the fall in the value of the dollar.

On the export side, there has been a rather steady increase, but far from high enough. Agricultural products continue to be the largest component, though the rise in manufactured exports from 11.5 percent in 1970 to 25.7 percent in 1977 is encouraging. The export performance of textiles, glass, and ceramics, and some metal products has been particularly good. Because of the large agricultural component, though, fluctuations in export earnings continue to be very great (in response to weather conditions).[36] There is also growing competition from other Mediterranean countries in specialized products such as citrus fruits, the demand for which in European countries is the fastest growing of all agricultural products. There has also been significant help through the development of markets in Middle East countries and in Eastern Europe for Turkish agricultural goods and consumer durables, though in percentage terms these areas have not increased much as Turkish customers during the 1970s. The bulk of exports continues to be to the EEC countries (49.5 percent in 1977 as compared to 40 percent in 1969). The continued strong performance vis-a-vis the EEC countries is, of course, important. They are the major hard currency areas. It is also here that Turkey will have to compete more strongly as integration with the EEC develops. As it becomes important for Turkey to greatly expand its volume of imports, the expansion of its non-European markets will also have to continue, though. The potential in these areas is considered very good.

The major causes of export shortfalls include very high domestic demand, insufficient attention to quality control in both industry and agriculture, weaknesses in marketing and distribution, inflexibility in adjusting to changing demand,[37] and insufficient and poorly coordinated government financial incentives to exporters. The fact that there are so many and varied causes makes the problem a very tough one to solve, and though many observers are of the opinion that entrepreneurs are now ready to respond to appropriate adjustments in tax credits and other stimuli (see, for example, the statement by Minister of Trade Teoman Köprülüler in *Yankı* , #384:21), that remains to be seen.

The Problem of the Common Market

In 1963, Turkey and the European Economic Community signed an

Association Act initiating a period which was to be followed by two stages of association leading to negotiation of conditions for full membership in 1995. The preliminary period was formally declared concluded in an Additional Protocol in 1970. Not long thereafter, Turkey formally applied for associate membership, and there began a period of negotiations about the specifics of mutual concessions which had been outlined in general terms in the Additional Protocol. The negotiations have generally not gone well, and while there are no signs that either Turkey or the EEC intend to withdraw from the arrangement, there is serious questioning on both sides.

There is little disagreement among either Turkish or foreign observers that Turkey's reasons for moving toward the EEC had a large political component. It was seen as an integral step in her continued movement toward full identification with the "developed" world, with the added incentive that one of Turkey's major rivals, Greece, was moving toward the same objective. A somewhat more economically based reason was that several of Turkey's major competitors in southern Europe (competitors for European markets) were also taking on closer relationships to the EEC, and they could not be allowed to gain too many comparative market advantages. All major Turkish political parties supported the move, and continue to do so, although all express dissatisfaction with some of the prospective terms of the association. The chief dissent comes from radical parties and factions of both left and right, who maintain that Turkey's sovereignty, and perhaps more importantly, her culture and identity will be seriously compromised.

Probably the most important problem is the effect on Turkish industrialization of full customs and trade integration. As noted earlier, Turkish industry is quite inefficient in many sectors and unable to compete with that of Europe, and most of the incentives offered by the Turkish government for better export performance have to date met with little success. A high percentage of the exports to the EEC countries continues to be in agricultural products, and the prospects are that under full association this pattern will be perpetuated, and the percentage probably increased.

The arguments for continuing on the path toward full membership (it seems generally agreed that the 1995 date will have to be put forward) are mostly economic. Those against continuation are in large part motivated by social, political, and, to some extent security concerns. There are several potential advantages in Turkey's continuation on its present course: (1) Availability to Turkish consumers of better quality and cheaper manufactured goods; (2) Privileged access to European markets for Turkish agricultural products, although, as noted, the fact that Spain, Portugal, and Greece are so close to joining the EEC may limit Turkey's gains in this regard. (The effects of Turkey's competitors joining the EEC are analyzed in detail by Manisalı, 1978. The protectionist policies of the current EEC members concerning their own agricultural products also indicate that Turkish gains might be limited.) (3) Continued access to Europe for Turkish workers; and (4) The possibility that some sectors of Turkish industry will be stimulated into greater efficiency and better quality by EEC competition, which effect would probably occur during the transition period. (On the other hand, at least one Turkish economist has pointed out that Europe fears Turkey on precisely these grounds, that there would be a flood of workers, cheap agricultural goods, and a requirement under the terms of internal relationships in the EEC structure for very large amounts of aid to Turkey from the other members.)

On the potentially negative side, the most serious possibility is that Turkish industrialization might be all but halted, and that Turkey would thus become an agricultural appendage of Europe. Among the chief problems here would be social and political matters. Being an agricultural appendage smacks of the very neocolonialism about which there was so much complaint in the waning days of the Ottoman Empire, and would certainly not be the kind of dignified association which a proud Turkish nation envisages. There is also the security factor. In the event of war, Turkey could be cut off from vital supplies of military and consumer goods. There would also be major dislocations were Turkey to depart from its policy of alliance with NATO which it has followed since World War II. A major economic as well as social problem is the likelihood that unemployment would increase even more, even if the availability of work for Turks in Europe were to increase (which it appears not likely to do).

Debate on the future of the association continues to very lively among both economists and political leaders. As yet neither side (those who favor continuing unswervingly on the path to association and those who see the need for at least slowing down—only the radical parties openly favor abandoning the EEC venture altogether) has made a totally convincing argument for its case. But it is perhaps the most important economic decision which the Turkish Republic has had to face since its inception, and the most pivotal one in the shaping of Turkey's economic development in the Republic's second half-century.

Conclusions

The challenges of Turkish economic development are immense. A prediction by Baran Tuncer (1977) is that even under the most favorable assumptions Turkey's population in the year 2000 will be over 66 million (compared with 40 million in 1975), and that the need for jobs, urban facilities, education, food, and energy will be considerably greater than it now appears the economy will be able to supply. As indicated above, Turkey's economy is an area in which there has been a particularly visible contrast between high quantitative growth and serious inadequacies in structural changes, refinements, and reforms needed to meet the more sophisticated demands arising both from domestic modernization and from growing integration into the international economy. It has been suggested that an accurate description of Turkey might be a country which is politically developed and economically underdeveloped. While this description has some validity, it must be also pointed out that alongside the shortcomings there are many areas of industry, agriculture and commerce which are indeed dynamic and innovative. It is also true that during the past half-century many foundations have been laid upon which a modern economy can now be built. Perhaps one of the lessons of the Turkish experience is that the stage of "advanced underdevelopment" may be far more difficult than the initial stages on the road to economic modernity.

EIGHT

Government Institutions and Organization

An important factor in the modernization process is the effectiveness of the nation's governmental institutions, including policymaking by the legislature and the cabinet, implementation of policy through the executive and the bureaucracy, and the functioning of the judiciary. The criteria for appraisal of these institutions include efficiency and thoroughness of legislative functions, effectiveness of delivery of services, efficiency of operations (an important aspect of which is the role of local government), and equity of services (an important issue in Turkey in this regard is the problem of regional imbalances.)

Government Structure

The Constitution

Among the functions of a constitution are spelling out basic national values and establishing mechanisms for their realization. Two major values inform Turkey's constitution: that the Republic should be democratic, and that it should be a vehicle for progressive social change. The 1924 Constitution and its 1961 successor addressed both of these issues in ways which reflect the circumstances of their origins. (For the text of the 1924 Constitution see Geoffrey Lewis, 1955:197-210. The original text, before amendments, of the 1961 Constitution can be found in the *Middle East Journal*, Vol. XVI, No. 2, Spring 1962, pp. 215-38.)

The constitution of the so-called First Republic defined the state as a Republic and included provisions giving individual citizens broad legal and political freedoms. It also "fully incorporated the majoritarian (rather than the 'liberal') concept of democracy (which) holds that sovereignty is the 'general will' of the nation . . . and it is, as such, absolute, indivisible and infallible" (Özbudun, 1978a:50). This concept was implemented by conferring complete and unchecked power on the Grand National Assembly. The absence of a presidential veto, independent judicial review, or other checks and balances meant that the protection of these liberties was left almost entirely in political hands. This arrangement worked satisfactorily during the Ataturk years. The political establishment did in fact (with only few exceptions) exercise control over abuses of citizens by the government. Nor did much abridgment of political dissent occur, its absence partly facilitated, to be sure, by the simple reason that very few citizens openly questioned the Ataturk reforms.

The situation in respect to both legal and political rights changed decisively during the Democrat party rule of the 1950s. The opposition raised questions not only about the wisdom of government policies, but also about the very constitutionality of many of them (such as retreats from the RPP version of secularism), and disputes between the political parties were often couched in the most fundamental terms. In addition to there being no mechanisms to resolve these basic questions, there were also no legal obstacles to the propensity of a ruling party to react to perceived political threats by passing repressive laws against the press, the judiciary, the opposition party, and others. (For a detailed discussion of the above points in relation to the Ataturk and Menderes periods, see Savcı, 1958. On the repressive actions of the DP, see Weiker, 1963:10-11.)

It was for these reasons that the 1961 Constitution converted the structure of Turkish government to one replete with checks and balances, including a bicameral legislature, presidential veto, Constitutional Court, guarantees of autonomy for the universities, for news agencies, and for the administrative bodies of broadcasting and television, and more explicit spelling out of political rights and freedoms (for details see Özbuun, 1978b:23-26).

The differences between the two documents were smaller in regard to social goals of the nation. In 1937 the entire "Six Arrows" of Kemalism were inserted into the Constitution after they had been developed in successive RPP programs (see chapter 1 and Weiker, 1973:222-27), to say that the Turkish state was to be "republican, nationalist, etatist, populist, secular and reformist" (Article 2). The 1961 charter continued the same basic direction and also spelled out social and economic provisions in much more detail (in the fashion of many post-World War II constitutions). These "positive obligations," as one might call them, include rights to social security, housing, medical care, education, and the right to rest (paid weekends and vacations). There are also articles authorizing land reform, mandating equity in wages, promotion of cooperatives, and progressive taxation. Whether or not the Constitution should contain specific measures for implementing specific rights was hotly debated, but the basic tenets of what Article 2 calls a "social State" were not seriously questioned. (On the making of the Constitution see Weiker, 1963:chapter 4 and Dodd, 1969:chapter 8.) Another notable new provision was the mandating of economic planning.

The Legislature

The Grand National Assembly actually preceded the Republic itself, having been first convened under the auspices of the Defense of Rights

Society in 1920. The 1924 Constitution established a unicameral legislature, consisting of 450 members elected for a four-year term. In 1961 a Senate was added, the members of which are elected for six years, one-third of the members standing for reelection every two years. Senators must have university-level education. In addition to its 150 elected members, the Senate contains fifteen "contingent senators" appointed by the President. Former members of the National Unity Committee hold lifetime seats. Members of both chambers are elected at large from individual provinces, with each province assigned a number of deputies and senators according to population. The Assembly must be in session at least seven months each year. (Recently it has been in almost continuous session.) Representation on all committees, including the Chairmanship Council, must be allocated proportionally among the political parties. The Assembly has more power than the Senate in that the former receives and discusses bills first and can override Senate disapproval of a bill by repassing it (though a ⅔ majority is needed if Senate rejection was by that margin). The legislature also has broad powers to question the government, initiate investigations and interpellations (these powers are available to both chambers), and to pass motions of censure (a right reserved to the Assembly only). Debate is usually held largely on the basis of party "groups," each party with ten or more members having the right to form such a "group," whose spokesman receives priority in debates. (For details on Assembly organization see Dodd, 1969:196–204; and Özbudun, 1978a).

The independence of the legislature in the political process can be appraised by several criteria. In many ways its power is, of course, related to the distribution of party strength, and since party discipline is generally strong (Özbudun, 1978a:63–65) the frequency of questions put to the government, or of amendments to proposed bills depends mostly on partisan considerations rather than on considerations of independent legislative checks on the government such as might take place in a separation of powers structure. Nevertheless, the power to put questions to ministers is an important one that has frequently made the Assembly a forum wherein the government has had to defend itself. There are usually a large number of questions (one calculation found the annual average for the years 1961–1975 to have been 611 in the Assembly and 185 in the Senate; Ibid.:69). The powers of deputies to amend proposed legislation have also been used periodically and have made the Assembly an arena for intra- as well as interparty bargaining, particularly when the partners in a coalition government have not been able to agree (a rather frequent occurrence in recent years).

Appraising the independence of the legislature from another angle, the Assembly has little capability of its own in the way of research staffs or library facilities, though some of the political parties have developed considerable expertise in these areas. Still another measure of legislative independence is the introduction of "private bills." Özbudun and Eroğul have calculated that some 12 to 20 percent of the laws passed in recent

Assemblies originated elsewhere than the ruling government, and in a considerable number of instances, government and private bills have been combined (1978a:67–68). Özbudun also believes that "successful amendment motions," either at the committee stage or in the whole House on the motions of private members, "are far from being rare" (1978a:69). An "internal constraint," on the other hand, is the high turnover of legislators, which has been less than 50 percent only once since 1961, so that there has been relatively little opportunity for development of expertise among individual members of the Assembly (Ibid.:66, citing Tachau, and Kili, 1978b:36).

Vis-a-vis outside institutions and forces, the legislature has had a mixed record. On one hand, on several occasions when legislative authority has been directly challenged, the Assembly has defended itself strongly. One noteworthy incident occurred in 1973, when the armed forces attempted to impose their own candidate for President of the Republic. The Assembly almost unanimously opposed not only the officers' candidate, General Faruk Gürler, one of the authors of the "memorandum" of March 12, 1971, but it also approved a number of compromise proposals designed to avoid a total rebuff, such as the proposal to extend the term of incumbent President Cevdet Sunay, also a former general. Even when the legislators could not agree on any candidate after fifteen ballots, they were adamant in resisting this challenge to their very status.[1]

In the eyes of the general public, the legislature has, according to some recent research, acquired substantial general legitimacy as a result of being "actively involved in creating representative linkages and opportunities for more autonomous and self-assertive citizen participation" as well as specific policy making (Turan, et al., 1979:23. It was also found, however, that in comparison to the other countries in the study, Kenya and Korea, a low percentage of citizens as yet distinguish the legislature from other parts of the government). We have no evidence as to whether the Assembly's stature in public eyes has suffered from occasions such as when prolonged disagreement has taken place on matters having little to do with legislation (for example several occasions when it required a very long time to choose its presiding officers) and when physical violence has broken out among Assembly members.

Overall, the legislature has been and is a highly visible institution, and the deputies have not hesitated to use all of the powers and devices at their disposal. Its role as scrutinizer of policy has varied largely in relation to degree of the ruling government's legislative party strength, to be sure, but there is no doubt that the Assembly has acquired a high degree of legitimacy.

The Executive

The Presidency. Despite the fact that the Turkish system is a strong parliamentary one, considerable power has also at most times resided in the office of President. The extent of this power is closely related to political circumstances, including the personality of the incumbents, and the strengths and weaknesses of Prime Ministers, cabinets, and the Assembly. The 1924 Constitution made the Presidency a party office, the chief of state being elected by each Assembly for a concurrent term. Its three incumbents, Ataturk, Ismet Inonu, and Celal Bayar, were all men of great personal strength and influence. Under the first two, the Prime Ministers were decidedly second in power, and although in the Democrat decade Premier Menderes was often the more visible, there is do doubt that President Bayar was also very influential.

The 1961 Constitution attempted to separate the Presidency from party politics by giving the president a seven-year term, limiting the incumbent to one term, and requiring that he disassociate himself from his party and his status as a member of the Assembly or Senate. The first two presidents under the 1961 provisions were important in large part because of their prior positions, and were quite strong. General Cemal Gursel, former head of the National Unity Committee, held the office from 1961 until he became terminally ill in 1966, and he was followed by General Cevdet Sunay, chief of the General Staff. In 1973 Sunay was succeeded by Turkey's only president who has not directly represented either the ruling party or the armed forces, retired Admiral Fahri Korutürk (who had been a diplomat since his retirement from the navy in 1960 and a contingent senator since 1968), a compromise following the Assembly's rebuff of the armed forces attempt to impose their own candidate. Korutürk has not hesitated to play an active, visible, and often very constructive role, but because of his lack of a strong independent political base he is generally considered to be the weakest Turkish president to date. Presidential power is likely to remain closely interdependent with its particular political context. (A good discussion of the role of Presidents from Ataturk to Korutürk is to be found in Tamkoç, 1976. Tamkoç maintains that the role of Turkey's presidents has been particularly outstanding in foreign policy matters.)

The Cabinet and Administration. Structurally, the Prime Minister and Cabinet constitute the chief power center of the Turkish government (but, as noted, historical circumstances and weaknesses of these political institutions have demonstrated that, in fact, the Presidency can be a major power focus as well). The members of the Turkish cabinet have both collective and individual responsibility. Recent cabinets have generally had between twenty and twenty-five members, all drawn from the Assembly or Senate. It is permissible to go outside these bodies for cabinet members, but this has been done only during periods of "above-party" governments, in 1960–1961 and 1971–1973. Turkish Cabinet posts, as in many countries, are frequently distributed on the basis of political needs (one clear example of this practice took place in 1978 when RPP leader Ecevit was able to form a government by detaching ten deputies from the Justice party, all of whom were given cabinet posts), but, on the whole, Turkish ministers have been quite capable. The chief problems involve politicization of the administrative structure, and coordination of policy. On these matters there is room for much improvement.

There is a high degree of politicization in most branches of the administration. Most Turkish governments have not hesitated to use their patronage powers and their powers of discretion in authorizing projects to reward their clients and supporters. This kind of thing occurred to a limited extent during the Ataturk period,[2] but quite frequently thereafter. During recent coalition periods, the small ideological parties have sometimes taken strong advantage of the practice of giving cabinet ministers all but unlimited powers of appointment within the ministries they head, and some observers consider "infiltration" of ministries recently held by radical right-wing parties in the National Front cabinets to be one of the chief problems of current governmental operations. At the upper levels, where politicization may be more justifiable if the will of the voters is to be put into effect, it has also frequently been excessive. For example, the rate of turnover among the highest career officials of many departments appears to be very high, not only at the beginning of an administration but at other times as well. It is difficult to believe assertions that most of these changes are made for purely technical or professional reasons. (Even if that were the case, it would be an indication of still another serious administrative weakness.)

A second problem of administrative structure is efficiency.[3] Although bureaucrats in all countries tend to protect their own "turf," the Turkish government appears excessively plagued by both formalism and legalism. As pointed out in a 1962 study commission report (cited in detail by Dodd, 1969:225 ff.), there is very little delegation of authority by ministers, and the problem is compounded in that not only do even the highest level civil servants have little scope for taking independent actions or initiatives, but the ministers themselves usually have much of their time taken up with handling small matters and details. Deputy Prime Ministers have usually been too busy with political matters to perform coordinative duties, most interdepartmental committees are at the ministerial level, and the Prime Minister's office is poorly equipped with coordinators. The major potentially coordinating agencies, the Ministry of Finance and the State Planning Organization, are frequently bypassed.

At lower levels, administration is also affected by the presence of numerous corps of inspectors, both in the central offices and in the field. As noted elsewhere in this study, their role is visible in many areas of Turkish life, including the intense monitoring of the lesson-plans of teachers, the myriad steps which a petitioner to any government office must go through, and, in the private sector, the need for bank tellers to have each deposit or withdrawal verified by not one but two supervisors.

The Judiciary

For civil matters, there are three major judicial bodies: the Court of Cassation *(Yargıtay)*, Council of State *(Danstay)*, and the Constitutional Court. The latter was created by the 1961 Constitution, but the others have a history going back to Ottoman times (see Dodd, 1969:239 ff. and his source footnotes). The most important in general administrative matters is the Council of State, which has authority to review administrative decisions brought to it both by the public, and by civil servants in regard to matters affecting their own status. In recent years there has been increasing resort to the council, as Turks have become more attuned to the concept of rights and more aware of the possible remedies, and the council has become a significant check on what many consider to be administrative arbitrariness. There are frequent complaints, however, about the council's inefficiency, the failure of lower levels of administrative courts to comply with council rulings, and of the failure of the council itself to adhere to the law. Thus there has been an excessive number of appeals and a very high rate of reversal of rulings of provincial administrative councils by the Council of State proper (Dodd, 1969:240–41). There has also been some politicization through the judiciary appointive process, but the nonpolitical character of the council has been for the most part well maintained.

Increasing use is also being made of the Constitutional Court. The institutions empowered to bring cases to it include not only various official bodies but also the political parties. The RPP, which for most of the period since 1961 has been in opposition, has used this power frequently. Some use of the Constitutional Court has also been made by the universities, which are "autonomous establishments" under the Constitution and are also authorized by it to bring to the court cases "concerning their duties and welfare." The Constitutional Court has, in turn, taken to its role with vigor, and because some of the issues which have come before it have had political implications, it has become quite a controversial institution. Particular controversy has centered on the court's protection of the "autonomous establishments," which in addition to the universities included (until 1971) the Turkish Radio and Television (TRT).[4] The court's general tendency to support curbs on government power led to frequent and bitter complaints by the National Front governments of the 1970s that the Constitution was in fact unworkable. These disputes will probably wane only with the waning of intense political partisanship itself and as the court itself establishes over time its reputation as a carefully reasoning protector of the basic procedural and substantive integrity of government.

To sum up, the organization of Turkish government is highly developed, but functionally government remains very much subject to political, cultural, and other outside factors in numerous particulars of its operation. Its efficiency, effectiveness, and its ability to aid in some urgently needed reforms are thus often considerably less than what is needed for the formidable tasks it is being called on to undertake.

Local Government

There is little historical precedent for governmental decentralization in Turkey. In Ottoman times government included the *millet* system, whereby certain policy matters (such as personal status and the adjudication of many disputes) were administered by local religious communities, but for most public policy matters the provinces were under the jurisdiction of governors directly responsible to Istanbul. For personal as well as political reasons these officials were primarily oriented to centralization of government. It was the central government that kept them in power and sanctioned their local emoluments. In return the governors usually sought to strongly discourage separatist movements, and saw to it that revenues for the central government were maximized. (In addition, there was little or no concept of a city as an entity with the responsibility of providing its own governmental services.)

In the Ataturk period, the motivation for continued centralization was more positive, but the results were similar. Intent on national integration, modernization, and the implementation of the new Kemalist values, it was both functionally and ideologically undesirable to allow the development of strong local power centers. In the early years of the Republic, the emphasis was on large-scale nationally oriented projects such as railroad and road networks and State Economic Enterprises, in which local participation (either financial or administrative) was seldom appropriate. Local and municipal needs were given lower priority, in part because there were as yet few pressures on the government to do otherwise. That functional and ideological considerations tended to be mutually reinforcing contributed to the momentum of the rapid increase of concentration of power in Ankara. In addition, of course, this situation gave national political and bureaucratic leaders sizable resources for expanding their influence.

In regard to the autonomy of local government, Turkey is one of the world's most centralized states (Weiker, 1972:6). Most of the functions of province, city, and village governments, and the priorities to be given to each function, are mandated. Almost all their activities are subject to close monitoring and approval by the central government. They have all but no independent financial resources which might give them the opportunity for taking initiatives, to say nothing of policy independence. Although local government functions are shared in a formal sense by centrally appointed and locally elected officials, primacy is generally in the hands of the former. The administration of each of the sixty-seven provinces is headed by a *Vali* (governor) responsible to the Minister of the Interior, and the provinces are further divided into districts headed by *Kaymakams* (district administrators). At the province level there is also a "Special Administration" *(Özel Idaresi)*, with an elected Province General Council which has functions relating to "health and welfare, public works, culture and education, agriculture, animal husbandry and economic and commercial matters" (T.C., 1973:186). In practice, though, it has jurisdiction only in the areas which do not fall under the scope of the national government (of which there are numerous field offices in each province), such as construction and maintenance of a few province roads (Weiker, 1972:20). Its presiding officer and operating executive is the governor. The budgets of the 67 Special Administrations for current expenditures in 1976 totaled about 1034 million TL, less than a tenth of the total of corresponding municipal budgets (DIE #890, Tables 357, 358).

City governments are headed by a full-time mayor and a City Council. Although both are elected and have long lists of duties and responsibilities, they have only little real power or autonomy. Still organized under the Municipal Law of 1930, the council by statute meets only three times a year (though each meeting may have several sessions) for the approval of municipal budgets, city plans, construction programs, and taxation and fee schedules. In the interim the city is in the charge of a municipal committee consisting of several council members plus the heads of major city departments and presided over by the mayor, who is the city's chief administrative officer. On these authorities are mandated some fifty-four specific duties applicable to all cities, and up to twenty-six others for the larger ones.[5] Duties are divided into four categories: public health and welfare, public utilities, urban planning and land use, and miscellaneous, and may range from protection of the water supply to operation of places of public amusement. In most cities many, if not all, are carried out poorly.

An important reason for this poor performance is that the centralized structure includes a single national tax system which is heavily weighted toward both national priorities and central control, with the result that municipal budgets are almost impossibly inadequate. During the period 1962–1972, for example, the cities' financial situation deteriorated both relatively and absolutely. The per capita increase in municipal revenues of 50 percent, from 178 to 268 TL, was considerably less than the rate of inflation. The increase of total municipal incomes of 186 percent compared with an increase of total government revenues during the decade of 458 percent, the cities' share falling from 17.0 percent in the earlier year to 8.7 percent in the latter (SPO, 1973:Table 683). Equally restrictive is the pattern of sources of municipal income. In 1976, tax revenues accounted for only some 41 percent, of which only about half was levied by the cities and collected by them. Most of the remainder comes from rent on city property and the operation of city-owned business establishments. As a consequence, Turkish city governments must frequently concentrate far more attention on these activities than on local administration or public services. The national government limits the levels of property taxes and of fees and charges which the cities may levy, and has been extremely reluctant to raise them, with the result that the cities have been unable to take advantage of the astronomical rise in land values which has taken place in recent years. The large cities are further penalized in that, of the taxes collected by the national government and earmarked for return to the cities, only 80 percent is distributed on the basis of population, the other 20 percent being used as special aid to cities under 50,000 (Weiker, 1972:21–2).

A second major reason for the low quality of city services, the dearth of skilled personnel, stems partly from another aspect of centralized control. Turkish cities are tied into a nationally mandated and fixed personnel law which prevents them from offering high salaries. Provincial cities are thus unable to attract many qualified persons who, in the absence of such an incentive, are loath to leave the major metropolitan areas. In part, provincial cities, like ministries as discussed in chapter 2, have circumvented this restriction by hiring on a "contract" basis, but the problem remains generally unresolved. (On these problems, see Yasa and Geray, 1968.)

Villages are governed under the Village Law of 1924 by an elected Village Council *(Köy Derneği)*, which chooses a headman *(muhtar)*, and by a Council of Elders *(Ihtiyar Meclisi)*, consisting of between eight and twelve members plus the village *imam* and the village teacher ex officio (T. C., 1973:189). In addition to being responsible for the provision of village services, the *muhtar*'s duties include compiling statistics, issuing some documents, and aiding in tax collection. The village government also has limited judicial powers, such as settling disputes over small loans and mediating personal arguments (Ibid.). The quantity and quality of village government varies in relation to factors such as size, wealth, the traditionality of the social structure (though this is not to imply that traditional elders cannot also be vigorous and innovative), and individual capabilities. The village headman is often put into a difficult position when directives sent down from higher levels are disagreeable, such as was the case some years ago when mandated projects were to be carried out by requiring each villager to contribute several days' labor. In practice, most headmen appear to have taken on more of a role of advocate for their fellow villagers than of a government agent. This perhaps helps account for the finding, as noted in chapter 3, that village dwellers feel their local government is more efficacious than do residents of cities and towns.

Should there be greater decentralization? There are some arguments on both sides. On the side of continued central dominance is the fact that in several areas it is conceivable that changes would not necessarily bring improvement of services. For example, the dearth of resources, both financial and human, continues to be severe in the country as a whole. It will still be some time before the number of qualified planners and technicians will be sufficient so that the national, provincial and municipal bureaus can all be adequately staffed, and it is unlikely that even with greater financial resources most local governments could equal the quality of national agencies such as the Ministry of Reconstruction and Resettlement or the Provinces Bank *(Iller Bankası)*. These agencies have built up competent staffs for planning and project design and provide often excellent technical services to the municipalities.[6] It is understandable, therefore, that the emphasis of the first and second five-year plans focused more on coordination (both within the national government and among central and province and municipal administrations) than on decentralization. (For a summary of early plan ideas and proposals on this topic, see Yavuz, 1963:13–17.)

Financially, there is no certainty that decentralization in terms of increasing the powers of local government to levy their own taxes would result in an increase in total revenues available for local government services. It is by no means certain that local governments would generally increase taxes or make them more progressive. While one should not automatically assume, of course, that this would *not* occur, research indicates that in many countries it is national governments which have often played a useful role in overcoming resistance to local tax reform because they are less subject to particular local pressures. (For examples from several countries, see Heidenheimer, et al., 1975:84, 126, 171.)

In terms of efficient delivery of services, too, there is no necessary reason to believe that local administration would be an improvement (although the comparative advantages and disadvantages of national vs. local administration in this area can only be speculative). Regional planning, even under national auspices, has not made much progress, and problems of multiple jurisdictions and long-outdated boundaries are found in every metropolitan area.[7] Nor can one assume that decentralization would improve the selection of priorities, or the equitable distribution of funds. It is possible, of course, to contend that local leaders are more attuned to local needs. But there are many province representatives of national government agencies who are very much involved in, aware of, and sympathetic to the specific concerns of their communities. As for equity, which is very difficult not only to define but also to assess in relation to other important criteria, the potential for disruptive frustrations is becoming great. Within many communities, especially the larger cities, there is reported to be a growing resentment of the flood of new migrants and their ever-increasing claims on local services and resources. Pressures may well mount to assure that the needs of the middle-class neighborhoods are met first, and while persons from these neighborhoods still occupy positions of local power. Such tensions may increase rapidly if there is continuance of a tendency shown strongly by most governments since the start of the multiparty period to grant *gecekondu* areas funds out of proportion to other felt needs and to otherwise cater to their interests by policies such as legalizing squatter housing through retroactive granting of land titles.[8]

On the other hand, decentralization could bring benefits. It would, for example, increase political participation and governmental efficacy and responsibility.[9] Turkish central government officials are not completely unjustified in seeing themselves as "tutelary" to the municipalities (Keleş 318), though whether "tutelage" in the political sense of training for self-government is as justifiable as it might be for training in technical matters is, of course, controversial. Moreover, it is unlikely that tutelage for self-government can be very effective unless the pupils are allowed to practice by doing. This is particularly true in policy decision-making areas (see Weiker, 1973:chapter 4).

Another argument for decentralization is that it could lead to the mobilization of the rapidly growing energy and talent for self-improvement visible in many Turkish communities. Numerous Turkish cities are buzzing with energy. The political, social, and economic plans and activities of local officials and private individuals and groups in cities such as Sivas, Kayseri, Gaziantep, and Isparta are impressive (Weiker, 1972:passim). Sivas, to cite only one example, reacted to its defeat in the competition for Turkey's third iron and steel complex (it went to Iskenderun) by developing a scheme to mobilize local capital, including the sale of shares in small denominations to a large number of local residents, for financing an aluminum casting plant

(Ibid.:58). Locally led plans for the creation of industrial parks for small manufacturers were advanced in Kayseri and Eskişehir, though it was anticipated that financial obstacles would be considerable and much more work would be needed. Part of this activity, interestingly, stems from a spirit of competition among cities as a result of greater interurban contacts. Virtually all of the people interested in Turkish development on the local level complain of frustration over central controls.[10]

The inertia which has been built up is very great, however. As Keleş and Danielson remark, "the highly centralized political system has been able to resist major changes in the administrative and intergovernmental arrangements. At the same time, the system operates to keep most local people outside the administrative and political process. . . .Centralization is self-perpetuating since it serves the interests of most national politicians and bureaucrats as well as the more affluent sectors of Turkish society" (1980:345). To make major changes will take great political courage (and strength) then, as well as a major overhaul of institutions (and some concepts) which are deeply imbedded in Turkish political culture and administrative history. There are reasons to think that major decentralization would not necessarily serve the needs of Turkish development in all important respects, but there is also little doubt that unless at least incremental changes are made, many important potential new strengths will not be mobilized in the service of the Republic.

Regional Balance

A second problem with important structural implications, the continuing severe imbalance of development levels among different regions, has also become a subject of more and more public discussion in Turkey in recent years. Among the reasons for concern are (1) large-scale internal migration from the less-developed eastern provinces is adding to the already rapid rate of urbanization and causing intense pressure on urban facilities; (2) the contribution which the eastern provinces should be making to national economic growth is not forthcoming; (3) norms of equity and social justice are of increasing concern to many Turks; (4) radical parties (especially on the right) are receiving a higher proportion of votes in the less developed regions than elsewhere; and (5) as perception of inequality grows, there is renewed danger of disruptive stirrings in many eastern provinces with large Kurdish populations.

The general course of integration of the rural areas into the mainstream of Turkish life has been discussed in chapter 3. The eastern provinces were left behind during Ottoman times, in part because they were not in a position (geographically, economically, or politically) to take advantage of many of the stimuli which affected the more western parts of the country. Since the Republic, the east has fared better. It was given major attention in the extensive programs of railroad and road-building to link major cities and as many smaller ones as possible to the new national capital at Ankara. The

State Economic Enterprises included factories in Erzurum and Sivas, and industrialization of the east was listed as a major target of the five-year plans (Hershlag, 1968:83). The eastern area also shared in the creation of governmental and cultural centers such as the *Halkevleri*. But the amount of attention was initially relatively small. Primary emphasis was put on central Anatolia. Factors influencing relative low levels of developmental efforts in these regions included the prospects of quicker and larger returns in the already semideveloped central areas, the need to keep order in the largely Kurdish provinces of the east, which actively occupied a great deal of the attention of the authorities,[11] and, possibly, the RPP's at least tacit alliance with many large landowners of the eastern region.

During the multiparty period policies have varied. No very special favors were given to the eastern provinces during the Democrat period. Reasons included concentration of the Democrat governments on facilitating the growth of the private sector, which was concentrated in the more developed regions; the lack of a development plan or overall concept; and the DP's desire to maximize political support, which was potentially highest in the western parts of the country. During the period of planned economic growth after 1961, the authorities expressed serious concern with the problem of regional imbalance and also took some actions to correct it. In the words of Keleş and Danielson, "national development plans have sought to promote territorial social justice through more balanced distribution of public investments among regions" (1980b:288). On a per capita basis, investment in the east in some spheres has been proportionally higher than in the west.[12] Efforts in the first plan period included more rapid building of infrastructure, offering financial incentives to technical personnel to work in the east, and offering tax incentives to private industry for making investments there (Keleş, 1976b:153). In the second plan period, a new policy was attempted, identifying several cities as "potential growth centers" in which "major infrastructural and cultural investments were made to speed their transformation into 'great metropolises'" (Ibid.:154). None of these efforts was significant in either changing the overall pattern of public investments or in attracting private industry, however, and the third plan continued to recommend incentives, but "practically jettisoned the notion of regional planning" in favor of a more national approach of emphasizing investments "where they could promise the greatest return" irrespective of considerations of regional development (Ibid.:159).

There has been but small comfort for the east from all this, notwithstanding Keleş and Danielson's conclusion that "without these governmental efforts, even greater differences would exist among regions," and that "the initial regional development policies, as a report by the World Bank notes, 'were effective in spreading industrialization throughout Turkey.' ..." (Ibid.:55), and one striking phenomenon continues to be the very high rate of internal migration. Calculations from the 1970 census conclude that for the country as a whole during the years 1965–1970, 11 percent of the Turkish population had changed their place of residence. To a small degree, these figures represent short-distance movement from rural areas to nearby towns, but most movement was either interregional,. or migration from small communities to large cities, or both. In the eastern, southeastern and Black Sea regions in 1965–1970, only four provinces had even modest rates of in-migration, each attributable either to the presence of a growing metropolis (Gaziantep) or to special growth factors (very large investments connected with the Keban Dam project in Elazığ, or with military installations in Erzurum). The chief destinations of migration have been the three metro-politan areas of Istanbul, Ankara, and Izmir (which received about 40 percent of the total gross migration; SPO, 1978b:par. 228) and, more generally, the Marmara, Aegean, and Mediterranean regions. An analyst at the State Planning Organization has cited field studies (in the absence of more detailed statistical data) indicating that there is also "substantial" urban/urban interregional movement (Yener, 1977:6). Perhaps even more significant than the numbers are the characteristics of the migrants: some 35 percent of the males and 39 percent of the females are in the 15 to 24 age group, 87 percent and 64 percent respectively are literate, and 44 percent and 31 percent are primary school graduates (Ibid.:9). There can be no doubt that during the post-1970 years the rate at which the less developed provinces are being drained of their most dynamic elements has increased (see Keleş, 1976b:151–60).

We must note, of course, that government policies are only part of the reason for the continuing problem. Much is also attributable to natural conditions and to history. Geographically, eastern Turkey is predominantly mountainous, with relatively infertile soils, poor climate, including extremely harsh winters, and is quite isolated. Although some major trade routes crossed the region, the nature of the terrain lessened their effect—i.e., the poor internal communications inhibited the spread of commerce around the trade lines. This is a great contrast with central Anatolia, for example, where the effects of the establishment of Ankara as the national capital have been very widespread. The area's location had also made it the route for numerous invasions through the centuries, which, among other things, drove the population further into retreat and isolation, diverted trade patterns, and generally made the area relatively unattractive to the Ottoman governments, which penetrated other regions to a far greater extent (e.g., by seeking to control them militarily and administratively, which in turn also opened them up commercially and culturally). Among the demographic factors, probably the most important is the large number of Kurds, whose "natural integration" with the Turkish population has never really been accomplished, despite official denials of any special problems.

For eastern Anatolia as a whole, the fact that it entered the period of more rapid growth at so much lower a level than other regions, also meant that it was far less well equipped to respond by self-generating "multiplier" responses. To cite but one example, regional development policies have spurred urbanization in eastern Anatolia,[13] but the differences in urbaniza-tion among the regions (i.e., the absolute size of cities, and the numbers of

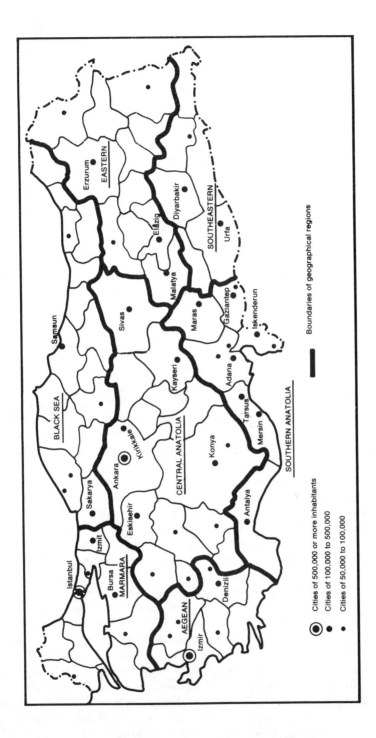

BLACK SEA

EASTERN

SOUTHEASTERN

CENTRAL ANATOLIA

SOUTHERN ANATOLIA

MARMARA

AEGEAN

Erzurum

Diyarbakir

Elâzig

Urfa

Samsun

Sivas

Malatya

Maras

Gaziantep

Iskenderun

Kayseri

Adana

Tarsus

Mersin

Kirikkale

Ankara

Konya

Sakarya

Eskisehir

Antalya

Izmit

Istanbul

Bursa

Denizli

Izmir

Boundaries of geographical regions

⊙ Cities of 500,000 or more inhabitants
● Cities of 100,000 to 500,000
• Cities of 50,000 to 100,000

urban centers in the region) remain great, and "what regional development strategies have not been able to deflect . . . is the strong pull of Turkey's largest urban centers, which continue to attract the lion's share of private and public investment to the west. As a result, the overall impact of urbanization is to sustain substantial regional disparities despite governmental efforts to redress these imbalances. And these regional differences, in turn, contribute significantly to the development of an urban system dominated by the large metropolitan complexes of Western Turkey" (Keleş and Danielson 1980b: 288).

It is not surprising that since the end of World War II, that is, since the beginning of the period when in addition to government-sponsored stimuli to growth Turkey has seen the growth of stimuli from the momentum of development itself, there has been a steady widening of the disparities among the country's various regions. Turkey has been characterized by analysts as divisible into three development levels: the developed areas of the Aegean, Marmara, and parts of the Mediterranean and western Black Sea; the middle levels of central Anatolia; and the least-developed regions of the east. The latter are found roughly east of a line drawn north to south through the province of Sivas. Since the regional problems with which Turkish policy-makers are most concerned are centered in the eastern regions, and since central Anatolia appears to be making significant advances and is generally no longer considered to be a problem so far as social and economic integration is concerned, the following analysis will focus on the east and contrast that region with the remainder of the country as a whole.[14]

Table 8-1 shows some of the regional differences.[15] Quantitatively, measurable government services are, for the most part, equitable, and many of the differences have explanations which, while possibly regrettable, are not necessarily wholly unjustified. Teacher-pupil ratios for elementary schools are quite similar for east and west. There is also now virtual equality in the per capita number of health officials, most of whom are government personnel. There has been an approximately equal rate of improvement over time in the number of hospital beds per capita, though in 1978 thirteen of the seventeen eastern provinces still fell below the national average on that item (nine did so by more than 50 percent). In terms of use of resources, the sharply lower overall percentage in the east may to some extent be justified (although it is still not something to be proud of) by the fact that the eastern areas are far more rural, so that even if more hospitals were built, the amount of access for much of the region's residents might not really be increased. Far less justifiable is the fact that in 1974–1975 some 25 percent of the villages in the east were without schools, as compared with 5.4 percent for the west (DIE #812:131). Some aspects of agricultural services are also disturbing. Fertilizer is used by over four times as many farmers in the west as in the east. About twice as many farmers in the west use insecticides. Seventy percent of those farmers who do not use fertilizers or insecticides say they do not do so because of expense, unavailability, or lack of knowledge as to how to use them. There are great disparities in visits by agricultural personnel (29 per-

TABLE 8-1a
Regional Differences

	1960		1965		1970		1975–77	
	East	West	East	West	East	West	East	West
Education								
Elementary school								
students per teacher	37.7	51.7	—	—	39.4	38.3	36.4[a]	33.1
Literacy Male (%)	36	57	—	—	52	73		
Female (%)	9	28	—	—	21	45		
Health:								
Persons per								
hospital bed	820	549	—	—	775	459	700[a]	450[a]
Urban population								
per hospital bed			—	—	232	184		
Persons per doctor	8,401	2,487	—	—	5,838	2,302	5,065[a]	1,706[a]
Persons per nurse,								
midwife, health								
official	4,737	2,730	—	—	1,307	1,161	1,211[a]	1,204[a]
Dependency:								
Percent of popula-								
tion ages 0–14			47.2	40.8	48.7	40.8		
Registered Marriages:								
Number per popula-								
tion over 14 yrs.	—	—	—	—	.0037	.0060	.0116[c]	.0389[c]
Registered Divorces:								
Number per								
registered marriages	0.74[d]	.100[d]	—	—	.033	.081	.068	.095
Vehicles								
Number per								
100,000 population								
Cars	20	174	—	—	59	418	372[b]	1,527[b]
Buses	18	44	—	—	53	101	98[b]	216[b]
Trucks	64	181	—	—	104	323	267[b]	755[b]
Radios:								
Per 1000 population			—	—	39.7	98.3	47.3[b]	117.7[b]
Labor Force:								
% in agriculture			—	—	80	65		
Income			—	—			1973	
per household					Eastern Anatolia		All Turkey	
					16,665 TL		24,694 TL	

SOURCE: DIE publications.

[a]1975.

[b]1977.

[c]Per total population. 1975 population by age and province not yet available.

[d]Total population, province and district centers.

TABLE 8-1b
Regional Differences (in percent)

MTV Table	Item	East[a]	West
26	Own, share, or rent tractor	14.5	18.1
28	Use fertilizers	15.1	64.4
31	Use insecticides	38.6	65.3
66	Villages with or attached to co-op	25.8	69.0
184	Villages with shortage of drinking water	75.8	69.0
189	Report health good or very good	64.5	71.3
38	Villages never visited by agricultural personnel	62.7	22.2
166	Read newspaper once a week or more	28.4	53.9
168	Listen to radio once a week or more	45.5	64.1
57	Villages in which change occurred in last ten years	37.1	50.6
98	Villages with seasonal unemployment	83.9	78.5
104	Age at first marriage 15 or less	30.7	23.4
130	Less respectful behavior of youth toward the aged	29.7	42.4
	Favor scolding or beating to punish same	46.5	39.8
134	Villages without schools	27.0	6.4
	Villages with reading rooms	3.0	18.5
161	Desire university education for daughters	28.7	29.5
	Desire only primary education for daughters	34.3	36.7
162	Desire professional occupations for sons	45.5	39.5

[a]East includes Northeast, Southeast, East central regions.

TABLE 8-1c
Regional Differences (in percent)

Item	East	Other regions
Marriage registered legally	53	72–93
Marriage arranged by family	83	73–82
Ideal number of children for a family like hers (in numbers)	4.51	3.00–4.02
Best age for a girl to get married (in years)	16.88	17.36–17.82
Unconditionally disapprove of family planning	44	26–37
Husband does not allow men and women to sit together while visiting	61	52–54 (except Medit. 29)
Husband does not allow wife to go out without a scarf	98	95–98
Husband generally makes decisions about which friends to associate with	70	56–65 (except Black Sea 44)
Husband generally makes decisions about how to spend family income	69	59–64 (except Black Sea 46)
Most important requirement for success in life is patronage and luck	88	92–98
Ever performs namaz	86	86–89
Performs namaz once or more daily	80	65–78

SOURCE: Srikantan, 1973.

cent of the villages in the west but only 13 percent in the east reported visits more than once a month, and 22 percent in the west but 68 percent in the east said they were never visited: SPO, MTV:Tables 28–32, 38).

There are other important indicators, statistically measurable but not as directly tied to government policy, which might be called more "autonomous." They are important in that they constitute much of the base on which more rapid development may be built. On some of these indicators the differences are being narrowed. The SPO study of income distribution mentioned in chapter 7 found that while the 48 percent higher income per family in the west in 1973 actually was a slight decrease from the difference in 1968 (SPO, 1976:37n2), the importance of that decline was offset by the larger average family sizes in the east, and by the fact that the small size of the difference is more a result of continuing low income in the country as a whole rather than of higher incomes in the east. Some of the uses to which this wealth is being put may also be indicative of important trends concerning equality. Although all the figures for communication facilities in the east are still far below those of the west, it is notable that there were considerably faster rates of growth in the east than in the west between 1970 and 1977 in the ownership of cars and only slightly slower growth in ownership of trucks (which are available mostly to the wealthy). Concomitantly, growth in buses (on which the poorer groups are most dependent for transportation) was slightly slower than in the west, and the east had substantially slower growth in radios (which are likely to be the most easily available means by which the poorer groups can keep in touch with the wider world).

On other indicators the data is less ambiguous and less promising for more rapid "take-off" in the east. A serious matter is that in value added in manufacturing industry per capita of population, eastern Anatolia showed a *decrease* of about 5 percent between 1968 and 1974, compared to increases in every other region. A similar trend took place in growth of "large" manufacturing establishments (ten employees or more.)[16] Differences between east and west in the dependency ratio increased by a quarter in the period 1965–1970 alone, the result not of a rapid improvement in the west but of a significant worsening in the east. In literacy, eastern men gained as many points as western men between 1965 and 1970, but women in the east fell from 19 points behind their western sisters in 1965 to 24 points behind only five years later.

Perhaps most striking and potentially significant, however, are the small differences on some of the attitudinal measures which we have. There are similarly high levels of ambition for social mobility by eastern and western Turks for themselves (e.g., wanting to settle in cities) as well as for their children (in education and occupation). There are also claims (if they are to be believed) of favoring the "new" over the "old," and demands for education. (On the rapid increase in the demand for education, see Aral, 1980:496). There is little doubt that many people are pursuing these goals most vigorously.

The choices facing policymakers on issues of regional imbalance are not easy. Although policies giving primary emphasis to overall national growth or to policies concentrating on regional equity and social justice are not necessarily mutually exclusive, the shortage of both financial and human resources makes the problem of direction politically and economically sensitive. On the side of stressing national growth is the fact that a high proportion of Turkish economic growth will ultimately still be based on the private sector, which is for the most part determined to go to the regions in which it can get the quickest and largest returns; the fact that the multiplier effect from public and private investments will for some time continue to be greatest in the already more developed areas; and that the continued shifts of population to the west will not only give the west increased political strength, but will also give added weight to arguments that the areas with the most people ought to get the most services. It is the opinion of at least one insightful Turkish economist that the eastern provinces now have high enough income, skills, markets, and other characteristics to make investments their profitable (Mükerrem Hiç, personal communication), but, as noted in chapter 7, there is as yet little evidence that investors and private entrepreneurs share this view.

The arguments for greater attention to the problem of regional balances are both economic and political. In economic terms, it is clear that if the east is ever to get to a "take-off" point for self-sustaining and self-multiplying growth, it will require very sizable short-run public investments.[17] The political arguments are that there are now increasing signs of potential unrest as the consciousness of their own underdevelopment grows among the region's residents. The unrest has to date been surprisingly small, but opportunities (and motivations) are becoming greater. As earlier noted, the eastern regions are voting disproportionately in favor of the radical right-wing parties. Reports of renewed Kurdish consciousness are also increasing sharply, albeit the reports are still for the most part informal and unofficial. In any case, the problem of regional imbalance is likely to remain one of the more vexing concerns of Turkish policy for some time.

NINE

The Modernization of Turkey: Today and Tomorrow

To conclude this study we must now bring together our findings on the individual aspects of Turkish modernization discussed in the preceding chapters, and offer, however gingerly, some prognoses for the Turkish Republic's second half-century. As was indicated in the Introduction, much of the answer may lie in whether Turkey's short-run problems can be solved before the basic long-term societal strengths which developed during the Republic's first half-century are eroded.

Turkey's Achievements

Turkey's achievements may be summed up as follows:

1. The maintenance of a democratic political system for over a quarter-century with virtually no interruption of more than a short-term "repair" nature.
2. A firm sense of national identity and confidence.
3. The integration of virtually all of the population into the mainstream of national life and national identification, and often even into the international context, via numerous factors including the vast growth of the mass media, transportation and communication, and a national economy.
5. Preservation, alongside modernization, of many basic traditions, including those of religion, folkways, and ties of kinship and regional origin. Retention of these traditions has helped cushion the trauma of many Turks subjected to rapid changes of many kinds.
6. An education system which, if not always impressive in its quality, is certainly so in its extent.
7. Emergence of a large amount of interest articulation by a large number and variety of groups.
8. The institutionalization of political parties and of a party system based on two large parties, which are both able to draw support from a variety of groups through the aggregation of interests, to be relatively moderate in their

policies, and to compete successfully for the broad middle of the political spectrum.

9. Reduction of the role of nonpolitical forces in the governmental process, the role of the military being the most outstanding example. (It is well to reiterate that Turks do not generally consider a military role in politics as illegitimate per se. It is also true that some public problems may appear to be more easily handled by nonpolitical means. But on the whole, reliance on institutions which do not have to subject themselves to public approval has many potentially undesirable effects.)

10. A responsive electoral system kept viable through extensive participation in the political process by Turkish voters.

11. The emergence of modern interest issues and the simultaneous decline in importance o earlier issues of basic social values and ideologies, which, among other things, were causes of deeply divisive social and political cleavages. Also, an impressively low amount of popular support for extreme views and for radical parties on either the left or the right.

12. The firm rooting of the concept of secularism in virtually the entire population, even if there is still considerable debate about its specific requirements.

13. A great deal of economic growth and development dynamism, often at quantitative rates which few other nations (developing or deeloped) have matched.

Turkey's Shortcomings

Turkey's shortcomings can be summed up as follows:

1. Far from perfect social mobility, and inequality of opportunity to enter the middle class. As a result, it has not yet been possible to utilize the full potential for leadership and initiative among the Turkish people. In addition, there is potential for disruptive frustration as nonelite expectations expand to include nonmaterial objectives such as power and status.

2. Continuing regional imbalances of considerable size, which may lead to consequences similar to those stemming from inadequate social mobility and inequality of opportunity, as well as to the less developed regions becoming a drag on national economic development and a potential area of political unrest and/or radicalism.

3. Poor quality of much of Turkish education, shortcomings in meshing educational efforts with manpower requirements, and a continued relatively low rate of literacy.[1]

4. Persistence in politics of factionalism, personalism, and patron-client relationships which encourage the basing of political decisions on matters other than issues and party programs.

5. The existence of enough potentially unstabilizing support for political radicalism to be troublesome, even though extremism is not yet a threat to the regime or to the integrity of the state. Part of this problem may be attributed to political happenstance: the two large parties have for some time been so even in strength that the minor radical parties have frequently held a balance of

power and thus gained increased attractiveness. Extremism has also led to increasing urban guerrilla violence, which is proving very difficult to control.

6. The failure of interest groups to encompass some major segments of the population, most particularly the peasants. The agricultural sector has done well in terms of increased income generally, but its lower strata have not.

7. An inefficient bureaucracy, which also continues to manifest a considerable amount of elitism, thus reinforcing the perception of many Turks that a major issue in politics continues to be that of center vs. periphery.

8. Serious and currently growing economic problems.

Why the Achievements?

1. Some legacies of history: the Republic began with leaders who had a considerable sense of national identity and who were politically and administratively experienced. There were, as well, important foundations for reforms which would later be carried out during the Republican period.

2. Geography and demography: Turkey has few ethnic or religious minorities; until fairly recently it had few population pressures and the area of land available for agriculture was expandable; it has many natural resources, including some very fertile agricultural regions; much of its land area is fairly easily accessible; and in moving the center of political-administrative gravity to Anatolia, Ataturk made it significantly easier to take advantage of many of these things than it might have been from the old capital.

3. Ataturk at the outset permanently defined geographical and psychological boundaries for the state which for all practical purposes excluded any question of the nation's identifying with alternate identities such as pan-Turkey or pan-Islam.

4. During the latter part of the single-party period, after authority had been established, the leaders of the Turkish Republic undertook a deliberate program of "tutelage," which succeeded in deepening feelings of national identity among the entire population and created conditions important for later movement toward a more open political system. Although these efforts often fell short of success in directly tutoring both elites and masses to behave "democratically," they did succeed in (a) legitimizing the idea of a constantly widening circle of political participation both by the general population and by competing groups among the elite, (b) establishing broad ideological guidelines as to what doctrines and, to some extent, what programs were beyond the pale of Kemalism, thus (c) convincing most members of the elite that those trained under the aegis of the Republic in the single-party period could later be trusted not to endanger the Kemalist revolution itself.

5. At the outset of the multiparty period, after the 1950 election, the Democrat party demonstrated that it could adhere to conservative social and cultural policies, and simultaneously preside over rapid economic growth, an economic situation in sharp contrast to the doldrums of the 1930s and 1940s. For the general population, this served to demonstrate that there could be material improvement without cultural and social reforms as drastic as the RPP had insisted on during the single-party years. For Turkish political leaders, it demonstrated that such a policy mixture had great voter appeal.

When it then became clear later in the 1950s that economic performance would be at least as important in the minds of voters as social and cultural issues, the Democrats were inhibited from moving strongly toward the right. As a result, a sizable public sector of the economy was retained, secular education continued to be expanded, etc. Similarly, in the 1960s, as the RPP began to seriously examine itself after several successive electoral defeats, it also decided that the middle of the road (albeit its left side) was appropriate. It did not reassert its earlier coolness toward religion. It toned down its bias toward centralization of political and economic power, and eschewed drastic reforms. Interest aggregation rather than polarization began to carry the day.

6. The existence of sociocultural "cushions" against the shock of rapid change, on which more below.

7. The ability of Turkish democratization to persist through time until the deep personal and historical hostilities of the earlier years could be forgotten.

8. Substantial economic growth during the multiparty period which helped legitimize the Republic and persuade the people that "modernizing" activities such as migrating to cities, accepting secular education, and adopting new agricultural techniques were acceptable and productive.

9. The momentum of development, which has led to new demands and aspirations, which in turn have acted as new stimuli to developmental and self-sustaining growth.

10. Analogous to the situation of Japan about a century earlier, the initial generation of leaders of the Turkish Republic were able to take advantage of a period in which mass pressure for rapid and widespread changes were not yet severe, neither on the part of the masses themselves nor as part of the ideological baggage of the elites in the name of the masses. Nations which began their development (or independence) at the end of World War II rather than World War I have not usually had the luxury of a quarter-century's breathing spell.

11. The conviction of most Turks that open politics does work and that although a nonelected or "nonpolitical" government might cater better to their particular interests, the risks to Turkey's social fabric and body politic (among which is the risk that their particular interests would not, in fact, be catered to) are simply too great.

Why the Shortcomings?

1. Continued elitism, i.e., failure of the elites to become true agents of modernization, either by actively encouraging popular participation in the process, or by treating non-elites as equal partners in it.[2] This shortcoming, one which is probably universal in elite-mass relationships, is reinforced in Turkey by strong cultural tradition. It is also related to the understandable reluctance of elites to preside over the diminution of their own power or status. Of course, we must note again that the degree to which this is a shortcoming may be somewhat ambiguous. Strong (elite) leadership continues to be desired by many people around the world, particularly as social change continues to lead to situations in which nonelite individuals must make a greatly increased number of political and personal decisions without much guidance from

established norms and institutions. Also, it is by no means clear that "followers" always know their own interests better than "leaders" do, particularly their long-term ones, and followers are certainly less well equipped than leaders to turn general values and interests into concrete plans and policies. Still, elitism in Turkish society remains greater than it should be if the rising level of follower pressure is to be dealt with with optimum effect.

2. Despite great advances, human and material resources (including financial resources) remain insufficient.

3. There is frequently poor planning, coordination, and implementation of policies and programs.

4. Rapid emergence of mass demands has resulted in additional strains on economic growth, industrial production, creation of new employment, etc., before a sufficiently solid structure could be laid for absorbing those demands.

5. There has been great reliance of "natural" development, i.e., great impetus has been given to unrestricted flow of private investment into the already more developed regions, to the concentration of advanced education in those areas, to the acquisition of agricultural technology by the already richer farmers. Little attention has been paid, on the other hand, to measures which might somewhat limit free choice of occupations but which could better mesh the distribution of educational resources with national manpower needs. Again, however, the net result of all this is ambiguous. For example, although neglect of less developed areas has had undesirable consequences, it is also true that the developed regions are now ready to and capable of supplying the bulk of investment capital necessary to maximize national economic growth and to take fullest possible advantage of economic multiplier effects.

The question of regional imbalances also illustrates more general dilemmas. It is problematic whether a democratic government can redistribute wealth regionally to a much greater degree than is now being done in Turkey. It is also debatable whether it would be justified in doing so in view of the fact that a relatively greater proportion of the population is increasingly locating in the already more developed regions. It is also conceivable that urban problems rather than problems of regional imbalance are the ones more likely to get out of hand in the near future. If there is a clash between long-term and short-term needs and demands and if pursuing the former means less ability to meet the latter, democratic governments, unfortunately, are possibly the least well-equipped forms to make decisions in favor of the long term.

6. Attention to basic economic reforms has been attenuated by the Turkish experience of being bailed out of financial difficulties by outside forces— World Bank pressures in 1958, for example, and the plenitude of foreign aid and remittances from Turkish workers in Europe. Such happenstances, some observers contend, have encouraged Turkish governments to all too quickly forget the need for basic reforms. (Perhaps what is needed is a long-term challenge, painful as that might be, such as the economic problems concomitant with Turkey's forthcoming integration with the EEC, to force the nation to face up to the necessity of basic economic reform.)

7. The increasingly important and sometimes negative role of international factors, which are only to a degree controllable by Turkey itself. For example, there is certainly a brain drain, visibly demonstrated by the large number of Turkish professionals (particularly doctors and engineers) residing outside

Turkey. Another "international" source of problems is the necessity, only recently realized, of competing in world markets as the economy becomes more and more dependent on imports and as foreign exchange from other than export earnings becomes less available.

Growth Vs. Modernization, or the Functionality of Traditions

Has Turkey "modernized," or only grown? That is, has the past half-century brought only quantitative changes, or has there been structural and qualitative change as well, change which will enable the country as a whole, and groups and individuals within it, to cope with new situations arising from continued development?

On some indicators of "modernization" the answer is unequivocal. Certainly there is no doubt that major structural changes have taken place on many of the social and economic indices listed in the Introduction of this book. There have been rapid urbanization, industrialization, advances in the use of technology, and replacement of local-based perspectives and institutions by ones which are nationally based (and often internationally based). All of these things at the least provide the setting in which other changes, in attitudes and ways of thinking, might follow. One such change has been the emergence of material interests and benefits as primary political issues, replacing earlier issues based on ideology, fundamental values such as religion, and deep-rooted historical rivalries, issues which led to the very deeply polarizing situations of not many years ago.

On other indices, however, despite predominantly "modern" settings like cities and factories,[3] it is notable that "traditions" have also survived. As noted above, one might conceive of this blend of tradition and modernity as a set of "cushions" against the potentially very severe psychological dislocation growing out of rapid change. It is possible to say only with little precision—and with even less certainty—whether the benefits of some of these "cushions" outweigh their short-term or long-term drawbacks, a difficulty which is related to the problem of possibly contradictory criteria for success. But nonetheless, some suggestions about their role in Turkish development are useful for this analysis.[4]

1. *Involuntary association* continues to permeate even those sectors of Turkish society which have become geographically mobile. As noted in chapter 3 of this study, the neighborhood associations found in most cities are in great part based on kinship, a place of origin, or a religious institution. Residential patterns also reflect these relationships to a significant degree. Whether they do more to smooth or to retard the integration of new migrants into urban life is something on which we need much more research, but prevailing opinion is that they do a great deal of the former, and that when the new urbanites are ready to move out (often through upward social mobility) they are able to do so without undue difficulty.

There are also some important specific benefits stemming from this blend of tradition and modernity. One is that the connections which are maintained between the new urbanites and their home villages help bring to those still in rural areas new ideas and new ways of improving their material situations. They often channel financial resources (remittances) into the villages as well. (Of course these contacts can also work to quicken even more the rate of urban migration, a paradox which makes an energetic rural development policy all the more urgent.)

2. Although "modern" subjects such as science and technology are being increasingly taught, traditionality in the methodologies of the educational system is also prevalent. Most obvious is the continuance of much learning by rote. More generally, there remains an overall emphasis on discipline and conformity rather than on innovativeness, originality, or criticism. Such "self-protective" tendencies on the part of older generations may be found to some degree in all societies, of course, and they may even be cited as functional for reducing generational tensions. For Turkey specifically, one can argue that they at least temporarily function as such because other relationships between superiors and subordinates which current Turkish students encounter (for instance, in most employment situations) are still largely based on principles such as promotion by seniority, conformity to established patterns, and obedience to authority. On balance, however, most critics consider that the dampening effects on the innovational propensities of the new generation of Turks are the most serious effect of traditionalism in Turkish education.

3. Traditionality in business (as detailed in chapters 2 and 7) is undoubtedly dysfunctional for Turkish development.

4. The role of religion is also an important "cushion" against the strains of rapid change. While religion may have had dysfunctional aspects for earlier modernization, one can reasonably assert that it is far less dysfunctional today. The chief reason for this is that although many difficulties are still being encountered in defining precisely what the relationship between religion and the state should be, most Turks have now become comfortable with being personally religious and at the same time "modern" and "scientific." One of important aspects of this dualism is that it is found among Turks in the middle class, whose modernity and often politically and socially "progressive" attitudes cannot be doubted, as well as among the lower strata, where such a separation was all but unheard of in earlier times. It is also important that the personal religiosity of fellow Turks is now accepted without prejudice by all members of the society. In the perspective of both Islamic and Turkish Republic history, the arrival at such a modus vivendi is no small achievement.

Turkish Capabilities

Among the many social-science theories about requirements for successful modernization, one which may be particularly useful in highlighting some important aspects of the Turkish experience is that of "capabilities." It has been suggested that political systems can be assessed in terms of their capabilities to extract, regulate, distribute, redistribute, symbolize, and respond. (For a concise exposition of capabilities theory, see Almond and Powell, 1966, chapter 8.)

Extractive capability is the capacity to transfer resources from private purposes to public ones. In two areas Turkish extractive capability is rather low: taxation, and the channeling of skilled personnel to the less-developed regions and rural areas.

As was discussed in chapter 7, it is generally agreed that the amount of tax revenue obtained by the Turkish government is considerably below potential. Major deficiencies include the low level of taxation on income from agricultural products, heavy reliance on indirect taxes, and failure to reform the structure and levels of taxation on urban land and real estate. Reasons for this situation include historical factors (the desire to relieve farmers and peasants from earlier oppressive tax burdens), political ones (favoring particular groups of political supporters, such as was done by the Democrat party in the 1950s), and economic ones (the need for large amounts of revenues which were most readily available through excise and customs levies, and the desire to stimulate particular sectors of the economy). Many of these things could be justified, but it is unfortunate that one of the legacies which the single-party period left to the multiparty one was a tax structure whose basic premises were so firmly established that it now requires much political strength and courage to change it in more than incremental ways. The consequences of this situation have now become even more serious. One result of the failure to extract sufficient tax revenues has been that in order to reach investment targets of the five-year plans, governments have had to resort to an excessively high level of deficit financing, with resulting inflation. Since this is a political cost which even the moderate right-wing governments of recent years would surely have liked to avoid, and since they frequently had the chance to make basic changes in the tax structure, it seems not completely unjustified to conclude that *unwillingness* to make the reforms which so many observers consider necessary is in fact *inability* to do so.

The other aspect of low extractive capability, inability to channel skilled personnel to areas in which there is the greatest need, has also been discussed elsewhere in this study. Part of the problem is related to the simple fact that there is a great shortage of skilled people, so that even if, for example, provincial cities were allowed to sharply increase salaries and thus be better able to compete for skilled personal with the metropolitan areas, the situation might still not be relieved. But here too, it is not too much to say that the strength with which established patterns endure at least borders on incapability to extract.

High regulative capability has long been a mainstay of the Turkish concept of government. Detailed regulations guide every aspect of Turkish public administration and affairs. This tendency has been facilitated by the traditionally authoritarian nature of elite-mass relationships, the legacy of strong emphasis on control and conformity which was seen as necessary during the implementation of the Ataturk reforms, and by the longstanding competence of the civil bureaucracy (which was in turn a legacy from the Ottoman Empire as well as an outgrowth of the ability of the bureaucracy to attract many of the most talented members of the society). Some observers feel that regulative capability is now in decline, however, because (a) the quality of bureaucrats is declining in conjunction with the rise of attractive alternative career lines, (b) the complexity of Turkish society has grown to such an extent that the scope of what needs to be regulated is almost too big to be manageable by even the best of systems, and (c) the dispersal of political power has encouraged citizens to find ways to circumvent the regulative structure. (For these insightful suggestions I am indebted to Professor Ilter Turan, of Istanbul University.)

The effects of both high regulative capability and of its possible decline are mixed. Most Turks see a high degree of regulation as normal, natural, or inevitable, and it does not bother them greatly. Outsiders usually see it as stifling, inhibiting to innovation, and a cause of low productivity both in the public and private sectors. One should not necessarily assume, however, that if the amount of regulation were reduced, there would soon be a significantly higher amount of innovation and initiative. There would be some, certainly, and those self-development-minded leaders who can be found in many Anatolian cities are quite justified in their frustration with the extensive web of centralized regulations in which they are enmeshed. Decentralization, which would involve less regulation, is in the view of some observers one of Turkey's most pressing organizational needs. But it can also be argued that in a period when great changes are still needed, the maintenance of high regulative capability can be an asset, and that the major criterion of regulation's defensibility may lie in whether the policies which regulation effects are better than ones which would exist were many activities less stringently supervised.

Distributive capability of Turkish government has also been quite high, as measured by the degree to which virtually all groups of the population have experienced gains during the Republic's first half-century. Although there may not have been major improvement in the general equality of wealth, social facilities, or opportunities for access to them—indeed a major study just completed has come to the conclusion that "the distribution of material goods (income, wealth, and services) in Turkey is highly unequal, that on the whole "public policy [in the 1950–75 period] has not led to significant reductions in inequality," and that "a full 30 percent of all households are in the extreme poverty group" (Özbudun and Ulusan, 1980:10–12)[5]—there can also be no doubt that the absolute increase in goods and services for almost the entire population has been dramatic.

The many factors which have enabled this sizable increase in goods and services have been detailed in preceding chapters. Not all can be unequivocally termed "healthy" (e.g., the willingness to accept a great deal of deficit financing), but there seems no doubt that high distributive capability has been and continues to be one of the major assets of the Turkish Republic. It has had positive results for regime legitimacy. It has also stimulated the economic momentum which has in turn quickened economic "multiplier" effects. Herein lies the difficulty as well, however, because the high level of distribution which the Turkish public has come to expect may become a burden if the amount of resources available for distribution declines while the level of expectations does not.

Redistributive capability (the ability to deliberately change the shares of public goods going to various groups of the population) is more difficult to measure and to evaluate. While there may not have been much redistribution in monetary income, there are also other areas to consider. As discussed in chapters 2 and 3, there have been visible, though still far from sufficient increases in the prospects of many Turks for social mobility (as measured, for example, by improved access of lower-class children to education). Other important redistributive developments include a general increase in nonelite political power, and the emergence of popular institutions such as trade unions. Not all groups have benefited from such phenomena to the same degree, of course, and the degree to which there has been redistribution in some of these areas is difficult to measure with precision—for example, how much of a *net* gain is a village school if the quality of city schools increases so much faster that the competitive gap between city-educated and village-educated youths in fact grows larger?

Among the reasons why redistributive capability has not received prominent emphasis in Turkey has been that so much of the popular demand for improvements could for many years be met by distributive capability. Another is that demand for major redistribution has begun to come only relatively recently from even some groups in the lower strata, as a consequence of radical ideologies beginning to become more widespread. It remains to be seen whether distributive capability as a way to blunt redistributive demands will decline sufficiently to lead to a serious expectation-achievement gap, or whether traditional conservatism and societal coolness to socialist ideas (an attitude which for many years was also officially encouraged) will give way rapidly, so that, as Özbudun and Ulusan hypothesize, there will be a sharp increase in the volume and strength of redistributive demands (1980:18–20), or whether major new class cleavages can still be avoided, as a result of renewed national economic growth, the continued spread of social services, or the persistence of "traditions."[6]

Symbolic capability has been and continues to be high. The many measures which Ataturk undertook to stimulate and/or restore national pride have had lasting effects. For all but a few Turks, Ataturk himself became a symbol of the new Turkey, though it must be added that in the Republic's early decades his name probably had negative symbolism for many, and it was only with his continued glorification during the period of less radical cultural change since 1950 that for at least some Turks positive characteristics have become part of the symbolism of Kemalism as well.

A second symbol which has become important is democracy itself. For many Turks democracy is seen as putting their country into a category distinctly above countries (some of which were also part of Ottoman Turkey) that are still not able to operate open political institutions. If multiparty politics breaks down, the cost to Turkey's symbolic capability could be great.[7]

Finally, there is *responsive capability*, on which this study has already commented extensively. In conceptual terms, a major dilemma is not whether to be responsive, but rather to what or to whom to respond. Turkish capability to respond to popular demands (material as well as social and cultural) has become highly developed. The many combinations of modern and traditional characteristics, of social conservatism and continuing reform, and the toleration of relatively slow change in some spheres which have emerged with this kind of responsiveness have been noted in this study as important reasons for many of the "healthy" aspects of Turkey's development in the past half-century. The leader-follower connections which have thus been built may be considered as one of the major assets for the future. To reiterate another major point of this study, however, an important question remains as to whether in some areas it might not have been more useful to have been more responsive to what might be called the demands of long-run modernization.

In sum, as capability theory projects, high levels of some (distributive, regulative, symbolic, responsive) have been helpful in making it possible to govern and develop despite low levels of others (extractive, redistributive). Fortunately, too, the high capabilities have included ones which answer both concrete demands (distribution of material goods) and what might be called "emotional" demands (policies combining economic growth with a more conservative social "tone" of government policy than was the case in the single-party period).

The Second Half-Century

What are the major problems and opportunities which Turkey will probably face in the future? Many of what might be called "second generation problems" will represent continuance of forces set in motion during the first half-century. They include:

1. Continued rapid increases in population.

2. Increasing international involvement, bringing such problems as more severe economic competition, pressures for foreign policy reorientation, and more Turks comparing their own nation with others.

3. Further increases in demand for consumer goods, as well as gradual change in the composition of that demand as incomes rise, away from basic (such as bread) to more specialized products (such as meat and industrial goods).

4. Ongoing rapid urbanization, with its difficulties (greater pressure on urban services) but also opportunities (access to better education, upgrading of skills, more availability of information).

5. Persisting and probably growing regional imbalances (and also imbalances within regions), which will probably lead to even greater migration to the more developed parts of the country.

6. The continuance of multiparty politics and of party competition for the broad middle of the political spectrum.

7. An increasing load on government, partly because of new fields in which government input will be demanded, and partly because the number of people who are integrated into the ever-more-independent economy and into society as a whole will continue to increase. Government policies will no longer leave large segments of the population relatively unaffected, as was the case earlier.

8. The likelihood that the changes which will be able to be brought about will be smaller, more incremental, less dramatic than in both the first quarter century and the second one (the multiparty period), so that it will become more important to concentrate on such things as efficiency, priority-setting, and making maximum use of the energies and talents of the entire population.

9. Competition for all resources will be more severe, and pressure group activity more militant. The latter may not, however, be immediately expressed in consciously class terms. That is, while it is likely that analysis of phenomena such as voting patterns will continue to show some patterns corresponding to what may be called class lines, competition will likely also be based on a multiplicity of groups, localities, factions, etc., thus providing enough cross-cutting ones to moderate those which could potentially be new deep fissures in the very fabric of Turkish society.

10. Many of the "cushions" against social and cultural trauma are also likely to continue to be effective, although it will also be necessary to provide more open channels for those persons who are most intent on and capable of mobility (geographic and social) and for the expression of more individualism and innovativeness.

11. It seems reasonable to expect that for the foreseeable future the greatest danger of radicalization will continue to come from the right rather than the left. The conservative parties still capture well over half the votes, and much of the RPP voting strength is based on its taking essentially moderate positions.

Although these phenomena are continuations of trends in the Republic's first half-century, these "second-generation" challenges also differ qualitatively from those of the past in several important ways:

1. They require a good deal of technical sophistication and fine-tuning of politics and administration.

2. They require the cooperation and involvement of a far larger number of people than was the case in the past.

3. They call for changes in some of the "traditional" attitudes which have been identified as not having as yet changed in response to noncoercive stimuli. That is, it may now be necessary to insist more strongly on changes of attitudes toward education, innovation, aggressive pursuit of export markets.

4. Solution to some of the economic problems may require, if not a sharp slowdown in economic growth, at least a period of greater austerity, and postponement of immediate gratification for the sake of long-term ends.

These kinds of challenges include many which a democratic government, as noted above, may be least well-equipped to meet. Yet Turkey seems determined that the democratic road will be the one it will follow. Is democracy a wise choice? This writer has no doubt that the answer is yes. One reason, of course, is that there is now little other realistic choice. To go back to a more authoritarian system would involve the need to repress many for whom open politics has become both functionally and normatively desirable, and it would likely bring very negative international repercussions in terms of Turkey's reputation and pride. All this would be a high price to pay indeed.

But there is also a deeper reason for optimism about Turkey's ability to succeed through democratic means. Turkey can be said to have been lucky in many ways—time, geography, demography, history were all significantly on her side. The very momentum of development and change has also been important, often at least as important as individual leaders or specific actions or policies. However, skilled leadership has also been a major asset, and it is not too much to say that among the most important of Turkish leadership skills has been the ability to come to terms with an unstoppable progression of increasing nonelite involvement in decision-making and direction-setting, and to lead the Turkish people toward acceptance of moderate policies and of mixes of old and new values.

Perhaps this was what was meant by the recent observations of two insightful Turkish intellectuals. One described the great dynamism he observed in his country and the vigorous discussion and questioning of all aspects of Turkish identity as "a great common learning experience." The other penetrated perhaps even further to the essence of the reasons for much of the success of Turkish efforts: "Turks succeed brilliantly when what they do is synthesize." That so large a number of Turks of all strata have become agents of modernization, not merely objects of it, is something of which Kemal Ataturk would certainly have been justly proud. It remains to be seen whether both leaders and followers will now have the wisdom, stamina, and perhaps, above all, the patience and tolerance to overcome relatively short-run problems, to bring about the many qualitative changes which must now be added to the quantitative growth, and to complete the many societal advances which have been begun. But if the lessons of the past are well learned, the reasons for optimism are well in evidence.

Notes

Introduction

1. On this dimension there are particular conceptual problems in the modern-traditional mix. It is clear that even in the societies we view as the most "modern," there is strong survival of traditional traits, family attachments, for example. It is also methodologically difficult to determine how to classify those people who, for example, choose to remain attached to their families (i.e., parents and relatives other than spouses and own children) and who might be described as "voluntarily" belonging to an "involuntary association." I hope that these ambiguities will not impede the general analysis found in this study.

2. This is another characteristic whose specification is particularly difficult, and it may well be more accurate to say that this is a trait of "Western" society rather than one which differentiates modern from traditional. This difficulty is at least partly a result of the fact that "modernization" is often conceived of as similar to "Westernization," either in the sense that what we define as "modern" is what Western society is seen to be, or in the sense that many individuals in "modernizing" countries are seeking in some degree to become like their counterparts in Western countries.

Chapter 1

1. Literally, "Father of the Turks" and so named by the nation in 1935.

2. Actually, there was comparatively little repression. During the 1920s there were some prosecutions for political offenses, but these were mostly in connection with overt rebellions, such as that of the Kurdish Sheikh Said in 1925. Several major opponents of Ataturk also went into voluntary or involuntary exile or retirement. On the whole, however, the record is not bad.

3. These borders are largely those of present-day Turkey; i.e., Anatolia and the Aegean, Mediterranean and Marmara regions, and the parts of Thrace which were controlled by Turkey and contained a Turkish majority. The only change in frontiers has been the incorporation of the disputed area of Hatay in 1939.

4. This was relevant on two social levels and in a number of ways. For the peasants it was necessary both to widen their focus beyond only their own locality and to narrow their universalist "Muslim" identity. For the educated classes, it was intended to reorient them away from viewing themselves as Ottomans toward identifying with the Turkish nation as a whole, and to raise pride vis-a-vis the West. In regard to the latter, Bernard Lewis has noted that Europeans for many decades have viewed Turks with disdain, which must surely have been frustrating and discouraging to eager young students going to the West. (1953:225.) It might also be mentioned

that to this day many Turks are convinced that Europeans view Greeks with more favor than Turks because the former are Christian and a part of "Western" civilization.

5. One of the more extreme efforts, for example, was the Sun Language Theory, which portrayed the Turkish language as the source of all other human languages (Weiker, 1973:231 n3). Although in the 1930s "school children took it all as gospel," Lewis Thomas has observed that "how light a dose of overt chauvinism nationalist Turkey has had, and how speedily she has shaken off most of it, can be measured by a foreigner who has lived observantly in other Balkan and Middle Eastern states as well as Turkey" (1951:84–5). These matters are not entirely a dead issue, however. Soon after the 1960 revolution there was a movement to again use as many "pure Turkish" words as possible, and it is not too much to say that today there are two almost distinct branches of the Turkish language, the old and new, used respectively by those generally identified with the political left and the political right (for illustrations see Weiker, 1973:233 n2).

6. Turkey entered the war on the allied side in 1945, just in time to qualify as a founding member of the United Nations.

7. The tidal wave of adulation among Turks was matched by worldwide praise which few other "developing" countries have received. See, for example, Robinson, 1951; Bisbee, 1950; Yalman, 1947; for a review of the factors which enabled Turkey to make its transition successfully. The best study in detail of the transition remains Karpat, 1959.

8. Ex-President Bayar was also sentenced to death, but his sentence was commuted, largely on grounds of his advanced age but possibly also in response to his dignified bearing throughout the trial. See Weiker, 1963:46.

9. All of these changes, however, are very uneven among various regions, and one of Turkey's major problems remains great regional imbalance in economic development and political and social structure. For a fuller discussion see chapter 8.

10. Although international affairs are of major importance among the factors influencing Turkey's ability to meet her new challenges, foreign policy per se is only generally related to the central theme of this study. It will be commented on in relevant sections of other chapters of this study, and only a few general facts will be given here. In the Ataturk period foreign policy was dominated by wariness of the Western powers as a result of the wartime experiences. At the same time, however, Turkey's face was turning toward the West in its quest for modernization. Relations with the Soviet Union were also relatively good, until the latter began to press for concessions in areas like the Straits. After World War II and the beginning of the cold war, Turkey aligned itself formally with the West, becoming a member of the Council of Europe in 1949, NATO in 1952, and the Baghdad Pact in 1955. In the early 1960s a more independent orientation was felt to be necessary, and a variety of steps were taken to loosen ties with the United States and to increase connections with Western Europe (toward which Turkey's economic relations were also moving after the advent of the Consortium for financial aid and the negotiations for Turkish association with the European Economic Community). Relations with the Soviet Union and with many of the non-aligned countries also were improved, one result of this being that the Soviet Union began to give Turkey economic credits. Disagreements with the United States over Turkey's actions regarding Cyprus caused strained relations on several occasions, most seriously in 1974 when the Ecevit government invaded the island in response to an attempted coup by conservative Greek army officers. The action resulted in an arms boycott by the United States which lasted until mid-1978. For good discussions of Turkish foreign policy in English see Vali, 1971; Harris, 1972; Kiliç, 1959; Karpat, 1975a; Ahmad, 1977: chap. 14; Weiker, 1973a.

Chapter 2

1. Movement toward election of younger deputies seems to come in conjunction with the fall and rise of a party's electoral fortunes. In 1950, DP deputies averaged five years younger than RPP deputies, but the average age of JP deputies has been steadily rising, if slowly, since 1961. Likewise, the average age of RPP deputies dropped sharply between 1950 and 1954, and has

remained steady, RPP deputies being on the average four years younger than JP ones. For the minor parties, Tachau found only very small differences for 1961, 1965, and 1969, and in 1973 the NSP had the youngest average age (but only two years younger than the RPP and six years under the JP). See Tachau 1973, and 1974:4 and Table II. In 1977, the average age in all parties was about the same. It might also be noted that indications are that Turkish legislators may on the whole be younger than those in the West (Schultz, 1973:571–90).

2. Unfortunately localism when defined by birthplace is not the best indicator we might wish for. Note, for example, that 11 percent of the 1920–57 deputies were born outside Turkey (there having been much migration of Balkan Turks back to Turkey proper after World War I). Perhaps length of family residence in a province would be a better measure, but we do not have it.

3. Özbudun studied leaders of the Justice, Republican, and Labor parties in three urban and three rural districts. There were major differences between his urban and rural findings, and also between the Labor party and the two major parties in both the urban and rural districts. For comparison purposes, therefore, I have selected only the urban leaders of the two major parties.

4. There are very few studies of Turkish towns. One recent one, however, found that the office of mayor was quite important, that much political controversy revolved around it, and that the mayor was usually an important figure in that he was the one who dealt with government authorities on numerous matters important to the town (Magnarella, 1974:134–5). Other town studies include Mansur, 1972; Benedict, 1974; and Yasa, 1969. (On the importance of village headmen see chapter 3.)

5. 1931: 104, 155.
   1938: 134, 779.
   1946: 222, 166.
   1963: 449, 869.
   1970: 665, 737.
   Mesut Gülmez, "Türk Kamu Görevlilerinin Siyasal Evrimi," *Amme Idaresi Dérgisi*, Eylul 1963. Data supplied by Metin Heper.

6. Much of this was just to facilitate constituents' day-to-day dealings with the bureaucracy, but it undoubtedly affected general power relationships as well.

7. Neither the liberal nor the conservative political parties have had difficulty in finding bureaucratic supporters during the past quarter century. In terms of reform philosophy, some ministries are regularly characterized as very "conservative" (e.g., education), while others have a far more "innovative" reputation (e.g., Reconstruction and Resettlement).

8. 1969:50–1. Bent noted that this is counter to the Roos' findings among Turkish provincial administrators that the more educated they were, the more they preferred a high income with high risk. Perhaps this is accounted for by the fact that the Roos' respondents consisted entirely of graduates of the high status Political Science Faculty, whose need for security is probably less than for administrators generally.

9. The persistence of tradition appears to extend even to a class of administrators who should be among the most "modern," i.e., those in the universities. In the case of the METU, which was supposed to become a model, there were, to be sure, political and ideological conflicts as a result of a high degree of radicalism among students and faculty and the hostility of the government to that institution, but Heper, in a study of its internal functions and decision-making, came to the overall conclusion that there were "promising developments," but that tradition loomed large (1974a).

10. For example, Turkish ministries employ "hundreds of inspectors to keep officials in line. In 1963 there were over 2,200 of these, and, while primarily intended to keep field officers compliant, their presence in Ankara is not without effect. Friction between bureaucratically oriented inspectors who see no value to innovation and more professionally oriented officials is virtually preordained and the depressant effect is freely admitted" (Bent, 1969:60). For a particularly vivid description of the tortuous path which petitioners to government offices must take, see Rustow, 1965:189.

11. Numerous studies testify to the disdain which many bureaucrats have for politicians. Heper's survey of bureaucrats of 1945–60 found that they viewed "the new political elite generally unfit to rule, and thought that educated, experienced, patriotic and honest people should contribute to policy-making" (1976b:516). Roos's survey of district governors in 1965 found that only one-third considered that politicians helped national development (1969:560). Businessmen, not traditionally respected in Turkish society, received considerably higher ratings (1971:Table 9-1).

Şerif Mardin has related these attitudes to his center-periphery formulation, i.e., that the center (the bureaucrats) see themselves as the elite as opposed to both the general population and the local leaders at the "periphery," this view reinforcing the bureaucrats' (and intellectuals') determination to make it hard for peripherals to penetrate into the ranks of the center. See his article in Milliyet, January 4, 1975.

12. For the purposes of this section I do not include in this group the esnaf, owners of small stores, repair shops, etc.

13. On the other hand, however, entrepreneurship was given a boost with the departure of large numbers of Greeks shortly after the end of the War of Independence and their replacement by Balkan Turks, who were considerably more business-minded than their compatriots who had spent their lives in Turkey proper. See Fallers, 1974.

14. Alexander found that 50 percent had previously been traders, 17.5 percent craftsmen or skilled workers, and 10 percent were sons of industrialists. Payashoğlu's sample was 34 percent merchants, 16 percent industrialists, 7½ percent esnaf. Of their wives, 47 percent also came from merchant or industrial families, and 49 percent of those were even from the same occupational subgroup. Forty-nine percent of the entrepreneurs who had partners drew them 100 percent from their relatives, only 15 percent drew them from kin in a proportion of less than 50 percent, and 62 percent foresaw that they would be succeeded in the management of their firms by a member of their own family.

15. This judgment was based on an admittedly narrow group, students in a middle-management course at Istanbul University, but Bradburn noted that the sample was in fact biased favorably in that a large number were graduates of the Village Institutes, whose n-Ach was expected to be much higher than average because many had left home at the age of 14 and may have thus been freed from the influence of an authoritarian father, a factor which tends (on theoretical and empirical grounds) to favor development of n-Ach. See also Bradburn, 1963b.

16. Ataturk involved his "Gazi" image on numerous occasions of potential crisis, for example in connection with controversies surrounding the Free party episode of 1930 and the reactionary Menemen uprising soon thereafter. See Weiker, 1973:93, 103. For a concise summary of the modernization of the military see Ward and Rustow, 1964:chap. 8-b.

17. A colonel today receives a salary equivalent to that of a General Director of a government bureau or ministry, and fringe benefits are also very liberal. Many officers have in addition done well in OYAK, an investment consortium which has plunged heavily into enterprises such as the Renault assembly plant.

18. Many members of the group, for example, "referred to extreme hardships they suffered during childhood" (Özbudun 1966:29). Twelve of the twenty-seven were sons of army officers, four were sons of civilian government officials, four of businessmen, and seven had fathers in in miscellaneous occupations. Only eleven came from the three major metropolises, Istanbul, Ankara, and Izmir, though this is probably explained by the greater likelihood that officers would have been stationed outside the major cities. My figures here differ slightly from Özbudun's (1963:118).

19. Kışlalı attributes the conservative tone of the armed forces' interventions in politics largely to the officers' lower- and middle-class backgrounds.

20. The Harbiye has adopted the West Point model of teaching a considerable amount of science and social science as well as more standard military subjects, and it makes use of some of the best professors from the Universities. Officers are frequently sent abroad for advanced training as well.

21. The low percentage choosing education in the 1973–74 data is in striking disparity with earlier studies. It may be explained by the fact that the 1973–74 study was among aspirants for University training (among whom teaching was never as desired as among lycee students as a whole) or it may be a reflection of the rise of other occupations since the mid-1950s. More data are needed.

22. It might also be useful if there could be some shifts within the health profession. The SPO estimates that in 1983 there will be an excess of some 5,000 doctors and 17,650 nurses (based on planned hospital capacity) but deficits of about 1,500 dentists, 8,700 pharmacists and 4,150 village midwives (1978b:176). I have not been able to locate manpower need estimates for other professions, except for engineers and technicians as mentioned above.

23. Abadan found that "in answer to an open question about what two specific things they as parents would try to teach their children, only 2% mentioned religion, and only 7% named religion as the area of activity which would give them the greatest satisfaction in life. Even when asked what they would do if disaster befell them, only 1.5% named religion" (1963:85). Hyman, Payaslıoğlu and Frey similarly found in 1957–58 that "when asked what accomplishments would bring them greatest pride, only one percent mentioned something in the sphere of religion, and all the emphasis is directed to contributions to the nation. . . .When asked about the two worst events that could conceivably happen, less than one per cent mentioned 'a loss of religious faith.' On the rating of the importance of the six sectors of life, the religious sphere received the lowest rating, even lower than amusement-and local citizenship activities" (1958:285).

24. To take only one example, in response to the question "As a parent, what two specific lessons would you try hardest to teach your children?" 20 percent answered "to be useful to the nation." In the Gillespie and Allport study only one country, Egypt, with 19 percent, approached the Turkish figure, and with the exception of Mexico, no other country exceeded 3 percent in this category (Hyman, Payaslıoğlu, Frey, 1958:283).

Chapter 3

1. The terms general population, people, lower strata, followers, are used more or less interchangeably in this chapter.

2. This is not to say, of course, that there has been no elite "guidance." As discussed in chapter 6, there was considerable indoctrination through the school system in the single-party period, and some contend it has not lessened much since then.

3. Non-Muslim millets often had far greater outside contacts, primarily because of their connections with Europe, but it is not clear how far down into all strata of these communities these wider horizons extended.

4. This neglect was general, though there have long been great regional differences in economic levels. The relatively accessible regions, such as the coastal Aegean, Marmara, and the Mediterranean, have been more advanced that the inland and eastern provinces for some time.

5. Four specific policies have been identified: "1. The transfer of the administrative and cultural center from Istanbul to Ankara. 2. The transformation of many provincial centers into modern administrative and cultural centers, thus introducing social changes to their hinterlands. 3. The construction of a railroad network to cover the country and replace the former 'tree form,' and the development of highways to support the railways. 4. The location of large public industries in small Anatolian towns." Tekeli, 1973:265, paraphrasing Rivlin 1965:1.

6. Rathbun (1972:103–7) notes that one of the characteristics of villagers as portrayed in literature right up to 1950 was their great isolation from politics and the nation at large.

7. It appears that size alone is not always an important variable, but its effect on efficiency of development measures is often apparent. The Village Survey found that differences were relatively small in fertilizer use between larger and smaller villages (p. 148), but size was a factor in that, for example, in 1968 only half as many villages over 1000 were without a cooperative as

compared with villages under 400 (p. 37) and 50 percent of the villages under 400 were never visited by agricultural personnel, compared to 20 percent of the villages over 1000 (p. 39). The Village Survey (hereafter MTV, Modernization in Turkish Villages), is a large study conducted by the State Planning Organization in 1970. In addition to it and to official statistics, we have several other studies. A major one was conducted by a team led by Frederick Frey in the 1950s and 1960s, and it, as well as several smaller ones which used quantitative and survey methods, will be cited. Since their findings generally are similar, we use the datà with some confidence. Since 1968, Village Inventories have been prepared by the Ministry of Reconstruction and Resettlement for each province, but to my knowledge these data have not been analyzed to enable us to bring the overall picture up to date.

8.   Weiker, 1973:178. For an excellent summary of the large number of studies see Kolars, 1962. On rural Turkey see also Beeley, 1969. A recent annotated bibliography of village studies (in Turkish) is Gül Ergil, 1968. It is quite possible that both favorable and unfavorable accounts were influenced by ideological considerations. The findings of the *Halkevi* reports probably reflect at least in some part the idealized picture of Turkish villagers painted by Ataturk in connection with his insistence that the villager is the 'efendi' of the nation. Edwin Cohn, on the other hand, has noted that not a few Kemalists, "bent on creating what they regarded as a modern Turkey and humiliated by the evidence of backwardness presented by Turkey's villages, tended to view the unlettered peasantry as an inert mass—indolent and stupid—that had to be forced to do what they, the elite, regarded as good for the country." The villagers, in turn, "conditioned by centuries of ill-treatment from a distant central government that did little or nothing for them, resented the condescending attitude of the members of the elite and the attempt of the latter to impose on them tasks that bore little relation to their own interests and aspirations" (1970:82).

9.   Rathbun, 1972:15–17. Part of Makal's problem appeared to stem from his own characteristics and from the particular situation, however.

10.   Keleş and Türkay (1962) asked for the date that various changes took place, and found that for most villagers, 1950 was the turning point. (See also Kolars, 1973:200.) The significance of this occurring simultaneously with the coming to power of the Democratic party is discussed in chapter 5. Fehmi Yavuz (1963:8–9) noted that "Up to the Second World War, efforts for promoting a well-organized administration and security in the village were of prime concern. During that period, no significant activities can be seen in the fields of economy, culture and public works."

11.   1963:80. That inequalities existed was well known. For example, a *muhtar* of a village near Kütahya, in an interview with the editor of *Milliyet* (26 February 1973) wondered why village schools had 170 days of instruction compared to 200 in cities, and why they did not receive the amenities provided to city schools, such as fuel, supplies, and tools for repairs. He also noted that all the improvements in his village were self-made, that the villagers practiced birth control on their own and did not have to be encouraged to do so by health authorities, and that it was general opinion in the village that workers who had migrated to cities were better off.

There are no hard data on the effects of disparities between the rural wealthy, middle and lower classes, though it is well known that the benefits of farm mechanization have been very uneven. As early as 1960 one study found that in the fairly rich Antalya region the benefits went to a very limited number of individuals, mostly those already in the upper income groups. But social and cultural effects from increased contacts with the outside world were being felt by all villagers, who as noted by Karpat were being "rapidly forced out of a lethargic state of mind and a stagnant life." Karpat further noted that "social differentiation had been suddenly speeded up and has taken on exclusively material forms," and that it was "no longer accepted as natural or pre-destined" (1960).

12.   A part of this may be attributable to teacher-villager relations, which in the view of the Survey "are not at the expected level and extent. It is possible to conclude that the villagers do not perceive the teacher as a leader and an intellectual guide who can be of any assistance in case of troubles. Only 9.1% of the villagers think of the teacher as the person best informed of what happens in the world. Only 12.5% stated the teacher as the person who brings change to the

village; (only) 30.9% consulted him in case of any need, and only 0.3% consult the teacher in case of difficulties" (p. 249). The most likely reason for this is the far greater power of the *muhtar* to obtain outside resources, though in terms of help with problems not requiring such resources, the comparatively minor role of the teacher is also related to the fact that those who are sent to villages are usually young and relatively inexperienced. Their average age was 26.1 years. Only 11.7 percent were over the age of 32. The survey also concluded that "although the villagers have positive attitudes toward education it is not possible to assert the same attitude toward the school" (p. 251).

13. This type of penetration is seen in virtually every part of Turkey: in only 35% of the villages did the Village Survey find no persons employed outside the village. About two-thirds of the wage workers were temporary migrants to cities, including 39 percent to the metropolises of Ankara, Istanbul, and Izmir. A significant number of the Turkish workers who have gone to western Europe went directly from villages.

14. Some observers still cite continuing lack of political sophistication of Turkish villagers. Among the reasons for low national efficacy, Özbudun observes, is Frey's characterization of the villager as one having "scant familiarity with the necessary mediating institutions, such as parties, and the world outside his village. 'He naturally applies his rather effective intra-village techniques for influence to the outside world and is usually rebuffed, or else he knows just enough of the difference between the two worlds to sense the futility of attempting to alter in even the smallest way the course of national events' " (1976:157).

15. At least one study concluded that this may be occurring. Leder (1976) found that in a town in the province of Manisa in the Aegean region, both "rightists" and "leftists" were able to cross boundaries of "solidarity groups" and successfully appeal to voters.

16. The exception to this statement is, of course, much of eastern Turkey, where the power of large landowners often remains very strong. In 1960 the National Unity Committee removed 55 *ağas* to compulsory residence in western Turkey and confiscated their lands for future distribution to peasants, but through legal tactics and political influence these landlords were able to return shortly after the reestablishment of civilian rule. Weiker 1963:144. Presumably, after these obstacles are removed, eastern villagers will begin to react to modernizing stimuli as their more westerly compatriots have.

17. The causes of urbanization include, as everywhere, both "push" and "pull" factors. As detailed in chapter 7, the pressure on agricultural land from rapidly increasing population has gotten severe. As a "pull," the greatly increased amount of information available to villagers regarding city life has had major effects. Levine has gone so far as to suggest that the "pull factors" are so strong that a third cause might now be conceptualized, "normative" migration—that is, migration that "becomes an accepted mode of behavior by many people" (1974:4).

18. Two criteria are used in Turkish official figures. One is that any settlement which is a province or district capital is classified as urban. Thus, in the 1975 census, some 190 places under 5,000 were included. The other is with 10,000 or more population, which is the criterion used here.

19. Keleş (1972a:16) has calculated as follows:

1950-100	Industrial Index (Nr. industrial workers) 1967	Urbanization Index 1967
Istanbul	240	178
Ankara	446	313
Izmir	139	174
Adana	179	246
Bursa	154	205
Eskişehir	170	194
Gaziantep	115	220
Konya	242	245
Kayseri	155	194

20.   The 20 percent figure is the one most often cited in the current press. But the figures are in some dispute depending on the basis of calculation. Not all are registered with the State Employment Service, which thus may understate the figure. On the other hand, many people find at least part-time employment in the so-called "marginal" sector.

21.   For example, by increasing the number of working members of the family even if it means that women work outside the home (a "modernizing" influence) or by having children leave school (undesirable in that it both increases the employment problem for adults and that it lessens the children's future chances). Another method is by entering the "marginal sector" of street peddlers, shoe-shiners, etc.

22.   Investment in housing was at a high of 34.5 percent of total investment in 1955, about 23 percent during the 1960s, and dropped to 17.6 percent in 1975 (Keleş 1978:137). Efforts to establish a financing system suitable for lower income groups and to channel small individual savings into the housing sector have so far been unsuccessful (SPO 1978b:par. 449).

23.   Literally, "put up during the night." Turkish custom is that any dwelling which is roofed before morning should not be torn down. Turkish government policy for gecekondu districts has varied over time between ignoring their growth, trying to prevent their growth, attempting to develop integrated plans for their improvement, and providing services and facilities on the basis of political patronage. Policy has generally been hampered by lack of funds as well as vacillation in goals. For a general history, see Heper, 1978:17–33. For a more detailed history and an overview of their development, see Şenyapılı, 1978:46–80.

24.   Keleş, 1978:189. He lists some 1970 percentages as Ankara 65 percent, Istanbul 45 percent, Izmir 35 percent, Adana 45 percent, Bursa 25 percent, Diyarbakir 20 percent.

25.   The quantitative dimensions are hard to measure and they vary considerably. As Kuran has pointed out, Karpat (1976) and Arı and Tütengil (1968) found a relatively high amount in Istanbul, Kongar observed a lower but still substantial rate in Izmir, and a significant amount of downward mobility was noted in a study in Istanbul and Samsun. For details, see Kuran, 1980:355–6.

26.   Karpat estimated the average family income in his three gecekondu areas in 1967 at about 8,200 TL, "which compares quite favorably with the national gross per capita income of 3,143 liras (in 1967). One may assume therefore that the squatters' income, although below the average of the established city dwellers, was substantially above that of the rural inhabitants and definitely much higher than that of many of their friends and relatives left in the native villages. This important development—the increase in living standards—was technically the immediate consequence of occupational change and had profound effects on the squatters' attitude toward the city" (1976:106).

27.   As Hart has put it, the amount of private money and man-hours of labor put into gecekondu housing is a great saving to the government, and should be welcomed as a national asset! (1963:2). In terms of residents' ambition, there appears to be a good deal of emphasis on self-reliance as a method of getting ahead. The ambitions of Hart's respondents were far more for small self-run stores or manufacturing establishments than for factory jobs, which were characterized as offering low wages, dull work, standard pay rates, and bonuses and promotions which were rare and often capricious (1963:9).

28.   There seems to be some evidence that the ideal of the extended family is more pervasive than had been believed, however, and that its prevalence is indeed related to class and economic status. Timur noted that the small number of extended families is inconsistent with the "very high proportion of peasants (80%), by their own admission, (who) aspire to live in an extended family which they see as an indication of prosperity and prestige" and that "extended families are prevalent among large landowners and among those who own middle-sized farms in rural areas and among artisans, retailers, etc., in the urban areas who have medium level of education" (1972:176). It is also noteworthy that among urban professionals, who have the highest percentage of nuclear families of any group (77 percent), there is still almost a quarter who did not have them (1972:175).

29.   These three things are generally seen by men as characterizing "common" women. On

the other hand, only 28 to 30 percent of the *gecekondu* men wanted to see their wives wearing a veil or *çarşaf* before leaving their houses, and it is likely that these symbols of the older Turkey will soon pass all but completely from the urban scene. Other things to which the men objected were what they call "city women's ways"—i.e., short, barber-cut hair (63 percent), fingernail polish (74 percent), and makeup (66 percent). Somewhat surprising is their general approval of women speaking publicly to men with whom they are acquainted (60 percent), and being together with men while visiting neighbors (64 percent). Presumably this is not approved of in regard to men with whom the husband has had no prior acquaintance (see Yasa, 1966:216–21).

30. Table 23. Unfortunately Timur did not break these responses down by SES, though her overall sample reflects the overall SES distribution of Turkey fairly closely.

31. But apparently the lower income husbands in Izmir managed to resist greater equality for their wives better than they withstood the same demands from their children. The 72 percent of those in the highest income groups who reported that their children had greater freedom than had been the case in their parents' families was matched by 74 percent of the lowest income families reporting the same thing. When broken down by neighborhoods, the change had taken place in 75 percent of the shanty families and in only 70 percent of the luxury area families, though it is likely that the 26 percent of luxury families reporting "no change" (compared to only 15 percent of the shanty families saying that) is accounted for by the fact that among luxury families there had been greater freedom in the previous generation. For a brief summary of why the Turkish "lumpenproletariat has not, as yet, been revolutionary," see Levine, 1973b. For more detailed analyses of the subject, see Levine 1973a and 1973c.

32. Some other data on these topics is also interesting. Kiray found the following in the Black Sea steel mill town of Ereğli:

Opinions on women working outside the home
(male family heads)

	All right to work	Can work half days	Must not work
Married women	16.5%	13.8%	68.8%
Unmarried women	40.9	16.1	42.1

She also found that the 15 to 24 age group was more liberal than older men, but that there were few differences related to education (1964:Tables 62, 63). Magnarella found in the town of Susurluk (population about 12,000) that 56.3 percent of his sample of adult men said that single girls should be allowed to work outside the home, but only 34 percent said the same of married women. He asserts that there are three fears: possible neglect of home and family, local concepts of honor and shame and "enhanced dangers of promiscuity," and "a potential challenge to male authority." He also found that on important decisions, 29 percent claimed they always consult their wives, 56 percent that they do so sometimes or often, 15 percent that they never do, and that the degree of consultation rose significantly with education (1974:100, 102).

33. The contrast is particularly striking when we note that in 1949 Richard Robinson found "not a single private social organization" in the city of Gaziantep (1951:432). A 1962 study of the already mushrooming iron and steel center of Karabük showed only about 100 associations, including four trade unions, five cooperatives, five welfare and charitable organizations, eleven clubs, and 72 "miscellaneous independent organizations" (Fındıkoğlu 1962:31–7).

34. A 1969–71 study by Dubetsky (1976) found that in at least one small Istanbul factory there had not been significant replacement of communal and personal loyalty by the more impersonal loyalties of occupation and class, and he further observed that employers in that kind of establishments sometimes continue to take deliberate steps to avoid hostility and to preserve "traditional" relationships, placing more emphasis on *bağlılık* (loyalty) than on skill and efficiency (though there are also, to be sure, many examples showing that productivity is the employer's primary concern).

35.   The one study I have found which is comparative is by Makofsky (1977), who concludes that class hostility (at least in one Turkish factory) tended to be associated with better education, better skilled jobs, and individual motivational factors far more than with dissatisfaction at work.

36.   The "brain drain" is more serious in professional categories. Turhan Oğuzkan found that as of 1970 there were some 907 Turkish scientists and engineers and 594 medical doctors with permanent residence in the United States alone, and an estimated 1,462 engineers and architects working abroad in 1968 (which was 9.6 percent of all Turks registered in those categories) as well as 150 Ph.D.'s (Abadan-Unat, 1976a:79–86).

37.   Rist estimated also that perhaps 15 percent had experienced some downward mobility (1978:50). This would certainly include the some 9,000 primary school teachers who went abroad as manual workers (Abadan-Unat, 1974:389).

38.   Germany has made some efforts to try to provide education for workers' children, and in fact has tried several approaches. In Bavaria teaching in the mother-tongue was stressed, while in Berlin an "integrationist" concept was used. In both cases, however, numerous problems of culture and philosophy were encountered. On these see Rist, 1978:chapters 9, 10.

39.   The survey encountered difficulties which among other things somewhat skewed the results in residence and employment in particular, but the magnitudes are such that there is no doubt about the sizable discrepancies between aspirations and actuality. See Paine, Appendix 3.

40.   Abadan-Unat, 1976a:169–70. Housing and real estate is considered the most profitable, dependable, and preferable field of investment, he found, though many workers also said they would like to invest in industrial and commercial enterprises. But there has been little government encouragement, nor was the government doing anything to channel investment into institutional rather than personal housing, the former being badly needed under the five-year plan. He concludes tht workers' remittances are not being used well.

Chapter 4

1.   A major reason is that the labor law allows membership in more than one union. Workers frequently neglect to withdraw from unions even if their primary allegiance is transferred to another one, and the federations and confederations neglect to report such withdrawals.

2.   This hostility seems not to have developed until the 1930s, however. At the Izmir Economic Congress of 1923, workers had been given recognition through separate representation, and in the Fourth Assembly in 1931, several persons included in the list of Ataturk's hand-picked candidates were specifically labeled as "workers" (Lewis, 1961:470; Frey, 1965:123). It was only when wariness of the new Soviet Union grew, and when the feeling of the need for national unity became very intense, that strong doctrinal hostility appeared in the RPP program. A stringent labor law was passed in 1932, and class-based organization was formally prohibited under Article 9 of the revised Law of Associations in 1938 (repealed in the new Law of Associations of 1946).

3.   Provisions of the labor laws were often not enforced, and the surplus of labor and high rate of unemployment, particularly during the depression years of the early 1930s, made it fairly easy for employers to evade their legal obligations. For a more detailed survey of the provisions of labor legislation during the 1920s and 1930s, see Hershlag, 1958:289–92 and Dereli, 1968:56 ff.

4.   The Democrats, if anything, outdid the RPP in providing benefits for workers. Among the DP actions were minimum wage legislation, introduction of a social security system, including a network of social security hospitals, and aid to gecekondu neighborhoods. Working class districts voted en masse for the DP throughout most of the 1950s.

5.   Not only were unions (and other organizations subject to the Law of Associations) forbidden to give aid to or receive aid from political parties, but under the political parties law

they were barred from even supporting a particular party or candidate for election. Dodd, 1969:11.

6. Karpat adds that there was probably also an element of self-protection. He ascribes the Democrats' failure to legislate the right to strike to the activity of other interest groups, and later to a large extent "because (the trade unions) expressed opposition to the government's inflationary policy which had lowered the workers' living standards" (1959:316). Probably some of the dislike of class-based association also lingered among the Democrats, most of whom were former members of the RPP.

7. The RPP did, however, make substantial gains in the working class area of Istanbul and other major industrial cities. For some figures see chapter 5.

Part of the conservatism is also tactical. It is only recently that it has become conceivable that the Turkish electorate may cease giving a majority of votes to the right-wing parties, and *Türk-İş*'s wish to remain on good terms with those most likely to control the government is understandable. Its avowed intent to fight for workers' causes by exerting influence on all political parties (Mumcuoğlu, 1980:388-9) is by no means unrealistic. Indeed, one can say that withholding direct support for any particular party may be more likely to win concessions than outright support.

8. For example, in 1970 the government sought to break DISK with a law that only unions representing at least one-third of the workers in a given industry could engage in collective bargaining. This sparked riots in Istanbul, which even the more conservative unions (which clearly would have benefited from the law) could not help but support. In another vein, observers noted that the JP eroded some of its support in 1977 by the simple failure to select any candidates for the assembly directly from *Türk-İş*, which was interpreted by some of the labor federation's leaders as a deliberate insult.

9. Tekeli found that of the twenty-one associations whose affiliation was identifiable, ten were with the RPP, ten with the JP and one with the DP. Part of the basis of factional identification of *esnaf* in Kayseri and Eskişehir also appears to be an expression of older group rivalries (Weiker, 1972:38, 55).

10. Ankara, 1963, Adana 1966, Kayseri 1967, Eskişehir 1968, Denizli 1973, Konya 1974, and Bursa and Gaizantep in process of organization at last report.

11. Öncü 1980:461, cites one estimate that although the Istanbul, Ankara, and Izmir chambers accounted for about 90 percent of Turkish industry and commerce, they constituted only 17 percent of the membership in the union's 1970 General Assembly.

Another source of distortion has been cited by Kıray. In her study of Izmir she concluded that many enterprises sought benefits "by mis-representing the value of their capital investment and gaining access into the Chamber (and hoping) to be eligible for better credit facilities and to enhance their prospects." She estimated that in the city of Izmir, Turkey's second-largest industrial center and a city of very considerable development and sophistication, on a key criterion roughly measuring "structural differentiation and organizational capacity," "53 percent of the enterprises registered with the Chamber of Commerce and Industry employed only a single person in an administrative capacity, and he was probably a part-time accountant" (1973:8).

Still another variant of such conflicts was found when Neyzi noted that in a survey in Istanbul in the early 1960s, the Association of Foundry Operators, a group made up mostly of very small operators, "did not want to reveal members' addresses because of fear that the Chamber of Commerce would meddle in their activities" (1973:141nl).

12. The degree of need for more funds is difficult to determine, though virtually all observers agree that it is considerable. Kili has calculated, for example, that the amount of aid to coöps from the Ministry of Village Affairs in 1975 averaged 370,000 TL per coöp, which apparently did little except provide for loans for seasonal cash flow problems (1976-7:72).

13. Various schemes for "community development" have been conceived and tried. Their success has also been limited, in part because of the dearth of both financial and human resources and in part because of the nature of the schemes. In contrast to enthusiastic plans for

"the development of initiative in small social units" about which both the first and second five-year plans spoke but which required either government initiative or extensive cooperation between villagers and outsiders (see SPO 1969:277–82), when projects of smaller magnitude have been attempted and when they have been geared to the needs perceived by villagers rather than by the developers, the record of performance is quite good. For examples of both successes and failures see Elbruz, 1974. See also Geray, 1966.

14.   It should be stressed that the members of the Turkish officer corps have never been united in their political views. During the Young Turk period there were as many military opponents of the regime as supporters of it. During the early Republic years there were no officers who basically dissented from the Ataturk reform program, but there were many who differed with him on various particulars and on some general aspects, such as the speed and radicality of desirable reforms. In the multiparty period, there was also a broad spectrum of opinion among officers with regard to the policies to be pursued either by civilian governments or by the military themselves during the periods of quasi-military rule in 1960–61 and 1971–73.

15.   For example, as late as 1960, the Menderes government attempted to prevent opposition leader Inonu from speaking at a political rally in Kayseri. Inonu succeeded in getting there because officers brought to the scene by the government continued to respect him as a former high military leader and passed him ceremonially through their ranks (Weiker, 1963:14, 37).

16.   This conclusion is analyzed in detail in Weiker, 1963, from which much of the material for this section is taken. For discussions arriving at a similar conclusion, see Karpat, 1970 and Özbudun, 1966.

17.   It is important to note, however, that the members of the NUC were far from radical in their social and economic views, although most were at least moderately left-wing. The most radical, actually, were on the right, a group of fourteen led by Alpaslan Türkeş (later founder of the National Action party), which included most of the younger members of the junta. They wanted to make some major nationalistic (and to some degree socialistic) reforms, but to do so by authoritarian means. When their aims became apparent, the rest of the NUC promptly purged them from the junta's ranks.

18.   The moderate influences in the military, clearly in control, took the lead in putting down two attempted coups by radical younger officers in February 1962 and May 1963, led by Colonel Talat Aydemir and several former officers who had been purged from the NUC. Aydemir was executed after his second attempt. Weiker 1963a.

19.   In 1973 the officers suffered an even more humiliating defeat when General Faruk Gürler, former Chief of Staff and the officers' hand-picked candidate to succeed President Cevdet Sunay (another general), was decisively rejected by the assembly. For a detailed account see Nye, 1973, and chapter 8 below.

20.   The section of Article 2 of the 1924 Constitution which stated that "the religion of the Turkish state is Islam" was dropped in 1928.

21.   Actually these retreats should be dated closer to 1947, since one of the first things the RPP did was to make some concessions in the area of religion. For an example, see page 122.

22.   When Koran courses were allowed to be conducted openly again in the multiparty period, it was discovered that the number which had been operating covertly might have been as high as 10,000, and that in 1960 and 1969 there were respectively 20,000 and 50,000 unauthorized ones in addition to the 6,000 officially authorized. Yavuz, 1969a:70–71.

23.   Actually, efforts in this direction had also been made as early as the nineteenth century when the Tanzimat reformers sought to win the loyalty of the non-Muslims of the empire by granting them full citizenship and rights. But these attempts failed because in the end neither the Muslim elites nor the general Muslim population were willing to accept removal of the distinction between themselves and non-Muslims, a distinction implanted in Islamic theology as well as in history.

24.   Figures calculated from DIE #710 show that nineteen provinces which contain the biggest cities and/or are in the western parts of Turkey had:

46.1 percent of the population in 1970;

66.2 percent of the registered marriages in 1972;

61.1 percent of the registered divorces in 1972;

There are indications that change is taking place more rapidly in rural areas of western Turkey than in even the urban areas of the east, but the data are still insufficient.

25. "Amnesty" laws to encourage *ex post facto* registration of marriages, divorces, and births have also been passed periodically, the most recent one about 1960.

26. Karpat's study of Istanbul *gecekondus*, for example, found that 66 percent of the women believed in the importance of voting (compared to 85 percent of the men). 1976:Table 8.1.

27. See, for example, a study of one of the highest social strata (some mother-daughter pairs in Istanbul, the daughters being university students) which showed that even though "the major social breakthrough has taken place in the mothers' generation (such as increased education), these social changes have not changed their own sex-role expectations fundamentally, and they are a generation of women trying to conciliate traditional and newer role demands." Cited in Kandiyoti 1978:25.

28. On some aspects of adjustment by women who have gone to Europe as workers or accompanying their husbands, see chapter 3 above.

Chapter 5

1. RPP membership figures are very scarce, in fact all but nonexistent for the 1920s. For 1935–36, party reports indicate that some 977,000 persons were eligible to attend party congresses, which was about 10 percent of the total population in the provinces covered by the reports. Weiker, 1973:194–98.

2. There were some obvious exceptions, perhaps the most prominent being Adnan Menderes, who was recruited personally by Ataturk after Menderes had come to his attention as leader of the Aydın branch of the Free Party of 1930. After that episode, Ataturk, in fact, gave orders that those who had performed well in the opposition were to be brought to his attention, but, again, there seems to have been little *systematic* effort at such recruitment, and it is doubtful that in its absence there was much real incentive for local leaders to perform well as a prerequisite for a political career. See Weiker, 1973:155–57.

3. The one area in which the RPP did tolerate the continued power of local notables was the eastern provinces, where the party exchanged support for some of its key policies by tacitly allowing landowners and *ağas* to retain much of their local power. As a result, until the late 1960s the RPP was able to retain a large percentage of the votes in those provinces, the most traditional in the country, and which Özbudun has described as having a peasantry which is "more voted than voting" (1976:162,182). It is only since the party's turning toward left of center that more aggressive policies toward social change in the east have been emphasized. For some recent examples of this emphasis, see *Yanki* #222.

4. The 1954 party Congress placed selection of candidates for the Assembly into the hands of the province organizations, rejecting a motion to allow even a small percentage be named by the national leaders (Kili, 1976:120). The same motion was again defeated in 1956 (Ibid.:124) but passed later. The DP by-laws allowed its General Executive Committee to nominate up to 20 percent "central candidates" (Frey, 1965:437). Since 1965 the Political Parties Law has allowed a party to name central candidates up to 5 percent of the total.

5. Ecevit was born in Istanbul in 1925. His father was a member of the National Assembly, his mother a well-known painter. After graduating from Robert College in 1944 he became a journalist, serving among other places in London, where he also studied Sanskrit and the history of art. In 1950 he became a political columnist and staff member of the RPP newspaper *Ulus*. In 1957 he spent several months at Harvard University, studying under Henry Kissinger. He has been a member of the Assembly continually since 1957. He is also an accomplished poet.

6.   Another similar but smaller defection took place in 1973, which resulted in formation of the Republicanist (*Cumhuriyetçi*) party, but that party never really developed and eventually merged with the Reliance party (Kili, 1976:341).

7.   It apparently required some time for this to take effect, and it was not until 1973 that the party executive council did not contain any members who had already been party officials before 1950. The 1973 council contained only six who were party officials between 1950–1960. The average age of the council fell from 51.3 in 1960 to 48.4 in 1973 (Kili, 1976:362).

8.   In July 1974 he had become a national hero by successfully invading Cyprus following the attempted coup d'etat there by conservative Greek officers.

9.   Frey, 1975:65. "Possibly the most striking and important characteristic of elite political culture in Turkey is a pronounced tendency to view the world in ingroup vs. outgroup terms." It is hard to say *how much* influence this has had, but "it is enough to note the grave significance of the friend-foe bias that pervades Turkish political life and leads to recrudescence of virulent inter-elite conflict every time the system is opened up to democratic competition." Frey: 67, citing Mardin and others who make similar observations.

10.   Celal Bayar (President, 1950–1960) was a veteran of politics as far back as the War of Independence and had held high offices including that of Prime Minister and Minister of Economics under Ataturk. Adnan Menderes (Prime Minister) was a wealthy landowner from the Aegean region, active in the Free Party of 1930 and personally recruited by Ataturk following that episode. Fuad Köprülü (Foreign Minister) was one of Turkey's most respected historians.

11.   Dodd 1969:25. As Karpat (1959:410) has also noted, "The Democrats discussed more fundamental issues and ideas only when forced to do so by circumstances and as an answer to other political parties."

12.   Farm mechanization tended, however, to disproportionately benefit the larger farmers (even though from the point of view of the national economy it was a positive step in that it became one of the bases for significant increases in agricultural production) and would soon be one cause of dislocating large numbers of peasants and generating severe "push" pressures toward rapid urbanization. See, for example, Karpat, 1960.

13.   The DP was, of course, also fortunate in being able to take advantage of other than political factors (extraordinarily good crop weather in the initial years, high world wheat prices stemming from the Korean War, sizable American aid) to maintain a high rate of industrial expansion and import of consumer goods.

14.   But these excesses are by no means the entire story. Simpson has pointed out that "not only was Turkey's industrial base substantially enlarged but large amounts of precious foreign exchange, previously spent on importing light industry goods, were saved. . . ." (1965:145) and that "one of the most striking results of [the agricultural] investments, increased incentives and improved distribution system was a rise of over 50 percent in Turkey's total agricultural output" during the period 1950–58. For a good account of this period see also, Tachau and Ulman, 1965.

15.   There were some earlier incidents of considerable vindictiveness such as the 1953 confiscation of many of the assets of the RPP on the grounds that they had been acquired illegally. But although relations between the two parties were usually tense, serious repression did not begin until things began to go badly for the Democrats in the latter part of the decade.

16.   The Republican Peasants Nation party will be mentioned below. The New Turkey party was formed by former DP dissident, Ekrem Alican, an able but also rather colorless politician whose chief program interest was the strong defense of private enterprise. Its political base in 1961 was mostly among local notables in some eastern provinces, a foundation which collapsed when its backers realized that the NTP would not become a vehicle to carry them to power. Its 13.7 percent of the votes and 65 seats in 1961 declined to 4 percent and 19 seats in 1965, and although it survived until 1973, it was never a significant factor, being neither ideologically distinct nor the vehicle for an attractive faction leader (which are among the things which have kept some of the other minor parties alive).

17.   Many analysts agree with Sherwood's observation that "the peasants (now) simply list mosques along with electricity, water, roads, educational opportunity for their children, and government support of agricultural prices as the things they expect from any government or party soliciting their votes" (1967:59). Signs of the waning of the issue of secularism as early as 1957, however, have been noted by Karpat (1961:458).

18.   Szyliowicz (1966b:487). We should note here that the JP in its early years did not appear to have the fundamental distaste for economic planning which the DP had. But in more recent years a central complaint by many in the business as well as academic communities in Turkey was that the JP government was virtually ignoring, if not directly sabotaging, the work of the State Planning Organization and was, instead, basing targets, projections, and strategies almost wholly on political needs.

19.   In this vein, the JP also kept alive the issue of amnesty and restoration of the political rights of the former Democrats, a spirited battle until a law restoring those rights was enacted in 1966.

20.   It is not clear how serious has been the effect of the government's inability to control urban violence. It may well be less important than economic policy shortcomings. Many of those persons who are directly affected by the urban guerrilla activity would not have voted for the Justice party anyway.

21.   Included among these was Feyzioğlu himself. A member of an old and prominent Kayseri family, he had been able to keep his party in a better position in that province than in most of the other areas of the nation, and has won re-election continually to date. It should be added that Feyzioğlu also had a considerable personal reputation among the press, among many deputies, and in the Ankara intellectual community, having been (among other things) at one time Dean of the Political Science Faculty, a respected professor, and one of the Democrats' prime targets in the days just prior to the 1960 revolution.

22.   The decline of minor parties in 1969 was due also to a change in the electoral system which the major parties had combined to put through. The change abolished the electoral law's "national remainder" feature in which the "unused" votes which parties polled under the proportional representation system were pooled nation-wide, and extra seats allotted. The Turkish Labor Party in 1965 obtained 13 of its 15 seats in this manner. Szyliowicz 1966.

23.   In 1973 the DP infuriated all the other parties when in the election for President of the Republic it insisted on maintaining Bozbeyli's candidacy through 15 ballots, although the chief issue was the struggle to thwart the attempt of the armed forces to impose their own candidate. See Tamkoç, 1976:58, Nye, 1977, and chapter 8 below.

24.   At various times since 1948, it has split, recombined, changed its name to the Republic Peasants Nation party and back, etc.

25.   Prior to 1945 the Law of Associations prohibited any organizations which were "class-based." All forms of Marxism, socialism and communism continued to be barred until 1961. On other leftist groups and parties and on some front organizations from time to time, see Landau, 1974:113–21, and his extensive bibliography; Harris, 1967; Tuncay,1967.

26.   The membership claimed by the TLP, on the other hand, which at its peak totalled about 12,000, was heavily nonelite: workers 27.4 percent, artisans and tradesmen 26.3 percent, agricultural laborers 9 percent, others 20.3 percent (Landau, 1974:132). The election returns, however, would seem to cast doubt on this claim.

27.   See note 22 above.

28.   In fact, the TLP suffered a greater decline in the urban areas than in the rural ones. The party's urban vote in 1969 was 3.2 percent, compared with 4.6 percent in 1965, and actually rose in rural areas from 2.4 percent to 2.5 percent (Özbudun, 1976:122). Much of its rural support appears to have come from the eastern provinces and because of the adherence of particular groups to the TLP for other than program reasons.

29.   Rather incongruously, leftist literature continues to be available in abundance. At least 25 leftist periodicals were recently available, including 11 weeklies, 6 monthlies, and 5

semimonthlies (See *Yanki* #309, 14–20 February 1977, p. 14). In January, 1979 such material was also prominently and openly displayed in many places, including large open-air bookstalls in Istanbul's Taksim Square.

30.   Like Demirel, Erbakan was an engineer, and thus both were somewhat of the new breed in Turkish politics. But in contrast to the JP leader, Erbakan had experience in the private sector (he had been General Secretary of the Union of Chambers of Commerce until he clashed with industrialists such as Vehbi Koç) and had strong ties in the conservative provinces of central Anatolia. For more details, see Landau, 1976.

31.   The Cyprus issue was central enough to involve all the parties, though on some other issues a greater separation of responsibilities had been possible through giving each partner control of specific ministries. Thus, for example, the NSP was given the Interior Ministry and some broad powers over activities of leftist and rightist groups as well as over the "moral" tone of some aspects of public life. In another particularly crucial area, education, it was possible to agree to classify "moral" education (a key demand of the NSP) as something peripheral to the general curriculum, and therefore not greatly disruptive to the educational process.

32.   Born in Cyprus in 1917, Türkeş graduated from the Military Academy in 1938. In 1944 he had a brush with the authorities, who alleged that he was a pan-Turanist, and though he was acquitted, his interest in that idea has apparently continued. In 1960 he became the chief public spokesman for the National Unity Committee, but was expelled from the junta in November on the grounds of opposing a return to civilian government. After a period of exile abroad he returned to politics via the Republican Peasants Nation party, which became the National Action party in 1969. See Weiker, 1963: 125-7, Landau, 1974:passim, Ahmad, 1977:passim.

33.   The only more or less sectarian party which has arisen in Turkish politics is the Unity party, which had its support largely in several Anatolian cities which had heavy concentrations of *Alevis*. The UP denied that it was chiefly a sectarian party, but most people regarded it as such. It began as "essentially a centrist party" in 1966 (Landau 1974:17) and sent eight deputies to the Assembly in the 1969 election. It was not effective, however, and after internal rifts which resulted in the victory of a faction which turned the party radically to the left, its vote declined by half (to 1.1 percent), and only one member was returned to the Assembly in 1973.

34.   Most recently, 5 TL for admission to the party, 1,200 TL for annual dues, 25,000 TL for individual gifts, and prohibitions on numerous kinds of nonparty organizations contributing to political parties. The bulk of party funds comes from the government, under a formula based on a party's percentage of votes in the most recent election. It ranges from 500,000 TL a year for a party which got to 5 to 10 percent of the votes, to 3.5 million TL for one getting 50 percent or more.

35.   It is still illegal for parties to have fully organized local branches, and they can be represented at that level only by individual employees or representatives. Some observers regret this, pointing out that useful political functions have thus only been partially restored.

36.   In 1973 in four key provinces, the vote for splinter parties far exceeded that for radical parties, in both towns and villages, while in the cities themselves (Ankara, Istanbul, Izmir, Adana) the radical votes were either very close to or greater than the splinter-party votes. Özbudun–Tachau, 1975:Table 6.

Chapter 6

1.   For Turkey, this refocusing involved not only villagers, but the "modern" segments of the population as well. For many years the urban elites were probably even less likely to be acquainted with villages than peasants were with the cities. The outlooks of the old elites were strongly influenced by Ottoman feelings of distinctiveness from even their own compatriots, and although Ataturk stressed nationalism, the urban elites were also diverted by the simultaneous desires for "westernization."

2.   The main stress was initially put on ending religious influence over education. Private

and foreign schools were allowed to continue to operate, though under close government supervision and with restrictions such as that Turkish history be taught only by Turks.

3. A relatively little-known aspect of the Izmir Economic Congress of 1923 was the enunciation of a series of goals for "agricultural education," which set out ambitious intentions and has been described as seeking "to liberate education from its classical bonds and force on it a direct stimulating role in the basic element of the national economy—the village agricultural unit" (Başgöz and Wilson, 1968:56-7). Much of this goal remains still to be realized.

4. See Kazamias, 1966:124-5; Kirby, et al, 1964; Frey, 1964:220-1; Karpat, 1959:377-80. Among the reasons why phasing out of the Village Institutes was started even under Inonu was that they were alleged to have been strongholds of radicalism, and it is true that some of the most ardent educational reform advocates are Village Institute products.

5. Unfortunately, many of the other projects did not get past the stage of pilot projects, despite vigorous efforts by a number of creative Ministers of Education. On some of the imaginative ideas and their failure to be implemented, see Frank Stone, 1970 and 1973.

6. Another factor may have been the relative slowness of attitudinal change in the villages, and the importance of development per se as a stimulus to modernization. As Szyliowicz has noted, "As late as 1952 about half of all villagers were either indifferent or hostile to modern schools, and in terms of rural priorities, education was considered less important than improvements in agriculture, health and credit facilities. [But] such attitudes, which indicate the limited impact of the Ataturk reforms upon village life, and the continuing strength of traditional values, soon began to change as economic, political and social change came increasingly to characterize rural society" (1973:329, citing the OECD's Mediterranean Regional Project Report).

Notable innovations of the 1960s included a large amount of vocational and literacy education given to draftees of the armed forces (Robinson, 1967:80-6), but some doubt has been cast on the effectiveness of these efforts by James Keyser (1969, 1974) who found that many of the men lost much of their literacy and skills because of absence of support when they returned to their villages. There was also the "Reserve Officer Teacher" program begun in 1960 by the National Unity Committee. In this venture some 11,000 graduates of lycee level schools were assigned to do most of their military service as village teachers. Many did an effective job (and gained important insights into and sympathies for the problems of Turkish villagers, which attitudes persist today among many of the former ROTs). Many were stimulated to become teachers. Most, however, encountered major difficulties because they were poorly prepared, because being both outsiders and young many had little status in villages, and because many were quite unhappy with their change from urban to rural living. The program was terminated in 1963, due in large part to its political unpopularity but also to hostility to it from some parts of the established educational bureaucracy. See Weiker, 1963:143-6 and Roos and Angel, 1968.

7. Of those taking the examination in 1974, only 28.5 percent were taking it for the first time (DIE #734, Table 45). For an analysis of the social background of the students taking the exam in 1974, see chapter 2.

8. Çukurova University in Adana (faculties of agriculture and medicine); Diyarbakir (medicine, science); Anatolia University, Eskişehir (medicine, basic sciences); Republic University, Sivas (medicine, science, social sciences); Selcuk University, Konya (science, humanities); Firat University, Elazığ (veterinary medicine, science, humanities); Bursa University (medicine, economic and social sciences, mechanics); 19 May University, Samsun (science, medicine, engineering). Inonu University in Malatya is not yet open. The staffing problems encountered by the universities established earlier outside the three main metropolitan areas do not augur well for rapid growth of the new institutions, however. The universities in Erzurum and Trabzon, after eighteen and thirteen years respectively, were still relying on a considerable number of commuting faculty from Ankara and Istanbul. The problems will be particularly severe in the new universities whose locations do not make them easily accessible. Thus, arrangements at Bursa, for example, are working out considerably better than in some of the eastern cities to which access by air during the winter is frequently extremely limited.

9. Part of their growth, though, was due to the nationalization of all private and foreign

schools above secondary level in 1971. There were many legitimate complaints that the private schools which had sprung up in profusion since the 1950s were offering extremely low quality education through policies such as accepting anyone who could pay the tuition, providing only the most minimal equipment and facilities, and hiring part-time teachers at the lowest possible salaries. It remains to be seen whether direct control by the Ministry of Education improves them substantially.

10.   Part of the basis for maintaining the difference in status is tradition and pride. It is also true that the difference in the quality of the faculties is great and that the academic level is frequently higher. There is less justification in the argument that the higher schools and academies are little more than vocational schools, for Turkish universities also offer very little if any liberal arts or general education components.

11.   Of some 47,000 registrants in 1974–1975, 39,500 took the examination, but only about 6,000 passed to the second year. Of the others, 14,500 repeated the first year and 20,000 reregistered but did not return. It was potentially an important way of spreading education, however, in that 62 percent of the students were in province capitals, mostly outside the areas in which college-level institutions are located, 20 percent were residents of district centers, and 18 percent of small towns and villages. For a full analysis, see Geray, 1977.

12.   In 1970–1971 only some 37% of city primary schools and 78% of village ones were on single sessions (SPO 1973:Tables 560, 562). Although I have not been able to locate later figures, there is no doubt that the situation has become far worse today (SPO 1978b:par.457) and I was assured in early 1979 that there are virtually no single-session public elementary schools in Ankara.

13.   The situation does not stem entirely from an increasing influx of lower-class students, however. Maynard earlier found that of 656,000 who entered primary schools in 1955 only 360,000 (55%) graduated five years later, that of 98,000 in the first year of middle school in 1957 only 56,000 (63%) were in the third year two years later, and that "throughout the last forty years consistently about 31% of the students in each (middle school) class have failed and had to repeat all the work of the class" (1964:9). Even among the students who later took the university entrance exams (in 1974), some 14.6% had taken more than the normal time to finish primary school, 33% needed one or more extra years in middle school, and 16.7% needed the same during their passage through lycee (DIE #734:34).

14.   In Turkish universities, examinations are given several times a year rather than only at the ends of the particular courses, and until recently there was no limit on the number of times students could attempt them.

15.   Again it must be pointed out that this problem is by no means limited to Turkey. The "democratic ideal" of teaching children to question the wisdom, values, and authority of the very generation which is teaching them is usually far from fully realized.

16.   There are numerous examples. They include the giving of examinations which test whether students have worked the arithmetic problems in the text rather than giving new ones which might ask them to apply principles. One result of this has been to lead students to resist attempts at the latter activity, and there is at least one case personally known to me in which students at a Turkish university (in a "prestige" faculty) walked out of a final examination in protest against the instructor asking them to go beyond the material printed in their text. For other examples see Cohn, 1970:105. For a general discussion of the problems resulting from rote teaching in Turkish schools, see the interview with Refia Şemin, Director of the Istanbul University Pedagogic Institute, in *Milliyet*, 12 January 1976.

17.   The situation is similar at the universities. While it is true that things like attitudes toward authority are already established by the time college age is reached, the persistence of rote teaching and the lack of encouragement of creativity is undoubtedly interpreted (usually correctly) as a presage of the characteristics needed to get ahead in institutions like the civil bureaucracy. Additional factors leading frequently (though by no means always) to poor teaching and to lack of individual attention include the huge size of many classes and low faculty salaries, which often force professors to "moonlight."

18.   Istanbul remains the home office of all important Turkish newspapers. The press is one of the few institutions which has not moved its center to Ankara, although the major dailies do now print editions in several major cities which contain local news and advertising.

19.   The murder of *Milliyet's* editor Abdi Ipekçi in 1978 was a grievous blow to Turkish journalism.

20.   Many newspapers have received some government assistance through the institution of official advertisements. Dating from the single-party period and inaugurated as a means of stimulating development of the press, both RPP and DP governments used these subsidies in partisan ways, with the result that in 1961 a nonpolitical Press Advertisement Association was created which has developed criteria for qualifying newspapers. Debate continues, though, about such points as the degree to which subsidies should be used to encourage the numerous very small newspapers, particularly in the larger cities. In 1978 some 278 million lira in official ads were placed in Turkish dailies. For an extensive summary of the history and issues see *Yanki*, #421, 9–15 April 1979, pp. 40–43.

21.   Tables 165, 166, and pp. 262–4. The data about which newspapers were read in villages reflect the general national picture. In 1968 *Hürriyet* captured about one-third of village readers despite the fact that it was available only in 16% of the villages, with the other mass circulation dailies getting around 12% each. 13% said they read whatever was available.

22.   *Akis* and *Kim*, which were both strong supporters of the opposition in the latter part of the 1950s and which therefore had a lively circulation, and *Yanki* which has been in existence since 1971.

23.   As late as the start of the second Plan in 1968 "only 36.8% of the country and 42.6% of the population (was) benefiting from radio facilities" (SPO 1969:634). By the end of that Plan period in 1972, however, there was at least one national station available to 87.5% of the population, and a regional one to 98.4%. SPO, 1973:612. For a general summary of the growth of radio facilities, see Abisel and Kocabaşoğlu, 1978.

24.   There were two kinds of literature involved. One was a small number of original works, the best-known of which was Namık Kemal's play *Vatan*, stressing the dual themes of freedom and fatherland (Lewis 1961:138). There were also a few novels of life among the Istanbul upper class, and some anthologies of poetry. The second was translations of Western literature, ranging from philosophy to the novels of Dumas, Zola, and others with antidespotic themes. The intentions of the translators were both to encourage political reform and to glorify the life which many of them had seen in exile in Paris and elsewhere. They did not advocate wholesale Westernization, however, in that they were also nationalists and strong advocates of Islam. For a general summary of literature of this period, see Menemencioğlu, 1973.

25.   There was, for example, Halit Ziya Uşakligil, whose *Mavi ve Siyah* (The Blue and the Black; 1897) "introduced into Turkish literature a character just emerging in society: the sensitive young man who must depend on his own enterprise for success, and whose dreams are crushed by the material realities of his environment" (Menemencioğlu 1973:17). Halide Edib, a woman who was soon to add military heroism to her literary fame, published several nationalistic novels, the most famous of which, *Ateşden Gömlek* (The Shirt of Flames, 1922), was based on her experiences in the army during the War of Independence and described, among other things, the heroism of many ordinary Turks. Others concerned themselves with social and moral issues of the day, as well as exaltation of patriotism and encouragement of Turkishness through stressing folk language and poetry, discussions of cultural history and the attributes of the Turks, linguistics, and pre-Islamic Turkish history (Ibid., 1973:passim).

26.   But their role was also limited because they were patronized largely by students, teachers, and civil servants, but not by workers or villagers, and their usefulness was further limited by the fact that in many libraries the books could not be taken out. It is not known how many of the volumes in these libraries were literature. Weiker, 1973:176–7.

27.   Not all the translations are classics, of course. Inspection of a Turkish bookstall will turn up a very large number of romances, mysteries, adventure stories, etc. They do, however, have an important effect in that they usually glorify modern ways, particularly those of newly

unfettered young people, and exalt urban life. Certainly no traditional parent would approve of them. Also included among the foreign literature are myriads of comic books.

28. The Turkish movie industry dates to the 1890s, but did not become a really significant force until the 1950s. Up to that time it was limited creatively by its domination by Muhsin Ertuğrul, a theatre director whose orientation to the stage resulted in "theatrical cinema in which the script was written as if it were meant to be performed on a stage, and stage genres such as melodramas or musicals were borrowed" (And, 1973:18). After World War II a number of new film directors emerged, but they were hampered in part by the small number of theatres, which made production uneconomic, and partly by censorship, which became severe at times during the late 1950s. The situation changed after the 1960 revolution, when controls were lifted, when audiences began to grow at a rapid rate (particularly as theatres expanded in provincial cities and towns), and when cinematography began to be taught at Istanbul and Ankara Universities and at the State Academy of Fine Arts. See T.C. 1973:453–8.

29. Current research on the effects of advertising on Turkish radio and television is being conducted by Dr. Oya Tokgöz of the Basın ve Yayın Yüksek Okulu and should be available soon.

30. Here Ataturk appears to have gone to excess. He banned all traditional Turkish music from the state radio, replacing it with music by the Presidential Symphony Orchestra. "The effects of this error are felt even today," Metin And has written, though one positive aspect was the stimulation of *true* folk music as contrasted to Ottoman music. See And, 1974. For an interesting musicological analysis, see Signell, 1976.

Chapter 7

1. TUSIAD, 1977:65, 74. There is some disagreement about these figures, but the ones cited here appear generally representative. The only major disruptions of this general growth rate were in 1958–1961, and as must mentioned, since 1977. There were also sizable variations in the performance of individual sectors of the economy, as will be discussed later in this chapter.

2. Yenal, 1973. In the words of another writer (Hershlag, 1973:4), the drive for autarchy in Turkey and many other countries "has frequently overshadowed all other criteria such as efficiency, rational allocation of resources, comparative advantage, and (at least in the short run) social considerations. . . ."

3. The "National Strategy" takes pains to point out that, "The wording in the preamble of the Turkish constitution 'exalting our Nation as a respected member of the community of world nations enjoying equal rights' reflects a basic ideal built upon Ataturk's call 'to reach the level of contemporary civilization.' This ideal has been expressly stated in the Second Five-Year Development Plan" (SPO, 1973a:par. 2.1.) While this is used as the basis for demanding considerable 'plan discipline,' it is specifically denied that it is also implies a goal of autarchy.

4. The Industrial Census of 1913 found only some 282 establishments, of which all except 13 (in chemicals) were in food processing, textiles, wood, and paper products. They employed only some 17,000 workers, and 85 percent were owned by non-Turkish minorities, many of whom left during the 1920s and created an entrepreneurial gap which began to be filled only much later (DIE #683:141–45).

5. It abolished the Capitulations (a series of treaties granting foreign powers special extraterritorial concessions in economic-commercial as well as judicial areas) but provided for only their gradual phase-out. Gradual phase-out had a positive aspect in that not all production ceased immediately, as occurred for example, when nationalization of port services and coastal shipping led to an almost complete paralysis of trade between many regions of the country early in the 1920s. Probably the most unfavorable provisions of the treaty were restrictions on full freedom of action on tariffs until 1929 and the saddling of the new government with much of the remainder of the Ottoman debt (Hershlag, 1958:20–25).

6. Although it is not fully clear why this strategy was chosen, the most likely cause was inability to do much else. As Hershlag points out, the government had very few budgetary

resources and "was therefore deeply concerned with finding new capital resources" (1958:49). Another probable cause was the leaders' preoccupation with other matters of political and social reform, which were at their height during the 1920s.

7. There was criticism that some of the plants were located in response to political criteria rather than economic ones, and there is probably some truth to this, but the increased dispersal was nevertheless important in giving at least some economic stimulus to other areas of the country.

8. In fact the government took great pains to deny any ideological (i.e., doctrinaire socialist) motives. See Weiker, 1973:249–53, Hershlag, 1958:75–97, Kerwin, 1951:23.

9. In part this was done through controls on such matters as the pricing and wage policies of private firms (Hershlag, 1958:134), ostensibly for reasons of social justice. It is likely, however, that another underlying motive was to inhibit competition with the SEEs, and it is clear that concentration of power in the hands of the bureaucracy was one factor which motivated the dislike of *etatism* by the Democrats and led to considerable changes in government economic policy in the 1950s.

10. These began in the 1920s through many measures, such as the establishment of the privately owned but government-stimulated Business Bank *(İş Bankası)* in 1924, the Bank for Industry and Mining in 1925, and the Law for the Encouragement of Industry in 1927. In the 1950s the measures ranged from establishment of the Industrial Development Bank in 1950 to a large array of tax incentives, customs provisions, favorable terms for purchase of land, etc. In addition, there was now a political regime generally sympathetic to the interests of private industry. There was also stimulation from the general momentum of development itself. On these points, see Hershlag, 1958; Krueger, 1974; and Singer, 1977, *passim.*

11. Iren, 1979:360. By 1942, when the law was repealed, 1,055 firms had benefited from it, but the total number of workers they employed was only 7,200 (Ibid.).

12. Part of the reasons for many firms not expanding is the matter of tax laws. As Codi analyzed the situation in 1962, above a certain level of receipts bookkeeping requirements get much more strict. Larger firms must hire accountants, which is an extra cost, and may reveal incomes to a third party, "a practice highly disliked in Turkey." There is also workers' insurance, a problem partly because payments are high for employers with over ten employees but also because record-keeping requirements become very complex. Large firms are also required to be members of the Chamber of Commerce, reveal sales and production figures, and get involved with record-keeping. Some expansion is accomplished by opening another store in the name of another family member, but it is impossible to take advantage of increased efficiency in such a way.

13. In 1976, out of 2,092 companies founded with capital of 5.5 billion TL, 1,172 with 2.986 billion TL (54%) were located in Istanbul, 330 with 1.076 billion TL (20%) in Ankara, 152 with 345 million TL (6%) in Izmir. Only some 20% of the new capital went to the entire remainder of the country, even though there were numerous cities which offered good human and logistical resources. It can be debated, to be sure, whether it is a greater contribution to economic development to produce with maximum efficiency (this being presumably at least one argument for locating in an already established center) than it is to stimulate the growth of new industrial centers.

14. Gülten Kazgan has suggested that optimum firm size for Turkey is 200-499 (1972).

15. On these problems as already visible in the *etatist* period, see Sarç, 1948:441–6. He advocated at that time a thorough rethinking of *etatist* policies.

16. There are also nonmanufacturing SEEs, such as the State Railroads, and marketing enterprises, such as the Soil Products Office. They are not included in the analysis in this section.

17. It is not fully clear how long the losses of the SEEs have been going on, and which ones ought to be charged to them. Several analysts have concluded that the problem is not so much one of operating losses as one of inability to capitalize their own reinvestment and expansion needs. Another contention is that separate calculations should be made for the manufacturing SEEs and the utility ones, such as the State Railways and Turkish Airlines. In addition to

Kazgan's analysis, see Schachter and Cohen, 1973, as cited in Kerwin, 1975:39.

18. Several analysts have concluded that nondevelopmental growth was able to continue only until about the end of the 1950s, that by 1960 all the land which was potentially arable had been put under cultivation, and that expansion thereafter had to come from elsewhere (Careys, 1972, Hirsch, 1970). And statistics do show that after rapid increases through the mid-1950s, the amount of land planted in grains increased virtually not at all (DIE 683:116).

19. But on another criterion, Eva and Abraham Hirsch found that their analysis "suggests that *per capita* agricultural output in Turkey increased primarily during the pre-war period and only little thereafter, and that the output of the typical peasant at present is probably no greater than it had been thirty years earlier" (1963:391).

20. Aresvik asserts that indigenous breeds have "low productive and reproductive capabilities and thus low input-output efficiencies." "Product output per animal unit is quite low as compared to the product output per animal unit of many important animal-producing countries. The average yield of cows' milk in Turkey is only 600 kilograms per year, and has increased very little in the last two decades" (1975:55).

21. Many analysts have pointed in this connection to even more readily available potential for expansion of poultry production, one of whose virtues is that it is not limited by factors of geography and space as is the raising of other livestock (Aresvik 1975:56).

22. Agricultural credit tripled in quantity between 1965 and 1972 alone (T.C., 1973:201) but still, according to the SPO in 1970, "the main problems to be solved (in agriculture) were the availability of credit for both dealers and farmers" (cited in Carey, 1972:55). In addition to greater amounts being needed, it appears that a serious problem arises from the fact that most loans to farmers are short-term. The Village Survey, for example, discovered that 43% of the respondents said they used their Agricultural Bank credits for "household needs" only 20% for purchase of agricultural inputs, 16% for purchases of agricultural equipment or investments in fields or animal husbandry (Table 65). According to Köksal, in 1968, 70% of the farmers could get less than 1000 TL from the Agricultural Bank, and 90% of the agricultural credit could not be used for financing long-term agricultural development projects. He adds that credit distribution among regions, interest rates, security of loans, terms of credit, were all problems which "create an unfavorable atmosphere for development" (1971:528). The Careys observe that this meant not only that "means of prompt repayment" must be found so that "recipients of the loans at the end of the year are often back where they started" (1972:54) but also that traditional private lenders, local notables for example, are able to continue their role at rates of interest which are often usurious. Cooperatives, which might perform such functions, are still few in number and often low in effectiveness.

23. A total of about 18 million acres of public land was distributed between 1923 and 1962 to about 375,000 landless and sharecropping families. The greatest part of this distribution took place under the DP governments in the 1950s. These numbers indicate that about half the farm families estimated to be landless or sharecropping (on at least part of their land) benefited from the distribution. See Aktan, 1966.

24. Eva Hirsch, for example, found that a significant difference in wheat yields showed up only for farms over 500 decares, and that barley yields did not differ even at that level. Size is only partially associated with the use of modern techniques, which often are more related to such things as mechanization and the ability to raise productivity of lands of lesser quality (1970: 93–95). That there is at least some of this relationship in existence was also found by Aresvik, who calculated that the yield of Mexican wheat on small farms was about 30% lower than on large farms under generally similar circumstances (1975:174).

25. Villagers also frequently use tractor-drawn wagons for travel to towns. Despite all these things, however, for villagers, roads were still at the top of the list of problems and needs mentioned by headmen and teachers in the Village Survey. The level of their expectations is indicated by the fact that 3/4 of the villages surveyed were less than two hours by the most commonly used means of transportation from the nearest district center *(ilçe)*, and the same proportion were within four hours of a province capital. On the other hand, only 30% reported no difficulties with road travel in any season (Tables 9–15).

26. Another factor driving a larger and larger percentage of transportation to motor vehicles is that many railroads are still single-track and schedules are poor and transportation slow.

27. Overloading of trucks is a particularly serious problem. The SPO attributes this in part to excessive competition which drives fares below their normal levels (1969:606).

28. At the end of 1977 the units tied to the cental grid included 64 (of 67) provinces, 1,608 (of 1,709) municipalities, and 11,259 villages (31.2%). SPO, 1978b:par. 38.

29. Yenal, 1973. Karpat has put it that "Industrialization in Turkey in its initial period was possible only by exploiting the internal markets, chiefly the rural ones. Heavy taxes were levied on agricultural products without regard to the peasant's ability to pay" (1959:102, citing evidence from Faik Ökte, *Varlık Vergisi Faciası*).

30. It is not clear whether this resulted in higher or lower taxes than were justified. Much was left to the discretion of the tax collectors. But in either case it would have added to the burden of other low-income groups. If the business taxes were too high, the small traders would have been bearing an inordinate share. If too low, the burden would have shifted to the remainder of the lower strata.

31. One specific calculation of some of this was done by the Hirsches, who found that the proportion of taxes collected from levies on wages and salaries was about the same as the proportion of taxable income in the nation derived from wages and salaries, indicating that taxes on these sources of income "are proportional instead of progressive," in that wage and salary income is found mostly in the lower-income groups, which also makes the pattern regressive (1966:348).

32. The only quantitative estimate which I have been able to locate was a recent report that in the agricultural sector both the RPP and JP governments since 1961 have periodically raised the exemption to the point where currently 99.5% of farmers are not taxed, and that in 1975 collections were 150 million TL compared to a calculated potential of 10 billion TL (*Yankı,* #257, 16–22 Feb. 1976:14–15).

33. It was permitted, according to two analysts, in part because Turkish leaders made "a differentiation between fighting against 'imperialism' and 'capitalism,' with the former predominantly occupying the thoughts of Turkish leaders," and was not "the rejection of the capitalist system as such but . . . hostility towards non-Muslim ethnic minority and Levantine commercial groups who had dominated the Turkish economic scene since the beginning of the nineteenth century" (Göymen and Tüzün, 1976:56).

34. Much of the material in this section is drawn from a manuscript in preparation by Professor Mukerrem Hiç, who kindly made it available to me.

35. At its high point, in 1974, remittances of $1,426 million were only slightly less than Turkey's export earnings that year. The more than 30% decrease in 1976 was, therefore, a serious blow.

36. For example, earnings from wheat exports were $9.8 million in 1972, $64.2 million in 1973, $27.2 million in 1974, and $120.2 million in 1977 (OECD 1978:54). In poor crop years, Turkey has even been a wheat importer.

37. Tobacco is a case in point. There has not only been a decline in worldwide demand, but also a shift in taste from Turkish to Virginia blends as the use of filter cigarettes has increased. Turkey has been unable to sell its tobacco surplus for much of the period since 1962, but production has continued to rise, in large part because the government has long bought the entire crop (Careys, 1972:49).

Chapter 8

1. Other examples include an attempt by the above-party coalition government of Nihat Erim in 1971 to increase the power of the government to amend laws by regulatory ordinances. It was rejected by a large margin of deputies, "intent on guarding the prerogatives of the Assembly." Özbudun 1978a:71.

2.   As noted earlier, political needs were often part of the criteria for locating State Economic Enterprises, though it must be said that winning followers to the Ataturk reforms was certainly an important and justifiable goal.

3.   For a detailed discussion of some aspects of this problem, see Yavuz, 1963. A reorganization of one area took place in the mid-1960s with the creation of the Ministry of Village Affairs, which has done much valuable work, but which, according to some observers, has not really been able to combat the determination of other ministries to retain control over many activities which they carry out in villages. In 1978 a Ministry of Local Government was created, the effectiveness of which remains to be seen.

4.   Although its immunity from partisan politics was safeguarded, its independent policy powers were greatly reduced. See chapter 6.

5.   Under the Municipalities Law any community with more than 2,000 inhabitants can become classified as a municipality, and many have done so in order to take advantage of more favorable financial treatment. This very low size requirement, plus the fact that many of these communities have functionally very few "urban" characteristics, has caused additional conflict and complication in trying to reform municipal administration under a single law and framework. See Weiker, 1972:20ff.

6.   A program of services to cities has also been developed by the Turkish Municipalities Association (*Türk Belediyecilik Dernegi*), which runs training courses, publishes a very good journal, and has carried out numerous projects and conferences to deal with topics of specific concern to local officials and others.

7.   On regional planning in Turkey, see Rodwin, 1970: chapter 4. Regional planning has been given attention since the early 1960s, but the third five-year plan moved in the opposite direction in that it recommended that regional development plans for particular areas no longer be prepared because they were not compatible with the unity of national development. Whether Turkey is at the stage of national integration where the country as a whole can be used as a planning dimension would seem in doubt. See also, Geray, 1970.

8.   In the 1977 local elections the RPP won 721 mayoralties, compared to 568 in 1973, a large number of them at the expense of the Justice party. A number of the new mayors of larger cities have advocated policies decidedly emphasizing priority to benefits for the lower socioeconomic districts.

9.   The restricted powers of local government may be a reason why voter turnout in local elections is low: 69.3% in 1963, 59.4% in 1968, 56.0% in 1973 (DIE #825:128).

10.   See also Fallers, n.d.:29–30. He found that local initiative was clearly evident in the community he studied, but that it has to be expressed outside the framework of municipal government because the scope of the latter was so restricted.

11.   A serious Kurdish insurrection took place in 1925 and the Turkish government has been uneasy about this problem ever since. See Lewis, 1961:260–1.

12.   As N . Ölçen has shown (1967:274–78), however, the pattern of investment in this period was based on more than just regional preference. In both east and west, provinces with low population density and natural resource availibility were given low levels of public investment, while those getting the greatest shares included Istanbul, Ankara and Zonguldak. On the whole, in the years 1963–1966 there was considerable correlation between the levels of development of provinces and their share of public investment.

13.   See Keleş and Danielson, 1980:Table 9.18. Since 1960, urbanization in the southeastern region has been the highest in the country. In 1965–1970 the east ranked second and in 1970–1975 fourth, and for the decade as a whole ran substantially ahead of the Marmara, Aegean, and Black Sea regions in percentage terms, although not in absolute numbers.

14.   The definition of the eastern area used here is based on the seven-region classification used by most analysts (although some also use a nine-region division, and various combinations of provinces based on both location and socioeconomic levels). The provinces included are Adıyaman, Ağrı, Bingöl, Bitlis, Diyarbakır, Elazığ, Erzincan, Erzurum, Hakkarı, Kars,

Malatya, Mardin, Siirt, Tunceli, Urfa, and Van. For the bases of regionalization, see Srikantan, 1973, and Keleş and Danielson, 1980b:notes 31, 34, 35. For a more complex analysis based on some 69 factors, see Albaum and Davies, 1973.

15. I must hasten to point out the very gross nature of these data. They are aggregate, and frequently conceal substantial differences within both the eastern regions and the country as a whole, and, of course, they indicate little beyond general quantities. They are for the most part, however, important in that quantitative differences are usually substantial.

16. The increases were:

	1968	1973	Percent Change
Aegean & Marmara	1,278 TL	2,078 TL	+63
Interior Anatolia	222	261	+17.5
Black Sea	578	596	+ 3
Mediterranean	474	702	+25
Eastern Anatolia	191	181	− 5

Source: SPO 198b:par. 48 and Table 57.

17. One problem area in which there are as yet few signs of change is the decided reluctance of most urban, educated Turks, such as teachers and engineers, to work in the least-developed areas, even when considerable financial incentives are given them. Efforts at inducing doctors, for example, to spend even short periods in some less-developed "model" provinces have encountered severe obstacles, as have attempts to assign university faculty members from Ankara or Istanbul to new institutions in places such as Erzurum. As a result, those civil servants (including teachers) who are assigned to the eastern areas are usually the youngest and the least experienced, a situation which tends to reduce even further their prestige among the villagers and, correspondingly, their effectiveness.

Chapter 9

1. Although the high adult illiteracy rate will be a serious problem for some time—the figures for 25 to 29-year-olds (below) are serious—it appears to be largely a failure to "catch up," as shown by the uninterruptedly worsening figures for success age groups:

Adult illiteracy, by percentage

Age group	Male illiterates	Female	Total
25–29	16.0	48.2	28.9
30–34	16.3	56.4	36.3
35–39	22.1	52.6	44.1
40–44	27.4	70.8	48.8
45–49	31.4	72.8	51.2
50–54	36.9	76.9	56.8
55–59	43.2	80.3	61.7
60–64	52.7	86.2	70.1
65 and over	66.2	90.9	79.4

Source: DIE #825: Table 34.

2. Frey, in fact, has gone so far as to say that " ... perhaps Turkey's central political

problem at present is how to deal with these strong residual tendencies toward elitism in the face of much newer but comparably strong pressures toward structural and cultural pluralism." (1975:43-4).

3. It is well to repeat here that it is not really very fruitful to try to specify what levels must be reached by various indices for a country to be called "modern." The predominant thrust of many of the characteristics is really all which can be reliably examined.

4. This "simultaneity" has sometimes been termed "neotraditionalism," and although it is not a new discovery, it is fortunately receiving increased attention by social scientists. A stimulating conference, for example, took place in 1978 at Rutgers University on "The Role of Traditionalism and Neo-Traditionalism in the Modernization Process." For earlier work on this subject, see, among many others, Apter, 1960, and Rustow, 1967:117 ff.

5. The income line used for this calculation was 12,000 TL annually. Analyzing the poverty group, Derviş and Robinson found that some 56 percent were farmers, 17 percent unskilled labor, 13 percent artisans, and 6 percent government employees. Very great inequalities within the urban and within the rural sectors were also found (Özbudun and Ulusan, 1980:11).

6. An additional problem is the degree to which redistribution is functional to development, as speculated on in earlier chapters. From the viewpoint of social justice there may be no denying that increased redistribution is desirable, but from other points of view there are many open questions, such as whether it will stimulate so much demand that there is both increased inflation and a too heavy shift of resources to consumption rather than investment.

7. Of course older symbolisms, such as Islam, have not been completely replaced.

BIBLIOGRAPHY

Abadan, Nermin (1961) *Universite Öğrencilerinin Serbest Zaman Faaliyetlen* (Leisure Time Activities of University Students), Ankara University, Siyasal Bilgiler Fakültesi.

———(1963) "Values and Political Behavior of Turkish Youth," *Turkish Yearbook of International Relations,* pp. 81–102.

———(1966a) "The Turkish Election of 1965," *Government and Opposition,* Vol. I, No. 3 (May), pp. 335–44.

———(1966b) *Anayasa Hukuku ve Siyasî Bilimleri Açısından 1965 Seçim Tahlili* (The 1965 Election from the Viewpoint of Constitutional Law and Political Science), Ankara University, Siyasal Bilgiler Fakültesi.

———(1969) "Turkish Workers in West Germany: A Case Study," Ankara University, *Siyasal Bilgiler Fakültesi Dergisi* XXIV, No. 1, pp. 21–49.

Abadan-Unat, Nermin (1973) (with Ahmet Yücekok) "Religious Pluralism in Turkey," Ankara, *Turkish Yearbook of International Relations,* X, pp. 24–49.

———(1974) "Turkish External Migration and Social Mobility," in Benedict, Tümertekin and Mansur (q.v.) pp. 362–402.

———(1975) "Major Challenges Faced by Turkish Women," International Islamic Center for Population Studies, Cairo, mimeographed.

———(1976a) *Turkish Workers in Europe 1960–75,* Leiden: E. J. Brill.

———(1976b) (with others) *Migration and Development: A Study of the Effects of International Labor Migration on Boğazlıyan District,* Ankara: Ajans Turk Press.

———(1977) "Implications of Migration on Emancipation and Pseudo-Emancipation of Turkish Women," *International Migration Review,* Vol. 11, No. 1 (Spring), pp. 31–57.

———(1978a) "The Modernization of Turkish Women," *Middle East Journal,* Vol. 32, No. 3 (Summer), pp. 291–306.

———(1978b) "Women's Movements and National Liberation: The Turkish

Case," Uppsala, Sweden, 9th World Congress of Sociology, mimeographed.

——(1979) (editor) *Türk Toplumunda Kadın* (Women in Turkish Society), Ankara: Türk Sosyal Bilimler Dernegi.

Abisel, Nilgün and Uygur Kocabaşoğlu, (1978) "Radio and Television in Turkey," *Current Turkish Thought* (Istanbul: Redhouse Press) No. 34.

Ahmad, Feroz (1977), *The Turkish Experiment in Democracy 1950–1975,* Boulder, Colo.: Westview Press.

Aktan, Reşat (1966), "Problems of Land Reform in Turkey," *Middle East Journal,* Vol. 20, No. 1 (Summer), pp. 317–34.

Albaum, Melvin and Christopher S. Davies (1973), "The Spatial Structure of Socio-Economic Attributes of Turkish Provinces," *International Journal of Middle East Studies,* Vol. 4, No. 3, (July), pp. 288–310.

Alexander, Alec P. (1960) "Industrial Entrepreneurship in Turkey; Origins and Growth," *Economic Development and Cultural Change* Vol. 8, pp. 349–65.

Almond, Gabriel and G. Bingham Powell, (1966), *Comparative Politics, A Developmental Approach,* Boston: Little-Brown.

Alpay, Güven, (1976) "Labor Perspectives," *Current Turkish Thought* (Istanbul: Redhouse Press), No. 26.

And, Metin (1973) "The Arts in Republican Turkey with Special Reference to Modernism and Nationalism," University of Chicago Conference on Fifty Years of Modernization in Turkey, mimeographed.

——(1974) "Gelecek 50 Yılda Türk Sanatları Nasıl Bir Gelişim Gösterebilir?" (What Kind of Development Will Turkish Arts Be Capable of in the Coming 50 Years?) Hacettepe University Conference on the Development Trends in the Coming Fifty Years in Turkey, mimeographed.

Apter, David (1960) "The Role of Traditionalism in the Political Modernization of Ghana and Uganda," *World Politics* Vol. XIII No. 1 (October) pp. 45–68.

Aral, Sevgi, (1980) "Social Mobility in Turkey." *Political Economy of Income Distribution in Turkey,* New York: Holmes & Meier, pp. 481–99.

Aresvik, Oddvar (1975), *The Agricultural Development of Turkey,* New York: Praeger.

Arı, Oğuz and Cavit Orhan Tütengil (1968), "Istanbul'a Göç ve Çalışma Hayatına Intibak Araştırması" (Migration to Istanbul and Adjustment to the Occupational Milieu), Istanbul Univ., *Ikitisat Fakültesi Mecmuası* 4.

Ataöv, Türkkaya, (1967) "The Place of the Worker in Turkish Society," Ankara Univ. *Turkish Yearbook of International Relations,* pp. 85–147.

Aybay, Rona (1977) "Some Contemporary Constitutional Problems in Turkey," *British Society for Middle Eastern Studies Bulletin,* Vol. 4 No. 1, pp. 21–27.

Aydınoğlu, Ismail Hakkı, (1976) "Manpower and Employment Policies under the Five Year Plans and Emigration," in Abadan-Unat 1976a (q.v.) pp. 104–32.

Başak, Zafer (1977) *Diş Yardım ve Ekonomik Etkileri Türkiye 1960–70* (Foreign Aid and Its Economic Effects in Turkey 1960–70). Ankara: Hacettepe University.

Başgöz, Ilhan and H. E. Wilson, (1968) *Educational Problems in Turkey 1920–1940*, Bloomington: Indiana Univ. Press.

———(1973) "The Free Boarding *(Leyli Meccani)* Schools," in Karpat 1973, (q.v.), pp. 203–23.

Beeley, Brian W. (1969) *Rural Turkey: A Bibliographic Introduction*, Ankara: Hacettepe Univ.

Benedict, Peter (1974) *Ula, An Anatolian Town*, Leiden: E. J. Brill.

Benedict, Peter, Erol Tumertekin and Fatma Mansur, eds., *Turkey: Geographic and Social Perspectives*, Leiden: E. J. Brill, 1974.

Bent, Frederick (1969), "The Turkish Bureaucracy as an Agent of Change," *Journal of Comparative Administration*, Vol. 1, No. 1, (May), pp. 47–63.

Berger, Morroe, (1957) *Bureaucracy and Society in Modern Egypt*, Princeton Univ. Press.

Berkes, Niyazi (1964) *The Development of Secularism in Turkey*, Montreal, McGill Univ. Press.

Bilmen, M. Sitki (1976) "Educational Problems Encountered by the Children of Turkish Migrant Workers," in Abadan-Unat 1976a (q.v.) pp. 235–52.)

Bisbee, Eleanor (1950) "Test of Democracy in Turkey," *Middle East Journal*, Vol. IV, No. 2 (April), pp. 170–82.

Bradburn, Norman (1963a) "Interpersonal Relations Within Formal Organizations in Turkey," *Journal of Social Issues* XIX (January), pp. 61–7.

———(1963b) "N Achievement and Father Dominance in Turkey," *Journal of Abnormal Psychology*, Vol. 67, No. 5, pp. 464–68.

Bulutay, Tuncer, Serim Timur and Hasan Ersel (1971), "Türkiye'de Gelir Dağılımı 1968," (Income Distribution in Turkey 1968), Ankara Univ., Siyasal Bilgiler Fakültesi.

Bulutoğlu, Kenan (1970), *100 Soru'da Türkiye'de Yabancı Sermaye* (100 Questions about Foreign Capital in Turkey), Istanbul: Gerçek Yayınevi.

Carey, Jane Perry and Andrew Galbraith Perry (1971) "Turkish Industry and the Five Year Plans," *Middle East Journal* Vol. 25, No. 3 (Summer) pp. 337–54.

———(1972) "Turkish Agriculture and the Five-Year Development Plans," *International Journal of Middle East Studies* Vol. 3, No. 1 (January), pp. 45–58.

Çavdar, Tevfik et al, (1976) *Yüksek Öğrenime Başvuran Öğrenciler 1974 Sosyo-Economik Çözümleme*, (Socio-Economic Analysis of Students Applying for Higher Education in 1974–75) Ankara: State Planning Organization.

Çeçen, Anil (1973) *Türkiye'de Sendikacilik* (Unionism in Turkey), Ankara: Özgür Insan Yayınları.

Chambers, Richard L. (1964), "The Civil Bureaucracy in Turkey," in Ward & Rustow (q.v.) pp. 301–27.

Codi, Michael (1962) "Disincentives Which Inhibit the Growth of Small Business in Turkey," USAID report, mimeographed.

Cohn, Edwin J. (1970) *Turkish Economic, Social and Political Change, The Development of a More Prosperous and Open Society,* New York: Praeger.

Daver, Bülent (1967) "Secularism in Turkey," Ankara Univ., *Siyasal Bilgiler Fakültesi Dergisi,* Vol. XXII, No. 1, pp. 55–66.

——(1969) "Political Rights of Women," Ankara Univ., *Siyasal Bilgiler Fakültesi Dergisi,* Vol. XXIV, pp. 111–20.

Davison, Roderic (1963) *Reform in the Ottoman Empire, 1856–76,* Princeton Univ. Press.

——(1964) "Environmental and Foreign Contributions to Modernization in Turkey," in Ward & Rustow (q.v.), pp. 91–116.

——(1968) *Turkey,* Englewood Cliffs: Prentice-Hall.

Dereli, Toker (1968) *The Development of Turkish Trade Unionism,* Istanbul Univ. Faculty of Economics.

Derviş Kemal and Sherman Robinson (1980) "The Structure of Inequality in Turkey." *Political Economy of Income Distribution in Turkey,* New York: Holmes & Meier, pp. 83–122.

DIE (Devlet Istatistik Enstitüsü) (State Institute of Statistics)
380: 1959 Annual.
568: 1965 Census.
580: 1968 Annual.
670: 1971 Annual.
672: 1970 Census by Administrative Division.
676: Developments in National Education 1942–72.
683: *Türkiye'de Toplumsal ve Ekonomik Gelişmenin 50 Yılı* (50 Years of Turkish Social and Economic Development.)
710: 1973 Annual.
715: (National Education Statistics, 1972–4.)
734: *1974 Universitelerarası Seçme Sınavı Anketi Sonuçları* (Results of 1974 Inter-University Entrance Examination Survey).
750: 1975 Annual.
812: Education Statistics, Start of 1973–4 Year.
817: Election Results 5 June 1977.
825: 1977 Annual.
841: *Türkiye Nüfus Araştırması 1974–75* (Turkish Population Research Project 1974–75).
850: 1978 Statistical Pocket Book.
890: 1979 Annual

Dewdney, John (1976) "Agricultural Problems and Regional Development in Turkey," in Hale, 1976 (q.v.) pp. 91–106.

Dodd, Clement H. (1969) *Politics and Government in Turkey,* Berkeley: Univ. of California Press.

Dubetsky, Alan (1976) "Kinship, Primordial Ties and Factory Organization in Turkey: An Anthropological View," *International Journal of Middle East Studies,* Vol. 7, No. 3 (July), pp. 433–51.

——(1977) "Class and Community in Urban Turkey," in van Nieuwenhuijze, ed., *Commoners, Climbers and Notables, A Sampler of Studies on Social Ranking in the Middle East,* Leiden: E. J. Brill, pp. 360–71.

Ecevit, Bulent (1966) *Ortanın Solu* (Left of Center), Istanbul, numerous editions.

——(1973) "Labor in Turkey as a New Social and Political Force," in Karpat, 1973 (q.v.) pp. 151–81.

Ekin, Nusret (1977) "Economic and Social Factors Affecting Industrial Relations in Turkey," Istanbul Univ., *İşletme Fakültesi Dergisi,* Vol. 6, No. 1, pp. 33–67.

Elbruz, Leyla Sayar, (1974) "The Changing Order of Socio-Economic Life: State-Induced Change," in Benedict-Tumertekin-Mansur (q.v.) pp. 139–55.

Erder, Necat (1973) "Educational Policies of the Republic 1923–73," University of Chicago Conference on Fifty Years of Modernization in Turkey, mimeographed.

Eren, Nuri (1963) *Turkey Today—and Tomorrow, an Experiment in Westernization,* New York: Praeger.

Ergil, Doğu (1975) "Secularization as Class Conflict: The Turkish Example," *Asian and African Affairs,* Vol. 62 Part I (February), pp. 69–79.

Ergil, Gül, (1968) *Köylerimizde Yapılan Araştırmalarla Ilgili Izahlı Bibliyografyası* (Annotated Bibliography of Research on Our Villages), Ankara, State Planning Organization.

Ergüder, Üstün (1980) "The Politics of Agricultural Price Policy in Turkey." *Political Economy of Income Distribution in Turkey,* New York: Holmes & Meier, pp. 169–95.

Fallers, Lloyd A. (1974) *The Social Anthropology of the Nation State,* Chicago: Aldine Publishing Co.

——(no date) "Notes on an Advent Ramadan," mimeographed.

Fermi, Laura (1968) *Illustrious Immigrants,* Chicago, Univ. of Chicago Press.

Fındıkoğlu, Fahri Z., (1962) *Karabük,* Istanbul Univ. Fakülte Matbaası.

Fişek, Kurthan, (1976) "Administration in Turkey: Structure, Basic Problems," *Current Turkish Thought* (Istanbul: Redhouse Press), No. 28.

Frey, Frederick W. (1964) "Education," in Ward & Rustow (q.v.) pp. 205–35.

——(1965) *The Turkish Political Elite,* Cambridge, MIT Press.

——(1967a) "The Propensity to Innovate Among Turkish Peasants," Rural Development Research Project, Report No. 7. (MIT Center for International Studies).

———(1967b) "Social Structure and Community Development in Rural Turkey, Village and Elite Leadership Relations," Rural Development Research Project, Report No. 10.

———(1968a) "Socialization to National Identification Among Turkish Peasants," *Journal of Politics* Vol. 30, pp. 934–65.

———(1975) "Patterns of Elite Politics in Turkey," in George Lenczowski, ed., *Political Elites in the Middle East,* Washington, American Enterprise Institute, pp. 41–82.

Geray, Cevat (1966) " 'İlçe' as a Unit for Planning and Execution of Community Development in Turkey," in *Regional Planning, Local Government and Community Development in Turkey*, Ankara, Turkish Society for Housing and Planning, pp. 167–217.

———(1970) "Problems of Local Administration at the Regional Level in Turkey," Ankara Univ., *Siyasal Bilgiler Fakültesi Dergisi*, Vol. XXV, pp. 1–11.

———(1977) "Yaykur Uygulaması," (The Implementation of Correspondence Education) in *Basın ve Yayın Okulu Yıllık 1974/76,* Ankara University, pp. 29-48.

Gökçeer, Fikri, (1978) "Yerel Yönetim Seçimlerinin Sayısal ve Siyasal Değerlendirilmesı," (Numerical and Political Analysis of Local Elections), *İller ve Belediyeler* (Türk Belediyecilik Derneği, Ankara) #393–4 (July-August), pp. 234–44.

Goode, Richard (1961) "Taxation of Saving and Consumption in Underdeveloped Countries," *National Tax Journal*, Vol. XIV No. 4 (December), pp. 305–22.

Gorvine, Albert, see Payashoğlu, Arif

Göymen, Korel and Gürel Tüzün (1976) "Foreign Private Capital in Turkey: An Analysis of Capital Imported Under the Encouragement Law 6224," Ankara, Ortadoğu Teknik Universitesi, *Gelişme Dergisi*, #11 (Spring) pp. 55–80.

Grant, James P., (1971) "Marginal Men, The Global Unemployment Crisis," *Foreign Affairs* Vol. 50, No. 1 (October) pp. 112–24.

Hale, William M., ed., (1976) *Aspects of Modern Turkey*, London, Bowker. (His article entitled "Labour Unions in Turkey: Progress and Problems," pp. 59–74.)

———(1978) *International Migration Project Country Case Study: The Republic of Turkey*, Univ. of Durham, International Migration Project.

Halman, Talat (1972) "Turkish Literature in the 1960's, "*Literary Review* Teaneck, N. J.: Fairleigh Dickinson Univ., Vol. 15, No. 4 (Summer), pp. 387–402.

———(1976) *Modern Turkish Drama, An Anthology of Plays in Translation*, Minneapolis: Bibliotheca Islamica.

Halpern, Manfred, (1963) *The Politics of Social Change in the Middle East and North Africa*, Princeton Univ. Press.

Harris, George S. (1965) "The Role of the Military in Turkish Politics," *Middle East Journal*, Part I Vol. XIX, No.1 (Winter) pp. 54–66, Part II Vol. XIX, No. 2 (Spring) pp. 169–76.

———(1967) *The Origins of Communism in Turkey*, Stanford Univ. Press.

———(1972) *Troubled Alliance: Turkish-American Problems in Historical Perspective*, Washington, American Enterprise Institute.

Hart, C. W. M. (1963) "Peasants Come to Town," Istanbul, Economic and Social Studies Conference Board, mimeographed.

Heidenheimer, Arnold, Hugh Heclo and Carolyn Teich Adams, (1975) *Comparative Public Policy, The Politics of Social Choice in Europe and America*, New York: St. Martin's.

Helling, George (no date) "Changing Attitudes Toward Occupational Status and Prestige in Turkey," mimeographed.

Heper, Metin (1974) "Decision-Making and Information Flow Systems at METU, Ankara," UNESCO, *Planning the Development of Universities* III, pp. 411–23.

———(1976a) "The Recalcitrance of the Turkish Public Bureaucracy to 'Bourgeois Politics,' "A Multi-Factor Political Analysis," *Middle East Journal* Vol. 30, No. 4 (Autumn) pp. 485–500.

———(1976b) "Political Modernization as Reflected in Bureaucratic Change: The Turkish Bureaucracy and a 'Historical Bureaucratic Empire' Tradition," *International Journal of Middle East Studies*, Vol. 7 No. 4 (October), pp. 507–21.

———(1977) "Negative Bureaucratic Politics in a Modernizing Context: The Turkish Case," *Journal of South Asian and Middle Eastern Studies*, Vol. 1 No. 1 (Sept.) pp. 65–84.

———(1978) *Gecekondu Policy in Turkey*, Istanbul, Boğaziç University Publications.

Hershlag, Z. Y. (1958) *Turkey, An Economy in Transition*, The Hague: Van Keulen.

———(1973) "Autarchy, Etatism and the Public Financial and Banking System in Turkey," University of Chicago Conference on Fifty Years of Modernization in Turkey, mimeographed.

Hirsch, Abraham and Eva Hirsch, (1963) "Changes in Agricultural Output per capita of rural population in Turkey 1927–60," *Economic Development and Cultural Change*, Vol. XI, No. 4 (July) pp. 372–94.

———(1966) "Tax Reform and the Burden of Direct Taxation in Turkey," *Public Finance* Vol. XII, No. 3 pp. 337–63.

Hirsch, Eva (1970) *Poverty and Plenty on the Turkish Farm*, New York: Columbia Univ. Press.

Hoell, Margaret (1973) "The Ticaret Odası 1885–99," Ph.D. dissertation, Ohio State University, unpublished.

Hyland, Michael, (1970) "Crisis at the Polls: Turkey's 1969 Elections," *Middle East Journal*, Vol. 24, No. 1 (Winter) pp. 1–16.

Hyman, et al., see Payaslioğlu.

Inalcik, Halil (1964) "The Nature of Traditional Society in Turkey," in Ward & Rustow, (q.v.) pp. 42–63.

Ipekçi, Abdi and Ömer Sami Coşar, (1965) *Ihtilalın Içyüzü* (The Inside Story of the Revolution), Istanbul: Toker Matbaası.

Iren, Cihat (1979) "The Growth of the Private Sector in Turkey," in

Mukerrem Hic, ed., *Turkey's and Other Countries' Experience with the Mixed Economy.* Istanbul Univ. Faculty of Economics, pp. 357–432.

Issawi, Charles (1965) "The Arab World's Heavy Legacy," *Foreign Affairs*, Vol. 43, No. 3 (April) pp. 501–12.

———(1966) *The Economic History of the Middle East 1800–1914*, Univ. of Chicago Press.

Kagıtçıbaşı, Çiğdem (1975) "Modernity and the Role of Women in Turkey," *Boğaziçi Univ. Journal* III. pp. 83–93.

———(1977) *Cultural Values and Population Action Programs: Turkey*, UNESCO, October 14, 1977.

Kaldor, Nicholas (1963) "Will the Underdeveloped Countries Learn to Tax?" *Foreign Affairs* Vol. 41, No. 1 (January) pp. 410–19.

Kandiyoti, Deniz (1974) "Some Social-Psychological Dimensions of Social Change in a Turkish Village," *British Journal of Sociology* XXV (March), pp. 47–62.

———(1977a) "Women's Place in Turkish Society: A Comparative Approach," *Current Turkish Thought* (Istanbul: Redhouse Press) No. 30 (Spring).

———(1977b) "Sex Roles and Social Change: A Comparative Appraisal of Turkey's Women," *Signs*, Vol. 3, No. 1, pp. 57–73.

———(1978) "Women in Turkish Society," Ankara, Turkish Social Science Association.

Karpat, Kemal (1959) *Turkey's Politics, The Transition to a Multi-Party System*, Princeton Univ. Press.

———(1960) "Social Effects of Farm Mechanization in Turkey," *Social Research* XXVII, pp. 83–103.

———(1961a) "The Turkish Elections of 1957," *Western Political Quarterly*, Vol. 14 (June) pp. 436–59.

———(1961b) "Contemporary Turkish Literature," Fairleigh Dickinson Univ., *Literary Review*, Vol. 4, No. 2 (Winter), pp. 287–302.

———(1962) "Recent Political Developments in Turkey and their Social Background, " *International Affairs*, Vol. 38, pp. 304–23.

———(1963) "The People's Houses in Turkey," *Middle East Journal*, Vol. XVII, Nos. 1 & 2, (Winter-Spring), pp. 55–67.

———(1964) "The Mass Media," in Ward and Rustow (q.v.)

———(1967) "Socialism and the Labor Party of Turkey," *Middle East Journal*, Vol. XII, No. 2 (Spring) pp. 157–72.

———(1970) "The Military and Politics in Turkey 1960–64," *American Historical Review* LXXV No. 6 (October) pp. 1654–83.

———(1973) (ed.) *Social Change and Politics in Turkey*, Leiden: E. J. Brill.

———(1975a) (ed.) *Turkey's Foreign Policy in Transition*, Leiden: E. J. Brill.

———(1975b) "The Politics of Transition: Political Attitudes and Party Affiliation in Turkish Shantytowns," in Engin Akarlı and Gabriel Ben-Dor, eds., *Political Participation in Turkey*, Boğaziçi Univ. Publications, pp. 89–120.

——(1976) *The Gecekondu: Rural Migration in Turkey,* Cambridge Univ. Press.

Kasnakoğlu, Zehra, (1978) "Türkiye'de 1968 Gelir Dagılımında Nesillerarası Etkileşim Üzerine," (On Intergenerational Influences on Income Distribution in Turkey in 1968,) Orta Doğu Teknik Universitesi, *Gelişme Dergisi* 19, pp. 50–59.

Kazamias, Andreas M., (1966) *Education and the Quest for Modernity in Turkey,* Univ. of Chicago Press.

Kazgan, Gülten (1972) "Structural Change in Turkish Manufacturing Inustry," in Mukerrem Hiç, ed., *Problems of Turkey's Economic Development,* Istanbul Univ. Iktisat Fakültesi, pp. 351–74.

——(1979) "Türk Ekonomisinde Kadınlarin Işgücüne Katılması Mesleki Dağılımı, Egitim Duzeyi ve Sosyo-Economik Statüsü," (Turkish Women's Labor Force Participation, Occupational Distribution, Education and Socio-Economic Status), in Abadan-Unat 1979 (q.v.) pp. 155–89.

Kazgan, Haydar, (1972) "A Brief Survey of State Economic Enterprises in Turkey," in Mukerrem Hiç, ed., *Problems of Turkey's Economic Development,* Istanbul Univ. Iktisat Fakültesi, pp. 97–160.

Keleş, Ruşen, (1972) (with Orhan Türkay), *Köylü Gözü Ile Türk Köylerinde Iktisadi ve Toplumsal Değişme,* (Economic and Social Change in Turkish Villages Through Villagers' Eyes), Ankara Univ. Siyasal Biligiler Fakültesi.

——(1972a) *Urbanization in Turkey,* Ford Foundation, International Urbanization Survey Report.

——(1972b) *100 Soru'da Türkiye'de Şehirleşme, Konut ve Gecekondu* (Urbanization, Housing, and *Gecekondus* in Turkey), Istanbul: Gerçek Yayinevi.

——(1975) "Social Stratification in Izmir," in Turkish Social Science Assn., *Social Change in Izmir,* pp. 97–120.

——(1976a) "Investment by Turkish Migrants in Real Estate," in Abadan-Unat, 1976a (q.v.) pp. 169–78.

——(1976b) "Regional Development and Migratory Labour," in Abadan-Unat, ed., 1976b, pp. 139–62.

——(1978) *100 Soru'da Şehirleşme,* 2nd edition.

——(1980a) (with Michael Danielson) "Allocating Public Resources in Urban Turkey." *Political Economy of Income Distribution in Turkey,* New York: Holmes & Meier, pp. 309–46.

——(1980b) (with Danielson) "Urbanization and Income Distribution in Turkey," Ibid., pp. 267–307.

Kerwin, Robert (1951) "Private Enterprise in Turkish Development, *Middle East Journal* Vol. 5 (Winter), pp. 21–38.

——(1979) "Management Experience in Several Nations With Mixed Economies," in Mükerrem, Hiç, ed., *Turkey's and Other Countries' Experience with the Mixed Economy,* Istanbul Univ. Faculty of Economics, pp. 45–75.

Keyser, James M. B. (1969) "Military Modernization and Its Effects on

Conscripts from Rural Turkey," NATO Conference on Special Training for Multilateral Forces, Brussels, pp. 239–54.

——(1974) "Upgrading Rural Health Standards, A Turkish Case," *Social Science and Medicine*, Vol. 8.

Kili, Suna (1976) *1960–75 Döneminde Cumhuriyet Halk Partisi'de Gelişmeler*, (The Republican Peoples Party 1960–75) Istanbul, Boğaziçi Univ. Press.

——(1977) "Türkiye'de Örgütleşme Sorunu ve Örgütsel Dengisizlik" (The Organizational Question and Organizational Imbalance In Turkey,) *Boğaziçi Univ. Dergisi*, Vol. 4–5, pp. 63–77.

——(1978a) *Çayırhan, Social Change and Political Behavior in a Central Anatolian Village*, Boğaziçi Univ. Publications #148.

——(1978b) "1977 Seçimlerinin Siyasal Davranış ve Partiler Yönünden Özellikleri" (Political Aspects of the 1977 Election and Particularities about the Parties), *Boğaziçi Univ. Dergisi*, Vol 6, pp. 25–39.

Kılıç, Altemur, (1959) *Turkey and the World*, Washington: Public Affairs Press.

Kinross, Lord, (1965) *Ataturk*, New York: William Morrow.

——(1977) *The Ottoman Centuries*, New York: William Morrow.

Kıray, Mubeccel (1964) *Ereğli, Ağır Sanayından Önce Bir Sahil Kasabası, (Ereğli*, A Coastal Town Before Heavy Industry) State Planning Organization.

——(1968) "Values, Social Stratification and Development," *Journal of Social Issues*, XXIV No. 2, pp. 87–100.

——(1970) (with Jan Hinderink) *Social Stratification as an Obstacle to Development*, New York: Praeger.

——(1972) *Örgütleşemeyen Kent* (The Unorganizable City), Ankara: Sosyal Bilimler Derneği Yayinlari.

——(1973) "Business Organizations and Development," *Turkish Yearbook of International Relations* X (1969-70), pp. 1–23.

——(1974) "Social Change in Çukurova: A Comparison of Four Villages," in Benedict et al. (q.v.) pp. 179–203.

——(1975) "Business Structure and Its Spatial Patterning," in *Social Change in Izmir*, Turkish Social Science Assn., pp. 1–96.

——(1976) "The Family of the Immigrant Worker," in Abadan-Unat, 1976a (q.v.) pp. 210–34.

Kirby, Fay et al. (1964) "The Village Institutes in Turkey," *Comparative Education Review* VIII, pp. 41–7.

Kışlalı, Ahmet Taner (1976) research report in *Yankı*, #296, 15–21 Kasim, pp. 11–13.

Kolars, John (1962) "Community Studies in Rural Turkey," *Annals of the Association of American Geographers*, Vol. 52, No. 4 (December) pp. 476–89.

——(1967) "Types of Rural Development," in Frederic Shorter, ed., *Four Studies on the Economic Development of Turkey*, London: Frank Cass, pp. 63–88.

——(1973) "The Integration of the Villages into the National Life of Turkey," in Karpat (q.v.) pp. 187–202.

——(1974) "Systems of Change in Turkish Village Agriculture," in Benedict et al, (q.v.) pp. 204–35.

Kongar, Emre (1972a) "Some Comparative Characteristics of Gecekondu Families in Izmir," Middle East Technical Univ. *Studies in Devt.* No. 4, pp. 643–56.

——(1972b) *Izmir'de Kentsel Aile* (The Urban Family in Izmir), Turkish Social Science Association.

——(1975) "Characteristics of the Urban Family," in Turkish Social Science Association, *Social Change in Izmir,* pp. 203–60.

——(1976) *Türkiye'de Toplumsal Yapısı* (Turkish Social Structure), Ankara: Cem Yayınevi.

Krane, R. E. (1975) *Manpower Mobility Across Cultural Boundaries, Social, Economic and Legal Aspects, The Case of Turkey and West Germany,* Leiden: E. J. Brill.

Krueger, Anne (1974) *Turkey,* New York: National Bureau of Economic Research.

Kudat, Ayşe (1974a) "International Migration to Europe and Its Political and Social Effects on the Future of Society in Turkey," Hacettepe Conference on the Development Trends in the Next Fifty Years in Turkey, mimeographed.

——(1974b) *Sociological Impacts of Turkish Migration,* International Institute for Comparative Social Studies of the Science Center, Berlin.

——(1975) *Stability and Change in the Turkish Family at Home and Abroad: A Comparative Perspective,* Berlin center.

Kuran, Timur (1980) "Internal Migration: The Unorganized Urban Sector and Income Distribution in Turkey 1963–1973," *Political Economy of Income Distribution in Turkey,* New York: Holmes & Meier. pp. 347–76.

Landau, Jacob (1974) *Radical Politics in Turkey,* Leiden, E. J. Brill.

——(1976) "The National Salvation Party in Turkey," *Asian & African Studies,* Vol. 11 #1, pp.

Leder, Arnold, (1976) *Catalysts of Change: Marxists versus Muslims in a Turkish Community,* Univ. of Texas Center for Middle Eastern Studies.

Lerner, Daniel (1958) *The Passing of Traditional Society,* Glencoe: The Free Press.

Levine, Ned (1973a) "Old Culture-New Culture: A Study of Migrants in Ankara, Turkey," *Social Forces* 51 (March) pp. 355–68.

——(1973b): "The Revolutionary Non-Potential of the 'Lumpen': Essence or Technical Deficiency?" *Institute of Development Studies Bulletin,* No. 213 (October) pp. 43–52.

——(1973c) "Value Orientations Among Migrants in Ankara, Turkey: A Case Study," *Journal of Asian & African Studies* VIII, pp. 50–68.

————(1974) Rural-Urban Migration and Its Effects on Urbanization Over the Next Fifty Years, Hacettepe Univ. Conference on Development Trends in the Next Fifty Years in Turkey, memiographed.

Lewis, Bernard (1953) "History Writing and National Revival in Turkey, *Middle Eastern Affairs* IV.

————(1961) *The Emergence of Modern Turkey*, Oxford Univ. Press.

Lewis, Geoffrey (1955) *Turkey*, New York: Praeger.

Modernization in Turkish Villages (see State Planning Orgn.)

Magnarella, Paul (1973) "The Reception of Swiss Family Law in Turkey," *Anthropological Quarterly*, Vol. 46, No. 2, pp. 100–116.

————(1974) *Tradition and Change in a Turkish Town*, New York: Schenkman.

————(1976) (with O. Türkdoğan), "The Development of Turkish Social Anthropology," *Current Anthropology*, Vol. 17 No. 2 (June) pp. 263–74.

Makal, Mahmut, (1954) *A Village in Anatolia*, London, Valentine, Mitchell.

Makofsky, David (1977) "In the Factories: The Development of Class Consciousness Among Manual Workers in Istanbul," *Urban Life* Vol. 6, No. 1 (April) pp. 69–96.

Manisalı, Erol (1979) "The Imapct of Foreign Economic Relations on the Mixed Economic Structure of Turkey," in Mukerrem, Hiç, ed., *Turkey's and Other Countries' Experience With the Mixed Economy*, Istanbul Univ. Faculty of Economics, pp. 517–57.

————(1978) "Enlargement of the European Community and Turkey," *Foreign Policy* (Ankara) Vol. VII, No. 1–2, pp. 51–67.

Mann, Charles K. (1977) "The Impact of Technology on Wheat Production in Turkey," Middle East Technical Univ. *Studies in Development* #14 (Winter), pp. 30–48.

Mansur, Fatma (1972) *Bodrum, A Town in the Aegean*, Leiden: E. J. Brill.

Mardin, Şerif (1962) *The Genesis of Young Ottoman Thought*, Princeton Univ. Press.

————(1966) "Opposition and Control in Turkey," *Government & Opposition*, Vol. I, No. 3 (May) pp. 375–88.

————(1969) *Religion as Ideology*, Hacettepe Univ. Publications.

————(1971a) "Ideology and Religion in the Turkish Revolution," *International Journal of Middle East Studies*, Vol. 2, No. 3 (July) pp. 197–211.

————(1971b) "Some Functions of Religion in the Ottoman Empire," United Church Board for World Ministries, Abstract for Cultural Understanding, No. 9.

————(1973) "Center-Periphery Relations: A Key to Turkish Politics?" *Daedalus*, Vol. 102 #1 (Winter), pp. 169–90.

Matthews, A. T. J. (1955) *Emergent Turkish Administrators*, Ankara, Türk Tarih Kurumu Basımevi.

Maynard, Richard E., (1964) *Education in Turkey*, American Board for World Ministries, Istanbul.

McClelland, David C., (1967) *The Achieving Society,* Glencoe: Free Press.

Meeker, Michael (1971) "The Black Sea Turks: Some Aspects of their Ethnic and Cultural Background," *International Journal of Middle East Studies,* Vol. 2 No. 4 (Oct.) pp. 318–45.

Menemencioğlu, Nermin (1973) "The Pre-Republican Literary Tradition," Univ. of Chicago Conference on Fifty Years of Modernization in Turkey, mimeographed.

Mıhçıoğlu, Cemal (1969) *Universiteye Giriş ve Liselerimiz* (University Entrance and Our Lycés), Ankara Univ., Siyasal Bilgiler Fakültesi Yayinları.

Mik, Ger and Mia Verkoren-Hemelaar (1976) "Segregation in the Netherlands and Turkish Migration," in Abadan-Unat 1976a (q.v.) pp. 253–83.

Miller, Duncan R. (1976) "Exportation of Labour and its Implications for Turkish Wage and Education Policy Formation," in Abadan-Unat 1976a (q.v.) pp. 154–68.

Mülayim, Ziya Gökalp (1977) "Recent Developments in Agricultural Cooperation in Turkey," *Year Book of Agricultural Cooperation,* Oxford, Plunkett Foundation for Cooperative Studies, pp. 199–210.

Mumcuoğlu, Maksut (1980) "Political Activities of Trade Unions and Income Distribution," *Political Economy of Income Distribution in Turkey,* New York: Holmes & Meier, pp. 377–408.

Neyzi, Nezih (1973) "The Middle Classes in Turkey," in Karpat 1973 (q.v.) pp. 123–50.

Nye, Roger P., (1977) "Civil-Military Confrontation in Turkey: The 1973 Presidential Election," *International Journal of Middle East Studies,* Vol. 8, No. 2 (April) pp. 209–28.

Oğuzkan, Turhan (1976) "The Scope and Nature of the Turkish Brain Drain," in Abadan-Unat 1976a (q.v.) pp. 50–73.

Okyar, Osman (1975) "Turkish Industrialization Strategies: The Plan Model and the EEC," Hacettepe Univ. Seminar on the Turkish and Other Countries Experience with a Mixed Economy, mimeographed.

Ölçen, N. (1967) "A Follow-Up Study: The Implementation of the Investments Foreseen in the First Five-Year Development Plan,' in S. Ilkin and E. Inanç, eds., *Planning in Turkey,* Ankara, Middle East Technical University, pp. 279–308.

Öncü, Ayşe (1980) "Chambers of Industry in Turkey, An Inquiry Into State-Industry Relations as a Distributive Domain," *Political Economy of Income Distribution in Turkey,* New York: Holmes & Meier, pp. 455–80.

Onulduran, Esin (1974) *Political Development and Political Parties in Turkey,* Ankara Univ., Siyasal Bilgiler Fakültesi.

Organization for Economic Cooperation and Development, *Economic Surveys, Turkey,* Nov. 1974 and Nov. 1978.

Özankaya, Özer (1966) *Üniversite Öğrencilerinin Siyasal Yönelimleri* (Political Characteristics of University Students), Ankara Univ., Siyasal Bilgiler Fakultesi.

Özbay, Ferhunde (1979) "Türkiye'de Kırsal/Kentsel Kesimde Eğitimin Kadınlar Üzerinde Etkisi" (The Influence of Rural-Urban on Women's Education in Turkey) in Abadan-Unat 1979 (q.v.) pp. 191–219.

Özbudun, Ergun (1966) *The Role of the Military in Recent Turkish Politics,* Harvard Univ. Center for International Affairs.

———(1970) "Established Revolution vs. Unfinished Revolution: Contrasting Patterns of Democratization in Mexico and Turkey," in S. Huntington and C. Moore, eds., *Authoritarian Politics in Modern Society,* New York: Basic Books, pp. 380–405.

———(1975) (with Frank Tachau) "Social Change and Electoral Behavior in Turkey; Towards a Critical Realignment?" *International Journal of Middle East Studies* Vol. 16, No. 4, pp. 460–80.

———(1976) *Social Change and Political Participation in Turkey,* Princeton Univ. Press.

———(1977) "Izmir'de Siyasal Parti Yöneticilerinin Sosyo-Economik Nitelikleri," (Socio-Economic Characteristics of Political Party Leaders in Izmir), Ankara University Hukuk Fakültesi, *Prof. Dr. Osman Fazıl Berki Armağanı,* pp. 629–65.

———(1978a) "Parliament in the Turkish Political System," *Journal of South Asian and Middle Eastern Studies,* Vol. II No. 1, pp. 44–73.

———(1978b) "Turkish Constitutional Law," in Tuğrul Ansay and Wallace, eds., *Introduction to Turkish Law,* Oceana Publs.

———(1980) ed. with Aydin Ulusan, *The Political Economy of Income Distribution in Turkey,* New York: Holmes & Meier.

Paine, Suzanne (1974) *Exporting Workers, the Turkish Case,* Cambridge Univ. Press.

Payaslıoğlu, Arif (1957) (with Albert Gorvine) "The Administrative Career Service in Turkish Provincial Government," *International Review of Administrative Sciences,* Vol. XXIII, pp. 467–74.

———(1958) (with Herbert Hyman and Frederick Frey), "The Values of Turkish College Youth," *Public Opinion Quarterly* Vol. 22, pp. 275–91.

———(1961) *Türkiye'de Özel Sanayi Alanındaki Müteşebbüsler ve Teşebbüsler* (Private Enterprises and Entrepreneurs in Turkish Industry), Ankara Univ., Siyasal Bilgiler Fakültesi.

———(1964) "Political Leadership and Political Parties," in Ward and Rustow, (q.v.)

———(1977) "ODTU Idari Ilimler Fakültesi Amme Idaresi Bölümü Mezunları Üzerinde Bir Inceleme," (An Examination of Graduates of the METU Public Administration Program), ODTU *Gelişme Dergisi* #14 (Winter), pp. 49–70.

Pool, Jonathan and June Starr, "The Impact of a Legal Revolution in Rural Turkey," *Law and Society Review,* Vol. 8, No. 4 (Summer) pp. 533–60.

Poroy, Ibrahim (1972) "Planning with a Large Public Sector: Turkey,"

International Journal of Middle East Studies, Vol. 3, No. 3 (July), pp. 348–60.

Rathbun, Carole (1972) *The Village in the Turkish Novel and Short Story 1920–1955,* The Hague: Mouton.

Reed, Howard (1955) "Turkey's New Iman-Hatip Schools," *Welt des Islams,* n. s. IV.

——(1957) "The Faculty of Divinity in Ankara," *Muslim World, Vols. XLVI and XLVII.*

——(1975) "Hacettepe and Middle East Technical University: New Universities in Turkey," *Minerva,* Vol. XIII, No. 2 (Summer) pp. 200–35.

Rist, Ray C. (1978) *Guestworkers in Germany, The Prospects for Pluralism,* New York: Praeger.

Rivlin, Malcolm (1965) *Area Development for National Growth, The Turkish Precedent,* New York: Praeger.

Robinson, Richard D. (1951) "The Lesson of Turkey," *Middle East Journal,* Vol. V, No. 4 (Autumn), pp. 424–38.

——(1967) *High-Level Manpower in Economic Development, the Turkish Case,* Harvard Univ. Middle East Monographs XVII.

Rodwin, Lloyd (1970) *Nations and Cities, A Comparison of Strategies for Urban Growth,* Boston: Houghton-Mifflin.

Roos, Leslie L. (1968a) (with George W. Angell) "New Teachers for Turkish Villages: A Military-Sponsored Educational Program," *Journal of Developing Areas* Vol. 2 No. 4 (July), pp. 519–32.

——(1968b) (with Frederick Frey) "Elite-Mass Relationships in Turkish Village Development," paper, American Political Science Association, mimeographed.

——(1969) "Development and Distribution, An Attitudinal Study of Turkish Local Administrators," *Economic Development and Cultural Change,* Vol. 17 No. 4 (July) pp. 552–66.

——(1971) (with Noralou Roos) *Managers of Modernization,* Harvard Univ. Press.

Rustow, Dankwart A. (1957) "Politics and Islam in Turkey 1920–1965," in Richard N. Frye, ed., *Islam and the West,* The Hague: Mouton, pp. 69–107.

——(1959) "The Army and the Founding of the Turkish Republic, *World Politics,* Vol. XI No. 4 (July), pp. 513–52.

——(1964) "The Military," in Ward & Rustow (q.v.)

——(1965) "Turkey: The Modernity of Tradition," in Lucian Pye and Sidney Verba, eds., *Political Culture and Political Development,* Princeton University Press, pp. 171–98.

——(1966) "The Development of Parties in Turkey," in Joseph LaPalombara and M. Weiner, eds., *Political Parties and Political Development,* Princeton Univ. Press, pp. 107–33.

——(1967) *A World of Nations,* Washington: Brookings Institution.

——(1969) "Ataturk as State Founder," in *Prof. Dr. Yavuz Abadan'a*

Armağan, Ankara Univ., Siyasal Bilgiler Fakültesi, pp. 517–73.
——(1973) "The Modernization of Turkey in Historical and Comparative Perspective," in Karpat (q.v.)
Saran, Nephan (1974) "Squatter Settlements *(Gecekondu)* Problems in Istanbul," in Benedict et al, ed. (q.v.) pp. 327–61.
Sarc, Ömer Celal (1948) "Economic Policy of the New Turkey," *Middle East Journal,* Vol. II No. 4 (October) pp. 430–46.
Savcı, Bahri (1958) "A General View on the Legislative-Executive Relationship in Turkey," Ankara Univ. Faculty of Political Science Institute of Administrative Sciences.
Sayarı, Sabri (1975) "Some Notes on the Beginnings of Mass Political Participation," in Engin Akarlı and Gabriel Ben-Dor, eds., *Political Participation in Turkey,* Boğaziçi Univ. Publications, pp. 121–34.
——(1976) "Aspects of Party Organization in Turkey," *Middle East Journal,* Vol. 30, No. 2 (Spring), pp. 187–209.
——(1978) "The Turkish Party System in Transition," *Government and Opposition,* Vol. 13, No. 1 (Winter) pp. 39–57.
Saybaşılı, Kemali, (1976) "Chambers of Commerce and Industry, Political Parties and Governments: A Comparative Analysis of the British and Turkish Cases," Middle East Technical University, *Studies in Development* #11 (Spring) pp. 117–38.
Schachter, Gustav and Bruce Cohen, (1973) "The Efficiency of State Economic Enterprises in Forging Development in Turkey," *Annals of Public and Co-operative Economy,* Vol. 44, No. 2 (April—June) pp. 165–79.
Schulz, Ann T. (1973) "A Cross-National Examination of Legislators," *Journal of Developing Areas,* Vol. 7, No. 4 (July) pp. 571–90.
Şenyapılı, Tansı, (1978) *Bütünleşmemiş Kentli Nüfus Sorunu* (The Question of Incomplete Urbanization), Ankara, Middle East Technical University.
Shaw, Stanford and Ezel Kural Shaw (1977) *History of the Ottoman Empire and Modern Turkey,* Vol. II, Cambridge Univ. Press.
Sherwood, W. B. (1967) "The Rise of the Justice Party in Turkey," *World Politics,* Vol. XX, No. 1 (October) pp. 54–65.
Signell, Karl (1976) "The Modernization Process in Two Oriental Music Cultures: Turkish and Japanese," *Asian Music,* Vol. VII, No. 2, pp. 72–102.
Simpson, Dwight J. (1965) "Development as a Process: the Menderes Phase in Turkey," *Middle East Journal,* Vol. XIX, No. 2 (Spring), pp. 141–52.
Singer, Morris (1977) *The Economic Advance of Turkey 1938–60,* Ankara, Turkish Economic Society Publications.
Srikantan, K. S. (1973) "Regional and Rural-Urban Socio-Demographic Differences in Turkey," *Middle East Journal,* Vol. 27, No. 3 (Summer), pp. 275–300.
State Planning Organization (1969) *2nd Five-Year Development Plan.*

——(1973) *Üçüncü Beş Yıllık Kalkınma Planı* (3rd Five-Year Development Plan).
——(1973a) *Strategy and Basic Targets of Long-term Development in the Third Five-Year Plan.*
——(1974) *Modernization in Turkish Villages* (MTV).
——(1976) *Gelir Dağılımı 1973.* (Income Distribution 1973)
——(1978a) *Developments in the Economy of Turkey 1963–78.*
——(1978b) *Dördüncü Beş Yıllık Kalkınma* Planı (4th Five-Year Development Plan).
Stirling, Paul (1965) *Turkish Village,* London: Weidenfeld and Nicolson.
——(1976) "Cause, Knowledge and Change: Turkish Village Revisited," in Hale, ed., *Aspects of Modern Turkey* (q.v.) pp. 75–89.
Stone, Frank (1970) "A Pioneer in Turkish Village Revitalization," *Hacettepe Univ. Bulletin of Social Sciences and Humanities,* Vol. 2, No. 2 (December).
——(1973) "The Evolution of Contemporary Turkish Educational Thought," *History of Education Quarterly,* (Summer) pp. 145–61.
Stone, Russell, (1973) "Anticipated Mobility to Elite Status Among Middle Eastern University Students," *International Review of History and Political Science* (Meerut, India) Vol. X, No. 4 (November) pp. 1–17.
Sugar, Peter, (1964) "Economic and Political Modernization," in Ward & Rustow, (q.v.)
Sülker, Kemal (1968) *100 Soru'da Türkiye'de İşçi Hareketleri* (100 Questions about Labor Movements in Turkey), Ankara, Gerçek Yayınevi.
Suzuki, Peter (1976) "Germans and Turks at Germany's Railroad Stations: Interethnic Tensions in the Pursuit of Walking and Loitering," *Urban Life,* Vol. 4, pp. 387–412.
Szyliowicz, Joseph (1966a) *Erdemli, Political Change in Rural Turkey,* The Hague: Mouton.
——(1966b) "The Turkish Elections 1965," *Middle East Journal* Vol. 20, No. 2 (Autumn) pp. 473–94.
——(1971) "Elite Recruitment in Turkey: The Role of the Mulkiye," *World Politics,* vol. XXIII No. 3 (April) pp. 371–98.
——(1973) *Education and Modernization in the Middle East,* Ithaca: Cornell Univ. Press.
——(1975) "Elites and Modernization in Turkey," in Frank Tachau, ed., *Political Elites and Political Development in the Middle East,* New York: Schenkman, pp. 23–68.
T. C. (Türkiye Cumhuriyeti) (Republic of Turkey) (1962) *Karayolları Genel Müdürlüğü İstatistik Bülteni* (Statistical Bulletin of Turkish Roads.)
——(1973) *Türkiye Yıllık* (Turkish Annual) (Başbakanlık.)
——(1978) *Yıllık Ekonomik Rapor* (Annual Economic Report)
——(1979 Malı Yılı Bütçesi Tasarısı İle Birlikte TBMM'ne Sunulmuş) (Submitted to the Assembly with the 1979 Budget.)
TUSIAD (Turkish Industrialists and Businessmen's Association) Turkey:

An Economic Survey, 1977, 1978, 1979.

Tachau, Frank (1965) (and Haluk Ülman) "Turkish Politics: the Attempt to Reconcile Modernization and Democracy," *Middle East Journal* Vol. XIX, No. 2 (Spring) pp. 153–68.

——(1973a) "Turkish Provincial Party Politics," in Karpat (q.v.)

——(1973b) "The Anatomy of Political and Social Change: Turkish Parties, Parliaments and Elections," *Comparative Politics,* Vol. 5, No. 4 (July), pp. 551–73.

——(1974) "Turkish Political Parties: Towards a Reconciliation of Modernity and Tradition?" Hacettepe University Conference on Development Trends in the Next Fifty Years in Turkey, mimeographed.

——(1975) (with Ergun Özbudun) "Social Change and Electoral Behavior in Turkey," *International Journal of Middle East Studies,* Vol. 6, No. 4 (October) pp. 460–80.

——(1977) "Social Backgrounds of Turkish Parliamentarians," in van Nieuwenhuijze, ed., *Commoners and Climbers, Social Ranking in the Middle East,* Leiden: E. J. Brill.

Tamkoç, Metin (1973) "Stable Instability of the Turkish Polity," *Middle East Journal,* Vol. 27, No. 3 (Summer) pp. 319–41.

——(1976) *The Warrior Diplomats,* Salt Lake City: Univ. of Utah Press.

Tansky, Leo (1967) *US and USSR Aid to Developing Countries* (A Comparative Study of India, Turkey and the UAR) New York: Praeger.

Tekeli, Ilhan (1973) "Evolution of Spatial Organization in the Ottoman Empire and Turkish Republic," in L. Carl Brown, ed., *From Medina to Metropolis,* Princeton, Darwin Press, pp. 244–73.

——(1977) *Bağımlı Şehirleşme* (Dependent Urbanization), Ankara, Mimarlar Odası Yayınları.

Tekeli, Şirin (1979) "Türkiye'de Kadının Siyasal Hayattaki Yeri," (The Place of the Woman in Turkish Political Life), in Abadan-Unat, ed., (q.v.) pp. 393–413.

Thomas, Lewis V. (1951) *The United States and Turkey and Iran,* Harvard Univ. Press.

Timur, Serim (1972) *Türkiye'de Aile Yapısı* (Family Structure in Turkey), Hacettepe Univ. Yayınları.

Tinto, Vincent (1977) "Perceptions of Occupational Status and Career Aspirations among the Turkish Elite," *International Journal of Middle East Studies,* Vol. 8, No. 3 (July) pp. 329–38.

Tunaya, Tariq (1952) *Türkiye'de Siyasî Partiler* (Political Parties in Turkey), Istanbul University.

Tuncay, Mete (1967) *Türkiye'de Sol Akımlar 1908–1925* (Leftist Currents in Turkey 1908–1925) Ankara University, Siyasal Bilgiler Fakültesi.

Tuncer, Baran (1967) "An Overview of the External Financing Mechanisms of the Turkish Economy," *Turkish Yearbook of International Relations,* pp. 1–13.

——(1973) "The Impact of Foreign Private Investments on the Turkish Economy," *Turkish Yearbook of International Relations,* pp. 85–101.

———(1975) "External Financing of the Turkish Economy and its Foreign Policy Implications," in Karpat 1975a (q.v.) pp. 206–24.

———(1977) *Turkey's Population and Economy in the Future,* Ankara, The Development Foundation of Turkey.

Turan, Ilter (1978) "The Development of Political Violence as a Feature of Political Life in Turkey," *Current Turkish Thought* (Istanbul: Redhouse Press) #37 (Winter.)

———(1979) "Legislatures and Social Change: A Cross-National Study of Kenya, Korea and Turkey," Univ. of Iowa Comparative Legislative Research Center, Occasional Paper No. 14.

Türk Kooperatiiflicik Kurumu (1976) *Kooperatiflerin Ekonomik ve Sosyal Kalkinmadaki Rolü* (The Role of Cooperatives in Economic and Social Development), Ankara.

USAID (1973a) *Agriculture 1962–72,* mimeographed.

———(1973b) *Economic and Social Indicators:* Turkey.

Ulusan, Aydın (1980) "Public Policy Toward Agriculture and Its Redistributive Implications," *Political Economy of Income Distribution in Turkey,* New York: Holmes & Meier, pp. 125–67.

Uras, Güngör (1977) "Economic Perspectives," *Current Turkish Thought* (Istanbul, Redhouse Press), #32 (Fall).

Vali, Ferenc A. (1971) *Bridge Across the Bosphorus, The Foreign Policy of Turkey,* Baltimore: Johns Hopkins Press.

Varlıer, Oktay (1978) *Türkiye'de Tarımında Yapısal Değişme Teknoloji ve Toprak Bölüşümü* (The Role of Technology and Land Distribution in Turkish Agricultural Structural Change), State Planning Organization.

Ward, Robert and Dankwart Rustow, eds., (1964) *Political Modernization of Japan and Turkey,* Princeton Univ. Press.

Weiker, Walter F. (1963) *The Turkish Revolution 1960–61,* Washington: Brookings Institution.

———(1963a) "The Aydemir Case and Turkey's Political Dilemma," *Middle Eastern Affairs,* Vol. XIV, No. 9 (Nov.) pp. 258–70.

———(1968) "The Ottoman Bureaucracy: Modernization and Reform," *Administrative Sciences Quarterly,* Vol. 13, No. 3 (December), pp. 451–70.

———(1969) "Turkey's Election May Bode Ills," *MIDEAST,* Vol. IX No. 6 (December) p. 10–13, 32–34.

———(1972) *Decentralizing Government in Modernizing Nations: Growth Center Potential of Turkish Provincial Capitals,* Beverly Hills, Sage Professional Papers in International Studies 02–007.

———(1973) *Political Tutelage and Democracy in Turkey, The Free Party and Its Aftermath,* Leiden: E. J. Brill.

———(1973a) "I Have Enough Troubles with My Friends—Dilemmas of American Relations with Turkey," in Yale Ferguson and Walter Weiker, eds., *Continuing Issues in International Relations,* Pacific Palisades, Calif., Goodyear Publishing Co., pp. 245–62.

Yalman, Ahmet Emin (1947) "The Struggle for Multi-Party Government in

Turkey," *Middle East Journal* Vol. I, No. 1 (January), pp. 46–58.

Yasa, Ibrahim (1966) *Ankara'da Gecekondu Aileleri* (Shantytown Families in Ankara), Ankara, Sağlık ve Sosyal Yardım Bakanlığı.

———(1968) (with Cevat Geray) "Basic Problems of Small Municipalities in Turkey, a Case Study," Ankara Univ. *Siyasal Bilgiler Fakültesi Dergisi* Vol. XXIII, pp. 117–135.

———(1969) *Yirmibeş Yıl Sonra Hasanoğlan Köyü* (The Village of Hasanoglan 25 Years Later), Ankara Univ. Siyasal Bilgiler Fakültesi.

Yavuz, Fehmi (1963) "Cities and Villages in the Republic of Turkey," Istanbul, Economic and Social Studies Conference Board, mimeographed.

———(1969a) *Din Eğitimi ve Toplumuz* (Religious Education and Our Society), Ankara: Sevinç Matbaası.

———(1969b) "Unbalanced Development in Turkey," in *Prof. Dr. Yavuz Abadan'a Armağan,* Ankara Univ., Siyasal Bilgiler Fakültesi, pp. 657–72.

Yenal, Oktay (1973) "Economic Policy of the Turkish Republic: Half A Century of Economic Nationalism," Univ. of Chicago Conference of Fifty Years of Modernization in Turkey, mimeographed.

Yener, Samira (1977) "Internal Migration and Its Policy Implications in Turkey," State Planning Organization.

Yücekok, Ahmet (1972) *Türkiye'de Dernek Gelişmeleri* (The Development of Associations in Turkey), Ankara Univ., Siyasal Bilgiler Fakültesi.

Yürükoğlu, Kadir Tanju (1975) "Economic Perspectives," *Current Turkish Thought,* (Istanbul, Redhouse Press), Winter.

Index

Agriculture, 195–202; agricultural organizations, 98–100; effects of mechanization, 268n12

Akbaba, 169

Alevis, 125, 270n33

Associations: involuntary, 246; in politics, 90, 93, 141; local, 73, 107; Law of Associations, 264n2, 269n25

Ataturk, xiii, 1–8, 24, 37, 101, 105, 111, 120, 121, 134, 161, 163, 164, 196, 222, 225, 226, 228, 243, 250, 258n16, 267n2, 274n30

Aydemir, Talat, 266n18

Balance of Trade and Payments, 214–6

Baltacıoğlu, Ismail Hakkı, 152

Bayar, Celal, 9, 132, 225, 256n8, 268n10

Bölükbaşı, Osman, 137

Borders, 243, 255n3

Bozbeyli, Ferruh, 136

Bureaucracy, bureaucrats, 29–34, 127, 225–6, 243

Çakmak, Fevzi, 101

Capabilities, 247–51

Capital, foreign private, 209–13

Capital formation, 206–13

Capitulations, 51, 274n5

Center-periphery, 50, 258n11

Cinema, 176–7

Cities: conditions of, 64–6; government, 229–32; Ankara, 65, 80, 94, 137, 205; Eskişehir, 94, 232, 265n9; Gaziantep, 231; Isparta, 231; Istanbul, 65, 80, 137, 205; Izmir, 65, 80, 93, 137; Izmit, 94; Kayseri, 94, 116, 191, 231, 232, 265n9; Sivas, 231; Zonguldak, 94

Communications, 163–73, 206; oral, 164

Constitution of 1924, 5, 108, 221–5, 266n20; of 1961, 11, 89, 108, 171, 221–5

Cooperatives, 98–100

Cyprus, 16, 26, 256, 270n31

Demirel, Suleyman, 14, 15, 16, 103, 123, 126, 131, 132, 133, 136, 139

Democrat Party (1945–60), 8, 9–11, 22–4, 89, 90, 102, 121, 122, 123, 125, 127, 128–31, 170, 183, 188, 194, 196, 200, 233, 243, 244, 269n18, 273n20, 275n9, 276n23

Democratic Party (1970–   ), 14, 136, 146

Deputies, social backgrounds of, 21–7

Dewey, John, 152

DISK (Revolutionary Trade Unions Confederation), 88, 89, 91, 92

Ecevit, Bülent, 14, 15, 16, 17, 123, 124, 125, 126, 135, 267n5

Economic growth, 7, 9, 13–14, 181–4

Edib, Halide, 111, 273n25

Education, 151–63, 241, 242, 247; of deputies, 25; of women, 113–5; of workers' children in Germany, 83; in eastern region, 236, 237

Election laws, 269n22

Employer associations, 92, 95

Energy, 205

Entrepreneurs, 34–7, 95–8, 189, 191

Erbakan, Necmettin, 14, 138, 139, 270n30

Erim, Nihat, 96, 277n1

Ertuğrul, Muhsin, 274n28

Esnaf, 92–4

Étatism, étatist period, 6, 187, 189, 209

European Economic Community, 182, 216–8, 245

Executive, 224–6

Family structure, 69–72; among workers in Europe, 83

Feyzioğlu, Turhan, 14, 124, 135, 269n21

Foreign aid, 213–4

Foreign policy, international affairs, 124, 245, 251, 256n10

Free Party of 1930, 3–4, 120, 164, 187, 268n10

Freedom Party, 11, 130, 135
Galatasaray lycee, 152
Gecekondus, 66–73
Gökalp, Ziya, 1
Gümüşpala, Ragip, 132
Gürler, Faruk, 224, 266n19
Gürsel, Cemal, 13, 225
Hakkarı, 168
Halkevleri, see People's Houses
Industrial workers, 73; in Europe, 79–85
Industry, 184–95, 237. See also entrepreneurs, State Economic Enterprises
Inönü, Ismet, 8, 13, 15, 123, 125, 225, 266n15, 271n4
International Monetary Fund, 190, 214
Ipekçi, Abdi, 273n19
Izmir Economic Congress, 3, 186, 264n2, 271n3
Judiciary, 226–7
Justice Party, 12, 14, 16, 27, 89, 92, 96, 123, 125, 127, 131–4, 144, 171, 195, 278n8
Kadro, 137
Karaosmanoğlu, Yakub Kadri, 174
Kemal, Namik, 1, 273n24
Kemal, Orhan, 175
Kemal, Yaşar, 174, 175
Kemalism, 5–7, 222, 243
Koç, Vehbi, 97, 214
Köprülü, Fuad, 106, 268n10
Korutürk, Fahri, 225
Kurds, 57, 233, 234, 240, 278n11
Labor, 88–92. See also *DISK, MISK,* Turkish Labor Party, *Turk-Iş*
Land reform, 196, 200–2
Leadership, criteria for evaluation, 19, 244
Legal reforms, 2, 60, 111
Legislature, 222–4
Literacy, 154, 279n1; among villagers, 57–8, 159
Literature, 173–6
Livestock, 198–9
Local government, 227–32
Localism, 24, 26, 28
Makal, Mahmut, 54, 174
Mass media, 163–73, 178; see also individual media
Mayors, 28, 29
Menderes, Adnan, 9, 12, 132, 225, 267n2, 268n10
Military, armed forces: revolution of 1960, 11–12; attempted coups 1962–3, 13; intervention of 1971, 15; intervention of 1980, xv, 17, 104; social backgrounds, 37–40; role in Turkish politics, 100–5, 242
Military Academy, 40
Millet system, 50, 227
MISK (Nationalist Trade Unions Confederation), 88
Modernization, concept of xvii–xix, 19, 49, 87, 151, 163, 181, 246–7

Music, 177–8
Nation Party, 136
National Action Party, 14, 16, 25, 126, 127, 139–40
National Front, 16, 92, 131, 139, 227
National Order Party, 14, 16, 107, 138
National Salvation Party, 16, 25, 107, 108, 125, 126, 131, 136, 138–9
National Security Council, 13, 103, 104
National Unity Committee, 11–13, 39, 102, 103, 142, 208, 223, 261n16, 271n6
Nationalism, 5, 161
Nesin, Aziz, 175
New Turkey Party, 12, 132, 268n16
Newspapers and periodicals, 165–70; local press, 168
OECD, 183, 213
Okyar, Fethi, 3, 101
Ottoman period, 1, 21, 49, 100, 119–20, 163, 173, 227, 232
People's Houses, 4, 54, 121, 154, 164, 174
Political parties: 119–50; activities of, 141; functions of, 119; organization of, 140; province leaders of, 27; Political Parties Law, 140, 264n5. See also names of individual parties
Political party system, 14, 121, 150, 241
Political Science Faculty, 32, 35, 159, 257n8
Professional associations, 100
Progressive Republican Party, 134
Radio, 57, 170–2
Regional balance, 232–40, 245
Regional planning, 231, 233
Reliance Party, 14, 25, 124, 135, 136, 146
Religion, 2, 6, 105–10, 122, 139, 242, 247; among villagers, 59
Remittances, 84–5, 215
Republican Peasants Nation Party, 12, 132, 140
Republican People's Party, 2, 3, 4, 8, 12–13, 15, 16, 22–4, 26, 27, 89, 90, 92, 95, 120, 121–8, 148, 171, 191, 193, 227, 244, 265n7, 273n20, 278n8
Republicanist Party, 135, 268n6
Revolution of 1960, 11–12, 123, 130, 183
Robert College, 152
Saygun, Adnan, 178
Secularism, secularization: see Religion
Socialism, 5. See also Turkish Labor Party
Soviet Union, 213, 256n10, 264n2
State Economic Enterprises, 187, 192–5, 233. See also *etatism*
State Planning Organization, 12
Students, 40–46, 157, 158, 159, 162
Sükan, Faruk, 136
Sunay, Cevdet, 224, 225, 266n19
Tahir, Kemal, 175
Taxation, tax system, 207–9, 229, 248, 275n12
Television, 172–3
Theatre, 177

Transportation, 202–3
Tunç, Halil, 90
Türk-Iş, 88, 90, 91, 92
Türkeş, Alparslan, 14, 15, 139, 140, 266n17, 270n32
Turkish Confederation of Employer Associations, 95
Turkish Cooperatives Association, 99–100
Turkish Labor Party, 13, 14, 15, 91, 104, 124, 125, 126, 136–8, 269n22, 269n26, 269n28
Turkish Municipalities Association, 278n6
TUSIAD, 92, 97
Tutelage, political, 4–7, 243
Ülkü Ocakları, 140
Unemployment, 65, 184
Union of Chambers of Commerce, 95–7

United States, 213, 214, 256n10
Unity Party, 125, 270n33
Universities, 154, 157–8, 159–60
Urban migrants, 66–72
Urbanization, 63–6, 234
Uşakıgıl, Halit Ziya, 273n25
Utilities, 66, 205–6
Village Institutes, 152
Villages and villagers, 52–4, 54–60, 61, 142, 169, 170, 171, 230, 236, 271n6
Violence, political, xiv, 243
Voting behavior, 143–8; of *gecekondu* areas, 74–8; of villagers, 62; in local elections, 278n9
Women, 44, 67, 71, 82, 110–7
World Bank, 10, 183